Psychosocial Nursing Care of the Aged

Psychosocial Nursing Care of the Aged

Second Edition

Edited by

Irene Mortenson Burnside, R.N., M.S.

Research Associate
Gerontological Nurse Specialist Program
San Jose State University

McGraw-Hill Book Company

New York   St. Louis   San Francisco   Auckland   Bogotá   Hamburg
Johannesburg   London   Madrid   Mexico   Montreal   New Delhi
Panama   Paris   São Paulo   Singapore   Sydney   Tokyo   Toronto

PSYCHOSOCIAL NURSING CARE OF THE AGED

Copyright © 1980, 1973 by McGraw-Hill, Inc. All rights reserved. Printed in the United States of America. No part of this publication may be reproduced, stored in a retrieval system, or transmitted, in any form or by any means, electronic, mechanical, photocopying, recording, or otherwise, without the prior written permission of the publisher.

1 2 3 4 5 6 7 8 9 0   DODO   7 8 3 2 1 0 7

This book was set in English Times by Allen Wayne Technical Corp.
The editor was David P. Carroll; the production supervisor was Jeanne Selzam.
R. R. Donnelley & Sons Company was printer and binder.

Library of Congress Cataloging in Publication Data

Burnside, Irene Mortenson, date   comp.
    Psychosocial nursing care of the aged.

    Bibliography: p.
    Includes index.
    1. Geriatric nursing—Addresses, essays, lectures.
2. Geriatric psychiatry—Addresses, essays, lectures.
3. Aged—Psychology—Addresses, essays, lectures.
I. Title.
RC954.B87   1980   610.73'65   79-13044
ISBN 0-07-009210-9

ACKNOWLEDGMENTS

American Nurses' Association, *Standards: Gerontological Nursing Practice,* Kansas City, Missouri, 1978. Copyright 1978, The American Nurses' Association.

W. H. Auden, *The Age of Anxiety,* Random House, New York, 1946. Copyright, 1946, selected lines reprinted by permission of the publisher.

Carol Estabrooks, "Anatomy of a Death" (poem), *The Canadian Nurse,* October 1977. Reprinted by permission of The Canadian Nurse.

Thomas H. Johnson, *The Complete Poems of Emily Dickinson,* Little, Brown, Boston, 1960. Copyright 1960, selected lines reprinted by permission of the publisher.

Phyllis McCormack, "Look Closer" (poem). Reprinted by permission.

Carl Sandburg, *The People, Yes,* Harcourt Brace and Co., Inc., New York, 1936. Reprinted by permission of Harcourt Brace Jovanovich.

Sister Marilyn Schwab, "Implementation of Standards of Practice in Gerontological Nursing." Copyright 1977. Reprinted by permission of American Health Care Association, Washington, D.C.

Lois Wyse, "The Widow" (poem). Copyright 1978. Reprinted by permission of Edward J. Acton, Inc., New York.

For Dean,
a young man
who died among the aged

Contents

1

INTRODUCTION AND INITIAL APPROACHES

2

THE AGED PERSON IN THE COMMUNITY

3

THE AGED PERSON IN THE ACUTE CARE SETTING

4

THE AGED PERSON IN A LONG-TERM CARE FACILITY

5

PSYCHOSOCIAL NURSING: SPECIAL CONCERNS

List of Contributors

MARIA C. ABARCA, R.N., M.S.
Professor,
  Department of Nursing
University of Costa Rica School of
  Education
San Jose, Costa Rica

MARI ANNE BARTOL, R.N., M.N.
Geriatric Mental Health Specialist
Comprehensive Mental Health,
  Tacoma-Pierce County
Tacoma, Washington

JANET C. BLACKMAN, R.N.,
  M.S.P.H.
University of California School of
  Public Health
Los Angeles, California

DOROTHY RINEHART BLAKE,
  M.S., R.N., F.N.P.
Associate Professor,
  Department of Nursing
Sonoma State University
Rohnert Park, California

IRENE MORTENSON BURNSIDE,
R.N., M.S.
Research Associate, Gerontological
   Nurse Specialist Program
San Jose State University
San Jose, California

MARY LOUISE CONTI, R.N.,
M.S.
Clinical Specialist in Community
   Health Nursing
Long Term Care
Veterans Administration Hospital
Palo Alto, California

MARION B. DOLAN, R.N.
Executive Director
New Found Area
   Nursing Association
Bristol, New Hampshire

GENIE EIDE, R.N., B.S.N.
Administrator, Community Home
   Health Care Agency
Maricopa County Health Services
Division of Public Health
Phoenix, Arizona

BEVERLY HARRIS, R.N., M.S.
Health Services Agency
   County of Santa Cruz
Santa Cruz, California

JANET R. HOLLOWAY, R.N.,
M.A.
Assistant Professor,
   Department of Nursing
Intercollegiate Center for Nursing
   Education
Spokane, Washington

JULIANNE M. McWHORTER,
R.N., M.S.
Associate Vice President,
   Patient Care
The Jewish Hospital of Cincinnati
Cincinnati, Ohio

BARBARA A. MOEHRLIN, B.S.N.,
P.H.N.
Coordinator, Senior Health
   Promotion Project
Santa Clara County Health
   Department
San Jose, California

KATHERINE M. NESS, R.N.,
M.Ed.
Associate Professor of Nursing
St. Olaf College Department of
   Nursing
Northfield, Minnesota

DIANE HOLLAND PUPPOLO,
R.N., M.S.
Instructor of Nursing
Saint Joseph College
West Hartford, Connecticut

SHARON L. ROBERTS, R.N., M.S.
Associate Professor,
   Department of Nursing
California State University
Long Beach, California

LINDA D. ROBINSON, R.N.,
M.S., D.N.S.
Associate Chief, Nursing Service for
   Geriatrics
Veterans Administration Medical
   Center
Little Rock, Arkansas

NOËL ROBINSON, S.R.N.,
R.P.N., O.T.A.
Coordinator, Montefiore Homes
   for the Aged
Melbourne, Australia

MARILYN SCHWAB, O.S.B.,
R.N., M.S.N.
Nursing Consultant,
   Benedictine Nursing Center
Mt. Angel, Oregon

ANN HERBERT SHANCK, R.N.,
M.S.
Associate Professor,
  Department of Nursing
California State University
Hayward, California

MARY OPAL WOLANIN, R.N.,
M.P.A.
Geriatric Nursing Consultant
  and Educator
Associate Professor, Emeritus
University of Arizona
Tucson, Arizona

Preface

Psychosocial Nursing Care of the Aged is a collection of papers with these commonalities: (1) the emphasis is on psychosocial nursing care of the aged person, (2) all the chapters are written by nurses, and (3) the chapters are rich in clinical data. When this book was begun in 1971, my intent was to publish student work in gerontological nursing written while in a master's program. I felt that many students were doing exciting things with the aged population and receiving little recognition or reward for their pioneering efforts. I still happen to feel that way about master's level students, and this edition has been revised with that same perspective in mind, although some of the new chapters are by nurses who have been working with the aged for years.

The purpose of this book, as stated in the original preface, is to share nurses' thoughts and their experiences with the elderly client as they upgrade the psychosocial care of the aged. This book is intended for use by clinicians who are caring for aged clients in the acute hospital, extended care facility, intermediate care facility, community, or day care center. ADN students, baccalaureate students, graduate students, continuing education students, and in-service educators can use this book for supplemental reading; it is intended as a reader, not as a textbook. Burnside's *Nursing and the Aged* (McGraw-Hill, 1981) has been designed as a textbook.

It should be noted that the contributing authors have a variety of backgrounds: psychiatric, medical/surgical, community health, gerontological nursing, and education. This combination of contributors was intended to give the book a wide scope.

Many of the papers came across my desk while I was teaching master's students; others were referred to me by colleagues. Two I found on a trip around the world when I met nurses in other countries. The chapter by Abarca (Chapter 3) was a result of a one-to-one relationship conducted in Spanish; all the process recordings were then translated into English. Miss Abarca was on a World Health Organizaton fellowship at the University of California School of Nursing at the time. Robinson's chapter (Chapter 22) on the role of a coordinator was originally a paper presented in Tasmania. Chapter 13 by Wolanin and Holloway was a very well received presentation at the International Congress of Gerontology in Tokyo.

A special effort was made not to edit out the individual style of the authors, since a clinician's style may be an influential component of therapeutic success in working with aged persons. A professor of mine once said, "Every good clinician has style."

The first edition was translated into Japanese by Dr. K. Hasegawa, and that serves to remind me of the impact gerontological nursing, as it evolves in the United States, can have in other parts of the world.

As the aged population continues to increase and as nurses assume greater responsibilities in both the physical and psychosocial care of the aged (note that these two should not be dichotomized), the need for more literature, research, and resources continues. This book only begins to cover the many facets of health care of the aged client. The reader is referred to *Nursing and the Aged* for some important subjects that are not covered here: (1) assessment, (2) group psychotherapy, (3) normal aspects of aging, (4) mental health problems in late life, and (5) gerontological nursing research. The second edition of *Nursing and the Aged* and the second edition of *Psychosocial Nursing Care of the Aged* are intended to complement one another.

Twelve new chapters on the following subjects were added to this edition: interviewing the confused aged person (Chapter 2), psychosocial assessment (Chapter 6), the high-risk aged person in the community (Chapter 7), reminiscing groups (Chapter 10), geriatric day care centers (Chapter 11), health maintenance (Chapter 12), confusion states after hip surgery (Chapter 13), implementation of standards (Chapter 18), coping with chronic disease (Chapter 19), wandering (Chapter 20), incontinence (Chapter 21), and the role of a nurse coordinator in a geriatric complex (Chapter 22).

The first part of the book is about the initial interaction with the aged person and focuses on the importance of the initial approach and of communication with the aged person.

Part 2 is devoted to the aged person who is still living at home. The importance of maintaining persons in independent living situations is still a major issue in the care of the aged client.

Care of the individual in the acute setting is fraught with complications, especially in the intensive care unit. Part 3 deals with aged persons in the acute care facility.

Part 4 is about psychosocial problems in long-term care of the elderly client. Chapters about state hospital residents have been omitted from this edition because they are now out of date. The influx of aged state hospital patients into the "community" now creates problems in geriatric care; nurses will now need to address themselves to the proliferating "geriatric ghettos."

Part 5 focuses on nursing process and the special needs of the older client, and highlights those needs so that problems such as wandering and incontinence can be better understood. This section ends with a chapter about the role one nurse designed for herself.

I am grateful to the students who shared their papers. They shared what they found to be possible in their real clinical world as they cared for and about the elderly. Evelyn Butorac handled the editorial tasks and my occasional lapses of forgetfulness. Pearl Bladek and Charm Novak were the loyal typists. I acknowledged my children in the first edition, and this second time around I would once again like to express appreciation to Mark, Tonya, and Clark for encouraging their mother/editor.

If psychosocial care of the aged is increased or improved in any way because of this book, it will have fulfilled its main purpose. If any reader becomes interested in the aged client, another goal will have been reached, because motivating nurses to work with aged persons continues to be a challenge.

Irene Mortenson Burnside

Courtesy of Harvey Finkle.

Part One

Introduction and Initial Approaches

Involvement
with people
is always
a very delicate
    thing
it requires
    real maturity
to become
    involved
    and
        not
    get
    all
    messed up.

Bernard Cook

INTRODUCTION

Sometimes neophytes coming into the area of gerontological nursing are not quite certain what comprises psychosocial care. Therefore, a list of common problematic areas is included at the end of this introduction.

The communication problems that may arise in interaction with the elderly client can often be intensely frustrating for both the nurse and the client. These difficulties can prevent the formation of an informal working relationship, can prevent getting an adequate and in-depth history from the individual to make a nursing diagnosis, and can leave the nurse feeling uneasy, dissatisfied, and unsuccessful with his or her own communication patterns.

An interview has been defined as a "conversation with a purpose."* The importance of an easy, preferably conversational, approach to working with the aged person cannot be impressed enough upon the beginning practitioner. Nurses, for the most part, usually handle the technique of gaining information through conversation quite well; Part 1 of this book is intended to help sharpen those skills.

In Chapter 1, Burnside suggests three immediate assessments to be made by the interviewer during the initial overtures with the aged client.

Interviewing an aged client may raise the interviewer's anxiety if it is a new experience; the anxiety tends to be heightened if the aged person is confused or disoriented. Therefore, Chapter 2 describes interviewing techniques which may be effective with such a client.

Abarca, in Chapter 3, reveals some of the difficulties in interaction when there are cultural as well as communication barriers.

The importance of promoting independence and maintaining old people at home through support systems and a nurse-patient relationship is sensitively described by Robinson in Chapter 4.

Chapter 5 discusses communication disorders in the rehabilitation of the aged client, and points out that the amount of communication between patient and staff member is often minimal. That comment seems as true now as it was in 1971 when Shanck first wrote it.

The focus of Part 1 is on initial interactions or longer interviews with an aged person.

PSYCHOSOCIAL NEEDS OF THE ELDERLY†

Acceptance as a person—maintaining personal identity
Acceptance or rejection of illness
Aged vs. youth and cultural value systems
Alienation and segregation from community life
Ambulation—restricted mobility—confinement

---

*Anne F. Fenlason et al., *Essentials in Interviewing*, (rev. ed.), Harper & Row, New York, 1962, p. 2.

†Used with the permission of Donald Kristola, Social Work Consultant, Division of Professional Standards Review, Health Care Financing Administration, Department of Health, Education and Welfare, Region V, Chicago.

Anxieties
Communication—use of native language
Confusion and memory loss
Constructive use of time—boredom
Difficulty in adjustment to institutionalization—dependence
Discharge planning
Expression of feelings, e.g., anger
Expression of religious beliefs
Fear of unknown
Feelings of being unwanted—rejection
Feeling of death and dying
Feeling of no longer being useful
Hopelessness, depression, frustration
Inability to understand what is happening
Loneliness—isolation
Loss of confidence
Loss of control in life situations
Loss of esteem
Loss of functions—hearing, speaking, seeing, etc.
Loss of self-care and independence
Loss of status
Low morale
Maximize strengths of individual
No interested family
Participate in treatment plans
Reduction or loss of income (also concern for payment of services)
Response to treatment—motivate toward reasonable recovery
Role reversal
Self devaluation
Separation from family and home
Sexuality
Social death
Social withdrawal
Staff interpersonal relationships with patients
To be with an individual who shows a warm interest
Touch
Unemployed—current use of skills
Unfamiliar surroundings (abnormal living)

Chapter 1

Interviewing the Aged

Irene Mortenson Burnside

And even stumbling speech may strengthen a weak tongue.

Kahlil Gibran
The Prophet

Only a few practical and helpful articles can be found in the literature about interviewing the aged client.[1-3] However, the few existing articles help delineate the communication problems which must be considered in interviewing the aged person, and most particularly the handicapped, regressed, or frail elderly adult.

Panicucci, Paul, Symonds, and Tambellini described the use of expanded speech and the importance of self-pacing during communications with the aged.[3]

A condensation of this paper was presented at the Sixth European Congress of Clinical Gerontology, Bern, Switzerland, September 9, 1971, and later was published in B. Steinmann (ed.), *Gerontology*, Hans Huber, Bern, Stuttgart, Vienna, 1973.

Bergman's studies indicated that older persons have greater difficulty in understanding speech than younger people do.[4] This phenomenon is called *phonemic regression* by Gaeth.[5]

Bloom et al. have written a most useful paper which focuses on nonmedically oriented interviewers and the special difficulties ill elderly people have. These authors suggest methods to deal with the difficulties so that the interviewer can obtain needed scientific information.[2]

The need for skillful techniques when interviewing the very old person is described in an excellent article by Schmidt, which I highly recommend for anyone interviewing the frail elderly.[1]

Elsewhere I have written about communication problems in group work with the disabled aged and described the importance of nonverbal communication in group interactions in an article which focuses on the importance of the use of touch by the leader.[6,7]

The data for this chapter come from a project in which I interviewed elderly persons in four groups: (1) metropolitan hospitalized elderly, (2) suburban hospitalized elderly, (3) metropolitan senior center members, and (4) suburban senior center members. Interviews varied in length of time; for example, the very ill and weak in the hospitals could tolerate only short periods of time. The subjects in the senior citizen centers talked more readily, and some seemed to enjoy the conversations with the interviewer. In all of the interviews I found three factors needed to be determined at the outset. These were: (1) assessment of distance, both physical and psychological, (2) assessment of hearing, and (3) assessment of comprehension.

Originally, I had planned to use a seven-question form and simply ask the subjects each one of the seven questions, and then write down their answers. This proved not to be very successful for a variety of reasons. First, the persons in the senior center had been researched several times, and because they had been asked questions about their finances and incomes, some were resentful towards interviewers and researchers. Second, in the hospital settings, a couple of paranoid patients were very guarded and suspicious. Finally, the writing was distracting for both the interviewer and the respondent. For these reasons a conversational approach was the method used. Answers were recorded immediately after the interview in order to keep the information as nearly as possible in the words of the respondent.

Previous interviewing of the aged had been done by the writer to establish contracts for group work with the aged persons in a convalescent hospital,[8] and some of the communication problems that ultimately arose in that group work also became apparent during the individual interviewing which is described in this chapter.[9] Previous group work together with nursing experiences with the aged clientele provided the necessary background.

ASSESSMENT OF DISTANCE
Physical Distance

The immediate decision that must be made in beginning an interview with an aged person concerns the most effective and comfortable physical distance between interviewer and interviewee; it is important to measure the most effective distance for both persons to be heard. This means that "the small protective sphere or bubble that an organism maintains between itself and others" must be determined. Hall describes a personal distance or close phase as $1\frac{1}{2}$ to $2\frac{1}{2}$ feet.[10] This was often the distance I used in interviewing the elderly.

The interviewer's placement of self is important for several reasons. Older persons seem to respond more readily when they can look directly at the interviewer. This is in accord with Steinzor who suggests that people in a face-to-face encounter "which allows them to observe more of each other's behavior will follow one another in verbal behavior more often than people whose view of each other is limited due to the fact that they sit close together."[11] Someone has also suggested that female interviewers wear bright-colored lipstick when interviewing with the aged, so lips can be seen more clearly and therefore more easily read.

Frequently an aged person will say that the hearing in one ear is better than in the other. This may necessitate the interviewer changing positions so that he or she sits at the side of the aged person rather than the preferred vis-à-vis position. Simply asking the aged interviewee if he or she can hear what is said is the best way to determine how loudly to speak.

The respondent's vision should also influence the decision of the interviewer as to where to sit. If a patient has been diagnosed as having cataracts or glaucoma (the two most common eye diseases of the aged encountered during the described interviewing), one should sit closer than one would to a patient who sees fairly well.

The writer found it necessary first to determine the "territory" of the aged hospitalized person and, next, how far into that territory she could move. The analogy of territory can be carried one step further when one considers the boundaries of the nursing home. Wheel chairs and bedrails, for instance, became veritable fences that kept the interviewer at the periphery of the invalid's tiny territory. These accouterments of the invalid were sometimes insurmountable barriers.

Also it has been documented that aged persons in institutions select certain chairs as their own. Lipman writes, "Residents regularly occupy specific chairs in communal sitting-rooms, and [that] chair arrangements are rigidly maintained over time."[12] I respected such "territorial imperatives" when I interviewed.

Psychological Distance

Hall states, "How man uses and experiences space in everything from interpersonal relations to architecture is the focus of a budding science called proxemics."[13] The proximity of the interviewer to the aged respondent has more implications than the obvious one of hearing. Since proxemics also includes the interpersonal aspect (which I have termed the psychological distance), it became apparent in early interviews with the hospitalized elderly patients that it was important to sensitively and accurately measure psychological distance. When this distance was ignored, or when measurements were insensitive and, therefore, proximity was too close or not close enough, failure was inevitable. The aged individual refused to talk or else gave nonverbal cues indicating a stalemate had been reached, and no further information would be offered.

Measurement of psychological distance was found to be most difficult with the withdrawn, bedridden patient. Roberts, who described territoriality in relation to a schizophrenic patient, agreed with Pluckhan[14] and Minckley[15] that "the relatively new concept of territorial behavior is gradually gaining recognition from the nursing profession."[16] Newman feels that for a long time the nurse's territory has been recognized, but it is only recently that we have begun to acknowledge patient territory.[17] One should also consider Goffman's point about old persons and also the very young "being engaged at will" because they really have nothing to lose in the encounter.[18] This author states, "Here, then, *persons* are exposed, not merely incumbents, they are 'open persons.'" This seems to me particularly true of the institutionalized aged. I attempted to decrease the psychological distance during interviews by operationalizing Wax's "Reciprocity in Field Work." Wax states, "An interviewer who knows that he is giving something in return is much more likely to maintain his respect for himself and for his scientific endeavors." She talks about a field worker allowing the informant to "play the ego-enhancing role of an authority or teacher."[19] Frequently the aged *are* authorities, if only on the subject of survival and aging.

When there is reciprocity in the interviewing there is also respect for the informant. The importance of this is emphasized because the aged in our society generally receive little respect or admiration.

Patients imposed a psychological distance for several reasons: (1) diminished attention span, (2) physical exhaustion due to a debilitating illness, (3) poor interpersonal relationships, and (4) frequently a recent dosage of medication. Some patients withdrew by simply shutting their eyes. Others turned their heads away and looked in a direction away from the interviewer. At times patients became noticeably restless and fidgeted with bedcovers and garments. If there was a television turned on in the room, which was frequently the case, the patient became engrossed in the television program.

ASSESSMENT OF HEARING

If the person being interviewed is very hard-of-hearing and cannot or does not use a hearing aid, one must talk loudly close to the ear. This necessitates that the distance be short. Having to lean towards the person and move into his or her territory often requires an awkward position. Such a stance can be both tiring and disconcerting to the interviewer. For example, bedridden patients presented problems because they had siderails up (which is mandatory in the nursing home) and often they could not hear unless the speaker was very close. No bedrails were lowered, in an effort to keep controls constant. Also, bedridden patients interviewed did not seem to have much energy and tired easily. Moreover, their attention spans were often noticeably shorter than those of mobile, alert patients.

Messages were frequently garbled by the hard-of-hearing. A minimum of questions and instructions should be administered to anyone with a severe hearing impairment. There were only seven questions on my questionnaire, but when my frustration mounted it seemed that I had many more than that.

ASSESSMENT OF COMPREHENSION

Once the most effective distance had been established by the interviewees, it became necessary to determine their comprehension ability. Often a person mistakenly thought to be bright and alert would suddenly confront the interviewer with signs of disorientation, confusion, and total lack of comprehension of the spoken messages. A similar situation occurred some years ago while I was passing medicines on a geriatrics unit. A delicate little woman with sparkling bright eyes reached out her hand to take the paper medicine cup. When the cup was placed in her hand, she promptly pitched all of the pills over the side of the bedrail and began to chew on the small paper cup! One cannot simply look at the aged person and determine how responsive she will be.

Towards the end of an interview, I often became aware of disorientation or memory loss. One woman, for example, heard well and had responded with appropriate replies all through the interview; but then I began to compare the ages she had given. According to the information she supplied, her son would have been born when she was five years old! Yet, she gave the dates and figures so glibly that it was not until the end of the interview that her memory loss came into focus. It seems quite possible that she had learned to cover up her memory loss by slipping in whatever date came into her mind. Other old people interviewed tended to say rather simply and unabashedly "I don't remember," or "I guess I have forgotten." This is not to imply that one should always be guarded and suspicious, but rather that one should check data if there is even a slight doubt about accuracy. From the measurement point of view, checking with staff and other patients increases the reliability of data obtained in the hospital settings.

On one occasion early in the interviewing, an alert patient who overheard an interview cornered the writer later and made corrections: "She told you her husband had been dead for 3 months; that is not true, he has been dead for 8 months." In the case of this particular patient all answers were checked for validity. Subsequently, if one portion of the answer was incorrect or seemed "out of line," I checked the entire answer sheet against the chart, Kardex file nursing care plan, and with nursing staff.

Figures and dates given by the aged often created problems for the interviewer—e.g., it was often difficult to tell if the reported age was the patient's true age. Some persons actually seemed to relish adding on a few years. One might assume such persons desire to be really old, because it is true that the oldest residents in nursing homes enjoy prestige and publicity that other patients do not. Also, if longevity is a criterion for success among these persons, it is understandable that they would add a few years. Sometimes the aged persons just simply did not know how old they were; yet much of the other information they gave seemed to check out accurately.

The aphasic patient in the samples also presented problems. Three types of aphasia are defined: (1) motor or expressive aphasic, (2) sensory or receptive aphasic, and (3) global aphasic. Expressive aphasics cannot express themselves verbally, but they are not dumb; they can usually say "yes" or "no," and they do hear and understand. Two such patients were encountered during interviewing for this project; they were not interviewed. Receptive aphasia is more complex; it usually appears as a loss of comprehension of the spoken language, or of written words, or may be a combination of these. Global aphasia is due to extensive damage of the brain's speech center.[20] Two global aphasic patients were in the random sample of the interviewees.

Since the interviewer would have to decide whether the aphasia was motor, sensory, or global, and then design techniques for interviewing the aphasic, no attempt was made by this writer to interview any aphasic who fell into the sample. Using paper and pencil, and simplifying the interview format may have made such interviewing possible; however, lack of time and persons to assist in conducting the interviews automatically ruled out such an approach. Interviewing the aphasic who does comprehend can, however, be a real challenge.*

Out of 50 hospitalized patients originally selected for this sample, 6 were aphasic and 1 had dysarthria due to Parkinson's disease. Fourteen percent were uninterviewable due to aphasic conditions. If an interviewer intends to interview an aged hospitalized sample, the possibility of encountering aphasic patients should be given serious consideration. For any random sample or selection of aged patients, 50 percent more interviews should be attempted than are actually needed for the data analysis, since there will be aphasics, those who are not interviewable, and those who refuse. The sample will be high-risk in the sense that the interviewer does not know a priori which respondents will be capable of answering rationally or, for that matter, how many individuals will survive between the random selection and the completion of the interview. For example, in one study of hospitalized patients, two patients died shortly after a random sample of the patient population had been drawn; these two patients had been in the sample.

The interviewer had anticipated that the aged persons from senior citizen groups would comprehend easily and be readily available for interviews. They did comprehend well. However, in the large suburban center, the aged had had previous unhappy experiences with interviewers. As a result, their anxiety levels were very high, and some were quite concerned about being asked about their income, and other questions they regarded as "too personal." Refusals were high in one senior center for this reason; only a few declined because of illness or lack of mobility.

The comprehension ability of the respondent should be assessed rather quickly by the interviewer, otherwise valuable time is lost trying to understand persons who ultimately will not be able to produce accurate data. As previously stated, accuracy in interviewing the aged, particularly in regard to dates, requires constant vigilance on the part of the interviewer. If one has to stop frequently to validate pertinent data with other sources, then extra time needs to be allotted for this task.

Another reason for assessing comprehension ability is to ascertain how to best phrase one's questions to obtain desired data. It is necessary to consider: (1) cultural background, (2) approximate education, or intelligence of the interviewee, and (3) the best presentation of self to use.

Some persons reacted readily to warmth and closeness. Others were suspicious and guarded; with these persons it was best to go slowly, and the interviewer kept some distance and reserve, and set up several interviews in order to establish trust and rapport. Wax writes about the ". . . complex

---

* Leonard Pearson's film, *The Inner World of Aphasia*, is recommended for those who might be faced with interviewing aphasics.

task of identifying with an individual who is simultaneously trying to identify himself with you." She gives the marvelous example of two an-
thropologists interviewing Indians. Their first Indian interviewee began
with this question, "Well, how's your rapport getting along?"[21]

Some older persons were quite spontaneous. Just as an older person
can be very direct and abrupt, he can also be spontaneous, charming, and
warm. Occasionally some of the women threw their arms around the interviewer and gave her a hug. The hugs were seen as the patient's desire to
establish a close psychological distance during the interview. Friendly,
outgoing patients seemed to enjoy having their hand held during part of the
interview. Weinberg has stressed the importance of a handshake.[22] One can
detect tremors, tenseness, reluctance, and perspiration in the handshake.
The willingness to hold the proffered hand, or the eagerness to let go are
also cues for the interviewer. Eye contact was another means of increasing
contact with the aged individual. One grumpy old man who offered little information during the first two interviews changed when the interviewer
shared a candy bar with him in the third interview.

Sometimes the question had to be reworded into simpler phrases or
shorter sentences. Speaking slowly was also useful in increasing the comprehension of the respondent. Panucci's study on self pacing gave valuable
suggestions regarding the pacing necessary with an aged person.[23] One
begins to set the pace while assessing the comprehension of the person being
interviewed.

The aged person frequently confuses one word with another and
responds to the word he thought he heard. This can be annoying, even
though it may also create some delightfully funny situations. One does need
to keep in mind, though, that this type of response is often due to the
respondent having misheard the word, and not to actual confusion.
Bergman says, "It is readily apparent that the functional evidence of
presbycusis is a deterioration in the ability to understand speech.
Characteristically, audiologists and otologists daily see older patients who
complain that speech that is still heard is no longer clear."[24]

Pestalozza and Shore have also done research on this phenomenon,
described as phonemic regression by Gaeth, [25] and found that older people
have inferior ability in their speech discrimination when compared with
young subjects.[26]

There were also patients in the samples who were mentally ill or retarded. Sometimes immediate cues were discernible from their facial expressions, as in the mentally retarded. Sometimes the speech itself indicated
there might be problems in the interview.

One mentally retarded patient began the interview without much difficulty, but as she began to talk about her family, her anxiety became high.
Her speech became more rapid and more slurred until it finally became
unintelligible; the incompleted interview was terminated shortly thereafter.

Occasionally manifest behavior alerted the interviewer, as in the case of one hallucinating patient. Staring at the ceiling or in some direction away from the interviewer, and listening intently, were the initial cues in the hallucinating patient.

One very paranoid patient could not be interviewed, not because she did not comprehend, but because her suspicion of an "outsider" interrogating was rampant. Unfortunately the nurse on the ward introduced me as a "researcher." That word was a trigger signal for the hostility which followed. Still another psychotic, who was schizophrenic, presented such a "word salad" that the interview was terminated as soon as the interviewer could break in and make the termination possible. The staff's description of that patient belongs in archives of understatement: "She does ramble a bit." These patients were on rehabilitation wards, and caught me off guard, as I had not expected to find patients with such overt psychiatric symptoms on a "rehab" ward and receiving no psychiatric help.

The comprehension ability of the aged individual is maximized when the interviewer can pace herself to the aged. Often this means going more slowly. Older people need time to think and to reminisce occasionally. Since reminiscing is such a part of the adaptation of the elderly person, and since it serves a significant adaptive function, the interviewer needs to allow time for this. Gerontology theory bears this out.[27-30]

Glasser and Havighurst found in a study they conducted that reminiscence appeared to have been an adaptive behavior. "It is found to have the following functions: enhancing self-esteem; enjoyment of social relations; understanding younger people; maintenance of consistent self-concept."[31] McMahon and Rhudick in their study found that reminiscing "is positively correlated with successful adaptation to old age through the maintenance of self-esteem, reaffirming a sense of identity, working through and mastery of personal losses, and as a means of contributing positively to their society."[32]

While the elderly person is reminiscing about past life—losses, victories, whatever—the interviewer can often find the answers to some questions. Also, the life-style of the individual can frequently be determined by attentively listening to the aged person reminisce. As one becomes increasingly aware of the importance of reminiscing to the elderly person, I believe one becomes more tolerant about listening to "the good old days."

Too many questions irritate the elderly respondent, who would sometimes terminate the interview with statements like "I am busy, I can talk no longer," or "I don't wish to talk anymore." The latent content of this message seemed to be: You have pushed me too far; go away. Pacing oneself to the client is one of the difficult things to learn in interviewing the aged. It is not easy to determine the anxiety level of aged patients, so as to know the point beyond which they cannot go—e.g., one patient simply got up and went to the bathroom and never came back.

RECORDING INTERVIEWS

During the early interviews, the writer wrote notes while the aged person talked. Suspicious patients resented this, and imagined a collusion between the interviewer and staff. On occasion there were questions asked about the interviewer being a social worker. Other patients wondered what would happen to the information they gave. The conversational approach later developed by the writer was more effective. Because of the estrangement and loneliness these aged felt, many enjoyed talking, but not being interrogated. Eliciting desired information was done by occasionally refocusing or letting the interviewee talk for a long while, and then asking a pertinent question or two.

Not writing in the presence of the aged person meant that I had to write immediately after an interview in order to capture its essence. Early in interviewing, while still writing notes in the client's presence, two incidents happened. On the interviewer's sheet was a blank for religion. From the chart I had read a Chinese woman's religion as "Buddhist." The woman saw this on her questionnaire and was furious, since she was a devout Catholic. On another occasion a clever 86-year-old woman was discussing her vision. She promptly pulled the portfolio out of the interviewer's lap and proceeded to read what had been transcribed there to show the interviewer her degree of vision! These two incidents forced the interviewer into changing to a conversational approach with less use of direct questioning, and a less brusque, businesslike manner.

Two or three short interviews were ultimately more successful in producing information from hospitalized patients than one longer interview. A series of brief interviews served to increase the reliability of the data obtained, since confused or hazy areas could be repeated, and initially unanswered questions could be rephrased at a second or third interview. Patients became noticeably less anxious in the last interview, permitting the interviewer closer physical and psychological distance. The technique of several brief interviews also reduced the length of the patient's attention span that was needed for a complete interview. This method is time-consuming, but there seem to be no short cuts to take in interviewing aged people. Such interviewing requires perseverance, patience, and gentleness on the part of the interviewer.

THE RECIPROCAL METHOD

Wax has written an excellent article in which she talks about reciprocating with the interviewee. This seemed to be particularly important to remember with the aged, both in and out of hospitals, since increasing their input made the interview worthwhile for them, too. Just sitting with them for a few minutes and watching something outside their window gave them something in exchange for having talked with the interviewer. Sometimes coffee was shared, or a candy bar. Touch was another form of input previously described. Looking at cherished photos, mementos, or personal possessions of the aged person were other ways I reciprocated with the aged, because, as Wax writes:

> It is difficult for me to see how an interviewer who is not a sadist or a misanthrope can keep good conscience when, armed with a long list of dull questions, he proceeds to bore an informant for hours on end. An interviewer who knows that he is giving something in return is much more likely to maintain his respect for himself and his scientific endeavors.[33]

REWARDS

Interviewing the aged is not easy. It can be exhausting, time-consuming, and frustrating. For these reasons the interviewer needs to find some self satisfactions to sustain him or her, for the end result—the written study—is far removed when one begins such a research project. It was necessary for me to find rewards as the weeks passed, else the task became discouraging, monotonous, or boring. Sitting longer with especially interesting patients was one way to prevent monotony. One patient had been a talented singer and sang songs from a 1918 stage hit to the interviewer. Another patient vividly described the 1906 earthquake and fire, told of needing a fire permit to cook out in the streets, and described the vandalism that occurred during that catastrophe. Listening to the philosophy of the sages, distilled from 80 or 90 years of living, was part of the reward of interviewing these old people. Sharing their present existence was a privilege, but sharing their past world and bits of their lonely lives was an even greater one.

SUMMARY

This chapter discusses problems in interviewing the aged person. Several classic articles in the literature which are helpful are recommended to the reader. Early assessment in an interview with an aged adult should include these three important areas: (1) distance, both physical and psychological, (2) hearing ability, and (3) comprehension. The pacing of the interviewer must be adjusted to each individual interviewed on the basis of the assessment. The place of seating is also important and it is the interviewer who must do the accommodating in the interview setting. This is one difficult aspect to remember when interviewing the elderly person, especially if the interviewer's anxiety is high. Other aspects of interviewing the aged discussed in this chapter include: the pros and cons of note taking during the interview, the reciprocal method of field interviewing adapted to the aged client, and possible rewards for the interviewer.

REFERENCES

1 Mary Gwyne Schmidt, "Interviewing the 'Old Old,'" *The Gerontologist*, vol. 15, no. 6, pp. 544–547, December 1975.

2 Martin Bloom, Edna Duchon, Gertrude Frires, Helen Hanson, Georgine Hurd, Vivian South, "Interviewing the Ill Aged," *The Gerontologist*, vol. 11, no. 4, part 1, pp. 292–299, Winter 1971.

3 Carol L. Panucci, Penelope B. Paul, Jean M. Symonds, Josephine L. Tambellini, "Expanded Speech and Self Pacing in Communication with the Aged," *ANA Clinical Sessions* (papers), Appleton-Century-Crofts, New York, 1968, pp. 95–102.

4 Moe Bergman, "Changes in Hearing with Age," *The Gerontologist*, vol. 11, no. 1, part 1, pp. 148–151, Spring 1971.

5 J. Gaeth, "A Study of Phonemic Regression Associated with Hearing Loss," Ph.D. dissertation, Northwestern University, 1948.

6 Irene Mortenson Burnside, "Communication Problems in Group Work with the Disabled Aged," *ANA Clinical Conferences: American Nurses' Association*, Appleton-Century-Crofts, New York, 1970, pp. 125–131.

7 Irene Mortenson Burnside, "Touching Is Talking," *American Journal of Nursing*, vol. 73, no. 12, pp. 2060–2063, December 1973.

8 Irene Mortenson Burnside, "Group Work with the Aged," *Nursing Outlook*, vol. 17, no. 6, pp. 68–72, June 1969.

9 Irene Mortenson Burnside, "Communication Problems with the Disabled Aged," *ANA Clinical Papers* (1969), Appleton-Century-Crofts, New York, 1970, pp. 125–131.

10 Edward T. Hall, *The Hidden Dimension*, Doubleday, Garden City, New York, 1966, p. 112.

11 Bernard Steinzor, "The Spatial Factor in Face to Face Discussion Groups," *Journal of Abnormal Psychology*, vol. 45, p. 552, 1950.

12 A. Lipman, "A Socio-Architectural View of Life in Three Homes for Old People," *Gerontologica Clinica*, vol. 10, p. 89, 1968.

13 Edward T. Hall and Mildred Hall, "The Language of Personal Space," *House and Garden*, p. 103, April 1969.

14 Margaret L. Pluckhan, "Space: The Silent Language," *Nursing Forum*, vol. 7, p. 386, 1969.

15 Barbara Blake Minckley, "Space and Place in Patient Care," *American Journal of Nursing*, p. 511, March 1968.

16 Sharon L. Roberts, "Territoriality: Space and the Schizophrenic Patient," *Perspectives in Psychiatric Care*, vol. 7, no. 1, pp. 28–33, 1969.

17 Lucile Newman, personal communication, 1970.

18 Erving Goffman, *Behavior in Public Places*, Free Press, New York, 1963, p. 126.

19 Rosalie Hankey Wax, "Reciprocity as a Field Technique," *Human Organization*, vol. 2, no. 3, pp. 34–41, 1952.

20 T. R. Harrison et al., *Principles of Internal Medicine*, Blakiston, New York, 1958, pp. 370-371.

21 Wax, op. cit., p. 98.

22 Jack Weinberg, "Psychiatric Problems of Aging," lecture presented at Summer Institute of Gerontology, University of Southern California, Los Angeles, July 22, 1970.

23 Panucci et al., op. cit.

24 Bergman, op. cit.

25 Gaeth, op. cit.

26 G. Pestalozza and I. Shore, "Clinical Evaluation of Presbycusis on the Basis of Different Tests of Auditory Function," *Laryngoscope*, pp. 1136-1163, 1955.

27 Judith Liton and Sara C. Olstein, *Social Casework*, vol. 50, no. 5, pp. 263-268, 1969

28 Maxwell Gitelson, "The Emotional Problems of Elderly People," *Geriatrics*, vol. 3, no. 1, p. 139, January-February 1948.

29 R. Glasser and Robert J. Havighurst, "Functions of Reminiscence in Later Adulthood," paper presented at Twenty-fourth Annual Meeting of Gerontological Society, Houston, October 28, 1971.

30 Arthur McMahon and Paul H. Rhudick, "Reminiscing Adaptational Significance in the Aged," *Archives of General Psychiatry*, vol. 10, no. 3, March 1964.

31 Glasser and Havighurst, op. cit.

32 McMahon and Rhudick, op. cit., p. 297.

33 Wax, op. cit., p. 98.

BIBLIOGRAPHY

Atwood, Hudson: "Communication Problems of the Geriatric Patient," *Journal of Speech and Hearing Disorder*, vol. 25, pp. 238-248, 1960.

Bakdash, Dianne P.: "Communicating with the Aged Patient: A Systems View," *Journal of Gerontological Nursing*, vol. 3, no. 5, September-October 1977.

Bermosk, Loretta S.: "Interviewing: A Key to Therapeutic Communication in Nursing Practice," *The Nursing Clinics of North America*, vol. 1, pp. 205-214, June 1966.

Bernstein, L., and R. Dana: *Interviewing and the Health Professions*, Appleton-Century-Crofts, New York, 1970.

Brill, Naomi: "Basic Knowledge for Work with the Aging," *The Gerontologist*, vol. 9, no. 3, August 1969.

Brink, T. L.: "Guidelines for Counseling the Aged," *The New Physician*, vol. 26, no. 10, October 1977.

Cannell, C. F., and R. L. Kahn: "Interviewing," in G. Lindzey and E. Aronson (eds.), *Handbook of Social Psychology*, 2d ed., vol. 11, Addison-Wesley, Reading, Mass., 1968.

Kahn, Robert, and Charles Cannell: *The Dynamics of Interviewing*, Wiley, New York, 1957.

McLeod, W. R.: "Making the Most of the Interview: Psychological and Psychiatric Aspects," *Patient Management*, vol. 2, no. 7, pp. 9–16, July 1978.

Mitchell, J.: "Disorder of Communication in the Older Patient," *Gerontologica Clinica*, vol. 6, pp. 331–340, 1964.

Sheppe, W. M. Jr., and I. Stevenson: "Techniques of Interviewing," in H. I. Lief, V. F. Lief, and N. R. Lief (eds.), *The Psychological Basis of Medical Practice*, Harper & Row, New York, 1963.

Webb, E. J., D. T. Campbell, R. D. Schwartz, and L. Sechrest: *Unobtrusive Measures*, Rand McNally, Chicago, 1966.

Chapter 2

Interviewing the
Confused Aged Person

Irene Mortenson Burnside

We, the simplest and vaguest of us, know that we are other and better than we appear.

Florida Scott-Maxwell
Measure of My Days, p. 122

The previous chapter dealt with the initial assessments to be made when interviewing an elderly client. This chapter, while it embraces many of the principles covered in Chapter 1, will focus only on the interview with a confused older person, perhaps one of the most difficult and draining of all interviews or interactions with older clients. But, as we will have to realize constantly,

> Mental confusion is the very stuff of geriatric medicine. Four features make it bulk so large: its great prevalence (it accounts for just under half of all admissions to geriatric wards); the large variety of diseases which can provoke it; its socially disabling effects when long continued; and the very large demands it makes on medical and social resources.[1]

19

The material for this chapter has been developed from a variety of interviews with confused older persons: interviews used to make contracts for group work with the elderly,[2] and interviews with confused older people in both formal classroom settings and informal workshop settings.* The persons interviewed, although confused and disoriented, always completed the interview, even though interviews were brief when the person displayed overt anxiety. In fact, the client's anxiety level determined the length of the interview. In the continuing education workshops, first an alert aged person was interviewed, then a confused person. These interviews served as a comparison and contrast exercise for the students. After each interview the participants were encouraged to look at the overt strengths of the aged individual who had been interviewed. As one student astutely observed, "Confusion can be penetrated."

McLeod reminds us that one has to be selective in gathering data since there is such a plentitude of data offered and/or observed.

> It is well to be aware that the process and content of an interview are influenced by the psychological set and expectations of the two participants. We select some information and the rest we either do not register or, if observed, we discard. The "noted" data comes to the "foreground" while the rest recedes to the "background." This "foreground-background" tension is always changing as the needs of both parties in an interview change or are satisfied.[3]

THE INTERVIEW

One of the first things one must consider in any interview with the aged, but especially in an interview with a confused older person, is the best place to interview the client. This is true in interviewing in a senior center, home, office, clinic, or institutional setting. External stimuli must be kept to an absolute minimum. The room must be assessed for the following conditions:

1 A comfortable chair for the client.
2 A table, large enough and at the correct height for the aged person to write on if written material is to be obtained.
3 Enough space, especially if there are wheel chairs or walkers.
4 Correct room temperature; no drafts; air-conditioner turned low.
5 Coat rack, or place to hang hat or coat.
6 No distractions during the interview, e.g., phone calls.
7 A minimum of extraneous noise in the environment, e.g., intercom blaring or radio playing; televisions should be off, because the television can provide an excellent way to avoid eye contact.
8 A restroom should be nearby if the client has very high anxiety or a urinary problem.
9 Water should be available.

---

*I am indebted to Linda Bertsch Cardenas for helping me to refine and operationalize teaching techniques for the continuing education short term seminars.

Many old people do not drink adequate fluids during the day and dehydration and malnutrition can contribute to confusional states. Interview time can be used to encourage fluid intake. If anxiety is high, there has been a long wait for the old person, or it has been a long time since a meal, tea or coffee may be offered. For a fearful, frightened person, this may increase sociability and increase trust in the interviewer.

In certain cases, interviews may be done in a resident's room, usually because of illness or immobility. The interviewer should maximize privacy and comfort, and be careful to avoid invasive actions, for example, moving newspapers or magazines being saved, or moving personal possessions such as bibles, photographs, and letters.

The reader is referred to the excellent work of Smith and Gray-Feiss on cues that aid a person to retrieve information or to learn new responses or gain new information.[4]

Gain Rapport Quickly

It is important to try to gain rapport immediately and to discover the "acceptance area," or the "rejection area." This awareness will help you position yourself correctly in relation to the client.

Assessing Distance

Because of severe hearing or vision loss, many old persons, especially the frail elderly (whether confused or not), will allow you to work very close to them. However, cues of rejection mean that you have moved in too close and they feel either threatened or uncomfortable or both. Or you may have moved in close to them physically too rapidly; early closeness may be unacceptable. Later in the interview physical closeness may be well tolerated. *When in doubt, approach slowly.*

Eye Contact and the Handshake

Gaining and maintaining eye contact is helpful for several reasons. The interviewer can become aware of possible visual problems. One can actually see the clouded eyes, the cataracts, or the keyhole appearances sometimes apparent after some cataract surgery. Also, the interviewer must watch carefully for teariness, actual tears which leave the corner of the eye. Tears are most often due to sadness, but one must remember they can also be due to watering of the eye. And, of course, they can also be tears of happiness or gratitude. Eye contact also gives indications about the trust level or the state of withdrawal in the interviewee. Eye contact should be intense and sustained over the time of the interviews.

The handshake is another clue to the receptivity or hesitancy of the older client. The clinging handshake may indicate fright or dependence needs.

When I interview in front of the students, holding the hand becomes an excellent barometer I use to indicate the rising and falling anxiety of the interviewee.

Assessment of Vision and Hearing

Since the previous chapter discussed the need to assess hearing and vision loss to determine where to sit, it will not be covered here. It goes without saying that interviews should always be conducted with the interviewer comfortably seated—anything else implies haste or lack of interest. If the aged client talks about having a "good ear," sit on that side of the individual. Talk into the aged person's ear if necessary.

Regarding vision, move slowly towards the person and ask the interviewee to tell you when you are visible; stop when the person states you are in range of vision. If the interviewee has speech difficulties, simply request a nod of the head when you are seen. It is helpful to blind persons if they know exactly where you are placing yourself in relation to them. It is also helpful to let them touch your face, hair, hands, and arms, but do this only if you are comfortable with such tactile movements during an interview.

Place Self in Best Space

Place yourself in the best location for an interview. Observe where the client is sitting or lying and also the "fences" that may enclose the person, e.g., a walker, crutches, bedrails, or wheelchair. An interview at the bedside means the interviewer may have to rearrange chairs, footstools, or bedside tables to get in closer. Permission to rearrange should always be asked first, since it is the interviewee's territory and offers some control or choice in the situation. The reply may even indicate some spunk. Also, moving objects and furniture may confuse the blind or visually impaired (see Figs. 2-1 to 2-3).

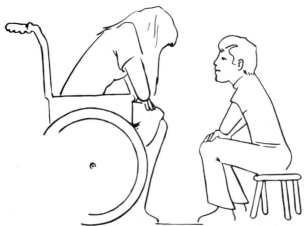

Figure 2-1 Position for an interviewer to use with an aged individual who is in a wheelchair and quite withdrawn.

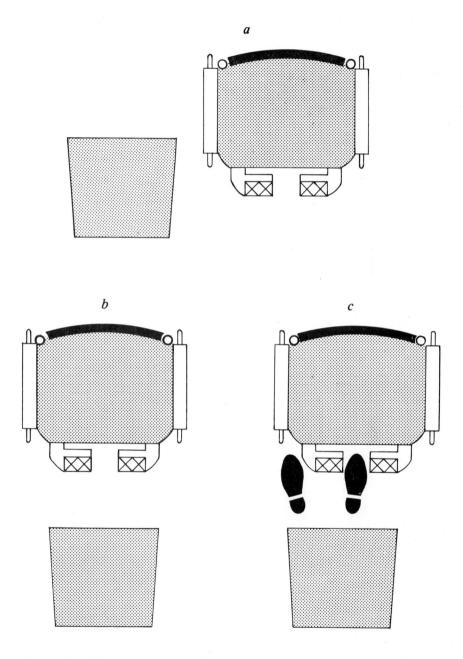

Figure 2-2 (*a*) A common placement for an interviewer to use with an old person in a wheelchair. (*b*) A position for an interviewer who wants to ensure eye contact. (*c*) The best position to use with older persons in wheelchair who are blind, hard-of-hearing, or sensorily deprived.

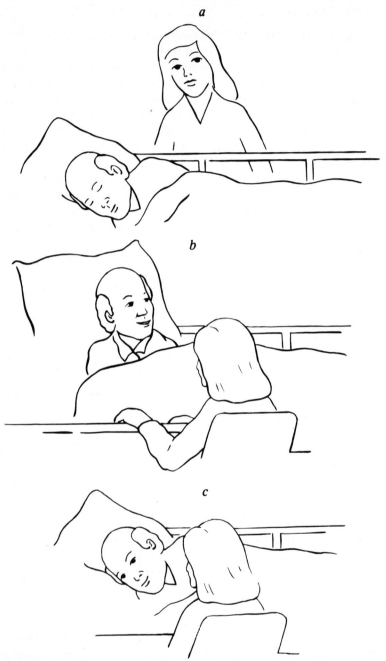

Figure 2-3 Positions used with bedridden patients. (*a*) This is an awkward and ineffective position to use with bedridden aged patients. (*b*) This is a better position, but the nurse is still not close enough for frail, visually impaired, or hard-of-hearing patients. (*c*) This is the best position because the nurse is close to the patient.

The Pace of Interviewer

Self-pacing for the interviewer is necessary simultaneously in two areas—physical and cognitive. Moving too quickly in either area will fluster, annoy, anger, or depress the confused patient. The easiest way to trigger a "catastrophic reaction"[5] or to encourage false answers and confabulation* is not to allow time for response. The confused person must have time to gain or regain composure, or time to figure out who you are; that in itself can be a formidable task for a confused person. Slowing body movements may take some self-discipline on the part of the interviewer; the same is true of the necessary cognitive pacing.

Most of us have at one time or another been in the company of someone we considered very brilliant, who thought more rapidly than we did. If we can recall our own behavior and response in such encounters, then we may have greater empathy for the regressed, confused, or disoriented client we interview. As one aged person said to a nurse, "Slow down. You make me nervous." It is also well to remember that an interviewer who slows down too much on the cognitive level with a very sharp oldster can expect some caustic comments. Woe unto you if you should ask one of the alert ones who the President of the United States is!

Accept Kindness, Thanks, Praise

Nurses (and other care providers) often seem to have great difficulty accepting praise or appreciation; in fact, they may be downright uncomfortable accepting the praise. Old people know how to express their gratitude par excellence; it is part of the professional's reward in working with them. Buber said, "The older one becomes, so much more grows in one the inclination to thank."[7] Student nurses may have difficulty in accepting gratitude or praise and may need help. Confused individuals will often express their appreciation or gratitude in a nonverbal manner as in the following example.

CASE EXAMPLE 1   Mr. G was a 62-year-old man on a research ward. All of the men there had Alzheimer's disease. I was an observer; the staff members were in the office listening to the change-of-shift report. I tried to converse with Mr. G; he could not speak to me. I was getting nowhere. He finally smiled at me and then leaned over and kissed me gently on the cheek.

Control of Interview

While the interviewer must maintain control of the interview and provide the structure needed by confused individuals, it helps to be comfortable and

---

*Confabulation is "a filling in of gaps in memory by free fabrication (as in Korsakoff's syndrome)."[6]

nonthreatened when the interviewee asks you questions. One goal is to increase the self-esteem of the confused individual; it can be increased if you are willing to place yourself in a learner's situation and have the interviewee teach you. The stance of the interviewer as a learner is not an easy one to assume; as one begins, it is especially difficult to know how much control to exert.

The control of the interviewer is a loose sort of control; the control is there, but may not seem obvious.

Robert Frost once described freedom as "moving easy in the harness."[8] Moving easy in the harness during interviews is especially good advice if you are stopping by patients on a confused evening.

Search for the Positive

The old ballad about emphasizing the positive and eliminating the negative is not only a good song, but it is also sound advice in working with the confused elderly person. While one usually will not eliminate the negative, one can certainly play it down, or ignore it, and strive to reward the positive.

> **CASE EXAMPLE 2** Mr. H was an 80-year-old alert black male, who asked to be called "Tiny" in the first interview. He had suffered a stroke which had left him paralyzed on the left side, and also with an annoying raucous laughter during which he opened his mouth very wide. The higher his anxiety, the louder the laughter, which often was inappropriate. The laughter was at first unnerving but the interviewer ignored it, and waited for him to respond. She then rewarded him for the response with touch, praise, or a smile. "Tiny" soon was able to share previous life experiences, although slowly and with effort.

Listen to Themes

Even during what sounds like babbling and incoherency, words can often be deciphered. Listen for semantics that suggest a theme, that is, words heard frequently about one subject, for example, death. Listen also for the choice of semantics—the choice of words; words which portray sadness, depression, abandonment, etc. Other words may indicate a life-style, for example, in a farmer's use of the expression, "I thought they sold the farm" to describe a baseball play. Use of colloquial terms from certain parts of the United States is another clue. Is the interviewee a loner, or a gregarious individual? How does the person relate to others? Here is an example of a "common past": Prior to a group demonstration for a continuing education class in Kansas, I interviewed two confused elderly women together. They revealed a common past. They had been institutionalized in the same extended care facility for several years and were close friends. They had assumed the important role of confidante for one another. They would turn to one another to verify the story they just told, "You remember that, don't you, Rosetta?" Rosetta would nod, smile and say, "Sure, I took care of your little boy then." It seemed to be an adjustment or coping device—a way to pretend that at least one continuous friendship existed, to show there was a confidante. Perhaps this did serve to provide a continuity in life in the face of many drastic changes.

Nonverbal Behavior

The interviewer must be especially cognizant of important nonverbal behavior in confused clients: lonely/depressed cues, body posture, the gait of the person, tears, tremor, and obvious disabilities. The nonverbal communication will have more accurate meaning than words one is trying to decode. Often when working with a confused person the nonverbal is a crude but accurate indication of the thoughts, as in the following example.

CASE EXAMPLE 3   Anna, a 78-year-old woman, was being interviewed for a continuing education seminar. Her anxiety was high in the initial contact. The interviewer had coffee with her and later walked with her to the front of the class. The interviewer noted how quickly she spotted the only two men in the room and repeatedly called one of them "Bob." The interviewer gave her the correct names of both men and explained who they were.

During the interview Anna talked about "a man from Dodge City." She repeated this several times. Then, as the interviewer could not seem to make sense out of the conversation, Anna put her first finger up with an obvious phallic sexual gesture saying softly, "Well it was like this." The interviewer's anxiety was already high so she took both Anna's hands, held them, and chose to divert the subject immediately. The interviewer simply did not feel up to handling sexuality in that teaching interview.

Later, students in the front row said they had missed the words about "the man from Dodge City" because Anna spoke so softly. A change in voice tone is often a good indicator of the seriousness or "secretiveness" of the event being described. Students also missed her hand gestures. The interviewer had quickly taken her hands and held them, and chose to ignore the sexual data as McLeod mentioned earlier.

Anna was then given her accordion. When the accordion was placed in her lap, and ready to play, Anna closed her eyes and played a very melancholy and sad rendition of "Laura." The confused woman sat very calmly and played the song twice for a rather stunned and impressed class. Two students in the front row cried.

Use of Reminiscing

Anna also was an example of a confused person who endeavored to reminisce during an interview. In a later interview the interviewer could have tapped into Anna's memories of this man. Although one cannot always accomplish successful reminiscing strategies with the confused elderly person, it is worth a try in any interview or one-to-one interaction. Lewis and Butler say this: "Life-review therapy need not be ruled out because of brain damage. The Goldstein catastrophic reaction, resulting from overwhelming stimuli, can be minimized or avoided if the therapist proceeds carefully and observantly."[9]

Anna was also a good example of awareness of the present situation and trying to relate it to the past and other experience. During the interview with any confused aged person it is well to remember that the output or behavior of a person is the product of a wide range of past experiences, current sensory input, and the here and now experience, as has been well stated by T. S. Eliot:

> Time past and time future
> What might have been and what has been
> Point to one end, which is always present.[10]

Beginnings and Closures

Beginnings and closures are important in interviews and though little is written about them except in psychiatric literature, students may need some help in this area. Good beginnings help:

1 To increase orientation (decrease pseudo-recognition)
2 To increase structure of the interview
3 To decrease anxiety
4 To increase social graces and amenities often
5 To assess sociability for the interviewer

Confused persons can fool an interviewer in the first few sentences if they confabulate or have managed to retain successful adaptation through the use of social graces. The following case study is typical of the ability of interviewees to handle the "good-bye," and their occasional reluctance to discontinue an interview which had been a warm, nonthreatening interaction.

CASE EXAMPLE 4   Mrs. N is a 94-year-old white female, widowed, who has lived in an intermediate care facility since March 1976.

Mrs. N has been slightly confused since she entered the facility, and this confusion has increased in the past year. She is able to ambulate, feed herself, and can usually find the bathroom. She is oriented most of the time as to place; however, there are times when she doesn't seem to realize where she is. She is oriented to person but not to time. She has one relative, a niece, who visits frequently. Mrs. N usually recognizes her but she cannot remember her name. Mrs. N has a tendency to be "bossy" at times, especially at the dining table. There are times she realizes she is not thinking straight and then she will become agitated or "weepy." She responds well to love and kindness. A tranquilizer medication, Haldol $\frac{1}{2}$ mg PRN, is given only when absolutely necessary for extreme agitation.

This information accompanied a frail 94-year-old woman who was interviewed in a workshop held in a motel 18 miles from the intermediate care facility where she lived. She tolerated the drive and interview well and these observations were made:

1 Feared move or abandonment (said she "was not packed yet" when the driver arrived to pick her up).

2 Tried to figure out who the driver was, a young attractive coordinator of a continuing education program who also had a solid background in gerontology and health care.

3 Always knew in which direction the driver was traveling, for example, stated "south" as soon as the driver turned.

4 Commented on the landscape of Kansas; on the flatness of land, plowed fields, shops, color of trees, truly enjoyed the drive.

5 Turned to the class to wave good-bye, then still waved good-bye out in the car in the motel carport, saying, "I don't suppose they can see me anymore, but I will still wave at them" (To hold onto the experience as long as she could?).

It is well to remember that the interviewer may also be trying to improve a low self-esteem which may be directly related to the confusional state as in the above case study. Or if not that, often an extreme embarrassment if the older person is aware of the confused state. One colleague pointed out about one elderly individual that "in her own state of deterioration she could not recognize or tolerate deterioration in others."[11]

Sideleau has done an excellent job in organizing helpful strategies for interviewing and interacting with the confused disoriented person. Her finely tuned interventions are to be found in Tables 2-1, 2-2, and 2-3.[12]

SUMMARY

The basic problems involved in interviewing the confused aged client are not well covered in the literature; however, an increasing amount of material is

Table 2-1 Nursing Goals and Interventions—Client Problem I

Client problem: Disorientation, increasing demands on coping mechanisms.
Nursing goal: Ameliorate disorientation and the concomitant increased demands; foster the development of less primitive coping mechanisms.

Nursing interventions
1 Frequently orient to time, place, and person, using clocks, calendars, and visual aids.
2 Establish a set, well-known routine for the client to follow.
3 Address the client by name and title (e.g., "Good morning, Mr. Tate") to reinforce a sense of identity.
4 Repeat basic information frequently during the day.
5 Orient the client when he or she wakes up during the night.
6 Do not agree with the confused client's incorrect statements, argue, or insist on your viewpoint.
7 Correct the client gently but not insistently.
8 Do not allow the client to ramble incoherently.
9 Respond to the client openly and honestly.
10 Create a calm, quiet, and unhurried atmosphere.
11 Speak slowly and distinctly.
12 Moderate or avoid stressful situations to decrease stimuli which would destroy perceptions or cause sensory overload.
13 Convey warmth and concern.
14 Respond patiently and consistently.

Source: Barbara Flynn Sideleau, "Response to Clients with Organic Brain Syndrome," in Judith Haber, Anita M. Leach, Sylvia M. Schudy, and Barbara Flynn Sideleau (eds.), *Comprehensive Psychiatric Nursing,* McGraw-Hill, New York, 1978, pp. 492–493. Used with permission of McGraw-Hill.

Table 2-2 Nursing Goals and Interventions—Client Problem II

Client problem: Exhibits disturbed dysattention.
Nursing goal: Ameliorate factors which contribute to dysattention.

Nursing interventions
1 Look directly at the client when communicating.
2 Position self in client's line of vision when communicating.
3 Give clear, distinct, simple directions in a step-by-step fashion.
4 Direct conversation toward concrete, familiar subjects.
5 Provide simple activities that will encourage purposeful motion.
6 Repeat messages slowly, calmly, and patiently until the client shows some signs of comprehension.
7 Vary media and/or words to fit the client's ability to comprehend the message.
8 Modify environmental stimuli which affect attention.

Source: Barbara Flynn Sideleau, "Response to Clients with Organic Brain Syndrome," in Judith Haber, Anita M. Leach, Sylvia M. Schudy, and Barbara Flynn Sideleau (eds.), *Comprehensive Psychiatric Nursing,* McGraw-Hill, New York, 1978, pp. 492–493. Used with permission of McGraw-Hill.

Table 2-3   Nursing Goals and Interventions—Client Problem III

Client problem:	Need to defend against catastrophic fear reaction, profound depression, or aggressive assaultiveness.
Nursing goal:	Avoids a catastrophic fear reaction, profound depression, or assaultive aggressiveness.

Nursing intervention

1 Support client's efforts to ignore or deny intellectual impairments.
2 Avoid confrontation of inappropriate behavior and probing for feelings.
3 Communicate in a way that does not increase the client's awareness of deficits, need for defensive coping mechanisms.
4 Accompany the client when he or she wanders, gently providing guidance back to the specified area.
5 Avoid use of restraints and/or incarceration, which will cause greater feelings of inadequacy and helplessness.
6 Interpret suspicious behavior as a possible regression to a lower level.

Source: Barbara Flynn Sideleau, "Response to Clients with Organic Brain Syndrome," in Judith Haber, Anita M. Leach, Sylvia M. Schudy, and Barbara Flynn Sideleau (eds.), *Comprehensive Psychiatric Nursing*, McGraw-Hill, New York, 1978, pp. 492–493. Used with permission of McGraw-Hill.

available on instruments to use in testing the older person for confusion and disorientation.[13-16] This chapter has not covered those it has shown but how to plan and implement an interview with a confused old person.

The milieu is important in any interview, but it is even more important with the aged confused client. The interviewer should gain rapport rapidly in the interview so as not to lose the interest and attention of the client. Quick assessment of vision and hearing is necessary; the reader is referred to Chapter 1. The interviewer must also select the best space to place self. The pace of the interviewer has to be adjusted to the physical, cognitive pace of the aged individual. One cannot hurry the interviewee; the necessary adjustments will have to be made by the interviewer. While the interviewer needs to maintain control of the interview, it should be done with firm kindness and appear as uncontrolling as possible. The interviewer is advised to always search for the positive—for the accordions for the Annas—and remember Tillich's suggestions:

> The other person cannot be controlled like a natural object. Every human being is an absolute limit, an unpierceable wall of resistance against any attempts to make him into an object. He who breaks this resistance by external force destroys his own humanity; he never can become a mature person.[17]

REFERENCES

1 J. C. Brocklehurst and J. Hanley, *Geriatric Medicine for Students*, Longman, New York, 1976.

2 *Elderly: Group Process and Techniques*, Duxbury Press, North Scituate, Mass., 1978.

3 W. R. McLeod, "Making the Most of the Interview: Psychological and Psychiatric Aspects," *Patient Management*, vol. 2, no. 7, pp. 9–16, July 1978.

4 K. Smith and K. Gray-Feiss, "Memory Development: An Approach for Responding to the Mentally Impaired Elderly in the Long-Term Care Setting," paper presented at the Gerontological Society 30th Annual Scientific Meeting, San Francisco, November 19, 1977.

5 Kurt Goldstein, *The Organism*, American Book, New York, 1939.

6 *Webster's Third New International Dictionary of the English Language (unabridged)*, Merriam, Springfield, Mass., 1961.

7 Martin Buber, in Ruth Nanda Anshen (ed.), *A Believing Humanism: Gleanings by Martin Buber*, Simon and Schuster, New York, 1967, p. 225.

8 John Ciardi, *How Does a Poem Mean?* The Riverside Press, Cambridge, Mass., 1959.

9 Myrna I. Lewis and Robert N. Butler, "Life Review Therapy: Putting Memories to Work in Individual and Group Psychotherapy," *Geriatrics*, vol. 29, no. 11, pp. 165–173, November 1974.

10 T. S. Eliot, *The Four Quartets*, in *Collected Poems*, Harcourt, Brace & World, New York, 1970, p. 175.

11 Bernita M. Steffl, personal communication, 1978.

12 Barbara Flynn Sideleau, "Response to Clients with Organic Brain Syndrome," in Judith Haber, Anita M. Leach, Sylvia M. Schudy, and Barbara Flynn Sideleau (eds.), *Comprehensive Psychiatric Nursing*, McGraw-Hill, New York, 1978, pp. 492–493.

13 R. L. Kahn, *Psychological Aspects of Aging in Clinical Geriatrics*, Lippincott, Philadelphia, 1971.

14 R. L. Kahn, A. I. Goldfarb, M. Pollack, and A. Peck, "Brief Objective Measures for the Determination of Mental Status in the Aged," *American Journal of Psychiatry*, vol. 117, p. 326, 1960.

15 Eric Pfeiffer, "OARS Multidimensional Functional Assessment Questionnaire," Duke University Center for the Study of Aging and Human Development, Durham, N.C., 1975.

16 G. Nosie Honigfeld, "History and Current Status of Its Use in Pharmacopsychiatric Research. Psychological Measurements in Psychopharmacology," *Modern Problems of Pharmacopsychiatry*, vol. 7, pp. 238–263, 1974.

17 Paul Tillich, "Existentialism, Psychotherapy and the Nature of Man," *Pastoral Psychology*, vol. 11, no. 6, pp. 10–18, 1960.

BIBLIOGRAPHY

Bakdash, Dianne P.: "Communicating with the Aged Patient: A Systems View," *Journal of Gerontological Nursing*, vol. 3, no. 5, pp. 29–32, September–October 1977.

Cahall, Jean B., and Diana Smith: "Considerate Care of the Elderly: Little Things Mean a Lot," *Nursing '75*, vol. 5, pp. 38–39, September 1975.

Gerdes, Lenore: "The Confused or Delirious Patient," *American Journal of Nursing*, vol. 68, no. 6, June 1968.

Gresham, Mary: "The Infantilization of the Elderly: A Developing Concept," *Nursing Forum*, vol. 15, no. 2, pp. 195–210, 1976.

Hall, Edward T.: *The Hidden Dimension*, Anchor Books, New York, 1969.

Hirschfield, Miriam: "The Cognitively Impaired Older Adult," *American Journal of Nursing*, vol. 76, pp. 1981–1984, December 1976.

Moses, Dorothy V.: "Reality Orientation in the Aging Person," in Carolyn E. Carlson (ed.), *Behavioral Concepts and Nursing Intervention*, Lippincott, Philadelphia, 1970.

Weymouth, Lilyan T.: "The Nursing Care of the So-called Confused Patient," *Nursing Clinics of North America*, vol. 68, pp. 709–715, December 1968.

OTHER RESOURCES

Concept Media: "The Confused Person: Approaches to Reality Orientation," Concept Media, Costa Mesa, Calif., 1973. (film)

Eisdorfer, Carl, and Leon Epstein: "Workshop on Aging," *Organic Brain Syndrome I, Organic Brain Syndrome II*, Sandoz Pharmaceuticals, East Hanover, N.J., 1976. (brochure and quiz booklet)

Gaitz, Charles M., Ray V. Varner, Welton Calvert, and Maurice E. Linden: "Realistic Expectations and Treatment Goals in Caring for the Impaired Elderly," scientific exhibit, AMA 126th Annual Conference, San Francisco, 1977. (brochure)

Goldfarb, Alvin J., and Shervert Frazier: *Aging and Organic Brain Syndrome*, McNeil Laboratories, Camp Hill Road, Fort Washington, Pa. 19034. (film and booklet)

Films

Return to Reality, 16 mm, color, 35 min., 1972. Mrs. Dorothy Scarbrough, R.N., M.S., Chief, Reality Orientation Training Program, Veterans Hospital, Tuscaloosa, Ala., 35401.

December Spring, 16 mm, b/w, 29 min., 1973. Mrs. Dorothy Scarbrough, R.N., M.S., Chief, Reality Orientation Training Program, Veterans Hospital, Tuscaloosa, Ala., 35401.

A Time to Learn: Reality Orientation in the Nursing Home, 16 mm, color, 28 min., 1973. Mrs. Dorothy Scarbrough, R.N., M.S., Chief, Reality Orientation Training Program, Veterans Hospital, Tuscaloosa, Ala., 35401.

Chapter 3

One-to-One Relationship Therapy: A Case Study

Maria C. Abarca

And there she stood, as strange as
   something loaned,
Slowly growing old and blind,
   and was not prized.

Rainer Maria Rilke

Philosophers and writers have discussed the inner feeling of loneliness and its effects on human beings. Existentialism closely relates the sense of non-being with loneliness, emptiness, and alienation from the world. "To the lonely person, the opposite of loneliness—closeness and relatedness to people—always appear to hold a potential threat."[1]

   This chapter about loneliness will be illustrated with clinical data from my process recordings of Mrs. E, who was a diabetic, blind, and had no knowledge of the English language. She was 65 years of age. Since I was a native of Costa Rica studying in America, I did all the interviewing in Spanish, then wrote English process recordings for my instructor, and for data to use in this chapter.

CAUSES OF LONELINESS FOR MRS. E

Blindness is a condition which in itself can cause despair; the sense of in-security and dependence is increased; and there is anxiety and the feeling of being alone in utter darkness. Despair was common in my patient, as is re-vealed in the process recording,

Nurse: What are you thinking?

Patient: Nothing. I can't think. I only pray. I never think about any-thing. For instance, I never think about my blindness; if I think about it I become desperate.

The patient used the defense mechanism of suppression. Understand-ably, she became desperate when she thought about being blind. If the pa-tient is alone and loses sight, the blindness reinforces the sense of loneliness.

One can quite easily understand the sense of loneliness in elderly people who live away from their relatives, and who sometimes face their situation without the possibility of living this stage of life peacefully. People need to feel their lives are not in vain.[2] As Hall says, "The paramount emotions of unhappy senior citizens probably are the feeling of not being needed—a sense of uselessness—and its co-partner, loneliness."[3]

My patient had lost her sight. She had a chronic illness. She had only a nephew who visited her infrequently. As I wrote the process recordings, I became increasingly aware that she revealed her feeling of not being needed, her sense of uselessness.

Ruesch says that disabilities such as blindness and chronic disease can increase neurosis if the patient does not compensate for these disabilities with acceptance, adaptation, and understanding.[4] If one adds to these problems the fact that my patient did not know the English language and did not have anyone who spoke her own language, one can more easily imagine her sense of loneliness and despair. I would agree with Buhler who says: "In his struggle to find beliefs and values, the individual feels lonely, even desperate; he feels he no longer belongs with those who feel part of tradition and establishment."[5]

Anxiety

"Anxiety strikes us at the very core of self-esteem, it is what we feel when our existence as selves is threatened."[6] What is more threatening to ourselves than the feeling of being lonely? The separation from other significant persons, and the lack of communication, are threats to our sense of belonging, or to being in our world. The threat of loneliness is a root of anxiety. The reality of being lonely can be denied; in fact, this is one way of coping with the anxiety.

The patient or client may behave as a conformist or may become depressive, have fantasies, illusions, or hallucinations. Fromm-Reichmann reminds us that loneliness plays an essential role in the genesis of mental disorders.[7]

Old people feel rejected when they are away from significant persons, and this feeling in itself is a source for anxiety. My patient had experienced rejection throughout her life. The most significant incident occurred a few days after her marriage. Her husband left her 10 days afterward with promises which he never fulfilled. This experience when she was 17 years of age was a traumatic one, although she emphatically denied its significance. Her subsequent feelings of rejection, loneliness, and lowered self-esteem may be linked to this episode in her early life. In the hospital she still felt rejected, anxious, and lonely. As she told me, "I have a nephew and neither he nor his wife come to see me. I don't have anybody and I am blind." The feeling of "nobody loves me," or "nobody cares for me" was stated in her own words.

Depression

The loss of a loved person or a loved object results in feelings of grief. Such a loss brings feelings of loneliness and emptiness. Frequently this emptiness is experienced in the person's inner world. The emptiness is within, and the person feels depressed.[8]

My patient's first loss occurred when she lost her parents; she was 5 years old and she was adopted. She again suffered separation when she was interned in a private elementary school and lived away from her parents. Then at 17 years of age she married and lost her husband in rather an unusual way; he left for the United States and never returned. At the age of 60, she gradually lost her sight. All these were deprivations which increased her loneliness.

Rubins says, "Some persons may not be aware that they are lonely; others may be peripherally aware of some such feeling but may try to exclude it or deny it. It may be experienced not primarily as loneliness but as depression or anxiety."[9] Once, when the patient wanted to do something by herself and could not, she said:

Patient: Oh! God, Why am I blind? (Despair and sadness) I don't know why does God punish me so much.

Nurse: Do you say that God punishes you?

Patient: Yes, sometimes I fight with him. Listen, I am blind because God wants me to be blind, there is no justice in heaven or on earth. I am not a drunkard or murderer, and he punishes me in this way. . . . (Anger)

Nurse: You look angry now. . . .

Patient: Yes, I am. And sometimes I talk to God in this way and I pray, "Oh, God, if you would want, with a breath of life, you could open my eyes."

Despair, anger and sadness were all present in the patient's verbal communication.

Illusions and Hallucinations of Mrs. E

The clinical data show the close relationships between loneliness and false perceptions. Hall says, "Loneliness and a sense of uselessness lie behind these feelings. They can make any of us feel that no one likes us, no one wants us; if 'they' do not like us or want us, 'they' must dislike us, . . . they are trying to poison or destroy us."[10] The patient said, "The men from the radio and TV tell me dirty things; I am not a saint, but I am good, and they persecute me." Her lack of communication aggravated the feeling of loneliness and the patient then "talks to the radio," as she said. The interviews revealed that the hallucinations and illusions were more frequent when she was alone:

Patient: When I lived with a friend, the spirits bothered me. Suddenly I felt like I was shot and I screamed, but nobody was over there.

Nurse: Does this happen frequently?

Patient: No, about three times, but not now.

Nurse: Were you alone on those days?

Patient: All the time I have been alone. . . .

When she was in the hospital, she did not feel the "spirits" but she had illusions and hallucinations:

Patient: And now, those men tell me things. . . .

Nurse: Which men?

Patient: The men who work on TV programs.

Nurse: What kind of things do you say they tell you?

Patient: They tell me "dishwasher" and "housekeeping" only to bother me and other gossips. . . .

Nurse: Gossips?

Patient: They say that I am a bitch, a drunkard, and a revolutionary. I spoke with them, even though they don't answer me.

It seemed to me that the words "housekeeping" and "dishwashing" had a connotation of inferiority for her, although she could not consciously admit this. The feeling of loneliness reinforced her feeling of inferiority.

Psychodynamics of Loneliness

Intimacy needs seem to be the prime factor in loneliness. Peplau says:

> Loneliness is the result of early experience in which remoteness, indifference and emptiness were the principal themes that characterized the child's relationship with others. Because it is an unbearable experience, loneliness is always hidden, disguised, defended against, and expressed in other forms.[11]

The patient lived with the parents who adopted her when she was 5 years old; the relationship with them was described by her as a good one, especially with her mother. However, on weekends her parents wanted to take her to their home, but she did not go. She said, "I liked the school." One can speculate that if she preferred to stay in school rather than go home, she found more gratification at school, or else school life may have been less painful. She also said, "I am not a person who likes to touch others." I observed that she was distant; she never greeted by touching the other person, which is a common custom in Central America where she lived.

In the hospital her feelings of loneliness were increased by lack of communication. Her lack of knowledge of the English language greatly intensified her isolation. As she said in her first interview:

> I am happy that you talk with me, because I don't know the English, only to say: "good-bye" or "good morning" and the people here are good ones. I would like to tell them, "You are very nice," "How is your family?" or something like that and I can't. Then, . . . I am mute although don't want to be. Sometimes I talk alone, some prayers, because if I don't talk Spanish I am going to forget it. I have a year in this hospital but I don't know anybody who speaks Spanish.

She had feelings of insecurity and despair because of the impossiblity of communicating with the staff and the other patients. Muecke says,

> The consequence is a painful sense of isolation for patients who do not speak English; in an unfamiliar milieu like a hospital ward or clinic office, they cannot use the language. . . . Their isolation brings expressions of feelings of inadequacy . . . humiliation . . . anger . . . and helplessness.

The patient's experiences throughout her life established the basis for her loneliness, but I believe the lack of communication and hallucinations were linked with her isolation.

INTERVENTIONS

When a feeling is not pleasurable (and in the case of loneliness it is unbearable), a person may falsify reality as a defense. I observed different defense mechanisms used by this patient.

Patient: I feel desperate when I have to stay in the same place, when I am here I walk around the bed and when I am in bed I move from the one side to the other side.

Nurse: When you walk, do you relieve your desperation?

Patient: Oh, yes. I walk and I can breathe better again.

Nurse: Only in this situation do you feel like that?

Patient: Yes. I am not afraid of anything. (Denial)

The patient used the defense mechanism of denial, so I explored the way she controlled her anxiety.

Nurse: Regarding your experience when you were married, did you feel desperation?

Patient: No, because I didn't love him and I thought that something bad happened to him.

The patient denied and rationalized her feelings in this experience.

Patient: I don't have any friend, and it is better. That means that I never have bothered anybody. (Rationalization)

Perhaps rationalization made her loneliness easier to tolerate.

Nurse: . . . Do you feel lonely?

Patient: I have been alone all the time. I like loneliness; nobody annoys me.

Nurse: But . . . once in a while, do you need someone with you?

Patient: No, I am fine alone. I don't need anybody and I am not alone at all because here there are many people.

One finds she contradicted herself when she said, "I am not alone at all." Contrary to her initial words, she liked to know that she was not alone (although few people spoke her language).

Peplau says that the need to prove independence is a defense against loneliness.[13] Regarding her own independence, the patient said, "I am blind, but I can do many things. I can walk alone close to my bed and now I can go to the bathroom. I am not bothering them unnecessarily."

Conformism is one recourse that she had in order to deal with loneliness. Her religion gave her the faith which supported her:

Nurse: How do you feel when there are many people and much noise here?

Patient: Nothing. They don't bother me. You see, I get along with all situations. If I am alone, it is okay. If I am with someone, it is okay, too. I am a conformist with everything. If Jesus Christ suffered and died, why should I protest?

In the first step, I identified the patient's loneliness. It was easy to detect in this patient's circumstances because of the sense of isolation and inner vacuity. In the initial interview with the patient, I sought not only to increase the amount of communication but also to improve the patient's skills.

In this patient's case, the next step was to realize that the patient needed a consistent relationship in order to feel that she was an important person and that she was not alone. Another person, the nurse, knew her feeling of loneliness even though the patient could not admit the feeling. Thus, the patient's feelings of being rejected decreased. The patient needed a genuine contact with another person; someone to talk with and to understand her. Ultimately, I became an important person to the patient, for one day she said, "I told him (her nephew) that I have a friend who comes to talk to me."

To reinforce her ego strength, I used the therapeutic approach of evaluating the patient's techniques for coping with the "challenge of suffering." I hoped she would be able to face her suffering with strength. I needed to know the patient's past experiences in order to evaluate her life. An interesting point is made by Frankl regarding the challenge of suffering and the frequent explosive spiritual conflicts in the patient. He says: "They are (the doctors) confronted with philosophical problems rather than emotional conflicts. The demand for consolation exceeds the supply furnished by pastoral care. 'Preachers are no longer the pastors of the soul, but doctors have become such,' said Kierkegaard."[14]

As a part of the comprehensive care plan, I sought another person on the staff who could help meet this patient's need for intimacy. I needed to encourage the patient when she said that in spite of her blindness she could do many things, because being dependent increases the sense of uselessness, helplessness, and loneliness.

Another goal to be achieved was to diminish the illusions and hallucinations. My plan was to meet her need for communication in a consistent and meaningful way so that the frequency of false perceptions would be reduced. First of all, it was necessary to allow her to describe false perceptions. In this way, the patient felt that I was interested in her experiences. It was useful also to put reality under the patient's consideration, but always indicating that I understood that the experience was real to her. In this manner the patient felt that her feelings and perceptions were respected. The patient then could begin to realize that the reality of those voices was doubtful. Hall says, "If a worker . . . is interested in him, and is concerned about him, he may be encouraged to trust others more. And as his loneliness and sense of uselessness decreases, he will have less need to be suspicious or paranoid."[15]

One sign of improvement in the patient was noted one day when she looked very satisfied. I asked her about it and she said that she had had a visitor that week. During that interview, she did not talk about false perceptions or delusions of any kind. In our final session, she said that she did not talk with the men on the radio any more. With this patient, I tried to meet the needs I thought she expressed, in order to decrease her false perceptions.

PREVENTION OF LONELINESS

The loss of a loved object can be one cause of loneliness. This loss may be real or symbolic. A common example is the physical separation of a significant figure in the early stages of life. In the symbolic loss, for instance, the mother may be alive, but she is a distant object who does not have a close relationship with her child, or else she may frequently frustrate his need for intimacy and communication. Even in conservative families where the relationships between grandparents, parents, and children are more close-knit, the children sometimes live like isolated persons. What can one say, then, about the loss of emotional contact and face-to-face encounters in the modern family?

Our basic institutions are paying an exorbitant price for civilization. The price is emptiness and isolation. Man is surrounded by proof of his materialistic achievements, but there is an inner vacuity which man denies and attempts to extinguish (if he is able to do so) with unrestrained activity. I believe basically that the family as a social institution needs to be fortified.

Generally speaking, all nurses have a great opportunity to prevent the sense of loneliness or at least to avoid its increase in their clients. Hospitalization in itself is a cause of loneliness. The nurse in such a setting is the person who works with patients who are experiencing despair, loneliness, anger, dependence, and fear. To avoid a patient, for whatever reason, is to increase his feeling of rejection and loneliness.

As nurses, I think we must know how to deal with our own loneliness in order to be more helpful to the patient. A meaningful relationship can help in the development of maturity. Such a relationship can also assist the patient to face the challenge of living.

My work with Mrs. E was in some ways continued by staff, even though they did not speak Spanish. They decreased her isolation in an effort to decrease the hallucinations also.

SUMMARY

Loneliness is a problem of our century, and certainly has been discussed by philosophers, psychiatrists, and psychologists, but very little by the nursing profession. Loneliness can be due to a loss and its subsequent reactions, or it can be due to our culture and the sense of isolation in our time.

Physical disabilities, chronic illness, death, and pain affect people in a way that sometimes makes these conditions seem insurmountable. The relationship between loneliness and such behaviors as (1) depression, (2) anxiety, (3) anger, and (4) despair has been described in this chapter. The roots of loneliness in the specific patient were: (1) the lack of communication as a behavioral pattern, (2) successive losses, and (3) an intimacy need, which was very often frustrated.

The pathological aspects of loneliness of my patient became evident when she described hallucinations. She was lonely and isolated because of blindness and a language barrier.

Her defense mechanisms to cope with the unbearable feeling were denial and rationalization. Her religion helped her deal with the sense of loneliness and despair.

In order to prevent loneliness one must understand its possible causes. The professional nurse must have an awareness of her own way of dealing with loneliness, anxiety, and despair. Then she is better able to help patients or clients as they attempt to cope with these feelings even though in some cases they may not be aware of them. I have shared some of the ways in which I intervened successfully with one very lonely elderly woman.

REFERENCES

1 Hildegard E. Peplau, "Loneliness," in Dorothy Mereness (ed.), *Psychiatric Nursing,* vol. 2, Brown, Iowa, 1970, p. 59.
2 Viktor E. Frankl, *Psychotherapy and Existentialism,* Simon and Schuster, New York, 1968, p. 17.
3 Bernard H. Hall, "The Mental Health of Senior Citizens," in Dorothy Mereness (ed.), *Psychiatric Nursing,* vol. 2, Brown, Iowa, 1970, p. 125.
4 Jurgen Ruesch, *Therapeutic Communication,* Norton, New York, 1961, pp. 378–385.
5 Charlotte Bühler, "Loneliness in Maturity," *Journal of Humanistic Psychology,* vol. 1, no. 2, p. 170, Fall 1969.
6 Rollo May, "Contribution of Existential Psychotherapy," in Rollo May, Ernest Angel, and Henri F. Ellenberger (eds.), *Existence,* Basic Books, New York, 1958, pp. 50–51.
7 Frieda Fromm-Reichmann, "Loneliness," *Psychiatry,* vol. 22, p. 13, 1959.
8 Sigmund Freud, *General Psychological Theory,* Macmillan, New York, 1969, pp. 164–179.
9 Jack Rubins, "On the Psychopathology of Loneliness," *American Journal of Psychoanalysis,* vol. 24, no. 2, p. 154, 1964.
10 Hall, op. cit., p. 127.
11 Peplau, op. cit., p. 55.
12 Marjorie A. Muecke, "Overcoming the Language Barrier," *Nursing Outlook,* p. 53, April 1970.
13 Peplau, op. cit., p. 66.
14 Frankl, op. cit., pp. 90–91.
15 Hall, op. cit., pp. 127–128.

BIBLIOGRAPHY

American Foundation for the Blind: *A Step-by-Step Guide to Personal Management for Blind Persons,* 2d ed., New York, 1974.
_____: *An Introduction to Working with the Aging Person Who Is Visually Handicapped,* New York, 1977.
Cull, J. G.: "Psychological Adjustment to Blindness," in A. B. Cobb (ed.), *Medical and Psychological Aspects of Disability,* Charles C Thomas, Springfield, Ill.,1973.
Dickman, Irving R.: "The Foundation Assumes Responsibility," in Irving R. Dickman (ed.), *Outreach to the Aging Blind: Some Strategies for Community Action,* American Foundation for the Blind, New York, 1977.
Duncan, John L.: *A Guide to Expanding Social Services to the Blind under Title XX of the Social Security Act,* American Foundation for the Blind, New York, 1976.

Erikson, Erik H.: *Identity, Youth and Crisis*, Norton, New York, 1968.

Evans, Richard I.: *Dialogue with Erik H. Erikson*, Dutton, New York, 1969.

Francel, Claire: "Loneliness," in Shirley F. Burd and Margaret A. Marshall (eds.), *Some Clinical Approaches to Psychiatric Nursing*, Macmillan, London, 1969.

Fromm, Erich: *The Sane Society*, Fawcett, Greenwich, Conn., 1970.

Hill, Everett and Purvis Ponder: "Touch Technique," in *Orientation and Mobility Techniques*, American Foundation for the Blind, New York, 1976.

Kienning, Sister Mary M.: "Denial of Illness," in Carolyn E. Carlson (ed.), *Behavioral Concepts and Nursing Intervention*, Lippincott, Philadelphia, 1970.

Lisenco, Yasha: "Touch Contact and Verbal Instruction," in Yasha Lisenco (ed.), *Art Not by Eye*, American Foundation for the Blind, New York, 1972.

McGarry, Barbara D.: *Federal Assistance for Programs Serving the Visually Handicapped*, 3d ed., American Foundation for the Blind, New York, 1977.

May, Rollo: *Man's Search for Himself*, Norton, New York, 1967.

Miles, Barbara: "Social Therapy for the Elderly Blind," *Nursing Times*, vol. 63, no. 9, pp. 292–293, March 1967.

Perks, Jenefer: "Nursing a Blind Patient," *Nursing Times*, vol. 71, no. 44, pp. 1728–1730, October 1975.

Sullivan, Harry S.: *The Interpersonal Theory of Psychiatry*, Norton, New York, 1953.

OTHER RESOURCES

Organizations

American Foundation for the Blind
15 West 16th Street
New York, N.Y. 10011

Guide Dogs for the Blind, Inc.
P.O. Box 1200
San Rafael, Calif. 94902

Library of Congress
Division for the Blind and Physically Handicapped
Washington, D.C. 20542

Films

Sykes, 16 mm, color, 13 min
Filmakers Library, Inc.
290 West End Avenue
New York, N.Y. 10023

See No Evil, 16 mm, b/w, 15 min
Filmakers Library, Inc.
290 West End Avenue
New York, N.Y. 10023

Chapter 4

"You Don't Seems to Want to Understand": A Case History

Linda D. Robinson

We do not look at the aged as a class apart, but seek to ensure that they live full lives within the ordinary stream of the community.

Rt. Hon. Sain Macleod, M.P.

The practice of nursing involves the provision of personalized health care services to people who need assistance to attain or maintain their maximum health and well-being potential. The nurse acts on behalf of others in ways designed to make an important difference in their lives. If the nurse's acts are to be beneficial, they must be integrated in some manner with the patient's ongoing work of living. Perhaps the core of nursing lies in establishing a special, reciprocal, collaborative relationship with patients.

The work described in this chapter was based on a clinical posture of commitment to whatever was revealed by data generated during the observation and tender care of one person. In this posture the clinician accepts responsibility for the well-being of another. Appropriate clinical interventions are determined by examining the ensuing caring relationship. The clinician must select from a universe of potentially beneficial acts those which seem to fit best. What is thereby revealed is considered by the clinician to be more valid and pertinent to the case than previous scientific knowledge or research findings. Clinicians are more open to alternatives than they would be if they were committed to a particular theoretical stance. This clinical posture seeks to avoid: (1) "explaining away" the data, and (2) forcing data to fit a preconceived theoretical framework.

My work with Mr. A was grounded in a relationship characterized by mutual respect and influence, mutual sharing and involvement of lives, and mutual interest and enjoyment of each other. I had been visiting him in his home for several months prior to his admission to a nursing home. My original purpose for being there was to gather data for a research project. Although I had no intention of engaging in clinical intervention, I eventually became very involved in Mr. A's efforts to obtain care from the health system.[1] There was no unilateral intervention on my part. He would not permit me to act upon my assumptions about him without confirming my decisions with him.

THE NURSING HOME EXPERIENCE

In time, Mr. A became a nursing home resident, and a most unwilling one at that. He had been placed there by a physician who had decided that Mr. A was too old and infirm to live alone any longer. Because Mr. A had been so unwilling, he had been told by the physician that the arrangement was only temporary. Consequently, he anticipated being returned to his home as soon as he recovered from the serious illness that afflicted him. The physician preferred not to burden Mr. A with explanations and diagnoses and told him simply that he was a very sick man. Actually, he was acutely anemic at the time. In addition, Mr. A had chronic illnesses affecting every organ system of his body. Arthritic degenerative disease of the spinal column with compression fractures of thoracic vertebrae had left him painfully bent almost double at the waist and twisted to the left. His feet and lower legs had been deformed by war injuries. Walking was quite painful. Arteriosclerotic cardiovascular disease resulted in borderline cardiac compensation, atrial fibrillation, and poor peripheral circulation. He was legally blind with only shadowy peripheral vision remaining. An enormously enlarged prostate caused him annoying and embarrassing urgency and decreased force of urinary stream. Diverticulosis and emphysema completed the inventory of worn-out vital systems precariously balancing one another. That he had been able to manage adequately and alone in his own home for so long was indeed amazing to me.

Problems of Independence

A fiercely independent and self-reliant man, Mr. A had lived alone since he emigrated to this country in his youth. He had lost track of his family and had never married. He owned his own home and did his own chores. He had been a free-lance landscape gardener and had retired several years ago when he could no longer see well enough to work. His moderate savings and limited social security benefits provided him a frugal existence. At 85 years of age Mr. A had only a few friends who were able to help him obtain what he needed from the world outside his home. He had been able to run his own household by seeking assistance from his friends and by insisting upon a rigid ordering of all the items in his environment. There was a precise place or arrangement for everything from the cans of food on the pantry shelf to the coathangers in his closet. He knew where everything was, even the small jars of spices in the rack over the kitchen sink. Anyone who entered the house was expected to cooperate with his furniture arrangement and to move about in such a manner that he did not leave Mr. A's limited field of vision. Mr. A knew when things were out of place and reproached the offender; however, by tightly controlling the environment he was able to manage quite adequately and maintain his independence. Although friends did help by doing the shopping, taking him to the doctor, writing his checks, or cutting his hair, he was also able to do all these chores himself. The assistance he received enabled him to use his energy for more pleasurable things like cooking and talking on the phone. He conversed daily with many old friends who were now housebound with infirmities. Because of his vision and mobility problems, his activities kept him very busy each day.

Adjusting to the nursing home was very difficult for Mr. A. Not only was he continually bombarded by unfamiliar sounds, odors, and other sensations, but he had no control over anything. Events happened around and to him, but did not seem to include him. He resisted being swept along and attempted to control things by shouting. Although bed, chair, stand, locker, and floor space had been assigned to him, they did not belong to him. He could not lie on his bed in the daytime, but had to lie there all night. He could not keep his pajamas in his nightstand, but had to keep his shoes there. He discovered that the staff and other patients also had access to his space and impinged on his use of it. Another patient could take Mr. A's chair without asking permission. The nurse could rearrange the contents of his stand and remove all his bits of paper on which he had written vital telephone numbers. The orderly could take his razor and use it on another patient. The maid could rearrange his furniture to suit herself. He was not able to function independently because he could not rely on finding things where he had left them. Indeed, he was barely able to function at all.

Social Isolation

Compounding Mr. A's difficulty in adjusting to the nursing home was the element of social isolation. His friends found the home very difficult to get to and consequently visited him less frequently. He became increasingly concerned about the safety of his house and possessions. Without his friends he was unable to settle a lot of unfinished business. Mr. A saw no need to invest in forming new friendships because he anticipated returning soon to his own home. In addition, two of his roommates were comatose and the third one spent all his time playing cards down the hall.

Mr. A became a rather quiet, passive patient who did as he was told but who yelled in protest if prodded to hurry or physically pushed. He sat by his bed searching for his possessions in the stand, waiting for the day when he could go home. He refused to go on outings, saying that it was too painful to be allowed outside and yet denied access to his home. He chased the other patients away from "his space" and raged silently when the staff straightened his stand or furniture. His protests relative to his need for a specially ordered environment were ignored. His attempts to maintain order by complaining about the disorder or chasing offenders away were met with scoldings and a labeling of "uncooperative."

Sense of Powerlessness

Mr. A's perception of the situation was that he was powerless. He had to get well in order to regain his freedom. Yet the system seemed designed for his ultimate destruction. He thought that he was "falling to pieces." The physician would not even listen to his complaints, let alone discuss a release date with him. Mr. A was very frustrated and angry. The more angry he became, the harder he tried to control the environment and the people in it. The harder he tried, the more he was scolded. Then he sought to fight power with power. Since he perceived that he had no power or influence in the system, he sought a powerful ally. This was me.

The Nurse as Special Advocate

Mr. A believed that a nurse was a special advocate of patients and especially adept at interpreting their needs and desires to the physician. The nurse would be able to influence the physician so that the plan of care would be made most suitable for a patient. He thought that since I was a free agent and soon to be awarded a doctoral degree by the University of California, I might have great power to influence the patient care system. If a patient possessed such a powerful nurse, he would not be helpless against the system. Although I was not legally responsible for Mr. A's care, he held me somehow accountable for it by virtue of our past commitment to each other and my being "his" nurse. In our relationship we were responsible to and for each other. In addition, he trusted that I would understand his directing his frustration at me and would not retaliate by abandoning or otherwise punishing him. When I had first known him in connection with the research project, his initial reluctance to provide me with vital data had been overcome only after I had shared similar information from my life with him. Consequently, we had learned to know each other rather well and had developed a high degree of trust. Mr. A had gotten in the habit of giving me much advice on all aspects of my life. In his male Teutonic way he had been "taking care of me." That I was a nurse he knew, but he did not cast me in this role until he needed to combat the health care system. His friends did not possess the powers that Mr. A attributed to me, nor would they permit him to vent his anger on them without retaliating. Hence, they could not be of assistance in his battle for control and freedom.

Weekly Visits by the Nurse

I visited him in the nursing home weekly, according to his directive, and sought ways to relieve his mounting frustration. He would accept for trial only those solutions which we evolved together. A pattern quickly emerged in the content of our visits. First I would help him arrange his space and possessions in the pattern he found most useful. He needed to have his furniture aligned so that the bed was squarely in the corner of the room, and the chair and stand touching the same side of the bed at precise right angles to it. I usually found his furniture sitting at odd angles to each other and various distances apart, making it impossible for him to walk around the room or find anything. Then I would look for the missing items, either recovering them myself or asking the staff to search for them. Usually missing were: (1) Mr. A's razor, (2) his back brace, (3) his clothes, (4) his soap and tooth powder, and (5) his many slips of paper containing his notes and the telephone numbers of his friends. Even his teeth, glasses, and religious medals occasionally disappeared. Sometimes the items were located among the possessions of another patient, in the laundry or the lost-and-found office, on the wrong shelf of his stand, or on the person of another patient. Sometimes the items were not to be found at all.

After the environment had been rendered more acceptable, Mr. A would inquire in minute detail about the activities of my week. Then he would demand that I tell him something happy. In this he was really asking about the date for his release. However, I supplied him with a happy event from my own life, or an amusing one. Occasionally he had me make phone calls to his friends or write letters for him.

Near the end of my visits he would become excited, pound the floor with his cane, sputter incoherently, and finally explode with either "You don't seems to understand" or "You don't seems to *want* to understand." And the fight would be on. Raging and ranting through all the annoyances of the previous week and his worries, he would eventually focus on his need to go home, the harmful (to him) nature of the nursing home setting, and my obligation to do something about all of it, especially to arrange for his release. I would murmur apologetically and make mental note of possible interventions to discuss with him later. At the end of the tirade he would proceed to "win me back" confidently, either very gently or rather conspiratorially. He reassured me that it was not all my fault and that he was not really angry with me, but that I did have the potential power as his own nurse and his very dear friend to intervene and improve his situation. It took about 5 to 10 minutes for him to blow up and calm down.

Patient Suggests Interventions

We would then discuss how I was to intervene. He wanted only select complaints attended to each week. I did not negate his complaints nor reject my responsibility for the assigned errors and power. It seemed very important for him to be able to dominate me ("beat me down," as he put it) and then to restore me to my former position as his powerful ally. Mr. A would then send me forth with instructions for doing something about the system and I would leave him some suggestions for improving his situation. The majority of my suggestions were designed to get Mr. A to deal more directly with the staff instead of nursing his anger while waiting for me to arrive, perhaps six days after the incident. I reminded him that whenever he had made calm requests of the staff for such things as information about his bill, help in finding a missing item, a second serving of meat, or long johns instead of boxer shorts to wear under his trousers, his needs had been met promptly and graciously and that he had been spared the annoyance of waiting. He was most reluctant to deal directly with health care workers and tended to brood about things until his frustration exploded into loud accusations that he was being lied to, robbed, starved, and generally misused.

Fights Relieved Frustration

The fights seemed to relieve Mr. A's extreme frustration. He was quite relaxed and hopeful at the end of each. He picked fights only with me, never with the nursing home staff. In fact, he seemed to want to hide our fights from them. He then would be much less irritable, more cooperative, and less depressed for most of the week between my visits. There were several visits in which I provided something of great value to him. Although he was no less frustrated by his situation, on these occasions he did not pick a fight with me. One time I brought him a peach pie, his favorite food. Once I repaired his razor. Several times I took him home to attend to some of his affairs. Occasionally a friend of mine accompanied me to visit him. He could appreciate a shapely young woman and reveled in the extra attention that her presence afforded. As much as he enjoyed these special occasions, he made it very plain that he wanted to keep them as infrequent surprises and never requested them.

Lack of Control over Environment

Although I worked closely with the registered nurse in charge of Mr. A, there was little we could do to provide him with any measure of control over his immediate environment. The institution with its large group of non-professional staff and many volunteers was geared to the custodial care of helpless persons more than to the preservation and promotion of the concept of self-care. It took seemingly unavailable time to assist Mr. A in caring for himself or to listen to his explanations of his needs. The physician refused to tell Mr. A that the institutional arrangement was to be permanent, or to discuss alternative arrangements with me. The doctor thought it would be best for Mr. A to conclude for himself that he would never live at home again. He simply told Mr. A repeatedly that he was not well enough to go home. Mr. A was unwilling to challenge the physican openly. He believed that there was some oversight or error which caused the physician to persist in keeping him in the nursing home. Mr. A accused me of not presenting his cause effectively enough to the physician. He believed that physicians know what is best for their patients and that they will eventually cause this "best" to happen.

Allies among Staff Members

As months passed Mr. A did find several allies among the staff members who would assist him in being more independent. However, he never abandoned his fights and reconciliations with me, although he ultimately realized that there would be no escape from the nursing home. After almost a year away from home, Mr. A died quietly one evening. I was notified of the death by one of Mr. A's friends and attended the wake, funeral, and burial. At the wake I met many of Mr. A's friends and his nephew from Germany. I learned much from these people about Mr. A, especially of his life before I knew him.

THEMES AND ISSUES

By now the reader has probably identified several empirical themes and issues revealed in the story of my encounter with this marvelous old man. A few of these are order, independence, control, stress, privacy, isolation, mutual involvement, prolonged dying, survival strategies, and timing. Any single theme could be profitably examined for its clinical significance. However, for purposes of this brief chapter I have elected to focus on a single aspect of the clinical encounter—Mr. A's spontaneous use of the verbal fight as a therapeutic vehicle for coping with frustrations. I have searched the literature for discussions of similar phenomena, but the only clinical studies I found were those of Goldfarb,[2-5] who described a mode of individual psychotherapy he used with emotionally disturbed aged nursing home residents. Sessions were structured so that the patients would vent at the therapist their anger about care received, dominate him, and restore him at the end of the session as their staunch ally who would improve their situation. The result was a heightened sense of self-esteem and power for the patient, and a reduction in disturbed behavior.

There are three major differences between the work of Dr. Goldfarb and my work with Mr. A. The first difference is that Dr. Goldfarb assumed that his patients felt more helpless than they actually were in the nursing home setting. He further assumed that the subjectively helpless patient would seek or coerce aid from his care givers in much the same manner he had sought support from his parents as a child. Hence, pursuit and mastery of a parental figure would be a pleasurable activity to be maintained so long as the parent-surrogate did not disillusion the patient about his powers or possible availability. The illusion of mastery of the parent-surrogate would cause the patient to feel an increase in pleasure and self-esteem which would then lead to the real achievement of improved, socially acceptable behavior.

In the case of Mr. A, my assumption was that he was dissipating his limited energy and other resources trying to cope with a system that was not cooperating with his vital processes or making allowances for his individuality or his infirmities. He was helpless in his attempts to maintain order in his environment and to obtain information. His rising frustration and anger further impaired his ability to cope with the situation; his acts and verbalizations caused him to be scolded and punished by his care givers. My accepting his angry outbursts and allowing him to plan his strategy out loud gave him an opportunity to be his real self. Considering his age and his infirmities, Mr. A was an expert on survival. Mr. A did not see me as a parent figure. He saw himself playing parent to me most of the time. Our fights did not elevate Mr. A's self-esteem; they provided him with a safety valve to release anger verbally, the only way possible at the time. He then could work more constructively on his problems.

A second difference is methodological: Dr. Goldfarb deliberately provoked his patients to complain angrily, while I did not provoke Mr. A nor shut off his spontaneous verbal fighting. Dr. Goldfarb also saw his patients very briefly (less than 15 minutes per session) and rather infrequently (every 2 or 3 weeks), while I visited Mr. A for 2 hours each week. The fight was only a portion of my sessions with Mr. A, while the venting of anger was the substance of the sessions Dr. Goldfarb had with his patients.

The third difference is that Dr. Goldfarb encouraged his patients to view him as all-powerful and able to alter any part of their situation, including sending them home. I was not all-powerful nor did I pretend to be.

The reality of the power structure in health care today is that the physician is all-powerful. He controls the patient's access to health care services and the access of other health workers to the patient. At best, the nurse can be an advocate for patients in the case of physician-generated decisions about their care.

In spite of the above differences, the fact remains that certain institutionalized elderly persons appear to need to express their anger and frustration to a nonretaliatory, powerful health worker in order to be able to cope more effectively with whatever has aroused their anger and frustration.

The Fight Phenomenon

It is risky to generalize from specific cases. However, there seems to be an opportunity here for further examination of the fight phenomenon. Institutionalized aged persons are forced to learn to survive in a new setting at a point in time when they do not adapt readily. They may become very frustrated and angry in the process, which may result in their employing some behaviors that are not acceptable to staff or to other patients. As frustration and anger build, behavior can become "antisocial" and "punishable." The person may even become so unmanageable that transferral to a state mental institution would be considered the only solution. If the patient has an opportunity to express frustration and anger to someone who has the power within the institutional system to do something remedial, the cycle of ineffective behavior might be broken.

The most important interventive clinical act relative to patients like Mr. A would be to prevent the frustration and anger from accumulating. I propose that the professional nurse is the appropriate person to assess the situation of the elderly patient and to plan appropriate interventive strategy. The nurse could also help patients identify and define their anger and frustration, and be able to recognize his or her own feelings and respond in a deliberative manner to patients' outbursts of anger. An understanding of the dynamics of behavior would help the nurse recognize whether a patient experienced beneficial relief or became more excited and felt guilty after expressing emotions freely. In the latter instance, the nurse would be able to provide the needed controls. However, not all elderly patients are in institutions where they can have access to a professional nurse. All too often, the nurse-clinician is not consulted until the patient is already angry and displaying uncooperative behavior.

Persons Selected to Fight with   It is vital that patients be able to ascribe a large amount of institutional power to the persons with whom they "fight." In the absence of a professional nurse or a nurse-clinician, the person in the role of head nurse or charge nurse would be able to fulfill the power criterion. However, this person should be able to handle this hostility comfortably. Nevertheless, it is important for the person who listens to the outpouring of frustration and anger not to chide the patient for being ungrateful or to retaliate in some other way. Other staff members who happen to witness the fight should not remonstrate later with the patient about his behavior. Staff members should cooperate with whatever solutions are sought to alleviate patient frustration. Accepting the outpouring may be as beneficial as correcting all the grievances. The patient's energy, which was directed towards being indignant and angry, can then be redirected towards coping more effectively with the situation. In having grievances accepted, the patient's identity is reaffirmed. As I learned with Mr. A, many of the grievances can be easily remedied. Interventions should be discussed with the patient so that planning is a collaborative effort. Definitive actions can be taken to reduce frustrating circumstances.

Nurses who work closely over time with several very angry, erupting patients like Mr. A may find their own emotional reserves running short. They may need counsel and support from other professionals, such as the nursing supervisor, a psychiatric nursing clinical expert, or a mental health consultant.

Sensitivity groups for staff members might also be helpful. The goals of such a group would be (1) to have the members learn something about how each affects others with whom they interact, and (2) to explore their own reactions to the ways people react to them. As staff learn more about themselves in relation to others, they may become better able to allow patients to express their frustration and anger.

Fighting as Coping   It is important that the care of patients be in harmony with their ongoing lives, no matter how aged or infirm the patient, or what the setting may be. To pick a fight with or to complain belligerently to a truly powerful and nonretaliatory person who will do something remedial does appear to enhance the ability of certain aged persons to cope with living in institutional settings.

REFERENCES

1 I worked with Mr. A for 16 months in a variety of settings: an outpatient clinic, his home, a general hospital, a convalescent hospital, and a nursing home. An in-depth study of aspects of our collaborative endeavors is the substance of my doctoral dissertation.
2 Alvin I. Goldfarb, "Psychotherapy of Aged Persons: I. The Orientation of Staff in a Home for the Aged," *Mental Hygiene*, vol. 37, no. 1, pp. 76–83, 1953.

3 Alvin I. Goldfarb, "Psychotherapy of Aged Persons: IV. One Aspect of the Psychodynamics of the Therapeutic Situation with Aged Patients," *Psychoanalytic Review*, vol. 43, no. 2, pp. 180–187, 1955.

4 Alvin I. Goldfarb and Jack Sheps, "Psychotherapy of the Aged: III. Brief Therapy of Interrelated Psychological and Somatic Disorders," *Psychosomatic Medicine*, vol. 16, no. 3, pp. 209–219, 1954.

5 Alvin I. Goldfarb and Helen Turner, "Psychotherapy of Aged Persons: II. Utilization and Effectiveness of Brief Therapy," *American Journal of Psychiatry*, vol. 109, no. 12, pp. 916–921, 1953.

BIBLIOGRAPHY

Blumberg, Jeanne E., and Eleanor E. Drummond: *Nursing Care of the Long-Term Patient*, 2d ed., Springer, New York, 1971.

Chang, Betty: "Generalized Expectancy, Situational Perception and Morale among Institutionalized Aged," *Nursing Research*, vol. 27, no. 5, pp. 316–324, September–October 1978.

Donaghue, Shirley: "Geriatric Care: Assumptions to Throw Overboard," *The Australian Nurses Journal*, vol. 3, no. 9, pp. 36–38, April 1974.

Fuller, Sarah S.: "Inhibiting Helplessness in Elderly People," *Journal of Gerontological Nursing*, vol. 4, no. 4, pp. 18–21, July–August 1978.

Lester, Pamela B., and Margaret M. Baltes: "Functional Interdependence of the Social Environment and the Behavior of the Institutionalized Aged," *Journal of Gerontological Nursing*, vol. 4, no. 2, pp. 22–27, March–April 1978.

Levine, Myra E.: "The Intransigent Patient," *American Journal of Nursing*, vol. 70, no. 10, pp. 2106–2111, 1970.

Pease, Ruth A.: "Dependency and the Double-Bind in the Aged," *Journal of Gerontological Nursing*, vol. 4, no. 4, pp. 24–30, July–August 1978.

Storlie, Frances: "Unit 5: The Aged Poor," in *Nursing and the Social Conscience*, Appleton-Century-Crofts, New York, 1970, pp. 147–194.

Wolff, Kurt: *The Emotional Rehabilitation of the Geriatric Patient*, Charles C Thomas, Springfield, Ill., 1970.

OTHER RESOURCES

After Autumn, 16 mm, color, sound, 10 min., 1971, National Audiovisual Center, General Services Administration, Washington, D.C. 20409.

Chapter 5

Communication Disorders: A Problem in Rehabilitation of the Aged

Ann Herbert Shanck

Speech is civilization itself. The word, even the most contradictory word, preserves contact—it is silence which isolates.

Thomas Mann
The Magic Mountain

In many primitive societies the soul is imagined to leave the body at death or just prior to it; on the other hand, society drives out the remnants of the soul of the institutionalized old person while it struggles to keep the body alive.[1]

It has been my observation that, most of the time, the physical needs of the aged person are adequately taken care of by staff members, but the amount of communication between patient and staff is often minimal.

Routinization, inattention, and carelessness, and deprivation of communication —the chance to talk, to respond, to read, to see pictures on the wall, to be called by one's name rather than "you" or no name at all—are ways in which millions of once useful but now obsolete human beings are detached from their selves long before they are lowered to the grave.[2]

The emotional needs of the elderly person might be better met if we recognized that conditions we write off as confusion, apathy, depression, or "senility" might be the result of unrecognized or untreated communication disorders. One of the nurse's responsibilities is to establish effective interactions with the elderly; to do this, constant assessment of sensory losses is necessary. The importance of nursing interviews and nursing care plans cannot be overemphasized; both must be used. Continuous updating and daily assessment of sensorium is necessary. One possible consequence of not updating nursing plans is that necessary changes in the care of the patient may not be made.

The seriousness of the sensory losses in nursing home residents can well be seen from Tables 5-1 and 5-2. The data were compiled in a National Nursing Home survey.

Aging affects the efficiency of language just as other mental and physical skills. Normal aging causes aberrations in an individual's ability to communicate, handicapping personal adjustment and impairing social efficiency. The decreased language abilities associated with normal aging result from reduced hearing and visual acuity.[3] Often the old will deny having any visual or hearing handicap, or else the onset of such a handicap may be so insidious that clues to it may go unrecognized.

Unless speech returns spontaneously, aphasia, one of the common speech disorders, may become accepted in a patient or client.

COMMUNICATION DISORDERS

Three important communication disorders are discussed in this chapter: (1) speech and language disorders, (2) hearing impairment, and (3) visual impairment. By recognizing these impairments and what might be done to change or correct them, nurses can frequently assist the aged in increasing their environment contact, with a resulting improved emotional adjustment. Travelbee says that "it is through observation and communication that nurses ascertain the needs of patients—the first step in planning nursing intervention."[4] I observe many missed opportunities for assessing and improving communication problems with the aged person.

SPEECH AND LANGUAGE

Speech is one of the most important means of human communication. When he or she receives no encouragement in speech or conversation, the aged person often withdraws into a state of apathy and depression, because this is less frustrating than making the effort to converse.

Language is the basis of all human relationships. We make our thoughts known to ourselves, as well as to others, by this set of symbols.

Table 5-1 Number and Percent Distribution of Nursing Home Residents by Vision, Audition, Speech, and Dentition Status According to Sex: United States, August 1973–April 1974

Vision, audition, speech, and dentition status	Total	Percent distribution		
		Both sexes	Male	Female
Vision status				
All residents	1,075,800			
Sight not impaired	575,500	53.5	56.5	52.2
Sight partially impaired	362,000	33.7	31.5	34.6
Sight severely impaired	107,900	10.0	9.0	10.5
Sight completely lost	30,400	2.8	3.0	2.7
Residents using eyeglasses	670,400			
Sight not impaired	371,400	55.4	57.0	54.9
Sight partially impaired	226,600	33.8	32.0	34.4
Sight severely impaired	66,500	9.9	9.9	9.9
Sight completely lost	6,000	0.9	1.0	0.8
Residents not using eyeglasses	405,400			
Sight not impaired	204,100	50.3	55.9	47.0
Sight partially impaired	135,500	33.4	30.9	34.9
Sight severely impaired	41,400	10.2	8.0	11.5
Sight completely lost	24,500	6.0	5.2	6.5
Audition status				
All residents	1,075,800			
Hearing not impaired	729,600	67.8	66.9	68.2
Hearing partially impaired	280,300	26.1	26.7	25.8
Hearing severely impaired	55,200	5.1	5.2	5.1
Hearing completely lost	10,800	1.0	1.2	0.9
Residents using hearing aids	45,900			
Hearing not impaired	14,100	30.6	32.1	30.0
Hearing partially impaired	20,400	44.4	42.6	45.0
Hearing severely impaired	10,400	22.7	23.7	22.3
Hearing completely lost	—	—	—	—
Residents not using hearing aids	1,029,900			
Hearing not impaired	715,500	69.4	68.3	70.0
Hearing partially impaired	259,900	25.2	26.0	24.9
Hearing severely impaired	44,700	4.3	4.5	4.3
Hearing completely lost	9,700	0.9	1.1	0.9
Speech status				
All residents	1,075,800			
Speech not impaired	799,100	74.3	70.6	75.8
Speech partially impaired	155,200	14.4	16.8	13.4
Speech severely impaired	89,500	8.3	9.3	7.9
Speech completely lost	32,100	3.0	3.3	2.8
Dentition status				
All residents	1,075,800			
No dentures	388,800	36.1	46.8	31.7
Dentures and used them	632,800	58.8	48.7	63.1
Dentures but did not use them	54,200	5.0	4.5	5.3
Number of residents	1,075,800	1,075,800	318,100	757,700

Source: National Center for Health Statistics. Final estimates from the 1973-74 National Nursing Home Survey.

Table 5-2   Number and Percent Distribution of Nursing Home Residents by Vision, Audition, Speech, and Dentition Status According to Age: United States, August 1973-April 1974

Vision, audition, speech, and dentition status	Percent distribution			
	Under 65 years	65-74 years	75-84 years	85 years or over
Vision status				
Sight not impaired	70.6	62.3	53.8	45.0
Sight partially impaired	21.7	28.8	35.0	37.6
Sight severely impaired	5.0	6.3	8.9	14.0
Sight completely lost	2.7	2.6	2.3	3.5
Residents using eyeglasses				
Sight not impaired	65.6	63.3	57.1	49.9
Sight partially impaired	28.8	29.3	33.8	35.9
Sight severely impaired	5.4	6.5	8.4	13.0
Sight completely lost	—	—	0.7	1.1
Residents not using eyeglasses				
Sight not impaired	73.2	61.2	47.0	34.5
Sight partially impaired	18.0	28.3	37.5	41.2
Sight severely impaired	4.7	6.0	9.9	15.9
Sight completely lost	4.0	4.5	5.6	8.4
Audition status				
Hearing not impaired	88.4	80.3	70.0	55.2
Hearing partially impaired	9.2	17.0	25.5	34.8
Hearing severely impaired	1.6	1.9	3.8	8.7
Hearing completely lost	—	—	0.7	1.4
Residents using hearing aids				
Hearing not impaired	—	45.1	32.6	27.1
Hearing partially impaired	—	—	42.2	48.0
Hearing severely impaired	—	—	23.1	22.5
Hearing completely lost	—	—	—	—
Residents not using hearing aids				
Hearing not impaired	88.9	81.1	71.4	57.2
Hearing partially impaired	9.0	16.7	24.9	33.8
Hearing severely impaired	—	1.5	3.0	7.7
Hearing completely lost	—	—	0.7	1.3
Speech status				
Speech not impaired	58.6	70.7	76.2	78.2
Speech partially impaired	18.2	15.9	13.9	13.3
Speech severely impaired	15.5	9.7	7.4	6.7
Speech completely lost	7.6	3.8	2.5	1.8
Dentition status				
No dentures	74.2	48.6	30.5	25.9
Dentures and used them	22.3	47.7	64.4	68.1
Dentures but did not use them	3.4	3.7	5.1	5.9
Number of residents	114,300	163,100	384,900	413,600

Source: National Center for Health Statistics. Final estimates from the 1973-74 National Nursing Home Survey.

Expressive language is used to reveal our needs and thinking to others, while receptive language is used to understand what others say to us. Inner language is used when people think or talk to themselves.[5] The latter seems to be very common in aged persons.

Often, nursing care plans contain the diagnosis *aphasia*, and this term indicates to the health team that the person does not speak; but aphasia can take many forms and it is much more complicated than simply not speaking. The types of aphasia are as follows.

Motor or Expressive Aphasia

Motor or expressive aphasia prohibits verbal expression, spontaneous speaking or reading aloud. Aged persons can say only a few words and these may not be used appropriately. They often retain the ability to count or sing, even when there is little or no production of speech. Those who are aware of errors are often frustrated and embarrassed.

The client should be encouraged to use gestures for words even though they may not always be appropriate for the message—the client may become more proficient at it. The nurse can say the word as the aged person gestures in order to help him or her relearn a word. Attempts to force verbalization may only increase frustration.

An effort must be made to try to understand the client's attempts to talk. Wait for slow or delayed speech. *It is essential to respond in some way to all attempts to speak. Do not fake it when you do not understand; you could damage your rapport.*

Get the client to relax; suggest speaking more slowly. This may aid relaxation and may also help the listener to understand better. Ask questions that require only a "yes" or "no" answer until you get some clues about the client's message. Calm acceptance and understanding when the client has outbursts of automatic unwanted words such as swearing or meaningless cliches is important. Any other behavior only adds to frustration and embarrassment. Even involuntary words are speech and should not be repressed.

Do not provide the word when the client is struggling until it is very evident that it will not be found. Provide the correct word tactfully if the client comes up with the wrong word. This difficulty often decreases as available language increases.

Sensory or Receptive Aphasia

Sensory or receptive aphasia is more complex. It usually appears as:

1 A loss of comprehension of spoken language
2 A loss of comprehension of written words
3 An inability to write
4 A combination of any of these

Patients often speak volubly but misuse words. When they begin to speak, the first sentences are composed but, as they continue, their speech difficulty becomes increasingly evident. Such patients are difficult to rehabilitate because they cannot understand the therapist and, in fact, may become quite indignant because their jargon cannot be understood.

Techniques should be used that will enhance the understanding of language the client hears or reads. Sit or stand close and make sure you have the client's attention. Talk slowly and clearly in a normal voice unless the client has a hearing loss, using simple words in short phrases or sentences. Clients find it annoying to be shouted at and they also do not like it when the content or tone of voice is childish.

Allow ample time for processing what has been said, because understanding may occur if given enough time. Sometimes changing or rearranging words may help clarify the meaning. Writing is fine, if the client can read without becoming frustrated.

In order to appear capable, the client may pretend to understand, so be sure to verify responses. Let the clients know verbally and nonverbally when you understand their efforts. Clients may be especially tuned into body language so watch for nonverbal clues. Keep in mind that the ability to follow directions or to understand may vary from day to day, or even minute to minute.

Global Aphasia

Global aphasia is caused by extensive damage to the speech center of the brain; this is the most serious type of aphasia. Most patients suffering from global aphasia are speechless; they cannot read or write, and can understand only a few simple spoken words or phrases. The chances of rehabilitation are quite limited.[6]

Dysarthria may be confused with aphasia. The dysarthritic patient cannot make others understand him because the many muscles needed for articulation are affected by damage to the central or peripheral nervous system.[7]

INFORMATION GATHERING

There are a few simple procedures nursing personnel can use to assess aphasia, though the nurse must keep in mind that information gathering may be hindered by the difficulty in interacting with the patient. The nurse might begin by determining the patient's native language, cultural background, previous education, and present communicative ability. Most of this information can usually be obtained from family and friends. All information about the client's communicating ability should be recorded in detail on both the nursing care plan and the chart. This will reduce the need for frequent reexaminations.

Find out if the patient can say intelligible words spontaneously and in proper sequence. Can the patient understand what is said? If the patient cannot speak, does he or she respond to commands, for example, "Close your eyes," "Hold up your hand"? Can the patient read? Write spontaneously? If able to speak, can the patient name objects? Actions called for should progress from simple to complex. Be careful not to give negative nonverbal cues when doing an assessment. Keep questions simple, and review as necessary for the patient, who often can't remember from one situation to the next. Assessment could take place during daily physical care.

Keep communication situations, whether assessing or facilitating, as relaxed as possible. The client's efforts are usually more successful when calm and not under pressure. Stop and allow for rest period when there are signs of fatigue, stress, or discomfort. Avoid large groups when attempting to communicate and eliminate background noises such as television and radio. Do not discuss matters the client should not hear, or might misinterpret, in his presence.

Working with aphasic patients is extremely trying. Nurses can improve communication by increased understanding of speech and language disorders as well as communication techniques. They can also help the patient to communicate with someone other than themselves. They can assist family and friends to reduce their discomfort in their relationship with the client by explaining the general nature of language disorder and teaching communication techniques.

There is a need to structure and control the client's environment, and ideally the same nurse should work with a client from day to day. The elderly often become downright rigid. They like things in order, so routine becomes important; if it is provided, then they can concentrate on other things. Some elderly people may withdraw because of constant changes in personnel caring for them.

Utilize anything to establish some form of communication. Try pencil and paper, picture books, flash cards, gestures, remembering that some clients may be so apathetic that you would be fortunate to get a toe wiggle from them. Sometimes nonverbal communications such as facial expression, gesture, posture, touch, and silence are necessary for the severely brain-damaged. The same approaches may also be used in working with the patient or client with less severe communication disorders in order to prevent too much frustration with the rate of progress.

A language disorder is often interpreted by the client as well as society to be a result of diminished intelligence. This has to be emotionally devastating. Achieving communication is time-consuming and frustrating, but it becomes worthwhile when the client feels more in touch with those around. You will improve the overall emotional outlook and rehabilitation potential of your clients by understanding speech and language disorders.

HEARING IMPAIRMENTS

Often, speech and language disorders are complicated by hearing disorders. The world of silence and misunderstanding is a lonely one and is unnecessary for most people; however, many will not admit or do not realize that they cannot hear well. One study found that 70 percent of the patients who were admitted to hospitals for psychotic or maladaptive behavior had a hearing loss. Hearing loss restricts 30 to 50 percent of the population past 65 years of age.[8]

There are two kinds of hearing loss: conductive and sensorineural. For some, both types of loss may occur. Conductive losses which are caused by errors in, disease of, or injury to the outer or middle ear are more amenable to treatment than the sensorineural losses. These clients do not have problems with word discrimination and respond well to louder voices. Good results can often be obtained with surgery, amplification, or both.[9]

Presbycusis

Presbycusis is a sensorineural hearing impairment and a normal consequence of aging. It may be severe, but it does not lead to total deafness; it involves both ears equally. These losses, which are in the high frequency range, are rarely reversible. Any improvement is due to training the person's ability to adapt.[10] The condition is presently occurring sooner in life because of the assault of noise. Considerable research is being done to determine the exact cause of presbycusis. It is no longer believed to be due solely to aging, but rather to a multiplicity of factors that assault the hearing apparatus during a lifetime. Quite often the person is unaware of any hearing loss, denies it, or thinks the condition is temporary.[11] He or she may also think it is a sign of old age and therefore accept the loss.

The elderly usually find high notes impossible or difficult to hear. Consonants are in the high frequency range and vowels in the low. It is essential for intelligibility and understanding that the consonants be heard. To gain insight into what the elderly hear in speech, write a sentence and remove the *f*'s *s*'s, and *th*'s; the gaps will demonstrate what the older person misses. The first to go are *ch*, *f*, and *th*—then *t* and *p*. When all these consonants are removed, speech is disjointed and becomes a murmur or a rumble. This accounts for misunderstanding and misinterpretation, because the sentence is not heard as a coherent whole. The aged person must guess at what is missing and often makes the wrong guess, which alters the whole trend of the conversation, much to the distress and annoyance of all concerned.[12] Moreover, old people who have hearing impairment often think people are talking about them, which adds to distress and misunderstanding.

Any responses that make the nurse suspect deterioration of hearing should be reported, so that hearing ability can be checked. The nurse may, for example, notice changes in the ease of communication with the patient or client. A nurse may first become aware of change when the patient turns up the volume on television or radio. It is important to check with the family as to whether they have noticed any change in personality or attitude, or any changes in ability to communicate. Remind the family that these changes are usually subtle or slow in evolving.

Early Diagnosis

Early diagnosis is important. There may be a condition that can be corrected or treated. It is important for a patient to get a hearing aid before it is desperately needed to allow for training in listening. The aged person should be referred to a qualified audiologist, who can determine whether a hearing aid will be beneficial and which type of instrument will help the patient the most. Some persons have quite a collection of hearing aids, because they succumbed to highpowered advertising for these instruments.

Nurses themselves often know little about hearing aids. They should become familiar with the instrument, so they can make a daily check to see if it is working properly. The nurse can assist the patient with some of the more frequently encountered difficulties (listed below) and also help in adjustment to new sounds, such as amplification of background noise.[13] The user should be helped to realize that speech may be louder, but not necessarily clearer. The elderly have a tendency to:

1 Lose the batteries
2 Let the batteries run down
3 Become confused between new and used batteries
4 Refuse to wear a hearing aid
5 Have difficulty manipulating batteries and handling controls because of poor vision and manual dexterity

The American Hearing Society will lend hearing aids in cases when the owners' are lost or stolen.[14] The telephone company in some parts of the country offers three different services for people with hearing defects:

1 "Handicap Telephone"—the user picks up the telephone; the operator receives a ring and she dials the number for the person. Usually there is no charge for changing to this type of service and generally no monthly charge.
2 An amplifier to increase the voice of the speaker initiating the call. (The charge is minimal.)
3 An amplifier to increase the volume on the phone.

Nurses should use a sympathetic approach to the elderly with a hearing handicap and help others in their environment to develop such an attitude. Touch the person when you are going to speak to maximize awareness that someone is present; then he or she can focus on you before you speak. Essential points to remember include enunciating carefully, speaking slowly, and talking slightly more loudly than usual. The aged person can feel excluded or included, depending upon whether such simple measures are used. These actions can also help the listening ability of clients who do not wear hearing aids. Give your full attention; get used to speech patterns; do not say you understand when you do not. Lipreading or speech reading has been recommended for those with hearing difficulties, but often visual handicaps will prevent the aged person from benefiting from such instruction. However, if the client is able and motivated to learn, a lipreading program can be very helpful. As a nurse working with a lip-reader, your most important responsibility is not to obscure your face.

Although most factors responsible for sensorineural hearing loss pose no threat to longevity, the result compromises the client's ability to communicate. The aged client has enough psychosocial problems without believing one must be resigned to living with a handicap that isolates one from society. Hearing loss often leads the aging to withdraw from society. Friends and family misinterpret this withdrawal as unfriendly behavior, even though it may be done to avoid the frustration and embarrassment that result from being unable to hear or understand what is being said. The many achievements in the field of hearing rehabilitation have made it possible for the hard-of-hearing to improve their ability to communicate. It is imperative that nurses identify hard-of-hearing individuals and refer them for the necessary consultations.

VISUAL IMPAIRMENT

The principal causes of impaired vision are cataracts, macular degeneration, glaucoma, and diabetes, all of which are associated with aging. Presbyopia is not a disease but a degenerative change which results in the inability of the lens to focus. Many visual disturbances are linked to neurologic disorders that will not be dealt with here. However, one common visual defect often overlooked is homonymous hemianopia, in which one half of the visual field in each eye is lost.[15, 16]

Unawareness of hemianopia can complicate nursing care and rehabilitation. Individuals with this defect may not respond, and are poorly motivated to move the involved side during physical therapy. Its discovery often results in dramatic improvement.

The nurse's responsibility in a case of hemianopia, for example, would be to have items on the right easily available and within reach. He or she should stay in view on the right, and have food items on the tray in the right visual field. One of the best things a nurse can do is to simply have the person turn the head. Frequently, the person is inadvertently positioned so that the good visual field is directed toward a blank wall and the hemianoptic field is directed toward the door and the side from which nursing personnel approach. Reversing the bed motivates patients to begin to participate in their own care.

Nurses must remain alert to changing visual acuity in order to identify new visual problems in their aging clients. When were the eyeglasses last corrected? How long has it been since their eyes were checked? Do they wear eyeglasses? If so, where are they? Would magnifiers help? Who can supply assistance?

Possible reactions to diminished vision include depression, withdrawal, denial, resentment, and anger. An aged person may suffer from serious communication problems because of prior dependence on vision for receiving and processing information.

People with visual defects require more and brighter lighting. Night lights should be provided because of the inability to adapt to the dark. Rooms with light-colored floors, walls, and ceilings will reduce shadows and provide an even illumination. Brighter lights will improve reading ability. Nighttime hallucinations are a prime example of psychological reactions to trying to overcome the handicaps of subnormal vision, refractive errors, and insufficient illumination. Individuals with cataracts are annoyed by the glare of bright lights, which also distort objects.

I have observed in some institutions specific visual aids such as signs with huge, bold, black lettering to catch the patient's attention. Color can be used effectively to help patients with sensory aphasia. For example, paint doors different colors: one color for the bathroom, one for the dining room. Colored arrows can be painted on the floor for direction. One hospital used color coding—a color on a ceramic bracelet for the patient and a corresponding color on the door of the patient's room. Large black silhouettes of a man and a woman could be used on bathroom doors. One blind woman told me that if the silhouettes were slightly raised from the door surface, she could feel them. Giant number dials for telephones, which are inexpensive, may be purchased at stationery stores. They are easily installed and some are luminous.

Permitting a flashlight at the bedside for nighttime use and putting fluorescent tapes around light switches and on door handles may help reduce "confusion." The nurse should remember that problems with eyeglasses might include dirty lenses, incorrect lenses, the need for repair, and loss with no replacement. Three media which can be very useful in preventing isolation of the aged with low vision are the telephone, radio, and tapes.

Regional institutes are being set up by the American Foundation for the Blind to deal with problems of visual impairment and blindness in the elderly. The institutes are directed to those who work with older persons.[17]

Both hearing and sight are essential for perceiving the environment if a person is to function rationally. Vision loss affects environmental adjustment, while hearing loss seems to have a more serious impact on psychological functioning. Visual disabilities add to the isolation of the elderly. Moreover, whatever the perceptual loss, it leads to inappropriate responses which, in turn, result in a labeling of "uncooperative," "confused," or even "senile."[18] Nurses are in an ideal position to recognize problems of vision, allay patients' fears, and help them correct their losses.

The Importance of Family

The family is, of course, important; do not, however, expect them to answer for the patient. You should encourage the family not to maximize the patient's problems or treat him or her as a child, and remember that the family also needs help from the health team in coping. Sometimes the patient will "blow his top" in order to handle frustrations. Nurse and family must be aware of this or the entire nursing care plan may fall apart.

It behooves the nurse to improve listening skills, since practicing listening will increase an understanding of the patient's communication disorders. In caring for the aged, we must not be impersonal and must tolerate attitudes and behavior even though we may not always approve of it.

MULTIDISCIPLINARY APPROACH

The ability to adapt is characteristic of human behavior, but when old people are denied the right to understand, or to be understood, within the limits of their capabilities, they lose effective social control and cannot adapt in a healthy manner. The old person can no longer control environment, family, friends, or job. As a result, he or she may break down completely and become totally dependent; because of speech and language difficulties, the older person may withdraw from society, feeling a loss of self-esteem, and a lack of anything useful to offer. Finally, there is no way to "blow up"; all the frustrations and anxieties are bottled up inside and may be manifested in maladaptive behavior that puts the patient in a mental hospital or institution.[19]

Nurses can be the first to begin reversing the process by permitting the older person to establish an emotionally dependent relationship, which is necessary initially to reestablish contact. *There can be no relationship without communication.* Because the person usually has other disabilities along with communication disorders, a multidisciplinary approach is necessary. Other people involved might include audiologists, psychologists, psychiatrists, social workers, medical doctors, therapists (speech, physical, occupational), registered nurses, and paramedical personnel. Interpersonal gratification is available to patients from many sources, not just from nursing service. Busse and Pfeiffer state:

> We feel that no single discipline, whether it be psychological, sociological, biological, or economical can claim to offer a comprehensive explanation of how aged people act, think, and feel, or what the multiple determinants of their behavior are.[20]

Ideally, rehabilitation should take place in a medical center, but this is not always practical. However, periodic local workshops sponsored by the large centers would be of considerable value to personnel in suburban settings. Perhaps a regional speech therapist, such as are available in certain areas, could assess and evaluate patients and then instruct the staff how to carry on until the next visit. Could convalescent hospitals cooperate in providing rehabilitation education for their staffs? Perhaps the extended care center could become a therapeutic community! Could the convalescent hospitals be used as day care centers and outpatient clinics to keep the elderly patient in contact with helping others, as well as on continuous rehabilitation, and hopefully out of general hospitals and mental hospitals?

SUMMARY

Speech therapy can begin within a few days after a stroke; however, success has been demonstrated in aphasic patients who began therapy as long as 6 to 7 years after a stroke. Personnel need no special abilities to identify hearing and vision disorders; sometimes all that is required is that we adapt our speech and actions to the elderly person with no particular communication disorder other than being slowed down by age. Therapy staffs are usually understaffed, and younger patients often receive priority. If the nursing staff were familiar with the rehabilitation therapies available to the unit, they could help tremendously in increasing the emotional and physical well-being of the aged patient who receives little or nothing in the way of therapy.

Nurses who work in aged settings are special. For many nurses, it is all they can do to meet the physical needs of elderly clients. Hopefully, what has been said here will inspire them to probe deeper into communication disorders and improve upon assessment skills. In the process of enriching the client's existence, the nurse's work will be lessened by the increased participation of the aging in their own life.

REFERENCES

1 Jules Henry, *Culture against Man*, Random House, New York, 1963, p. 393.
2 Ibid.
3 Jane Sheridan, "Restoring Speech and Language Skills," *Geriatrics*, vol. 32, no. 5, pp. 83–86, May 1977.
4 Joyce Travelbee, *Interpersonal Aspects of Nursing*, Davis, Philadelphia, 1966, p. 100.
5 Irene Beland, *Clinical Nursing*, 3d ed., Macmillan, New York, 1975, p. 1008.
6 George W. Thorn et al., *Harrison's Principles of Internal Medicine*, 8th ed., McGraw-Hill, New York, 1977, pp. 137–142.
7 Ibid., p. 142.
8 Ralph Rupp, "Understanding the Problems of Presbycusia," *Geriatrics*, vol. 25, no. 1, pp. 100–107, January 1970.
9 Gerald Hirschberg et al., *Rehabilitation*, 2d. ed., Lippincott, Philadelphia, 1976, pp. 112–117.
10 Ibid., pp. 114–115.
11 Rupp, op. cit., p. 102.
12 E. C. N. Strong, "Deafness in the Elderly," *Nursing Mirror*, vol. 135, pp. 19–21, July 11, 1969.
13 Rupp, op. cit., pp. 105–106.
14 American Hearing Society, 919 18th Street N.W., Washington, D.C. 20006.
15 Gerald E. Fonda, "Ways to Improve Vision in Partially Sighted Persons," *Geriatrics*, vol. 30, no. 5, pp. 49–52, May 1975.
16 Michael J. Andriola, "When Visual Disturbances Are Linked to Neurologic Disorders," *Geriatrics*, vol. 31, no. 3, pp. 109–112, March 1976.
17 American Foundation for the Blind, 15 West 16th Street, New York, N.Y. 10011.
18 Virginia Stone, "Give the Older Person Time," *American Journal of Nursing*, vol. 69, no. 12, p. 1296, December 1969.
19 Joyce Mitchell, "Disorders of Communication in the Older Patient," *Gerontologica Clinica*, vol. 6, pp. 331–340, 1964.
20 E. Busse and E. Pfeiffer, *Geriatric Times*, p. 13, February 4, 1970.

BIBLIOGRAPHY

Buseck, Sally A.: "Visual Status of the Elderly," *Journal of Gerontological Nursing*, vol. 2, no. 5, pp. 34–39, September–October 1976.
Carstenson, Blue: *Speech and Hearing Problems among Older People*, Nos. 285–286, U.S. Department of Health, Education and Welfare, Administration on Aging, July–August 1978.

Corso, John F.: "Sensory Processes and Age Effects in Normal Adults," *Journal of Gerontology*, vol. 26, no. 1, pp. 90–105, January 1971.

Goehl, Henry: "Speech and Language Disorders," in F. H. Krusen (ed.), *Handbook of Physical Medicine and Rehabilitation*, 2d ed., Saunders, Philadelphia, 1971, pp. 145–167.

Goodpasture, Robert C.: "Rehabilitation of the Blind," in F. H. Krusen (ed.), *Handbook of Physical Medicine and Rehabilitation*, 2d ed., Saunders, Philadelphia, 1971, pp. 799–809.

Hallburg, Jeanne C.: "The Teaching of Aged Adults," *Journal of Gerontological Nursing*, vol. 2, no. 3, pp. 13–19, May–June 1976.

Kart, Cary S., et al.: *Aging and Health: Biologic and Social Perspectives*, Addison-Wesley, Menlo Park, Calif., 1978, pp. 60–73.

Keim, Robert J.: "How Aging Affects the Ear," *Geriatrics*, vol. 32, no. 6, pp. 97–99, June 1977.

Rush, Howard A.: *Rehabilitation Medicine*, 4th ed., Mosby, St. Louis, 1977, pp. 259–269.

Stryker, Ruth: *Rehabilitative Aspects of Acute and Chronic Nursing Care*, Saunders, Philadelphia, 1977, pp. 64–79.

Valenstein, Edward: "Nonlanguage Disorders of Speech Reflect Complex Neurologic Apparatus," *Geriatrics*, vol. 30, no. 9, pp. 117–121, September 1975.

OTHER RESOURCES

The Inner World of Aphasia, film—available from local branches of the American Heart Association.

The Stroke Patient, film strip with tapes.
Concept Media
1500 Adams Avenue
Costa Mesa, Calif. 92626

Aids & Appliances for the Blind & Visually Impaired (booklet).
American Foundation for the Blind
15 West 16th Street
New York, N.Y. 10011

Part Two

The Aged Person
in the Community

Aging is like a game of chess, in which individuals may be captured, but in which a few potent figures can still hold the field and even regain a new and powerful position.

Martin Grumpert

INTRODUCTION

Part 2 is focused on the aged patient who is still residing in the community. Blake describes her experiences with psychosocial assessments in Chapter 6.

Eide, a public health nurse, describes in Chapter 7 the role of the nurse who is dedicated to maintaining the older person's ability to reside at home against tremendous odds, and provides suggestions for the nurse when the elderly patient is discharged from a hospital. In Chapter 8, ways to improve continuity of care for discharged patients are suggested.

In Chapter 9, McWhorter describes her group work with grieving women during their throes of widowhood, in an outpatient clinic group in a large metropolitan hospital.

Blackman, in Chapter 10, describes her group leadership with aged persons who resided in the community, but attended a senior center in a suburban area.

Chapter 11 by Dolan is about day care centers and the important role they can play in keeping elderly people in their own homes. It should be noted, however, that day care centers for the elderly are still not very common at this writing.

A survey done by Moehrlin on the utilization of health care services by the elderly is described in Chapter 12 and the author lists implications for practice based on her research.

Chapter 6

Psychosocial Assessment of Elderly Clients

Dorothy Rinehart Blake

Is there such a thing as an impartial history? And what is history? The written representation of past events. But what is an event. . . . It is a notable fact. Now, how . . . to discriminate whether a fact is notable or not? He decides this arbitrarily, according to his character and idiosyncrasy, at his own taste and fancy—in a word, as an artist. . . .

Anatole France

The Garden of Epicurus

This chapter is geared to the assessment of the elderly person who comes to the nurse with one or more of the symptoms commonly associated with psychosocial problems, i.e., fatigue, insomnia, nervousness, anorexia, bad taste in the mouth, dizziness, depression, or a spate of somatic complaints involving multiple systems of the body. Disturbed interpersonal relationships occasionally prompt the client to seek help, but often a symptom that signals a physical or a psychosocial problem is the client's main concern.

The format for data collection presented in this chapter is a variation on methods found in medical physical diagnosis texts. The format is modified here to include topics pertinent to the psychosocial assessment of the elderly. I find the medical model of data collection expedient for obtaining the most information with the fewest questions. It has been refined by years of usage and is a tool that could be used to advantage by all nurses. I believe that nursing should enrich itself with whatever is useful from medicine, just as medicine is enriched by nursing's emphasis on psychosocial aspects of patient care.

ASSESSMENTS AS USED IN PROBLEM SOLVING

Assessments of any kind are primarily useful in the context of problem solving. Writing about assessment without a focal point predisposes an unwieldy mass of information. It is presumed that the reader will abstract from this chapter those materials that are useful to a specific client's needs. Only a nurse with limitless time and a bored but loquacious client would attempt to address every heading suggested under "Other Topics Pertinent to the Elderly." It is also presumed that it is not always possible to get the information necessary to make the best decisions because of a client's difficulty in communication, e.g., a hearing, speech, or memory deficit. The nurse may make an initial decision based on less than optimal information and revise the nursing plan if more data are later available from the client's family or friends. Often the constraint of time necessitates gathering the information in more than one interview, but the order of gathering the information should begin with "A Detailed Description of the Problem" and proceed to "Getting a Description of Associated Symptoms/Problems." It is not possible to know in what direction to proceed until a precise picture of the problem has been elicited. Making judgments without knowing what medications the client is taking, or without knowledge of the history of past health problems, can lead to poor or dangerous decisions.

A DETAILED DESCRIPTION OF THE PROBLEM

This information should be collected for any unsolved problem. The problem is whatever the client, the client's family, or the nursing staff state as being the problem or problems. Suppose the problem is loss of appetite and irritability. A detailed description of both is necessary. Specific details would include the following:

1 Duration of each problem, i.e., how long ago each began
2 Age of the client
3 Onset of each problem, events preceding the onset, whether the onset was rapid or slow

4 Characteristics of each problem; constant or intermittent, frequency with which they occur, duration each lasts when it occurs, other qualities specific to each symptom

5 Previous occurrence, diagnosis, and treatment of the problem

6 Factors which relieve the problem

7 Factors which aggravate the problem

8 Client's own treatment of the problem to date, with drugs, change in habits, and other solutions tried

9 Effects of the problem on the client's usual daily activities

CASE EXAMPLE: The daughter of an 80-year-old woman is concerned about her mother's poor appetite and irritability. Both of these problems began gradually at the same time, approximately 3 months ago; neither woman can recall any unusual factors preceding the onset. The irritability takes the form of sharp retorts to the daughter's questions about her mother's health and general well-being. The mother accuses the daughter of not really being concerned and even of wishing that she (the mother) were dead. The client is not always irritable, and when not so, she shows some of her usual humor. Her irritation is usually short-lived and she is apologetic about her acid answers. Her anorexia takes the form of a reduced appetite for all foods; she is not hungry and food does not taste as good. She felt this way 5 years ago after the death of her husband; she sought no treatment and gradually recovered her appetite and usual mood. She has been living with her divorced daughter since then. Her appetite and mood are worse on the weekends and better when she visits a married son, who lives 100 miles away. The daughter has unsuccessfully attempted to find out if something is bothering her mother and has tried fixing special foods for her. The mother is able to carry out her usual activities of self-care; she goes to a senior citizens' group and visits with church friends. The daughter says the anorexia is no worse than 3 months ago but that the episodes of irritability are increasing.

This detailed description of the two problems shows the likelihood of one underlying problem, as both began at the same time. The fact that the symptoms got worse on weekends and better away from the daughter is suggestive of a nonorganic problem. Since similar symptoms occurred after the loss of the husband, the nurse should look for a more recent loss or anticipated loss.

GETTING A DESCRIPTION
OF ASSOCIATED PROBLEMS/SYMPTOMS

At this point the nurse must use some judgment and imagination in choosing the multiple paths of questioning that could be pursued. The judgment will be based on the diagnostic possibilities that the nurse has already formulated. In the above instance, more somatic information is necessary, and there is already an indication for further searching for a psychosocial basis. My favorite pathfinder is *The Common Symptom Guide*, a paperback which lists the symptoms associated with all common somatic and psychological problems.[1] Ascertaining the presence or absence of these associated symptoms will aid in narrowing the focus of the search. In the case example cited, the associated symptoms of anorexia include weight loss, nausea and vomiting, change in bowel habits, melena, abdominal pain, and jaundice. A positive answer to several of these would necessitate a medical workup to confirm or rule out a gastrointestinal problem. If those associated symptoms were not present, or even if several were, the possibility of a psychosocial problem should be considered, and the next group of topics should be pursued.

SYMPTOMS COMMONLY ASSOCIATED WITH PSYCHOSOCIAL PROBLEMS

Sleep Disturbance

Difficulty in sleeping is often one of the first symptoms of depression, and the diagnosis must be considered when a disturbed sleep pattern is present. Feinberg points out that after adolescence the normal amount of total sleep time stays constant until old age. Even then there is only a slight, gradual tendency to less total sleep time.[2]

> Young and old have periods during normal sleep in which they approach waking up. Young people may wake up briefly and not even remember doing so; the elderly have a decreased intensity of sleep and are more likely to remember waking up more often than when they were young.[3]

People past middle age often spend more time in bed, but have fewer hours of continuous sleep, and may sleep a total of 6 or less hours during the night.[4]

Insomnia is a problem in falling asleep, more frequent awakenings, and decreased total sleep time. If insomnia is secondary to depression, early morning awakening is almost always present. Difficulty falling asleep is more often secondary to situational stress, anxieties, and pain. Frequent awakenings may be secondary to age, depression, and physical problems such as hypo- and hyperthyroidism, ulcers, angina, lung and cardiac disease, and degenerative joint disease of the back.[5]

Studies by Kales showed that 82 percent of insomniacs age 50 and older show depressive scales on the Minnesota Multiphasic Personality Index

(MMPI), and that older people tended to focus more on their sleep problems and to avoid looking at depression.[6]

In assessing sleep patterns, ask what time the person goes to bed, when they fall asleep, how many times they wake up, how long it takes to go back to sleep, and at what time they awaken in the morning. If they wake up early, ask if that is due to an alarm clock or if it is spontaneous and if they are able to go back to sleep.

If insomnia is a complaint and your later questioning about drug usage elicits a history of hypnotics which the person has recently discontinued, consider drug withdrawal insomnia, which can temporarily cause fragmented sleep and considerable anxiety about sleeping. People who have been on barbituates may also experience nightmares for a time.

CHANGE IN BODILY FUNCTION

Ask about changes in bowel habits, nausea, vomiting, diarrhea, melena, weight loss, cardiac palpitations, fatigue, headaches, fever, and shortness of breath. A positive answer to any of these questions means that physical illness must be considered as a possibility; remember that tension headaches are unusual in the elderly. Even a slight temperature elevation can signal serious disease in the elderly. The immune response of the aged is so decreased that an elderly person can die of an acute infection without having a fever.

CHANGES IN MENTAL STATE

Disturbances in Experiencing Pleasure

A decline in pleasure is also characteristic of depression. Ask the clients if food tastes good or if they eat from boredom or habit. Ask about sexual functioning and pleasure. Inquire about pleasure from social and family activities. If the client replies in the negative to those questions, ask what in life is pleasurable. If nothing is, determine if they can no longer do the things that once gave them pleasure because of lack of money, transportation, or energy, or if they discontinued their former activities because of lack of joy in them. Answers to such questions can be used to make an accurate diagnosis and also to make interventions at a later time.

If the client sleeps well and has a good appetite for food and sex, depression is an unlikely diagnosis; even if the person sleeps poorly but finds pleasure in food and people, depression is not likely.

Memory Impairment*

Ask if there is difficulty in remembering details or in concentrating and making decisions. If so, when did this start? Abruptly or gradually? What events preceded the onset? (Astute readers will recognize a rerun of the questions from "A Detailed Description of the Problem.") Ask for an example in which the difficulty occurred.

Loss of memory is especially frightening to the elderly, who dread becoming "senile," and realistically so, for memory impairment may be a symptom of chronic brain syndrome.

I tend to look at the person's life situation for causes of memory problems. If the problem is antedated by a major life change, I assume they are preoccupied by that change and I use that rationale in making nursing interventions.

Ask clients to choose the words that best describe how they feel much of the time: sad, angry, happy, self-confident, worried, cheerful, pessimistic. To get an estimate of how intensely they experience the mood, ask them to place themselves on a scale of 1 to 10, using the extremes of that emotion. For instance, "If 10 equals great joy and 1 equals the depths of despair, where would you rate yourself?" If they rate themselves as low, sad, or hopeless, then ask if life seems worth living. Do they think of dying? Of taking their own life? And if so, what plans have they made to do so?[7] Ask if they have changed their will or insurance policy recently. Suicide is the tenth most common cause of death in white males aged 60 to 64 and continues to be frequent although it is not among the top 10 causes after that. It is somewhat less common in older women, but it is a possibility whenever depression exists.

Appearance of Hallucinations; Delusional Thinking

Ask the elderly person about any possible paranoid or suspicious ideas regarding other persons, and neighbors especially. Ask about unusual thoughts or experiences with television, electricity, or the washer or dryer. Hallucinations or delusional thinking may come out in this type of questioning and help you uncover a psychosis. Paranoid ideation can occur in persons who have organic brain syndrome. And paranoid ideation can sometimes be missed even by a careful interviewer.

---

* Robert Butler and Myrna Lewis give an example of a screening questionnaire in *Aging and Mental Health*, Mosby, St. Louis, 1977, pp. 190–192. The Kahn and Goldfarb mental status questionnaire (MSQ) can be found in Irene Mortenson Burnside (ed.), *Nursing and the Aged*, McGraw-Hill, New York, 1976.

Figure 6-1 Both physical and psychosocial problems are cause for depression, and may require intervention. *(Courtesy of Harvey Finkle.)*

PAST HEALTH HISTORY

Older clients may have a voluminous history of past problems, which may be available to the interviewer. If not, inquire about:

1 Chronic illness. Ask if the client is getting medical care for any problems and if he or she has had past serious problems. Get a history of hospitalizations. Be especially alert to a recent, life-threatening illness or a neurological disorder.

2   Surgery. Note a recent major or mutilating surgery or transplant; either one can be followed by depression.

3   Injuries. Note especially a recent head injury.

4   Past psychiatric illness. Get details of diagnosis, treatment, hospitalization. Ask about suicide attempts or if the person has ever been on phenothiazides, mood elevators, tranquilizers, or seditives.

DRUG HISTORY

Prescribed and Over-the-Counter Drugs

Inquire about any medication taken daily. If the client is unsure, do whatever is necessary to get that information. The side effects of drugs are legion and must be considered. In one instance, an 82-year-old woman was admitted to the hospital for a skin infection. Her family had noticed a gradually increasing mental confusion and fatigue which began long before the cellulitis. Her prescribed medications were digoxin, hydrochlorothiazide, and lasix. She had severe hypokalemia from that combination; a replacement of the potassium loss restored her mental alertness and level of energy.

Antihypertensives such as reserpine, methyldopa, and perhaps propanolol may cause depression. Excessive amounts of vitamins A and D can cause fatigue. Other drugs that can modify behavior include steroids, thyroid drugs, amphetamines, major and minor tranquilizers, barbiturates, sedatives, antidepressants, and hypnotics. Consult references for central nervous system side effects of all the drugs the client is using.

Alcohol Intake

The elderly are not immune to alcoholism. Ask about specific amounts of alcohol consumed per day or per week. "A couple of drinks a day" is not specific enough. Find out if the client has ever abused alcohol. Look for chronic abuse and for recent increase in consumption. The latter is often indicative of increasing depression.

Caffeine Intake

There are 70 to 150 mg of caffeine in a cup of coffee and about half of that amount in tea. Over-the-counter headache and cold preparations and cola drinks often contain caffeine, which is a powerful central nervous system stimulant. About two cups of coffee is equal to the recommended therapeutic dose of caffeine when it is a prescribed drug. Overuse can lead to restlessness, disturbance of sleep, and palpitations, all of which may be mistaken for symptoms of psychosocial stress.

FAMILY HISTORY

Ask about parental death when the client was very young, and a family history of depression, suicide, psychiatric disorders, alcoholism, or any mental disorders. I often find present family information more helpful than facts from the past, but it can be helpful to know that children of alcoholics are more at risk for alcoholism or to recognize that a client came from a family rampant with psychiatric disorders.

SOCIAL HISTORY AND PRESENT ACTIVITIES

Ask about education, work history, and vocational interests past and present. Having the client describe a typical day from the time of arising until bedtime can provide a clear picture of the present situation and answer many of the questions posed under the topics which follow. Find out if a change in the daily routine has occurred in the weeks or several months preceding the onset of the symptom being investigated.

OTHER TOPICS PERTINENT TO THE AGED

1 Loss/separation experiences: Consider the cumulative effect of several losses. Consider actual and anticipated losses.
   a Death of a spouse (usually the most devastating loss).
   b Loss of other family, friends, or any significant person.
   c Alienation between client and family.
   d Loss of social status, job, income, job satisfaction.
   e Loss of useful purpose in life.
   f Loss of vigor, physical attractiveness, effortless bodily function.
   g Loss of pets, a home, automobile, any familiar object.
2 Food intake: Chronically inadequate diets can produce fatigue and loss of mental alertness.
3 Significant others: Who provides physical and mental touching?
   a Spouse: How satisfying is the relationship and what is the spouse's health status?
   b Children: How often are they in contact and how satisfying is the relationship?
   c Friends: Do they listen as well as talk?
   d Social groups: The older person who belongs to some groups is more likely to maintain good mental health.
4 Finances: Ask clients what they would buy if they had more money.
5 The need to feel useful: Ask directly, "What things in your life make you feel useful?"
6 Concern with death and dying: Sometimes the fear of becoming helpless and a burden is stronger than the fear of no longer existing. Some people have made their own funeral arrangements and take satisfaction in having relieved survivors of that responsibility.

Figure 6-2 The importance of pets in the psychosocial care of the older person, especially in the areas of assessment and relocation, has not been recognized. Consideration should also be given to the ill or dying pet, which may need a veterinarian. The photograph shows how one old man keeps his dog with him since he is unable to walk with or run after the dog. *(Courtesy of Harvey Finkle.)*

COLLECTING OBJECTIVE DATA

Doing a Physical Examination

The extent of the physical examination will depend on the nurse's skill in physical assessment. The following minimum data base is within the capacity of all nurses.

1 Personal appearance: dress, posture, facial expression, gestures.
2 Affect: often measured by the client's effect on the nurse, who may sense the client's sadness, anxiety, hostility partially by outward observations and partially by noting his or her own mood in response to the client.
3 Mentation: (Sufficient observations may already have been made in the previous interviewing.)
   a Speech: rate, clarity of answers, repetition, ability to focus on a topic.
   b Orientation: to person, place, time, day of the week, month of the year.
   c Memory and recall: of the data requested in the history, year the client was born, last three presidents.

    d   Unusual ideation: best elicited by asking the client to explain a common proverb.

    e   Signs of hallucinations.

4   Vital signs: Include weight; an unexplained gain may signal cardiac or kidney failure.

5   Cardiac examination: Note ability to lie prone without shortness of breath, pulse rate and regularity, presence of ankle edema (sacral edema if the client is bedridden). There is a tendency to bradycardia in the aged; a resting pulse above 80 can signal pathology.

6   Respiratory examination: rate, and auscultation if possible. Insufficient oxygen to the brain can cause fuzzy mentation.

7   Gastrointestinal examination: a rectal examination to rule out fecal impaction as the cause of anorexia or of vague abdominal complaints. Do stool examinations on several occasions to look for occult blood and anemia as a cause of fatigue.

8   Neurological examination: Watch the client's gait; observing buttoning and unbuttoning clothes can be a quick assessment of cerebellar function.

9   Other systems: Examinations will depend on the problem being investigated and the nurse's ability.

See Table 6-1 for a brief outline of assessment.

MAKING THE DIAGNOSIS: NURSING OR OTHERWISE

Proving the absence of a physical component is necessary in making the diagnosis of a psychosocial problem. Often both are present, especially in the elderly, and both deserve intervention. My most vivid example of this concerns a 72-year-old woman who dropped into the clinic with the complaint of chest discomfort and "feeling funny" of 15 minutes duration. She

Table 6–1   Brief Outline of Assessment

Gathering the data
1 Detailed description of the problem
2 Description of associated symptoms/problems
3 Symptoms commonly associated with psychosocial problems
a sleep disturbance
b change in bodily function
c changes in mental state
4 Past health history
5 Drug history
6 Family history
7 Social history and present activities
8 Other topics pertinent to the elderly client
9 Collecting objective data

had been running to see a parade and noted the chest discomfort as a group of boy scouts marched by. They were from the same troop as her grandson, who had died in an accident; the next day would have been the first anniversary of his death. The woman was distraught and tearful. I was sure that grief was the source of her distress and my first impulse was to halt the assessment process to assure her that grief could cause such symptoms, especially near the anniversary of such a loss. My mouth said those things, and we sat hand in hand in silence for a brief time.

I suddenly realized that I had no information about her past health history, that I had not done the most basic physical examination, and that two of the usual causes of angina—exertion and emotion—were present. Further assessment led to her being admitted to the coronary care unit with an ECG showing myocardial ischemia. *The assessment process is not complete if the nurse stops too soon* and this can be one of the more difficult lessons to learn. If the nurse cannot make a medical assessment, another health team member should be consulted. Often a somatic and a psychosocial problem coexist in the elderly; a client may be fatigued from an acute episode of congestive heart failure, or from a depression engendered by reaction to the illness.

Butler discusses emotional reactions common to the elderly. They make useful nursing diagnosis tools and help to clarify the focus of nursing interventions.

1   Grief.
2   Guilt.
3   Loneliness.
4   Depression: Exclude early organic brain syndrome, lead poisoning, brain tumor, recent influenza, recent severe illness or mutilating surgery, hypothyroidism, and adrenal insufficiency. The use of mood elevators can give dramatic relief to the insomnia and help restore enough energy to help the client work on the sources of depression.
5   Anxiety: Exclude hyperthyroidism, angina, paroxysmal nocturnal dyspnea, paroxysmal atrial tachycardia, tuberculosis, anemia, and hypoglycemia.
6   Sense of impotence.
7   Helplessness and hopelessness: Clients experiencing these feelings are at risk for developing a somatic disorder.
8   Rage.[8]

MAKING NURSING INTERVENTIONS

The detailed data base on which the nursing diagnosis was made can often provide clues as to what changes the client is responding to and guideposts for offering help. Remember that the client was coping before the present problem occurred; note what is different in the situation and plan accordingly.

A person with the ability to diagnose physical illness should be monitoring the client, since prolonged psychosocial stress predisposes to physical illness. Health maintenance is important in the aged as well as the young.

This section on interventions is shorter and less specific than the one on making the diagnosis. It is easy to make a long list of shoulds—the nurse should make positive interventions, the nurse should motivate the client to change, the nurse should help the client and family to find a better way to relate to each other. But, realistically, I am aware that not all clients (including nurses when we are clients) are willing or perhaps able to change. Auden says it in poetry:

> We would rather be ruined than changed,
> We would rather die in our dread
> Than climb the cross of the moment
> And let our illusions die[9]

As nurses, we can describe to the clients our perception of their problems, hold out a hand, and offer to work with them on the problem. The client must be moved to also hold out a hand to join in the endeavor. I wish us all godspeed in making the hand we hold out as engaging as possible.

REFERENCES

1 J. Watson, B. Walsh, R. Tompkins, and H. Sox, *The Common Symptom Guide*, McGraw-Hill, New York, 1975.
2 I. Feinberg, "Effects of Age on Human Sleep Patterns," in A. Kales (ed.), *Sleep: Physiology and Pathology*, Lippincott, Philadelphia, 1969, pp. 40–43.
3 Ibid.
4 Ibid.
5 John Brandner, "Sleep Disorders: Help for the Patients Who Can't Sleep," *Patient Care*, vol. 10, p. 105, February 1, 1976.
6 A. Kales and J. Kales, "Recent Advances in the Diagnosis and Treatment of Sleep Disorders," in Gene Usdin (ed.), *Sleep Research and Clinical Practice*, Brunner/Mazel, New York, 1973, pp. 71–72.
7 Robert N. Butler and Myrna Lewis, *Aging and Mental Health: Positive Psychosocial Approaches*, Mosby, St. Louis, 1977, pp. 41–45.
8 Ibid.
9 W. H. Auden, *The Age of Anxiety*, Random House, New York, 1946, p. 134.

BIBLIOGRAPHY

Anon.: "Assessing and Managing Dementia," *Patient Care*, vol. 11, pp. 90–116, November 30, 1977.

Anon.: "Treat Depression as the Curable Disease That It Is," *Patient Care*, vol. 11, pp. 20–77, March 1, 1977.

Burnside, Irene M.: *Nursing and the Aged*, 2d ed., McGraw-Hill, New York, 1981.

Chapter 7

Home Care for the Elderly

Genie Eide

In order to provide a comprehensive service for old people many different types of provisions are essential and as the best place for an old person is in his or her own house a wide variety of domiciliary services are required.

W. Ferguson Anderson

It is the urgent wish of most older people to remain at home. This was recently clearly established in a study by Brickner, who wrote:

> Older people have positive feelings about their own homes because there they are in a familiar environment. They can eat, watch television, sleep, and rise on their own schedule. They can keep the light on late, find the bathroom in the dark. Independence is limited only by degree of frailty.[1]

Maintaining the high-risk elderly in the community is challenging and rewarding for both clients and health care professionals. To accomplish this, however, the client's participation in the decision-making process is essential. Plans must be timely and should involve the use of all appropriate personnel and community resources.

The care of isolated, greatly impaired homebound elderly people is a national issue. Only new legislation will halt the trend toward institutionalization of the aged and make maintenance at home more feasible. It is the right of every individual in the United States to live in circumstances which allow for the fullest use of his or her capacities. The services necessary to promote physical, mental, and emotional health must be available, accessible, and adequate.

AT-RISK POPULATION

A recent report from the U.S. Department of Commerce states that 11 percent of the population, 23.7 million, is age 65 or older, which supports estimates that the nation's population is growing older. Herman Brotman's population projections for A.D. 2000 based on current trends were as follows:

> Not only is the older population growing faster than the younger, but the older population itself is aging, since the older part is growing faster than the younger part: between 1975 and 2000, the 55–64 age group will increase by 16 percent, the 65–74 group by 23 percent and the most vulnerable, the 75 + group, by 60 percent. [2]

In brief, by A.D. 2000, 30.6 million people, 15 percent of the total projected population, will be age 65 or older.

In light of this projection, physical and social planners should utilize all relevant information and resources to assist the aging population to manage in their own home with dignity and quality of life. The term *high-risk elderly*, as used in this chapter, denotes persons who have a deterrent to optimal functioning. More than 80 percent of all older people suffer some degree of activity limitation as a result of one or more chronic disease conditions requiring some medical supervision. These conditions include, but are not limited to, hypertension, heart disease, diabetes mellitus, respiratory disease, arthritis, and sensory impairment that results in the loss of ability to perform certain functions and activities of daily living. Approximately 17 percent of this group falls within the greatly or extremely impaired category, and 5.75 percent is homebound. Of the greatly impaired, 31 percent live alone.

The findings of Kane and Andersen on identified medical problems in the elderly isolate are shown in Table 7–1.

Table 7-1 Medical Problems Identified

	Isolates %	Non-isolates %	Extreme isolates %	Other isolates %
Chronic joint locomotor	28	36	20	31
Cardiac	18	20	14	19
Hypertension	16	19	16	16
Chronic respiratory	18	15	17	18
Neurological	6	12	7	5
Severe sight/hearing	12	13	12	12
Diabetes	4	3	—	6
Cancers	3	3	5	2
Excessive alcohol	7	5	15	4
Loneliness	26	11	35	23
Somewhat/very depressed	27	17	35	24
Somewhat/very anxious	21	17	25	20
N = 100%	225	271	60	165

For isolates v non-isolates

Neurological	$\chi^2 = 5.14$	df = 1	$p \cong 0.02$
Loneliness	$\chi^2 = 18.22$	df = 1	$p \cong 0.001$
Depression	$\chi^2 = 8.01$	df = 1	$p \cong 0.004$

Source: L. Kane and N. A. Andersen, "The Elderly Isolate," Australian Family Physician, vol. 7, March 1978. Reprinted by permission.

COST OF CARE

It is important to note that care costs vary with impairments. Similarly, care cost figures must assume quality of care. Pollack states that the mass media expose the indignities and dangers suffered by the elderly as a result of the poor quality of our nursing homes. One may conclude that home care is the setting of choice if it is also the least expensive. Nevertheless, inadequate housing and the lack of other basic needs may also cause suffering for the low-income elderly.[3]

The cost of providing care for chronically impaired elderly people in virtually every setting will vary according to the level of impairment and the quality of care provided. Moreover, the cost of care in most community settings will be influenced by the availability of services.

In December 1977, the Comptroller General's Report to the Congress compared home services to institutionalization, pointing out that until older people become greatly or extremely impaired, the cost for home services, including the large portion provided by families and friends, is less than the cost of care in an institution. As one becomes more impaired, the cost (or value) of home services increases as does the proportion of care provided by family and friends.

Families and friends provide over 70 percent of the value of services received by older people at the greatly impaired level—about $287 per month in services for every $120 being spent by agencies. For all levels of impairment, the value of services provided by families and friends is significantly higher than public agency costs. Greatly impaired older people who live alone have a higher probability of being institutionalized than those who live with spouses or children. Of those greatly impaired older people 31 percent do live alone and 76 percent of this group eventually enter institutions.[4]

THE VALUE OF HOME CARE

The concept of devising alternatives to long-term care facilities implies that more meticulous attention should be given to the person's care in the home. Using the services of the family, friends, and home health care should be the first alternative when an elderly person cannot manage alone. Priority should be placed on a continuity of effort through a multidisciplinary team approach to make the home not only the place of choice, but the place where adequate care can and will be provided as long as it is needed.

How often has it been said by family members or by the elderly themselves, "If I had only known about in-home services, the outcome could have been so different." Such statements are often made following an acute hospitalization. Today utilization review does not allow for convalescence or full recovery. The patient must leave, and the decision is not based on his or her functional ability.

Many patients could be helped to adjust to their situation through discharge planning, patient teaching, and home health care.[5] The home has always been the primary institution for care of the sick, disabled, and elderly; in the past, such care was rendered by family and friends. Reliance on institutional care in hospitals and nursing homes is a twentieth century phenomenon, as is the professionalization of home health care.

"Care of the Helpless Elderly at Home" is a moving account of a nurse's experiences when caring for her mother, a severely impaired and completely helpless patient who has required total care for the past 5 years. The author's mother cannot speak, but there is nevertheless communication. The article demonstrates the closeness, devotion, and love shared by a mother, father, and daughter.[9] Such examples document success in maintaining even the greatly impaired elderly in the home.

A study in the agency where I work revealed that of 224 patients receiving support care, 42 percent were discharged from service due to improvement and their ability to manage independently. I wonder how many elderly are discharged from nursing homes with sufficient improvement to manage independently.

The First Home Care Program

The first organized home care program in the United States was established by the Boston Dispensary in 1796. During the second half of the nineteenth century, visiting nurse associations began to develop home care programs. Following World War II, the first hospital-based home care program was established at Montefiore Hospital in New York City. In 1951, E. D. Rosenfeld, M.D., stated that the Montefiore Home Care Program, in addition to providing the necessary medical attention, reestablished the family unit without imposing upon it burdens which it was ill-prepared or unable to assume. (The program also made available additional hospital beds for patients in greater need at a cost comparable to home care.) Patients who were cared for at home enjoyed the continued presence of those who loved them best and respected them most. Cures take less time in such conditions, if only because the sick person's struggle to recover can be strengthened by the more personal kind of medical attention that can be provided in the home environment.[6]

Home Care Today

Following a study of long-term care and the testimony of hundreds of health consumers and providers in 1974, the U.S. Senate Subcommittee on Long Term Care concluded:

> If home health care services are readily available prior to placement in a nursing home, there is convincing evidence to conclude that such care may not only postpone, but possibly prevent more costly institutionalization. What is particularly appealing from the standpoint of the elderly, is that home health services can enable them to live independently in their own homes, where most of them prefer to be.[7]

Trager summed up the situation by noting that home care provided for the restoration of normal rights and privileges to persons who happened to be ill. We are a long way from providing these rights and privileges to all who need them. In 1975, $287 million (or 1 percent of the combined Medicare/Medicaid budget) was expended on home health care. Even though this figure increased to $786 million in 1978 due to increased utilization of services for disabled persons and for patients with terminal kidney disease, it is but a fraction of the sums spent for institutionalization of the elderly. Of available public funds for long-term care, 90 percent goes to institutionalized nursing care.[8]

Some legislators who are proponents of home health care are aware of the deterrents to providing home health care services for the elderly, and have proposed such changes in Medicare benefits as:

1 Unlimited visits under both Part A and B
2 Elimination of the 3-day prior hospitalization requirement under Part A
3 Elimination of the deductible requirement

HOME HEALTH CARE AND CLIENTS' RIGHTS

The American Nurses' Association, Division of Community Health Nursing Services, has developed a position statement in support of increased emphasis on health care at home and the integration of home care into the health care delivery system. This support represents a reaffirmation of one of the major purposes of the association—to work for the improvement of health standards and the availability of home care services for all who need them.

These are the ultimate objectives of all home health care agencies, but they will become a reality only when information about available services becomes accessible to consumers, physicians, and all professional staffers who assist the elderly with their plans when a disruption of homeostasis occurs. Home care builds on the resources of the individual and of the family. When they are in a familiar setting, individuals feel in charge of themselves and their recovery.

According to the American Nurses' Association, one of the basic principles of a national health policy is that "health is a personal responsibility and must be recognized as such in a national health policy."[11]

This is compatible with the first standard of the Patient's Bill of Rights as established in 1977 by the California Association for Health Services at Home. Standard I states: "The patient will receive the care necessary to help regain or maintain his maximum state of health and if necessary to cope with death."

THE GREATLY IMPAIRED AT HOME: THE MOST DIFFICULT CLIENTS TO MANAGE

There is no one best life-style for the greatly impaired, but they must maintain control over their own lives as long as possible. One of the most desired personal attributes is independence. As long as one can take care of even some of one's personal physical-maintenance needs, and have a voice in the decision making and planning of one's care, a sense of independence remains.

Some of the greatly impaired elderly do not have the ability to assess either the care they need or the care giver's ability to provide it. It is not too uncommon to hear an 80-year-old who is recovering from a cardiovascular accident say that his or her spouse can manage. (The spouse may be 85 and not too functional.)

In my experience as a home health care (HCC) administrator, the three types of greatly impaired elderly patients who are most difficult to manage in the home are:

1   Greatly impaired patients who are mentally competent, but need 24 hours of total care, which the care giver appears incapable of providing
2   Elderly impaired patients who could be managed at home with HHC and community resources, but whose home environment is unsafe
3   Elderly impaired patients who desire to remain at home and who have adequate family support systems, but whose systems will not provide the care needed, or even give the patient nourishment

The first type is illustrated by a case study of a client who receives service from our agency.

CASE EXAMPLE   Mrs. C, age 72, was admitted to hospital in July 1978 with two fractured femurs plus a fracture on the right tibia following a fall from her bed. Subsequently two long leg casts were applied.

The discharge planning team had been working with Mrs. C to persuade her to accept nursing home placement, at least until the casts were removed. Mrs. C and her sister, Miss N, absolutely refused. Both ladies were of sound mind and had the right of refusal.

On September 1, 1978, Utilization Review informed the physician that it was time for Mrs. C to leave the acute care facility based on a formula of calculated days. Secondary diagnoses included: (1) obesity (probably over 300 lb.); (2) incontinence of bowel and bladder (with Foley catheter), and (3) diabetes mellitus (insulin-dependent with restricted diet). Mrs. C had been admitted to the hospital with over 400 mg fasting blood sugar, decubiti on both posterior thighs from the top of the casts to the waist, and abdominal excoriation due to obesity and old site of insulin injections. Mrs. C's sister had the use of one hand and arm; the other arm was paralyzed and in a sling.

Prior to the incident, the two women had been living in the home of a niece. The niece had recently married and was determined to have full occupancy of her small home, leaving the patient with no place to go. Miss N had been unrealistic in planning to return her sister to her niece's home without first consulting the niece. Since the niece remained adamant, Miss N had to find a place to take her sister. An unfurnished house was found, and home health care ordered a hospital bed with a trapeze to be delivered. It was hard to believe that these two women would be able to manage alone even with home health care and access to community resources.

The client and her sister arrived in their new home on the Friday before Labor Day weekend. The home was bleak; there was no stove, no refrigerator, no electricity, no furniture or food. The temperature was 110° in the shade. The equipment men were setting up the bed, the home health care nurses were there to prepare it, and the physical therapist was present to supervise the move and assist the patient with the use of the trapeze. I was there to help cope and to pray for a smooth transition! When I arrived, the patient was waiting outside in the ambulance. At that moment Miss N decided that she didn't want her sister as she wasn't ready. I had to order Mrs. C to be brought in and put to bed. After all, this had been the sister's decision, and they had known all week that this day would arrive.

The older neighborhood ladies had arrived for prayer; Mrs. C was put into her bed shouting with pain, and someone was putting sheets on the windows for curtains. The physical therapist was attempting to get Mrs. C to use the trapeze to help position herself. The home health care nurse and I saw an old table in the alley, and brought it in for a bedside table. When a lull in the activity occurred, Mrs. C said, "Bring me my snuff." She was happy and was where she wanted to be.

Discharge Plans

Before Mrs. C left the hospital, the home health care staff members and I visited the patient and her sister and presented them with a formal agreement which specified the role of the field staff, the resources available, and the responsibilities that the home health care staff could assume. The agreement also detailed the responsibilities of the care giver. Briefly, the HHC staff would provide intermittent service 7 days a week for insulin injections, medication supervision, decubiti care, and personal care. Noon meals from the senior citizen center and Title XX Housekeeping Service were coordinated. The sister would be responsible for feeding the patient, keeping her clean, and turning her during the day and the night.

Even though Mrs. C's sister was reluctant to help with care in the beginning, she *is* providing personal care now that the aide service has been reduced.

The patient care plan was altered daily to meet the needs of Mrs. C, but professional team members approached the care as a group project.

Nurses frequently questioned their rights and responsibilities. They had to leave the patient knowing she might not be cleansed again until their return the following day. They also knew, however, that Mrs. C's basic needs were being met, that Mrs. C and Miss N had chosen this life-style.

Three months have passed. Mrs. C's condition has improved in these specific areas:

1 Decrease in pain.
2 The decubiti have healed.
3 The patient gives herself insulin in rotated sites.
4 The fasting blood sugar remains within normal limits.
5 The patient is selective of her diet, eliminating items she should not eat.
6 Both casts are off; only a splint remains on one leg.
7 Both Mrs. C and her sister show signs of regaining independence.

The field staff members consist of the public health (home health care) nurse, the home health aide, the social worker, the nutritionist, and the physical therapist. All have done an outstanding job with positive results.

In a case review with the staff, the nurse, as the team leader, had implemented Standards IV, V, and IX from Geriatric Nursing Practice Standards, which state:

IV. The nurse differentiates between pathological social behavior and the usual life-style of each aged individual.
 V. The nurse supports and promotes normal physiologic functioning of the older person.
IX. The nurse assists the older persons to obtain and utilize devices which help them attain a higher level of function and ensures that these devices are kept in good working order by the appropriate persons or agencies.[12]

In a recent conference with staff members, the consensus was that the most difficult aspects of the care were (1) the frustrations of the predictable problems, (2) the limited field staff available, and (3) the limited time to do all that could or should have been done.

The social service worker felt that the patient's attitude of being satisfied lying in bed and her lack of motivation were the most difficult problems to overcome. Care by the team has gradually decreased to visits three times a week for personal care by the health aide and three times a week by the nurse for monitoring care; care also includes skilled observation, medication supervision, and the carrying out of preventive measures sufficient to support the maintenance. The present goal of the client and team is for Mrs. C to return to her preaccident state of independence. This requires that the sister get Mrs. C up in a chair daily, using the Hoyer lift, and that the commode is used to attempt bowel control. When these objectives are accomplished, the nurse and aide foresee the need to continue weekly visits to maintain functioning at Mrs. C's maximum level. The team can accept that the client remain in her home, even though the care has had its limitations.

The team met with Mrs. C and her sister to discuss their thoughts about being at home rather than receiving nursing home care, and their feelings about how they had managed.

Mrs. C had been placed in a nursing home when her sister fractured her arm and was unable to care for her. Mrs. C admitted that during this time she was depressed, unhappy, and did not have good care. Her personal items were taken. Mrs. C and her sister became extremely angry, and Mrs. C finally left against medical advice. Both she and her sister had been promised Mrs. C could go to her private physician, only to have the decision reversed after the taxi arrived.

In response to questioning about leaving the hospital and being cared for at home, both Mrs. C and her sister expressed anger at the physician because Mrs. C had been discharged too soon. The staff's explanations about utilization review and Medicare rules and regulations, and their assurance that only nursing care was needed fell on deaf ears.

Mrs. C. felt that she was getting along better at home than she had in the nursing home. To emphasize her statement, she said, "My sister knows what upsets me and can understand my eating habits and emotional sore spots; we are very close; she loves me." Both women were grateful to the HHC staff for the emotional support, care, and concern they had provided. Mrs. C and her sister are looking forward with renewed interest to their future independence.

The charges by the Community Home Health Care Agency are $2100 for the 3 months, which included equipment and supplies. This is approximately $700 per month, which may be comparable to the cost of nursing home care. But the unknown factor is this: if Mrs. C had been sent to a nursing home, how long would she have remained there? Would she have been released and, if so, been able to manage with limited independence?

NURSES' RESPONSIBILITY FOR CONTINUITY OF CARE

The professional nurse is responsible and accountable to the patient for the quality of nursing care; as an integral part of that nursing care, every professional nurse has a responsibility to plan for the continuity of patient care.

Nurses in acute care facilities must think of discharge as more than an empty bed. Patients are discharged without convalescence; many patients, particularly the elderly, are sent home still needing nursing care and therapy services to ensure recovery.

Continuity of care is a series of connected patient care events or activities which are coordinated so as to render the best possible benefit to the patient. Well-planned, comprehensive, coordinated continuity of care prevents expensive duplication and fragmentation of service. Such care provides patients with the ability to reach their maximum level of wellness and to regain their dignity with the least amount of discomfort and emotional stress.[12]

Nurses are with their patients 24 hours a day. No one else on the multidisciplinary team has that privilege. Nurses know patients' attitudes toward their illness and their ability to function. They know the extent to which patients can provide self-care.[13]

The basis for making continuity of care a reality is discharge planning, which must begin prior to admission. Whenever possible, the physician must prepare patients for the expected outcome and let them know whether there will be any change in functioning following discharge from the hospital.

If we really expect this type of planning to occur, we need to teach the physician, the nurse, and the social worker what continuity of care is all about.

One method is to have student nurses, social service students, and medical students make home visits with public health and home care staff. These observations should help them develop a better understanding of how people can be managed at home, of the use of appropriate resources, and of the extent of impairment that can be managed at home.

Another method is to bring the patients to the students. For many years I used slide presentations showing the clients who received in-home services from my agency. These clients were elderly; many lived alone, some were greatly impaired, but all had a "common denominator"—remaining in their own home, no matter how humble it might be. I had the opportunity to show these slides to the Arizona State Legislature Committee on Health, House of Representatives, when the Arizona State Home Care Association supported a bill to provide public health nursing consultants to assist with developing home care throughout the state and to improve the quality of in-home services. I also presented the slides at the Health, Education and Welfare hearing, Region IX, in Los Angeles in 1976. On both occasions, the reaction was one of surprise; these committees had no idea that this kind of public service existed. Though reaction to it appeared favorable, the Arizona House bill did not pass and at that time Medicare had not yet increased its benefits for in-home services.

Last year I had the privilege of having the Public Broadcasting System of Arizona State University at Tempe prepare a 30-minute video tape that presented six patients receiving home health care from my agency. The dialogue between the patients and staff in the patients' homes was totally unrehearsed. The narrator provides information about discharge planning, the services that home health care can provide, and the availability of these services. This video tape is shown to all new personnel at the hospital and the home health care agency. A copy was given to the College of Nursing at Arizona State University and viewing by nursing students is required. The State Department of Health Services purchased several copies and has made them available for use throughout the state.

PROMOTING HOME CARE FOR THE ELDERLY

Public Law 93–641 mandates systematic planning for health care. If health care at home is to be developed to meet the need, health systems agencies must take an active role in identifying needs of the populations and assuring that adequate services are available and accessible.

Much of the current focus of health planning is on institutional services rather than on home care with alternatives. One prominent nurse said at a nurses' meeting in Texas several years ago that elderly Americans had to have tubes coming from all orifices and be confined to bed before the government could assist with their care. Many concerned legislators in Washington are issuing public statements encouraging care for the elderly in their own homes or place of residence. One strong supporter of home care, Representative Millicent Fenwick, said, "Of the one million elderly Americans who currently reside in nursing homes, an estimated 20–40 percent . . . do not require institutional care and might be able to stay at home with their family or with friends if adequate funds and community-based facilities were available to them." Her sentiments were shared by the late Representative Leo Ryan, who said, "It is clear that our existing government programs for the poor squander our dollars while failing to give [the] help to the elderly that the programs were created to provide."[14]

Services are necessary not only for rehabilitation and recovery, but also to prevent deterioration, to maintain the current capacity of the greatly impaired elderly when full recovery is not anticipated, and even to provide a peaceful death.

In October 1978, the Federal Council on Aging (FCA) recommended a new program of federal assistance for the frail elderly. FCA contends that better care at the community level would enable the frail elderly to avoid or postpone having to enter hospitals or long-term care facilities. Representative John J. LaFalce said, "It is time that we shape a national policy as dedicated to the improvement in the quality of life of our older Americans as our education system is to the overall well-being of our youth."[15]

REFERENCES

1 Phillip W. Brickner, *Home Health Care for the Aged*, Appleton-Century-Crofts, New York, 1978.
2 Herman Brotman, "Population Projections," *The Gerontologist*, vol. 17, no. 3, pp. 203–209, June 1977.

3   W. Pollak and J. Hiferty, "Costs of Alternative Care Settings for the Elderly,"
    in M. P. Lawton, R. J. Newcomer, and T. O. Byerts (eds.), *Community Plan-
    ning for an Aging Society: Designing Services and Facilities*, McGraw-Hill, New
    York, 1976.
4   "Home Health—The Need for a National Policy to Better Provide for the
    Elderly," Report to Congress by the Comptroller General of the United States,
    December 1977.
5   Bernita Steffl and Imogene Eide, *Discharge Planning Handbook*, Charles B.
    Slack, Thorofare, N.J., 1978.
6   "Organized Home Care," Montefiore Hospital, Bronx, N.Y., 1947–1962,
    March 1963.
7   "Home Health Care," Report on the Regional Public Hearings of the Depart-
    ment of Health, Education and Welfare, September 20–October 1, 1976.
8   *Geriatric and Residential Care News Monthly*, M. Mills and H. Schwartz (eds.),
    vol. 3, no. 11, p. 7, New York, November 1978.
9   Mildred Hogstel, "Care of the Helpless Elderly at Home," *Journal of Geron-
    tological Nursing*, vol. 3, no. 1, pp. 36–39, January–February 1977.
10 "Type, Length and Cost of Care for Home Health Patients," National League
    for Nursing Publication No. 21-1589, pp. 3–7, New York, 1975.
11 "Health Care at Home: An Essential Component of a National Health Policy,"
    American Nurses' Association, 1978.
12 "Standards, Geriatric Nursing Practice," American Nurses' Association, Kan-
    sas City, Mo., 1973.
13 Steffl and Eide, op. cit., p. 5.
14 *Geriatric and Residential Care News Monthly*, M. Mills and H. Schwartz (eds.),
    vol. 3, no. 9, New York, September 1978, p. 2.
15 *Geriatric and Residential Care News Monthly*, M. Mills and H. Schwartz (eds.),
    vol. 3, no. 8, New York, August 1978, p. 4.

BIBLIOGRAPHY

Kahana, Eva, and Rodney M. Coe: "Alternatives in Long-Term Care," in Sylvia
    Sherwood (ed.), *Long-Term Care*, Spectrum Publications, New York, 1974, pp.
    511–572.
Sheer, V. T.: "Homebound Geriatric Care," *American Journal of Psychiatry*, vol.
    131, pp. 104–105, 1974.

OTHER RESOURCES

Publications

*Legislative Approaches to the Problems of the Elderly: A Handbook of Model
    State Statutes.* Available from Legal Research and Services for the Elderly, Na-
    tional Council on Senior Citizens, 1627 K Street, N.W., Washington, D.C.
    20006.
National Capital Area Homemaker Service Training Manual. Prepared by the
    Homemaker Service of the National Capital Area, Inc., Washington, D.C.
    Available from AoA: DHEW Publication No. (OHD) 74-20103.

Standards for Homemaker–Home Health Aide Services. Available from the National Council for Homemaker Services, Inc., 67 Irving Place, New York, N.Y. 10003.

What Churches Can Do—Inter-Faith Opportunity Center (Hartford, Conn.). AoA Publication No. 903.

Organizations

National Council for Homemaker–Home Health Aide Services, Inc.
67 Irving Place
New York, N.Y. 10003

Nevada State Welfare Department: Homemaker Services
Carson City, Nev. 89701

STEP: South Snohomish County Senior Center
220 Railroad Avenue
Edmonds, Wash. 98020

Chapter 8

Continuity of Care for Elderly Discharged Patients

Mary Louise Conti

Continuity of care is a right

Bernita M. Steffl
Imogene Eide

This chapter is about the experiences of a community health nurse-coordinator of a 200-bed geriatric unit in a large veterans hospital, and describes a 7-month period of outplacing patients from this unit. Patients ranging in age from 45 to 88 are discharged from the hospital to (1) nursing homes, (2) boarding homes, (3) residential care homes, and (4) their own homes. A total of 35 men and women were placed during this period of time. The hospital had specifically designated an office for outplacement of patients, staffed by a community health nurse, a social worker, and a secretary. This was the first attempt at outplacement for this particular geriatric unit. I, as the community health nurse-coordinator, took on a new role as I combined my experiences and background in (1) community health nursing, (2) gerontology, and (3) community mental health.

As community health coordinator for patients in the long-term chronic illness section of the hospital, my task was to assist in formulating appropriate discharge plans which would provide continuity of care for the patient and thereby decrease readmissions to the hospital. At this time there was no plan to assess patients who might be discharged.

Most of the patients on this unit had been hospitalized for many years (the greatest length of time was 48 years). As the need for hospital beds became increasingly acute, discharge plans had to be considered; however, their long hospitalization had made these patients very dependent. Many of them suffered from the "institutional syndrome," characterized by dependency and a lack of initiative.[1] The social worker and I were advised by the acting chief of geriatric service that we could handle the discharges in whatever manner seemed most effective, and we were assured that we were not expected to meet a "discharge quota." This was an ideal opportunity to put into practice nursing philosophy about continuity of patient care.

The patients to be prepared for discharge had a combination of psychiatric and medical disabilities. The psychiatric condition was, in many cases, no longer the major problem for many of them, and they were being treated for various medical conditions. There were patients with (1) degenerative brain disease, (2) brain injuries due to trauma, and (3) stroke conditions with chronic confusion. Most of these aged patients were in this geriatric unit because there was nowhere else to place them.

This particular population was 75 percent male and over 65 years of age. There was a large number of men because the institution was a Veterans Administration (VA) hospital. Many of the patients had been in VA hospitals, state mental hospitals, or long-term care institutions the greater part of their adult life. The patients came from these places: (1) state mental hospitals, (2) homes where the bizarre symptoms they manifested could no longer be tolerated by family and friends, and (3) wards within the same hospital. The third group had received acute medical or psychiatric care, or both, in other sections of the hospital and were now "just waiting." One time I called a clinic doctor and explained to him that a patient was leaving the hospital to go to a nursing home. The doctor asked me again to identify myself. I repeated my name and position. He said, "I thought you said that building, but I didn't think *anyone* left there."

The degree of involvement with the families varied; some patients saw their family or friends often, others hardly at all. Family involvement was in any case limited by the visiting hours, which were restricted to three afternoons a week. There were patients who had families who did not seem to care, and never visited. There were others who were without known relatives or friends. The patients represented many ethnic groups and came from many different areas of the United States. Discharge plans had to consider the cultural and life-style differences of these patients, along with the feasibility of returning them to previous areas of residence.

If patients were to leave this unit and adjust to different living situations, it was apparent that a careful plan would have to be made and continual support would have to be provided by myself and the hospital staff. The elderly institutionalized patient often is unable to cope with all the stimuli within the environment and has low self-esteem.[2] I quickly realized that discharging long-term institutionalized patients from the hospital would mean an increased effort on the part of the patients themselves. In general, their abilities to adjust were decreased. I felt that in many instances the hospital staff would also require support, for the staff were often observed as being very protective of "their" patients. It is not uncommon for an individual staff member to attribute his or her own feelings to patients, or to displace personal fears and apprehensions onto the patients.[3] The staff member may be fearful about the patient leaving the hospital because he is protective of the patient, or he may be concerned that as patients are successfully discharged he will "work himself out of a job."[4]

The kind of patients I have just described are afraid of change. They have frequently felt rejected in their lifetime, resulting in a lowered self-esteem. "For those aged unaccustomed to expression of lonely feelings or sadness, they may turn feelings inward. In doing so the low self-esteem which may already exist is lowered even more."[5] This low self-esteem had to be considered when we instituted changes; we had to protect patients from feelings of rejection. The older patient usually has increased difficulty in adapting and adjusting to the rapidly changing environment, not only to the physical environment but to the psychosocial one as well.[6] Changing one's entire living situation can be frightening, especially to the aged; therefore, care givers instigating changes need to involve patients, their families, and the hospital staff. The patients were encouraged to discuss their feelings about leaving the hospital. We tried to help the staff to be well informed about the new living situation, so that they could provide reassurance.

The John Umstead Hospital in North Carolina established prerelease groups to allow patients to express feelings prior to their discharge. These groups met weekly under the guidance of a social worker; she acknowledged their fears and assured them that their feelings were normal. At the same time she invited them to help plan for a satisfactory living situation.[7] The provision of a supportive environment in which patients are able to plan for their future helps them feel they control their destiny. They are able to make decisions concerning the future and also to express fears about it.

In a study of brain-damaged residents in a home for the aged in Montreal, Canada, it was revealed that among the basic needs of the patients were the need for a stable pattern of daily activities and the need to depend. Because brain-damaged persons cannot use their brain adequately to make decisions and to assess their environment, they seek familiar routines which have been successful and safe in the past.[8] To help persons with limited neurological functioning adjust and accept change, we would have to retain much of what was familiar. I felt this could be accomplished (1) by providing the opportunity for expression of the patients' fears in a supportive environment, (2) by providing complete information regarding the patient when the change was made, and (3) by encouraging follow-up visits by hospital staff members after the transfer of the patient.

The following are case examples randomly selected from the 35 patients who were placed.

CASE EXAMPLE 1   Mrs. L was 68 years old and especially afraid of change; she had been hospitalized for 6 years. Prior to that, she had been in and out of institutions for 20 years. She required much assistance to walk, and spent most of her day in a wheelchair. A stroke several years previously had left her with indistinct speech and left-sided facial droop. Her hands trembled when she lit her cigarettes. Mrs. L, in spite of her sad appearance, was very vain. For example, she found the unironed hospital clothes distasteful, and she was adamant about her weekly trip to the hairdresser. She enjoyed talking with the staff, but she would seldom talk with other patients; in fact, she very carefully avoided all contact with them. Her previous medical history showed an emotionally labile woman who had attempted suicide once. She occasionally had temper outbursts which seemed to result from frustration about the rules of smoking, wearing certain clothes, and lack of individualization in the routinized hospital schedule.

Mrs. L was certainly not benefiting from the hospital environment; this fact was verified by the staff, her doctor, and her sister. Mrs. L's sister was very interested in her. During visiting hours she would push Mrs. L in her wheelchair around the grounds. Although the sister was aware that Mrs. L would not benefit from further hospitalization, she also expressed concern that Mrs. L would reject placement because of fear. We decided to allow Mrs. L's sister to help in the selection of a nursing home. The sister knew her tastes and was aware she needed an environment that would respond to her as a person and still meet all her physical needs. Several nursing homes were suggested; Mrs. L's sister selected one, and we agreed with her decision. We then approached Mrs. L. She was not convinced she needed a change and, in fact, became quite angry with her sister, so we suggested Mrs. L visit the nursing home and decide for herself.

Mrs. L was shown the facility and what was offered. The visit convinced her, since she felt her living situation would be tremendously improved. We agreed, and later that week she moved to the nursing home. At present, she relates to other residents in the nursing home and has developed new men and women friends. Her sister has supplied her with a new wardrobe of dresses, which are kept clean and well-pressed. She is always happy to see the staff from the hospital when we visit, and she proudly shows us around her new home.

As previously stated, the hospital staff often became very attached to their patients. Staff members had cared for some of them for many years; in fact, there were some patients whose only family was the staff. The nursing staff were understandably concerned about such patients and interested in their welfare away from the hospital. The general feeling seemed to be that the patients would not be as well cared for elsewhere. Involvement of the staff in discharge planning and in the follow-up of their patients, was important so they could see their patients doing well outside the hospital. In some instances previous hospital discharges revealed poor planning. Involving the staff in well-planned discharges would also allow them to share in the successes. On occasion, the nurses went along to assess nursing and boarding homes in the area for possible placement of patients. Such visits gave us an idea of both what was available, and of how to begin matching patients to a particular facility, rather than expecting the patient to adjust to the facility selected. It has been my experience that the latter is usually the case. As the staff became aware of what was available, they were also more able to assess appropriately both their own patients and incoming new patients for potential discharge. Visiting community facilities and their patients gave the staff an opportunity to be directly involved with discharge planning and follow-up. The process of discharging patients was not just something that was *done* to them. Successful placement became a matter of pride for all who were involved in developing and implementing the plan.

Careful follow-up was especially important in the case of elderly patients who were long-term and chronically ill and had been in the same institution for a number of years. The hospital staff knew special bits of knowledge about these patients, but many times written communication did not convey this knowledge. The personal involvement of hospital nurses with boarding home operators, community health workers, or nursing home staff opened more direct lines of communication. Much of the guesswork involved in caring for a new patient was eliminated for the new agency.

CASE EXAMPLE 2   Mr. W, a 78-year-old man, had been hospitalized for 2 years. He was admitted after he shot himself in a suicide attempt. He received medical treatment for the acute condition, and was subsequently transferred to the geriatric section of the hospital because locked wards were available there. The nurses became very attached to Mr. W. They were aware of his needs and his personality traits, and they knew the best methods of meeting those needs. He walked with the help of two canes, and was fiercely independent about his walking and his personal hygiene. His only interest was reading, and he preferred to do this alone in a room. He had been allowed to grow a healthy beard, which concealed a nasty facial scar, the result of the

suicide attempt. Mr. W vehemently disliked the hospital and de-
nounced everyone as "insane." His primary goal was to return to his
own home and live there *alone*, unbothered by others. Prior to his
hospital admission he had been a recluse and refused to admit anyone
to his home. He was absolutely alone, with no family or friends. He had
been employed by one firm for over 30 years; yet no one associated
with the firm could tell his court-appointed guardian more than his
name and the quality of work he had produced.

Mr. W would not be able to return to his own home. This decision
was made conjointly by the medical staff, the nursing staff, the social
worker, and the community health nurse. I discussed alternative plans
with Mr. W during many sessions, which gave him the opportunity to
think about the possibility of a different living situation. It also gave
him a chance to express his feelings. Explanations to patients do require proper timing, and Aasterud states: "In the case of a major event
that involves changes in living patterns and sustained psychological
stress, the person may require a period of time to plan adaptive
changes and to work through his feelings."[9] Near the hospital was a
facility licensed for the care of the mentally ill which would meet all of
Mr. W's needs and still provide him with the individualized care he
needed. Mr. W could have a room to himself—to be kept as he wished.

The head nurse and I transferred Mr. W, and the head nurse communicated his needs to the new staff. The nursing home personnel
were quite concerned about the fact that a man subject to such vocal
outbursts and abuses should have two wooden canes—potentially
lethal weapons! The head nurse assured them that striking out with
the canes had never been a problem and that Mr. W was only verbally
abusive. She also explained his need to be alone and his love of
reading, and even suggested the kind of novels that he enjoyed most.
She added that he responded very well to a one-to-one relationship and
needed much praise.

The nursing home staff then selected a volunteer who enjoyed
reading and who visited once or twice a week. The head nurse pointed
out the reason for Mr. W's beard and its importance to him. (Nursing
homes and other institutions prefer clean-shaven patients simply
because skin care and cleanliness is more easily accomplished.)
She discussed many of his other idiosyncrasies which, she admitted,
had taken time for her to learn and accept. Mr. W had a distinct and
somewhat unusual style, and we did not try to change him. For example, for many years he had worn his pajamas under his clothing during
the day and changed pajamas at night. When he was first admitted to
the hospital, he became quite distraught when the nurses insisted that
he remove his pajamas every morning. However, some patient staff
member listened to Mr. W's demands and complied. All the morning
uproar then ceased, and he has since worn his pajamas under his

clothing. The staff member here was able to see the importance of continuing Mr. W's usual life-style. The "Standards for Geriatric Nursing Practice" describe the discrimination process in assessing life-styles:

> In all human beings there is a continuum of behavior which is within a range of normal. It is difficult to discriminate between that which is normal and that which can be dangerous to the individual or others, such as the right of a person to have privacy and its extreme, which is withdrawal, and a person's right to independence and its extreme, which may be pathologic. Older persons have these behavior changes precipitated by changes in environment which place extra demands on them. The nurse uses fine judgment to identify that which is the usual life-style. The nurse finds out what the individual's life-style has been before she can determine that which is deviant.[10]

The head nurse was extremely helpful in this particular transfer. She also felt comfortable about visiting Mr. W in his new home, and talked with the nursing staff about changes she observed in him. Shared communication benefits the patient by promoting true continuity of patient care.

Many of the patients in this building have been unable to participate in the selection of their own appropriate living situations. Those who are capable, show judgment, and have definite likes and dislikes are encouraged to participate with the family in the decision making. The value of having patients become active participants in their care plan has long been recognized by nursing education. Fuerst and Wolff state: "The relationship of the nurse to the patient should be one of *mutual planning and consent*. It is disastrous for the nurse to assume an authoritarian role and place the patient in a position of a recipient of care which he may neither understand nor want."[11]

CASE EXAMPLE 3   Dr. R was a 70-year-old retired dentist. Following his stroke, his son encouraged Dr. R to live with him in a distant state. Dr. R lived with his son and his family for a short period of time, but this was unsuccessful. Dr. R began exhibiting behavior too difficult for the family to tolerate. He was then placed in a state hospital and subsequently transferred to our hospital. Dr. R expressed a feeling of not being wanted. He adamantly refused to socialize with other patients; he became very upset if his routine was changed. Dr. R was certainly not benefiting from the hospital environment.

Initially, I began talking with him casually in the hospital lobby or on the ward. He seemed to enjoy our chats. When I explained my job function, he seemed interested but did not seem to think a move was for him. Then I talked with Dr. R's son, who was very interested in his father, but realized how impossible it was for his father to return to his home. I suggested the son visit several nursing homes that might be suitable for his father, and he found two that he especially liked. I then talked with Dr. R about the possibility of transferring to a nursing home. He remained very skeptical, but thought that a visit to these places would be appropriate. We visited two facilities and Dr. R was quite pleased. He decided upon one of them, although not without much debate with his son and me. It was extremely interesting to watch a man who assured me that nursing homes were not for him to become so involved with the choice later. I have visited him frequently after his discharge and he remains happy with his choice.

For patients who have been in institutions the greater part of their adult life there will always be a risk in any outplacement plan. Failure of the patient to remain in the community should not be viewed as a failure on the part of the persons involved, but rather as an opportunity for them to learn how to formulate and refine future plans for patients. We cannot expect emotionally dependent persons to make a successful move to the community unless we provide adequate support and activities for them. Scoles and Fine state that the chronic mental patient has three main problems: (1) poor interaction skills, (2) poor skills in daily maintenance, and (3) poor motivation. If community placement is to improve the patient's condition, then a concentrated effort should be made to assist in these three areas. Day treatment centers are frequently used, for they allow the patient to adjust to the therapeutic community and to try out these learned skills on the larger community.[12]

Boarding home operators often view themselves as landlords who must provide rigid control. When patients are placed in boarding homes, the operator needs not only assistance in understanding their problems but support as well. These operators are frequently persons without medical training. If successful placements are to be made, then a working information exchange system needs to be developed between the operators and hospital. Many operators are afraid that if they don't "handle the situation," the patient will be removed from their home and they will, in effect, lose business. An atmosphere should be created which allows the operator to ask for assistance or information.

Occasionally patients will return to their own homes and/or to the care of relatives. Often the patient has been hospitalized because the relative simply could not manage any longer. As time passes, the relative may have a change of heart and want the patient at home. Care needs to be taken, however, in making a decision; one cannot just discharge the patient, expecting the relative to pick up after a long interim. The patient may be more limited than formerly in the performance of daily activities, or unable to perform at all. This change of living situation, like any other, may also produce initial confusion in the patient. Again, anticipatory guidance is very important for the family so that they may cope better with the patient.

If possible, the patient should be allowed to go home on a trial visit first. This visit allows patient and family to test out what they have learned and see what problems may occur. Following a trial visit the family and the patient should be allowed time to discuss with appropriate nursing personnel how the visit proceeded. Preferably this nursing person should have some understanding of the available community resources.

CASE EXAMPLE 4 Jean, 50 years of age, had been in the hospital for 30 years with a diagnosis of schizophrenia. She was ambulatory, but her leg muscles had degenerated from standing still for long periods of time. She stood still when her anxiety was high; any movement for her then was impossible. Jean needed constant reassurance and guidance.

She was aware that many of the patients were leaving the hospital and that we were assisting them in forming appropriate plans. *She approached us with the idea of her leaving.* We discussed the possibility with the doctor and the head nurse on her ward. A decision was made that placement should be in a boarding home where the operator could provide a great deal of support and attention. Jean visited the boarding home before her discharge, and we talked to her about the boarding home and community living.

We were all fearful that Jean's extreme dependence would make her return to the community impossible; for this reason the social worker and I planned frequent follow-up visits so that Jean would know that she had not been deserted by her previous home and family, the hospital. We thus continued to provide support for her; she also attended the hospital-affiliated day treatment center. Jean was seen once weekly, and frequently more often, during her first month in the boarding home. I met with the boarding home operator during these visits and provided her with anticipated behavioral patterns based on Jean's adjustment and reactions noted during hospitalization. It was true that Jean did have the problems we anticipated in the new living situation, but with reassurance and necessary interventions, Jean remained in the community. As of now, she has lived there for 4 months and has made friends with the other residents. There is certainly no guarantee that she will remain in the community, but we are working very hard to help her to do so.

CASE EXAMPLE 5 Mr. S, a 47-year-old man with multiple sclerosis, required nursing care for all his needs. He spent most of the day in a reclining chair or in bed. He was able to express his needs, but at times he was very confused. He had periodic skin breakdowns which were difficult to care for because he refused to vary his position. Mr. S came to my attention when his wife requested that she take him home. She was an intelligent woman who wanted very much to try to care for her husband at home.

I felt it was important that she understand exactly what would be involved in his care. Simply to talk about the average day, the time schedule, the restrictions, and other problems is often not sufficient, and was not in Mr. S's case. The head nurse on Mr. S's ward concurred with this opinion. We therefore consulted Mr. S's doctor and decided to arrange for a 2-day period when Mrs. S could spend time on the ward caring for her husband. This time on the ward would accomplish three things: (1) allow her to learn the procedures for skin care, catheter care, etc., (2) give her the opportunity to judge how involved her daily living activities would be with her spouse, and (3) help her gain some initial confidence in her ability to care for a debilitated husband. She learned quickly, and returned to her home in another city to plan for his discharge. A referral was made to a social worker in that city who had a great deal of experience with multiple sclerosis patients. It was agreed that he would visit Mr. and Mrs. S frequently to assist when necessary. Also, arrangements were made for an attendant to relieve Mrs. S of some of the care. As a result, the staff, who had initially felt very negative about Mr. S leaving the hospital, became somewhat reassured that Mrs. S would be able to assume the care. Unfortunately we were never able to assess this particular plan, nor evaluate its implementation, as Mr. S became quite febrile from an infection which resisted treatment. He was never able to return home.

The problem of appropriate "long-lasting" placement is a problem not only for the patient, but also for the hospital staff. If staff do not feel a patient should leave, they may talk discouragingly to the patient and thus set up a failure. A study done at Boston State Hospital on the factors involved in the discharge of chronic patients showed that staff as well as patients should be prepared for patient discharge. According to Chien and Sharaf, "Attendants in particular may often have the unspoken and unwarranted concern that census reduction also means staff reduction, that they will work themselves out of a job."[13] Attendants in this study were found to be the key personnel on chronic wards in determining the patient's fate.

I hoped to counteract the negative input to patients by involving the staff with the placements and the follow-up visits to their patients. This was successful with the staff who worked daytime shifts, but communication with the other shifts regarding the discharged patients was lacking. There were the additional problems of persons rotating shifts or having days off; all these factors prevented adequate feedback about persons out of the hospital. I also felt it was important that the patients in the hospital hear about those who were discharged, and learn that leaving the hospital is, in most instances, a pleasurable experience.

I solved this problem in part by taping recorded messages about patients in other facilities. All shifts could play the recording. This was only a partial solution, however. For example, tapes were seldom played by a single person if he or she had missed the change of shift. There was no opportunity provided for the patients to listen. Also, someone listening to a tape at 3 a.m. is very likely to sleep. I finally decided to publish a newsletter on a monthly basis entitled *Your Community Grapevine.* This newsletter was widely distributed and conveyed the news to all members of all shifts. It also enabled me to inform staff and patients about various facilities and activities available for persons living in the surrounding community. It was posted on the patients' bulletin boards, and was also read aloud in the reality orientation groups. I also began taking snapshots of patients in their new surroundings. These were posted on a bulletin board in an area where they would be seen by patients, staff, and visitors. Staff members began to request the patients' new addresses and instructions on how to get there to visit.

I feel these discharges have been successful for the following reasons:

1 The patient's individual needs are being recognized.
2 These needs are matched with the appropriate living situation, and referrals to community agencies are made if necessary.
3 The staff is involved in planning for placement, and receives adequate information on patients discharged.
4 The patient and patient's family are involved and, when possible, their preferences are taken into account.
5 The patients are given the chance to view and assess the new living situation before discharge plans proceed.
6 Channels of communication are opened between the hospital staff and the persons in the supervised living situations.
7 Follow-up visits by the community-health nurse and hospital staff are made at least once a month to assess the patient's adjustment, and, if needed, to provide assistance.

SUMMARY

Of the 35 patients—15 women and 20 men—placed in various nursing homes, boarding homes, homes for the aged, or their own homes, only 2 have required rehospitalization. One elderly lady was returned to the hospital by her husband for a 2-week period for evaluation of her medication. After this time, she again returned home with her husband. Another, a diabetic woman, required readmission from a nursing home for more extensive medical care of an infection of her foot.

All patients are visited at least monthly, and usually much more frequently. The staff—RNs, LVNs, and nursing assistants—have shown an interest in the patients outside the hospital. Initially the staff were encouraged to make follow-up visits with me to their patients, but now they are requesting to do this on their own. The staff seem to feel free to give suggestions to boarding home and nursing home operators, and do not automatically suggest a patient be returned to the hospital when a problem arises, which is what usually occurred in the past. The staff have begun to discuss with various patients the possibility of leaving the hospital, and have even encouraged some patients to initiate plans for leaving, and to approach either the social worker or myself. One head nurse, who has been conducting a group of patients on periodic excursions outside the hospital, became especially interested in her patients being able to leave the hospital. She began discussing this with the patients and one day said to me very proudly, "You know, almost all the men in my group have come to talk with you and the social worker about leaving the hospital."

REFERENCES

1 Ching Piao Chien and Myron R. Sharaf, "Factors in the Discharge of Chronic Patients," *Hospital and Community Psychiatry,* vol. 22, no. 8, p. 24, August 1971.
2 Roger G. Barker and Beatrice A. Wright, "The Social Psychology of Adjustment to Physical Disability," in *Psychological Aspects of Physical Disability,* Rehabilitation Service Series Number 210, Department of Health, Education and Welfare, Washington, D.C., 1953, p. 27.
3 Charles K. Hofling and Madeleine M. Leininger, *Basic Psychiatric Concepts in Nursing,* Lippincott, Philadelphia, 1960, p. 196.
4 Chien and Sharaf, p. 26.
5 Irene Mortenson Burnside, "Loneliness in Old Age," *Mental Hygiene,* vol. 55, no. 3, p. 396, July 1971.
6 U.S. Department of Health, Education and Welfare, *Nursing Homes Environmental Health Factors,* Washington, D.C., 1967, p. 25.
7 Ali Jarrahizadeh and Carol S. High, "Returning Long-Term Patients to the Community," *Hospital and Community Psychiatry,* vol. 22, no. 2, pp. 63–65, February 1971.
8 Louis J. Movick, "Programming for the Brain-Damaged Aged in a Long-Term Care Facility," *Hospitals,* vol. 39, no. 9, pp. 61–62, May 1, 1965.
9 Margaret Aasterud, "Explanation to the Patient," in James K. Skipper, Jr. and Robert C. Leonard (eds.), *Social Interaction and Patient Care,* Lippincott, Philadelphia, 1965, pp. 84–85.

10 American Journal of Nursing, "Standards for Geriatric Nursing Practice," *American Journal of Nursing*, vol. 70, no. 9, pp. 1895–1897, September 1970.
11 Elinor V. Fuerst and LaVerne Wolff, *Fundamentals of Nursing*, Lippincott, Philadelphia, 1964, p. 40.
12 Pascal Scoles and Eric W. Fine, "Aftercare and Rehabilitation in a Community Mental Health Center," *Social Work*, vol. 16, no. 3, p. 79, July 1971.
13 Chien and Sharaf, p. 26

BIBLIOGRAPHY

David, Janis H., Johanne E. Hanser, and Barbara W. Madden: *Guidelines for Discharge Planning*, Rancho Los Amigos Hospital, Inc., Downey, Calif., 1968.

Garrett, James R. (ed.): *Psychological Aspects of Physical Disability*, Department of Health, Education and Welfare, Rehabilitation Service Series Number 210, Washington, D.C.

George, Madelon, Kazuyoshi Ide, and Clara E. Vambery: "The Comprehensive Health Team: A Conceptual Model," *The Journal of Nursing Administration*, vol. 1, no. 4, 1971.

Kulys, Regina: "Discharge Planning," *Hospitals*, vol. 44, May 1, 1970.

Lambertsen, Eleanor: "Hospitals and Nurses Urged to Encourage Continuity of Patient Care," *Modern Hospital*, vol. 101, no. 1, July 1963.

Lindenberg, Ruth E.: "Approaches to Continued Care," *Nursing Outlook*, vol 11, no. 8, August 1963.

National Commission of Community Health Services: *Health Is a Community Affair*, Harvard University Press, Cambridge, Mass., 1967.

National League for Nursing: *Continuity of Nursing Care from Hospital to Home* (11–1228), New York, 1966.

Scoles, Pascal, and Eric W. Rine: "Aftercare and Rehabilitation in a Community Mental Health Center," *Social Work*, vol. 16, no. 3, July 1971.

Skipper, James K., and Robert C. Leonard: *Social Interaction and Patient Care*, Lippincott, Philadelphia, 1965.

Steffl, Bernita M., and Imogene Eide: *Discharge Planning Handbook*, Charles B. Slack, Thorofare, N.J., 1978.

Veterans Administration Department of Medicine and Surgery: *Program Guide to Nursing Care of the Long-Term Patient*, Washington, D.C., April 10, 1963.

Washburn, Richard W., and Elaine J. Smith: "A Continuum of Mental Health Services," *Hospital and Community Psychiatry*, vol. 22, no. 2, February 1971.

Chapter 9

Group Therapy
for High Utilizers
of Clinic Facilities

Julianne M. McWhorter

By the crowd they have been broken;
by the crowd shall they be healed.

L. Cody Marsh
Group Psychotherapy and the Psychiatric Clinic

The aged patient who makes frequent medical appointments in which no disease process can be defined and treated represents a challenge and a frustration to a care provider. The challenge may well be: "What do I do with these persons who insist they are sick, defend their symptoms, and occupy critical time required for the care of other patients?" The frustration is often that a need is being expressed that has to be identified in a reasonable time restraint, and a method to best address that need has to be found.

Vhile working in a comprehensive care clinic, I identified patients who utilized the clinic frequently. Actually, they were clearly identified for me by staff reactions when their name appeared on the appointment calendar—usually a sigh and cringe.

Each had multiple functional or psychosomatic disorders. They seemed to love coming to the clinic and insisted on their full share of the time of the receptionist, the nurse, and primarily the physician—often demanding more than could be given in a busy schedule.

Our current method of caring for these patients (make a medical appointment, conduct a physical examination, listen, and assure them they were well) did not seem to be effective. In fact, it set up a situation in which more symptoms had to be reported and defended, and dependency increased.

As a student reading volumes on psychosomatic medicine, I saw this set of circumstances as a good project. More accurately, I was in the position of seeing these patients, listening, and being completely frustrated by the experience. It became increasingly difficult not to be irritated when they walked in.

More from intuition than for any logical reason, I thought a group might be one answer. At least it would be effective in utilizing time and professional resources. So, I began to plot out the individual histories, look for common denominators, and pull out references to see if I could support my hunch.

THE FORMATION OF A GROUP

In order for me to make the decision to treat a person in a group setting, I needed to identify who that person was. I did that by sketching out a profile of each patient involved: current life situation, health status, mental status, interpersonal behaviors, expressed needs, and my evaluation of their motivation for treatment.

The following questions were then applied:

1 Why should each individual be considered for a group?
2 Are the individuals being considered compatible for effective group function?
3 What are their needs?
4 How might a group meet these needs?
5 Are there any other alternatives that would better meet these needs, either as expressed by the patient or identified by the staff and myself (who I will also refer to as "therapist").

With these questions answered, other considerations that arose were (1) the treatment goals, (2) the number of patients that could be effectively handled, (3) the duration of time allotted for therapy, and (4) the limitations of the therapist.

Selecting the Patients

Densen's criterion for a high clinic utilizer states that the patient requires predominantly supportive care in more than 10 clinic visits per year.[1] Silverman has identified the population of people widowed and over 60 years of age as having a high risk of developing mental illness.[2] The patients selected as possible candidates for group therapy were widows who had multiple functional or psychosomatic disorders, who made more than 10 clinic visits per year which were primarily supportive, and who had a mean age of 64.3 years. The statistical prognosis, the frequency of unscheduled visits to the clinic, and the rescheduling of appointments indicated that nursing intervention beyond attention to physical symptoms was needed. These factors met the criteria for a target population.

The Clinic "Personae"

The behavior patterns observed in these patients were very similar. Most had multiple complaints, many of which were functional and lacking in etiology. Headache, backache, nerves, lightheadedness, and fluttering in the heart were common symptoms.

The patients had few interpersonal relationships and little involvement in activities. This fits with research findings of Zigler and Phillips who linked somatizing with reduced social competence.[3] Each individual expressed feelings indicative of depression, and suffered from one or more realistic stresses caused by organic damage or focus on object loss.

These patients demonstrated remarkably similar modes of interacting with the staff. The predominant characteristics of their interpersonal relations were (1) demanding behavior, (2) use of psychosomatic symptoms, (3) anxiety, and (4) some evidence of cognitive disturbance, e.g., memory loss or preoccupation with the past. Both loneliness and the utilization of an illness to gain gratification could be inferred from observations and interviews.

Interestingly, all patients selected for the group spoke of themselves as independent. Perhaps they were, in dealing with their peers (you really have no way of knowing, only educated conjecture), but in the clinic they not only preferred, but demanded authority and leadership, giving dictates on what they needed to handle their discomfort and their daily problems in living. Commonly, they wanted to see their particular physician, who in each case happened to be male. Several worried about the doctor and nurses working too hard and often brought baked goods to their appointment.

As I will discuss later in the text, much of this behavior could be interpreted as replicating past behavior toward a husband.[4] The widow, as a patient, essentially transferred her feelings, behavior, and need for structure from object loss (husband) to a caring authority figure (physician). In this manner, the actual loss, the accompanying anger at being left alone, and the pain of grief could be denied, or expressed through physical complaints.

One further comment on dependency and somatizing: such dependency can probably be predicted. Comparative studies of psychologically oriented and somatically oriented individuals demonstrate that somatically oriented individuals were more dependent on authority, demonstrated lower ideals and goals for self, and had greater autonomic awareness than the psychologically oriented.[5] The authors of the study inferred that somatizing was used as a means of binding anxiety and minimizing the distortion of external reality. *It appears then that such patients may develop physical discomfort as a way of generating a personally acceptable explanation of their environmental situation and focusing their anxiety.* Less free-floating anxiety would then be manifest.

Patients' Use of Symptoms

According to these studies, physical symptoms would then provide these patients a channel for communication and a way of getting attention, a reason for not initiating activity, and a method of handling psychological pain and conflict. Illness legitimized the individual's presence in the clinic.

It is difficult in any case to walk into a clinic and state, "I'm lonely. I don't know what to do next. I need someone to talk to." I'm not even sure that these individuals consciously recognized that this may have been what they wanted.

Somatization enabled them to focus on a concrete complaint, which was probably easier to endure than looking inside themselves to determine what reactions and feelings were creating discomfort.

Gramlich states that grief and depression are often manifested in chronic physical complaints, particularly in the elderly individual.[6]

Thus, chronic physical complaints often mask an underlying emotional conflict and deny its resolution.[7] I've since become very attentive to what is between the lines when working with persons who have lists of ongoing symptoms not physically determinable.

With the exception of one 54-year-old woman who had problems with an adolescent son at home, the patients did not seem to be aware of any possible relationship between their anxiety, their somatic complaints, and their intrapersonal and interpersonal relationships. It's important to remember that these patients believed in their symptoms, and in fact experienced them. This cannot be minimized. Symptoms are real and distressing to the individual experiencing them, whatever the etiology. However, in treating such symptoms, one might suspect that the patient's relief from medication or a traditional medical appointment is likely to be short-lived. Couple this with a hurried and sometimes impatient and less than sympathetic staff (self included), and one realizes that the patient must be in a very distressing situation.

Summary of Patient Characteristics

The eight women finally selected for consideration in group treatment appeared to be homogeneous regarding (1) age, (2) sex, (3) marital status, (4) ego strength, and (5) use of clinic facilities. Their social history was similar: only one was from a large family; all reported rigid parental controls; and all had similar current life situations.

PRELIMINARY CONSIDERATIONS IN ESTABLISHING THE GROUP

The literature indicates that although differences in race, religion, intellectual capacity, and cultural background may initially create difficulties in a group, these are rapidly overcome, and within a short time patients align themselves according to previous emotional experience and problems rather than to similar background.[8-10] One patient had a diagnosis of schizophrenia. I had been warned about introducing an individual with such a diagnosis into a group. However, her behavior was appropriate; she was not disturbed by hallucinatory activity, and she was able to interact with others. (It's never a good idea to accept a diagnosis as sole criterion, or always to accept a diagnosis without inquiry.) I saw her as a potentially valuable catalyst to group function on the basis of her ability to accurately perceive and comment on the feelings and nonverbal behavior of others—an unusual trait in somatizing patients. So, I decided to give it a try. Psychosomatic illness, high dependency needs, and what appeared to be strong transference reactions were manifest in each patient. These factors are discussed in the literature as good indications for a group.[11]

To get started, each patient was seen individually and the idea of a group was introduced. The patients relinquished decision-making power to me after the first interview: anything I said was acceptable. Initially, and naively, I assumed this relinquishing of decision making to be the result of absolute trust in me as a therapist. I have since modified this assumption and find it incredible that I ever made it. What the behavior may have more accurately reflected was the response to a feeling that their visits to the clinic were in jeopardy, and an attitude of "I need and want this clinic and if this is the only way I'm going to get in here, I'll play your game. At least right now."

To explore the covert or hidden messages which occur in group process, Lieberman and Whitaker offer helpful insights.[12]

Identifying Patients' Needs

Bowlby sees bereavement as occurring in three stages: (1) the impact stage, where the system is focused on the original object; (2) the recoil stage, where disorganization of the person is accompanied by pain and despair; and (3) the recovery stage, in which a reorganization and redefinition of role takes place.[13] It was my assumption that these patients had not made a successful transition in the recovery phase, that they needed to learn skills in interpersonal relationships and make new role adjustments. The following factors formed the basis for this assumption: (1) activities were directed to the past rather than the future, (2) attempts were being made to recapture the deceased in spirit, and (3) irrational feelings about life, loneliness, and worthlessness were in evidence.

I saw tasks confronting these patients as (1) learning to live successfully without their marital partner, (2) finding a meaningful emotional life, (3) finding a meaningful social life, and (4) dealing realistically with stress. This represented a big order and one in which we all are participating to some degree. As I review them now, the tasks were unrealistic for the short-term group setting I had in mind. In addition, I'm not at all sure the basic assumption of arrest in the recovery stage of bereavement was accurate. Morath interprets such behaviors as clues that the individual may be operating in the impact stage, stating that the widow who makes such strong transference to the care giver is still denying the loss of her husband by projecting the feelings, interactions, and need for definition to the practitioner. She is thereby able to prevent full realization of the loss and is able to deny the accompanying anger and pain, which then finds its expression somatically.[14]

Accepting this interpretation, I saw the task confronting this group as the full recognition of loss that was basic to any further movement.

Since the patients' behavior in the clinic (demanding, advice-seeking, and structure-seeking) may well have replicated their interactions with the deceased, in retrospect I am inclined to accept the interpretation of Morath. Either interpretation supports a group therapy modality for treatment.

Current medical treatment was not working, and I saw no readiness for individual psychotherapy or counseling. Referrals to senior citizen or other social community groups were an option. However, these groups are utilized by people who are motivated and eager for such activity. Readiness for interpersonal contact usually occurs after the individual begins to feel alive again, and is aware of loneliness and a sense of separation. The patients I described needed to examine and express their grief. They were poorly motivated to resume social activity.

It might be appropriate to note here that it is not unusual for grief work to be arrested. Our society often does not permit an individual to vent feelings of bereavement and then deal with those feelings.[15] This may be illustrated by the following. One patient, a 65-year-old widow, was seen in the clinic 6 months after the death of her husband. She complained of pain originating in the abdomen and radiating to her back. This pain was accompanied by a burning sensation along her spinal column. She had no appetite and slept poorly. She was told by her relatives that she must be brave, that her husband would not have wanted her to cry. She had, in effect, been told to stop grieving.

I would refer you at this point to the works of Elisabeth Kübler-Ross, who describes stages of grief and grief work and offers many insights and suggestions to facilitate the process.[16-18]

The Special Needs of Widows   Silverman reports that widows need personal, unstructured, human encounters.[19] Therefore, the structure of traditional clinic care with its lack of personal involvement, and the often impersonal neutral environment of an office setting are potentially dysfunctional to the widow. Seeing a therapist individually is usually for the purpose of resolving psychological problems rather than a difficult life situation, and the women I identified did not recognize psychological conflicts as a difficulty or as a cause of their symptoms. According to Morath, widows require firm, personal, and structured direction initially, to be provided by the care giver through the process of transference.[20] The care giver would offer direction to help establish the structure that the deceased had provided, e.g.,: "I want you to get up at 8 a.m., cook bacon and eggs, eat that, then clean the living room, etc." Given order and predictability in the day, anxiety is reduced. Of course, a strategy to move the individual through the process of grieving and toward independence would need to be plotted.[21]

The results of a study by Silverman indicate that the most effective care giver for a widow is another widow, and the relationship often results in mutual assistance that makes movement toward health possible.[22]

I saw group therapy, properly handled, as a combination of all these elements.

STRUCTURE AND FUNCTION OF THE GROUP

The group was planned to consist of eight members, but to remain open-ended. It was to be a short-term group, and to meet weekly for 4 months. Because of the short duration of the group, and the participants' obvious lack of interpersonal skills and lack of motivation to look beyond symptoms, the group required a directive therapist. The degree of direction to be given remained flexible, and was contingent on the functioning of the group. The group was conceived as verbal, directive, and dealing with the here and now. Historically, this technique has been successful in assisting individuals to find an interest in life and to focus on the present and future. Moreover, the technique reportedly results in decreased symptoms and decreased use of clinic facilities, and has been found to be particularly useful in the treatment of psychosomatic patients.[23]

The nature of this short-term group required an emphasis on a commitment to work when the members did meet. In order to increase the effectiveness of this short-term group, we made a specific, concrete contract for each member.

Resistance to Group Involvement

Most patients tend to resist being in a group. The major source of resistance to this particular group, and an obstacle to group functioning, was the feeling of being "dumped" into a group and being deprived of individual attention by an authority figure. This problem was handled by encouraging regular medical appointments, and by setting aside time before or after a group session to check distressing symptoms or medication problems.

Pretherapeutic transference was another obstacle. The assumption seemed implicit that the therapist had all the answers and explanations concerning how to live more successfully. This attitude may have been due to the group members' long association with the medical model; it may also have resulted from their dependence on authority and demand for leadership.

Therapeutic Goals

The goal for this group was conceptualized as: "How do you let go of the past and form new relationships?" With these patients, the realization of this goal involved developing a new "I," or self-concept. The needs of these patients to be met by group therapy were identified as (1) attention to urgent problems in living, e.g., welfare, (2) improvement of self-image and raising of self-esteem, (3) increased ability to share with others, and (4) reduction in the use of physical symptoms of illness.

The group therapy was not intended to change basic personality trends, but rather to encourage a reorientation of attitudes. A group can facilitate such reorientation in the following ways:

1 Provide an opportunity to develop a group identity
2 Even when the client does not report any symptoms, give the client an appointment for a future visit
3 Provide an opportunity to analyze resistance as a means of avoiding working in the group, e.g., the use of physical complaints to allow the individuals to avoid dealing with their feelings
4 Encourage outside contacts for social and supportive encounters, with the possibility of later movement into community social groups

  5 Teach reality testing—a chance to recognize distortions of reality and test new insights

The Group Experience

Individuals respond expressively, and in a group they manifest all the significant roles and feelings they experience in their lives. The group therefore is a laboratory to ~ssess, modify, and test new behavior by trial and error. Several of these patients observed the similarity between the physical complaints of others and their own, and recognized the compulsive nature of these complaints. These patients had been engaged in long-standing struggles with doctors to prove that their symptoms were not psychosomatic or imaginary. Such a stance became increasingly less necessary in the group setting, because other patients were in the same position. With the obstacle of somatization reduced, the relationship between expression of feelings and relief of symptoms was gradually explored. The therapist interpreted somatic complaints as a resistance to dealing with underlying feelings. Rationalization for such feelings as failure, guilt, worthlessness, and loneliness may have been another reason for physical complaints. Several individuals demonstrated awareness to the point of asking for help directly and recognizing that they were welcome in the clinic with or without symptoms.

  There were no meetings in which every member was present. One patient became delusional, experienced hallucinatory activity, and was later hospitalized for congestive heart failure. Her treatment was followed up on an individual basis. A second patient stated that she realized she was afraid to try to live without her husband. She was encouraged to cry during a meeting, and did so for almost an hour. After this session her physical complaints decreased and she was eventually able to enroll in an adult education course. This patient was seen individually once after she left the group. She no longer had physical complaints, was actively participating in her adult education course, and had resumed social contact with friends. She felt that she could now talk honestly with her doctor and receive support from him.

  A third patient joined a senior citizens group and chose not to attend the clinic group. A fourth, aged 72, came to the clinic for 1 hour every 2 weeks and met with the clinic aide, whom she found supportive. This patient stated that she was lonely and wanted to meet some new people. A fifth patient, who identified feelings of guilt about her husband's death as the cause of her anxiety, was seen on an individual basis by the therapist. She no longer mentioned physical complaints. Two patients failed to come to the group at all, stating that they only wanted to visit their doctor. The eighth patient, a 54-year-old widow, was eventually able to verbalize her grief; she began going out socially and found a male companion. She had not been back to the clinic for 3 months.

Although the group was smaller, and its duration shorter than I had anticipated, group therapy appeared to be a catalyst for several patients to begin to identify their feelings, evaluate their behavior patterns, and share their feelings with others. These patients were able to resume social contacts and engage in outside activities. The consistent emphasis of *"physical symptoms are real and distressing, but often represent an expression of how you feel emotionally"* was successful. The use of physical complaints decreased, and the patients were able to talk directly about the feelings they were experiencing. Referral agencies, families, and the attending physician were contacted as needed to establish channels of communication, obtain information, and provide data. This resulted in improved continuity of care.

THERAPIST TECHNIQUES

The therapist for a group such as the one described in this chapter needs to maintain a patient, noncritical, and consistent attitude. The principal techniques of the therapist should include:

1 Emphasizing ego strengths.
2 Utilizing group members as auxiliary egos.
3 Focusing on reality.
4 Dealing with dreams and fantasy on a reality basis.
5 Engaging interrelatedness.
6 Encouraging relationships outside the group.
7 Utilizing outside people as needed for reality problems (e.g., social workers or medical consultants).
8 Recognizing transference as it occurs, and, when appropriate, identifying the behavior to the group. Such identification helps the group to deal with the behavior in the new context of understanding. It is not necessary to delve into the patient's past to find the origin of the transference.

SUMMARY

A directive-verbal type of group dealing with the here and now was the treatment chosen for eight widows who were identified as high utilizers of clinic facilities. The group was short-term for this selected number. The patients were a relatively homogeneous group with (1) psychosomatic complaints, (2) high dependency needs, (3) strong initial transferences to the therapist, and (4) reduced social skills. The lack of successful transition in the recovery phase of bereavement was identified as a source of anxiety requiring a possible redefinition of the individual. It was hypothesized that, through group therapy, group members would gain increased awareness of their feelings and a decreased need to use psychosomatic complaints as their primary mode of communication and means of dealing with stress.

This experience with eight widows, most of whom were elderly, indicated to me that short-term informal group therapy might be valuable in the outpatient clinic to assist patients in coping with difficult life situations. One physician I know discreetly engineered a situation in which patients such as those described here would wait together for their medical appointments. The office waiting room spontaneously evolved into an environment in which symptoms were shared, one-upsmanship of illness exhausted, and some meaningful dialogue initiated without a facilitator.

REFERENCES

1 Bernard Schoenberg and Robert Senescu, "Group Psychotherapy for Patients with Chronic Multiple Somatic Complaints," *Journal of Chronic Disease*, vol. 13, no. 6, p. 655, 1966.
2 Phyllis Rolfe Silverman, "Services to the Widowed: First Steps in a Program of Preventive Intervention," *Community Mental Health Journal*, vol. 3, no. 1, pp. 37–44, Spring 1967.
3 Edward Zigler and Leslie Phillips, "Social Competence and Outcome in Psychiatric Disorders," *Journal of Abnormal and Social Psychology*, vol. 63, no. 2, p. 270, 1961.
4 Donald R. Morath, President, Medical Health Services, Cincinnati, Ohio, from conversations on primary care, 1978.
5 Karl Rickles, Robert W. Downing, and Mildred H. Downing, "Personality Differences between Somatically and Psychologically Oriented Neurotic Patients," *Journal of Nervous and Mental Disease*, vol. 142, pp. 10–18, 1966.
6 Edwin P. Gramlich, "Recognition and Management of Grief in Elderly Patients," *Geriatrics*, vol. 23, pp. 87–92, July 1968.
7 Ibid., p. 89.
8 Irene Mortenson Burnside, "Group Work among the Aged," *Nursing Outlook*, vol. 17, no. 6, pp. 68–71, June 1969.
9 Paul Leiderman and Veronica R. Leiderman, "Group Therapy: An Approach to Problems of Geriatric Outpatients," in Jules H. Masserman (ed.), *Current Psychiatric Therapies*, vol. 7, Grune and Stratton, New York, 1967, pp. 179–185.
10 Schoenberg and Senescu, op. cit., p. 651.
11 Asya L. Kadis et al., *A Practicum of Group Psychotherapy*, Harper and Row, New York, 1963.
12 Morton Lieberman and Dorothy Whitaker, *Psychotherapy through the Group Process*, Atherton Press, New York, 1964.

13 John Bowlby, "Process of Mourning," *The International Journal of Psychoanalysis*, vol. 42, pp. 317–340, July–October 1961.

14 Morath, op. cit.

15 Ann B. Love, "Surviving Widowhood," *Ms.*, pp. 84–91, October 1974.

16 Elizabeth Kübler-Ross, *On Death and Dying*, Macmillan, New York, 1969.

17 Elizabeth Kübler-Ross, *Questions and Answers on Death and Dying,* Macmillan, New York, 1974.

18 Elizabeth Kübler-Ross, *Death: The Final Stage of Growth,* Prentice-Hall, Englewood Cliffs, N.J., 1975

19 Silverman, op. cit., p. 43

20 Morath, op. cit.,

21 Granger E. Westburg, *Good Grief*, Augustana Book Concern, Rock Island, Ill., 1961.

22 Silverman, op. cit., p. 37.

23 Schoenberg and Senescu, op. cit., p. 656.

BIBLIOGRAPHY

Bellak, Leopold, and Tokosoz B. Karasu: *Geriatric Psychiatry: A Handbook for Psychiatrists and Primary Care Physicians*, Section I and III, Grune and Stratton, New York, 1976.

Burnside, Irene Mortenson: *Working with the Elderly: Group Process and Techniques,* Duxbury Press, North Scituate, Mass., 1978.

Epstein, Leon: "Clinical Geropsychiatry," in William Reichel (ed.), *Clinical Aspects of Aging*, Williams and Wilkins, Baltimore, Md., 1978.

Hurder, W. P., John H. Lewko, and Alex J. Hurder: "Improving the Evaluation of Human Services by Separating the Delivery of Service from Service," *Community Mental Health Journal*, vol. 14, no. 4, pp. 279–290, 1978.

Schwab, Sister Marilyn: "Professional Nursing in the Care of the Aged," in William Reichel (ed.), *Clinical Aspects of Aging*, Williams and Wilkins, Baltimore, Md., 1978.

Steury, Steven, and Marie L. Blank: *Readings in Psychotherapy with Older People*, Center for Studies of the Mental Health of the Aging, U.S. Department of Health, Education and Welfare, National Institute of Mental Health, Rockville, Md., 1977.

Taylor, Robert B. (ed.): *Family Medicine: Principles and Practice*, Springer-Verlag, New York, 1978, chaps. 18, 23, 29, 39, 40, 43, and 78.

Williams, T. Franklin: "Assessment of the Geriatric Patient in Relation to Needs for Services and Facilities," in William Reichel (ed.), *Clinical Aspects of Aging,* Williams and Wilkins, Baltimore, Md., 1978.

Chapter 10

Group Work in the Community: Experiences with Reminiscence

Janet C. Blackman

Evening haze:
   when memories come, how distant
   are the bygone days.

Kito (1740–88): Buson pupil

During a recent return to school, I was anxious to step away from my background in acute care nursing and to become familiar with several community-based programs. Consequently, I found my way to a senior day care center where I worked as a volunteer for 8 months. For a part of that time I served as a group leader, and the purpose of this chapter is to set forth my experiences working with a group of elderly women. In the broader context, the nature of my work with the elderly group was mental health. More specifically the focus was the creation of an opportunity for reminiscence, resocialization, and life review in a small group setting.

A survey of the literature convinced me of the value of these therapeutic processes in expanding the quality of the elderly person's life. I became increasingly convinced of this as I came to know the group.*

* The author gratefully acknowledges the cooperation of the Palo Alto Senior Day Care Program.

© 1972 United Feature Syndicate, Inc.

REVIEW OF THE LITERATURE

In beginning my gerontologic reading, I found one of the earliest papers to be the most exciting. Linden and Courtney, who may not have received the recognition that is their due, struck me as front-runners of the innovative and positive orientation toward aging that now characterizes the literature, if not the reality. They observed that "little place is found in a mobile and aggressive society, except fortuitously, for individuals in the postreproductive phases of life."[1] However, it was their hypothesis that some of life's

most important tasks may begin only after parenting is a completed responsibility. They hypothesized:

> It may well be that the additional function of the adult of preserving culture, of
> maintaining the annals of history, of keeping alive human judgment, of main-
> taining human skills, of preserving and skillfully contriving the instruments of
> civilization, and of conveying all this to oncoming generations, is the
> postreproductive work of the human organism and that this realistic and
> valuable quality of the human mind is uncovered or manifested in the senescent
> individual.[2]

Linden and Courtney envisioned the life cycle as composed of two
halves, *evolescence* on the younger side of the middle of life and *senescence*
on the older side. (Those in evolescence are the E's, those in senescence the
S's.) They saw ours as an E-dominated culture with the requisite values being "movement, agility, quantitative productivity, exhibitionistic sexual attractiveness, and artfulness" rather than the "simple" S-values of
"deliberation, caution, quality, modesty and loyalty."[3] Not surprisingly the
E's and the S's have a relationship marked by conflict: the E's rebel against
the S's and

> S counterrebellion is a continuous restatement of old ideals, a tenacious attach-
> ment to the established and proven solutions, a reluctance to countenance
> social revolution, and an increasing awareness of the value of the past as a
> predictor of the future and an instrument of judgment.[4]
>
> It is therefore seen that the S attitude is simultaneously directed toward protec-
> tion of the E's against social perils and toward the preservation of a culture.[5]

Linden and Courtney suggested the direction of much research and encouraged efforts at therapeutic work with the elderly.

> For example, the enormous dependency needs and self-isolation of the senile
> respond remarkably to an independence-fostering program engineered in an in-
> tegrated group setting. In a large number of such people physical and psychic
> decline can be arrested or slowed. This is not designed so much for the purpose
> of extending longevity as it is to help promote some degree of serenity during
> the remaining period of life.[6]

Written in 1953, this set the stage for the later surge of interest in enhancing
the quality of life of our elderly.

Ten years later Butler published a paper which was to be a milestone in
the field of gerontology. Quite simply he presented a case for the value of

reminiscence, which previously had been viewed as an unfortunate tendency among the old, a nuisance or an annoyance in one's relations with an elderly person. "The prevailing tendency is to identify reminiscence in the aged with psychological dysfunction and thus to regard it essentially as a symptom."[7] Going further, Butler summarized the widely held disdain for reminiscence in the elderly: "In consequence, reminiscence becomes a pejorative suggesting preoccupation, musing, aimless wandering of the mind. In a word, reminiscence is fatuous."[8]

Butler, however, postulated that there was value in reminiscence, a behavior which has long been recognized as a characteristic of old age and as having greater frequency then than at other stages of life. Butler saw reminiscence as an outward manifestation of a larger psychic process that is exclusive to the aged. This psychic process he named the *life review*, which he saw as an inevitable attempt at resolution of a lifetime's conflicts in preparation for one's death.

> . . . I conceive of the life review as a naturally occurring, universal mental process characterized by the progressive return to consciousness of past experiences, and, particularly, the resurgence of unresolved conflicts; simultaneously, and normally, these revived experiences and conflicts can be surveyed and reintegrated. Presumably this process is prompted by the realization of approaching dissolution and death, and the inability to maintain one's sense of personal invulnerability. It is further shaped by contemporaneous experiences and its nature and outcome are affected by the lifelong unfolding of character.[9]

Butler attached considerable significance for adaptivity to reminiscence and the life review, but he also described psychopathological manifestations most likely to be seen when "the process proceeds in isolation in those who have been deeply affected by increasing contraction of life attachments and notable psychosocial discontinuities, such as forced retirement and the death of the spouse."[10] Specifically Butler predicted psychopathological manifestations in the form of anxiety, depression, and despair in three categories of individuals:

  1 Those who always tended to avoid the present and to put great emphasis on the future
  2 Those who have consciously exercised the human capacity to injure others
  3 Those who may be best described as characterologically arrogant and prideful[11]

Although, in 1963, the literature of psychotherapy carried warnings about psychotherapy for the aged group (implying the dangers of reviewing one's life), Butler felt otherwise and said so.

> The existence of a life review occurring irrespective of the psychotherapeutic situation suggests that the aged particularly need a participant observer, professional or otherwise, and that the alleged danger of psychotherapy should be re-evaluated.[12]

McMahon and Rhudick approached reminiscence in a different way. Defining reminiscence as "the act or habit of thinking about or relating past experiences, especially those considered most personally significant,"[13] they studied 25 male volunteers between the ages of 78 and 90, all Spanish-American War veterans. They used an hour-long nondirective interview, and categorized each subject's responses for content references to the past, the present, and the future. "Responses referring to the remote past were classified as reminiscences."[14] During the course of the interviews all subjects were scored for clinical depression, suspected depression, or no depression, using the criteria of prevailing affect of depression, evidence of loss of self-esteem, and expressed feelings of helplessness and hopelessness. Finally, all subjects were rated for degree of intellectual deterioration. Approximately 1 year later the group of veterans was resurveyed to determine deaths in the interval, and all data were then subjected to statistical analysis "to determine the relationship between the tendency to reminisce and (a) the degree of intellectual deterioration, (b) the presence or absence of depression, and (c) survival since the interview."[15]

The findings did not indicate any relationship between reminiscing and intellectual deterioration, and they suggested that the nondepressed group reminisced more than the depressed group. The resurvey yielded interesting data: 3 of the 4 subjects rated as depressed had died, 4 out of the 5 who were scored suspected depression had died, while only one of the 16 nondepressed subjects had died. These findings were significant at above the 0.01 level.[16]

While McMahon and Rhudick did not accept the universality of the life review, they saw reminiscence as an entity in its own right "positively correlated with successful adaptation to old age through the maintenance of self-esteem, reaffirming a sense of identity, working through and mastery of personal losses, and as a means of contributing positively to their society."[17]

The first nurse to write widely of her experiences in group work with the aged was Irene Burnside.[18] In a survey of 33 articles on the subject of group work with the aged, Burnside wrote: "Important traits in the group leader were: flexibility, warmth, perseverance, patience, and ability to listen."[19] In a later paper she recounted her experiences in working with a group of seven elderly patients in an extended care facility over a 2-year period. Her early goals for the group were to facilitate communication among the group members and to resocialize the withdrawn, long-hospitalized patients. She described Schatzman's use of the "heroic life" as a focus for discussions, pointing out to the elderly participants their innate toughness and proven ability to survive many difficult and devastating experiences. She learned to be more flexible in her interpretation of rules and regulations for health care of the aged; and she noted that her group members talked freely of death and dying, their own or that of spouses or friends.[20] In yet another paper Burnside described the constant theme of loss that was so much a part of group discussions.[21]

In a nursing text, Burnside, Taulbee, Hennessey, and Ebersole discussed other facets of group work with the elderly.[22] Ebersole, who has practiced and taught reminiscing and group psychotherapy with the elderly, states that:

> Group reminiscing is a psychologically sound method of intervention with the aged to promote group interaction; to stimulate perceptual, interpersonal, and intrapersonal awareness; and to assist the elderly in meshing their lives with others who have participated in the same significant eras and historical events.[23]

Her own observation has been that reminiscence increases following losses or at those points where certain segments of one's life are clearly "completed." She believes that this tendency supports the life review concept.

Ebersole identified four stages, or phases, which her reminiscing group went through: (1) trusting the leader (learning to trust), (2) establishing the importance of self, (3) extending trust to group members, and (4) working through conflictual material.[24] She supports the therapeutic value of listening.

> Nurses wishing to implement this form of group psychotherapy may question their ability to follow the client into areas of psychic vulnerability. Supportive listening and encouragement toward self-expression have never within my knowledge been detrimental. Psychic probing, confrontation, and interpretation are neither advisable nor necessary to accomplish the task of the reminiscence group. There may be tears and sorrow when recounting some episode of past loss and disappointment, but this most often has a healing effect. As nurses we need to accept the premise that listening and sharing are reparative. Interested listeners are often sorely lacking in the lives of the very aged who have outlived most significant others.[25]

Ebersole was the first nurse to make conscious use of group reminiscing in a therapeutic fashion.

Taking the point of view of another discipline, Lowy's paper is interesting on the subject of group work with the aged.[26] Recent efforts at a systematic study of different aspects of reminiscence may be found in the papers of Lewis and of Havighurst and Glasser. Lewis studied 23 males to determine "whether reminiscers showed an increased consistency, compared to non-reminiscers, between their past and present self-concepts following a form of stress."[27] Havighurst and Glasser studied a large sample of elderly people using a questionnaire to elicit self-reports on silent reminiscing. They think it likely that "there is a syndrome of good personal-social adjustment, positive affect of reminiscence, and high frequency of reminiscence."[28]

Yalom and Terrazas established goals for group work with psychotic elderly patients. Their primary goal was to rehumanize their patients' lives, and included the following objectives:

> To reduce the isolation of patients, to enable them to reexperience bonds with others, and to increase feelings of group morale or cohesiveness. The reduction of bizarre behavior, the strengthening of adaptive personality traits, and the resolution of specific ward problems are all appropriate therapeutic goals.[29]

Though their patients were psychotic, most of the material presented is applicable to other groups of elderly people. These researchers looked at group composition, stating:

> Mute patients can profit from group attendance. Nonverbal cues often indicate that these patients are actively involved in the group. A verbal group cannot absorb too many nonverbal members, however, and still maintain active interaction.[30]

Other topics dealt with were physical setting, the role of the therapist, common themes, group cohesiveness, and increasing interaction. "Since a major goal of therapy is to improve interpersonal communication, the therapist should continuously strive to increase the patients' awareness of each other and to encourage their interaction."[31] Later, on the same technique: "Therapists should help to point out similarities between group members. . . . Feelings of isolation and loneliness diminish when patients become aware that others are experiencing similar feelings."[32] In conclusion, Yalom and Terrazas acknowledged that there was widespread pessimism about therapeutic work with the elderly; however, they felt that the pessimism is unwarranted.

RATIONALE FOR FORMATION OF GROUP

Despite the contradictory views that have been expressed in the literature I find myself believing in the concept of the life review, although I accept that its importance may vary from person to person. I see it as a manifestation of psychological health when a person is able to puzzle over the twisted meanderings of a lifetime and simply accept the milestones *as they are* without judging or yearning for "the road not taken."[33] The kindness one allows oneself in finally understanding that the decision made 20 years ago was the best one could do at that point in one's life and the wisdom gained in that understanding are healthy and are the heart of the life review in its positive adaptive manifestation. I see the life review as an intrapsychic process largely hidden from the outside world, except insofar as interpersonal relationships signal the internal harmony of the individual. Therefore, I did not hope to encourage life review through a small group modality except by a circuitous route.

Instead I hoped to facilitate purposive verbal (and indirectly silent) reminiscence in a small group setting in the belief that a sharing of memories of past experiences might influence elements of that larger intrapsychic process, the life review. I would emphasize that it is important to view reminiscence as a therapeutic process, for only then will the group leader create a positive setting in which reminiscers feel that they have "permission" to explore and to share their memories.

Butler described the psychopathological manifestations of the life review, hypothesizing that their presence is more likely in the isolated individual.[34] I have spoken of the *sharing* of reminiscences, and it is the resocialization of withdrawn elderly persons that I also hoped to influence through the small group modality. Resocialization then was a key factor in my rationale for the formation of the group. Linden wrote:

> The emphasis in gerontologic group psychotherapy is on *resocialization* of the individual. There is a greater need for promoting tranquility, a potential for happiness, and a return of some degree of self-sufficiency in a group of people whose years are numbered, than for producing deep insights. A system of therapy and group management utilizing appropriate leadership presents a setting in which the poignancy of overdetermined defenses is diminished, repression of unconscious fantasies occurs, and object interest returns.[35]

Ebersole remarked that

major therapeutic assumption in the initiation of this group was that improved motivation for and skill in communication would enrich the lives and expand the possibilities for interaction beyond the group. Subsidiary to this main goal and contingent on it are (1) reduced feelings of isolation, (2) enabling the re-experiencing of bonds with others, and (3) increased feelings of power and cohesiveness. The aged will not accept each other without encouragement.[36]

I believed that the major benefit to be reaped from a resocialization process was the enhancement of self-esteem, and, as in the case of therapeutic reminiscence, I felt that to influence self-esteem might favorably influence the intrapsychic climate for the life review.

There were, then, three components in my rationale for the formation of a small group: resocialization, reminiscence, and the life review. It was my intention to actively encourage resocialization and reminiscence within the framework of the small group. If resocialization and reminiscence were cultivated, I postulated that the climate for the life review in group members would then be positively influenced. Furthermore, while I might do no more than hope for the working of the life review in group members, I felt confident of the innate value in resocialization and reminiscence; they could stand alone as therapeutic tools. That there was a need for resocialization in these elderly participants has not yet been demonstrated. The question will be addressed in the general description of the individuals I selected as group members.

GENERAL DESCRIPTION OF GROUP MEMBERS

One of my earliest observations was the marked reduction in socialization behavior in the center's population. The previous quarter's report had announced an average daily attendance of 20. Within that large group I saw little evidence of interpersonal communication. The majority of participants sat silently in the group, looking neither to the right nor the left. Verbal exchanges were more likely to occur between a participant and a staff member rather than between participants. Some participants called staff members by name, but rarely did a participant acknowledge another participant by name. Most unfortunate were the puzzled particpants who did speak to another person, but received no response because the participant to whom they directed their remarks was blind or deaf and never knew anyone was there.

It seemed to me that there was as much value to be gained in talking as in exercising or drawing and that any serious effort at facilitating conversation between participants must be conducted on a smaller scale. *In the group of 20 there were too many sensory losses and too much sensory overload, which seriously impeded efforts toward interpersonal exchanges.* I hoped to facilitate resocialization among the eight group members who would maintain continuing contact through semiweekly meetings. I had realized early in my experience that I could accomplish little that was therapeutic within the large population of the center. Unless I carefully focused on one or two individuals I found the day consumed with toileting and feeding activities, and moving participants from one room to another.

The eight women who comprised the group ranged in age from 70 to 88; the mean age was 80.75 years. Three were born in Europe, and three were first-generation Americans. All the women were Caucasians. Only two group members had attended the center for more than 6 months. One member had attended for 5 months prior to the beginning of the group, and the remainder had attended for no more than 3 months.

EARLY DEVELOPMENT OF A VIABLE GROUP

I enjoyed an advantage in the selection of group members, since I had already had a relatively long tenure at the senior day care center during which I had become acquainted with many of the participants. Even so, a viable group is not formed overnight. In the earliest stage of group formation, that of establishing a contract with each potential member, I approached each individual with a simple description of the small group as an opportunity to make closer friends and to be better able to talk with people away from the mainstream of the center. I gave the time and the dates for the meetings, which had been worked out earlier with the staff so as not to conflict with any scheduled activities or classes. I defined the duration of the group experience, so that each individual knew that it was time-limited and would not continue indefinitely. I described it as an all-woman group and confirmed the confidential nature of the time we would spend together. Perhaps most important, I *invited* each woman to participate, telling her that I felt she would be able to offer a good deal to the group. None of the participants I approached refused my invitation, although one lady hesitated and did not commit herself until the day of the first group meeting.

Yalom and Terrazas stated that "a cohesive group confers a sense of acceptance and belonging to its members. The therapist, accordingly, should continuously attempt to strengthen group cohesiveness."[37] And "the composition of the group should be kept fairly stable, since frequent turnover retards the sense of group identity."[38] I was anxious to create a stable and cohesive group. These issues, therefore, were in my mind as I selected potential members and decided that the group would be closed. The nature of a senior day care center is such that one does not have a captive audience. Participants may be sporadic in attendance because of ill health, doctor appointments, social engagements, or simply because they don't want to come.

The importance of regular attendance for group stability was brought home to me in the first 2 weeks of the group's existence when one or two individuals I had thought would be ideal group members were absent from the center. During those first 2 weeks I made some adjustments in my selections so that the group which finally established itself was composed of very faithful attenders. It was because of attendance that the group emerged in its all-female form. The greatest percentage of participants at the center were female; the handful of male participants were quite erratic in their attendance during my tenure at the center.

It was at the fifth meeting that a fully stable group appeared, and all data presented are based on that membership; attendance records were tabulated from the fifth meeting through the twenty-fourth (two meetings short of termination). The group was composed of eight members and dropped to seven members at the seventeenth meeting.

My experience demonstrated to me that it is to be expected that the earliest history of a group in a day care center will be unstable and that several meetings will elapse before a stable group emerges. Yalom and Rand have pointed out that one third of patients in group therapy drop out in the first dozen meetings, although that figure may indicate the exercise of more free will than one might expect to find in an elderly population.[39] Nonetheless, if a novice leader is prepared for early membership instability, leader flexibility can be maintained and anxiety modulated.

The work of a group leader begins long before the first meeting of the group. It is important to select members who can contribute in some fashion to the group as well as derive value from the group experience. In my first experience, I took into account my paucity of skills as a leader in evaluating potential members. I wanted a positive experience for myself and therefore did not select some of the more difficult participants with whom I would now be more willing to work should the occasion arise.

THERAPEUTIC APPROACH AND SUMMARY OF GROUP MEETINGS

The group of eight elderly women met for a total of 26 hours; the average attendance for the series of meetings was 85 percent. Meetings were held twice weekly for 1 hour, and all sessions were recorded on tape. I functioned as group leader without a co-leader primarily because no other person was available with any regularity.

My therapeutic approach involved many elements that have been recommended by Burnside for group work with the elderly. I recognized the importance of hellos and good-byes at each group meeting and of the use of people's names when I addressed them. I was careful to recognize and direct remarks to each group member at every meeting. I pointed out any absence during a group meeting, hoping thereby to increase the members' awareness of each other. Upon an absent member's return to the group I acknowledged that she had been missed by the group. This was an expressed area of concern for some group members, hinting at their diminished self-esteem. L once remarked to the group: "I don't believe anyone would miss me if I weren't here." The student of group dynamics will recognize this comment as indicative of the need for inclusion, defined by Schutz as the "need to establish and maintain a feeling of mutual interest with other people. This feeling includes (1) being able to take an interest in other people to a satisfactory degree and (2) having other people interested in the self to a satisfactory degree."[40]

Touch was another important component of my therapeutic approach. I touched group members frequently, and they in turn felt very comfortable in walking arm in arm, holding hands, or embracing me or other group members. None of these group members were living with spouses, a factor which indicated the loss of a profound source of intimacy in their lives. The use of touch is an intimate gesture which serves to respond to the need for affection postulated by Schutz.

Unlike the approach of Blake, who was verbally active and did not allow long silences,[41] I worked to increase my tolerance for silence without feeling a need to interject a comment. This is not to say that I was verbally inactive. I was, however, aware that a lapse into silence might allow a more reticent member to make a comment. Since it was my goal to facilitate communication between group members, I was sensitive to dialogues which developed between myself and a group member and, when they occurred, I tried to refocus the member's attention on her peer group. This was an important therapeutic stance which I took throughout the group meetings, since it had been my initial observation that participants interacted more readily with staff members than they did with each other. I felt that the leader-member dyad represented a superior-inferior or teacher-pupil relationship and was not as nurturing of self-esteem as was the dyad of two group members.

Many of the approaches I used tend to enhance cohesiveness, which has been defined by Yalom and Rand as "the attraction of membership in a group for its members" or "the resultant forces acting on members' stay in a group."[42] In describing the outcomes of cohesive groups, they wrote: "Of the many variables influencing the course of group therapy, one of the most salient is the cohesiveness of the group."

In reviewing my records of group meetings, I see that a recurrent theme was the presentation of factual information by each member about herself. Repeatedly, each member told the group where she was born, where she had lived, who and where her children were, and where she lived now. This behavior corresponded with the interpersonal need for inclusion as well as

phase II in Ebersole's experience of group work: establishing the importance of self.[43]

Reminiscing and resocialization characterized the general tenor of
group meetings; nevertheless, I was particularly interested in experimenting
with Ebersole's phase IV: working through conflictual material.[44]
Therefore, I was sensitive to expressions of anger or sadness. These emotions first surfaced at meeting 5 when L expressed annoyance over a recent
slight by her niece, and C was briefly tearful as she referred to her alcoholic
second husband. At that same meeting G walked out of the room after 45
minutes. The staff had predicted I would need to use an "open door" policy
regarding her attendance, and I was prepared to do so because of her
characteristic manifestation of restlessness. But, with the exception of one
other occasion, G remained until the conclusion of all meetings she
attended.

Meeting 11 coincided with the fiftieth anniversary of Lindbergh's flight
to Paris. L talked of the kidnapping and murder of the Lindbergh baby and
then moved on to the disappearance of Amelia Earhart and the Kennedy
assassinations. Death and violence were not unfamiliar topics for her, and
she characteristically said of them, "Oh my, it's awful . . . you don't know
what the world's coming to . . . it's terrible." C recalled the excitement of
being in Paris when Lindbergh landed, and twice led the group in a completely spontaneous and rather spirited rendition of the *Marseillaise*. Each
time, French-born A passionately joined in the singing and at each conclusion broke into deep sobs, explaining, "It is nostalgic to remember so
much." Meeting 13 coincided with Memorial Day, and again sadness and
talk of death came out during the meeting. L talked about war and referred
to many of her dead family members by name. M became somewhat tearful
after C sang a few bars of "My Buddy."

Meeting 18 was a birthday party for two of the group members, and the
morning was festive with cake and candles, candy and presents. Sadness
was expressed by C as she recounted being overlooked by another participant who had sent everyone else a postcard from Hawaii. During meeting
20 I pointed out the similar struggles that C and A had known in caring for
invalid husbands through long illnesses that ended in death. A said, "I had
a sick man for a long time . . ." and was briefly tearful. This meeting was
also interesting in its early moments while people were greeting each other;
when I walked into the room bringing coffee, I found nearly everyone smil-
ing and chattering away. It looked more like a women's morning coffee
meeting than the withdrawn group described previously.

In meeting 22, there was an expression of potent anger. L gave vent to
anger toward her niece over an incident that had transpired some 30 years
earlier when the niece (then 7 or 8) broke a favorite doll of L's. After
describing the incident she said, "So I was awfully annoyed with her, and I
can't stand her even now. You see, she was jealous because I thought more

of the doll than of her, and that can happen." And in reference to the harm that the niece might do now in the present, "If you break that, young lady, you're gonna get hell." Various group members responded to L with advice and counsel, including H, who said, "Let not the sun go down on your wrath."

During this same meeting an exchange occurred which demonstrated what Ebersole has described as phase III: extending trust to group members.[45] C was expressing her opinion that the English as a people were rude, and was challenged by A, who said, "I don't feel that way at all." This was followed by G's response, "I never went into anything like that." Each opposing viewpoint was maintained and, as Ebersole has described, "Nothing cataclysmic happened."

Following each meeting, I rated each member for her degree of participation. The group consisted of three active members, one mute member, and four members who were characteristically inactive or passive to varying degrees.

PRACTICAL CONSIDERATIONS REGARDING THERAPEUTIC GROUP MODALITY

Maney and Edinberg have noted the following:

> Most existing group treatment procedures are designed for clinical populations such as nursing home patients. Little attention has been paid to the needs of the majority of older adults who maintain themselves in the community. Most senior centers and golden age clubs do not offer small group experiences which facilitate deep interpersonal relationships.[46]

My experience concurs with this observation. At the time I began my group, no other groups were in existence at the day care center. The director of the center gave me a free hand to try whatever approach I wished, and the center's atmosphere was supportive of my efforts. However, I believe that the small group modality is not necessarily familiar to community gerontological workers. Knowing this motivates one to heed Burnside's warning about "sabotage" from the staff, well-meaning or otherwise (and it may certainly be well-meaning).[47] Early in my own experience with the group, I was asked to terminate a meeting early so that group members could attend a lecture on senior home repairs! Yet, only one of the group members lived in her own home. The courage of one's convictions about the value of group work with the elderly will aid the group leader to maintain the integrity of the group while gently demonstrating its efficacy to the staff.

My experience has also convinced me that nonpsychiatric nurses are generally unfamiliar with the nature of therapeutic group work. In early clinical conferences, while I was trying to plan and formulate the nature of my group work, a fellow student encouraged me to "do a health-teaching group and you can throw in some psychological stuff," while a faculty advisor commented, "Well, everybody knows that old folks like to reminisce. So what?" *I feel that it is important to be aware of the lack of understanding for or experience with the small group modality, because reading the literature does not prepare one for that.* Instead, one is impressed with the breadth of material on group work with the elderly and may begin work with naive expectations.

A question for further study is how best to encourage reminiscence in the face of profound memory loss. In my group, three individuals manifested remote as well as recent memory loss. Consequently many different ventures into purposive reminiscence were stymied by the inability of these members to recall past events, even important ones. I recognize that the brief duration of this group experience may have been inadequate to create the interpersonal bonding necessary for revealing oneself via group reminiscence. Nevertheless, I do not believe that the antithetical relationship of reminiscence and memory loss has been well explored.

EVALUATION OF SMALL GROUP MODALITY

In my evaluation of the efficacy of the small group modality at the senior day care center I focused upon the observable social behavior of group members. The life review is an elusive process to substantiate and therefore difficult to evaluate. While reminiscence can be qualitatively and quantitatively measured during group sessions or, in a more leisurely way, during the review of tapes, I did not have the necessary assistance for those procedures. Nor did I wish to impose my own bias upon such an assessment.

It seemed feasible, therefore, to solicit the assistance of experienced staff members in assessing observable social behavior, both before the group sessions began and just before their termination. Furthermore, I thought that the utilization of an independent assessment would provide more objective psychosocial data on each participant and might reveal interobserver inconsistencies.

I devised a simple 14-point questionnaire in order to elicit information about each individual regarding her social behavior with other participants, and (less comprehensively) with staff members. Before the group sessions began and near their termination (week 12) two questionnaires for each group member were distributed among staff members for completion. No attempt was made to match group member to staff member in each of the two assessments. That is, if a staff member completed a questionnaire on the same group member in both assessments, that matching was random rather than designed. The staff members whose aid was solicited were experienced workers at the center, and either salaried personnel or volunteers (with one exception, they were students of professional programs). Because several students completed clinical placements at the center during the group's time span, the same staff members were not necessarily respondents to both assessments.

Not surprisingly this social behavior assessment did not demonstrate the efficacy of a small group modality. However, I believe the results can be utilized in the further development of a meaningful evaluative tool for clinical work. The results of both assessments as well as pertinent personal data on each group member are presented in Table 10-1.

Table 10-1   Personal Data on Group Members and Results of Social Behavior Assessment Questionnaires

Name of participant	Initial assessment	Termination assessment	Sensory/Memory deficit	Living arrangement
C Age: 71 Separated	25/35	27/36	None	Residential care
K Age: 88 Widow	11/14	Left group at meeting 17	1 Right hemiplegia 2 Blind 3 Slight deafness	With children
G Age: 81 Widow	17/20	13/15	Memory loss	With children
L Age: 70 Single	33/—	26/31	Chronic schizophrenia simplex	Residential care
A Age: 83 Widow	14/—	17/25	Memory loss	Retirement home
H Age: 85 Separated	15/31	14/17	Slight deafness*	With children
M Age: 81 Widow	3/8	3/8	1 Parkinson's disease 2 Essentially mute 3 Wears hearing aid	Own home with non-family care providers
N Age: 87 Widow	8/12	11/15	Memory loss	Retirement home

* Diagnosis of attending MD: staff assessment inconclusive (one "yes," one "no").

On the questionnaire, a total score of 39 was possible. However, a high value did not conclusively indicate a high level of interpersonal social behavior because of the presence of two negatively slanted questions which were included to elicit manifestations of hostility or withdrawal. Therefore, exclusion of those questions allowed a total possible score of 33 as indicative of a high level of social behavior in the areas assessed. Still another question could appropriately have been answered "yes" or "no" rather than quantitatively, thus dropping to 30 the score indicative of a high level of social behavior. One may therefore interpret scores of 30 to 33 as indicative of high-level social behavior without associated hostility or withdrawal.

It was apparent that the range of scores was wide (see Table 10-1) and that some group members either increased or decreased their scores in the second assessment. M's scores were quite stable in the second assessment, as were C's, although their two sets of scores were markedly disparate when compared. C's scores, while stable between assessments, demonstrated an interobserver inconsistency of 9 to 10 points in each assessment. I believe this phenomenon can be interpreted as indicating the staff's greater skill in assessing regressed maladaptive behavior as compared to assessing more positive, though marginal, adaptive behavior. M and C represented two opposing ends of the spectrum of social behavior. M displayed essentially *no* social behavior, and little evaluative finesse was necessary to confirm that observation; therefore, her scores demonstrated interobserver consistency on both occasions.

C, however, was capable of a wide range of social behavior and exercised her capabilities in different ways with different people, which is, after all, characteristic of the lone elderly person with diminished self-esteem. It requires greater skill, patience, and time on the part of the professional to assess the older person with a capability for varied responses, and I believe this explains the interobserver inconsistency in C's scores.

The subtle upward shift in N's scores is likely related to her long tenure at the center, which allowed staff members to get to know her better. Her group membership corresponded to her initial attendance at the center.

It is possible that a long-term group experience (more than 1 year) might have demonstrated an increase in positive social behavior. *Group leaders need to consider making commitments to long-term group work with the elderly, and finding methods of evaluating their results.*

REFERENCES

1 Maurice E. Linden and Douglas Courtney, "The Human Life Cycle and Its Interruptions: A Psychologic Hypothesis. Studies in Gerontologic Human Relations I," *American Journal of Psychiatry*, vol. 109, no. 12, pp. 906–915, June 1953.

2 Ibid., p. 908.
3 Ibid., p. 913.
4 Ibid., p. 908.
5 Ibid., p. 910.
6 Ibid., p. 915.
7 Robert N. Butler, "The Life Review: An Interpretation of Reminiscence in the Aged," *Psychiatry*, vol. 26, no. 1, pp. 65-76, February 1963.
8 Ibid., p. 66.
9 Ibid.
10 Ibid., p. 69.
11 Ibid., p. 70.
12 Ibid., p. 74.
13 Arthur W. McMahon and Paul J. Rhudick, "Reminiscing: Adaptational Significance in the Aged," *Archives of General Psychiatry*, vol. 10, no. 3, pp. 292-298, March 1964.
14 Ibid., p. 293.
15 Ibid.
16 Ibid.
17 Ibid., p. 297.
18 Irene Mortenson Burnside, "Group Work among the Aged," *Nursing Outlook,* vol. 17, no. 6, pp. 68-81, June 1969.
19 Irene Mortenson Burnside, "Group Work with the Aged: Selected Literature," *The Gerontologist,* vol. 10, no. 3, pp. 241-246, Autumn 1971, part 1.
20 Irene Mortenson Burnside, "Long-Term Group Work with Hospitalized Aged," *The Gerontologist,* vol. 2, no. 3, pp. 213-218, Autumn 1971, part 1.
21 Irene Mortenson Burnside, "Loss: A Constant Theme in Group Work with the Aged," *Hospital and Community Psychiatry,* vol. 21, no. 6, pp. 173-177, June 1970.
22 Irene Mortenson Burnside (ed.), *Nursing and the Aged,* McGraw-Hill, New York, 1976, chaps. 16-20.
23 Priscilla Ebersole, "Reminiscing and Group Psychotherapy with the Aged," in Irene Mortenson Burnside (ed.), *Nursing and the Aged,* McGraw-Hill, New York, 1976, p. 214.
24 Ibid., pp. 221-223.
25 Ibid., p. 223.
26 Louis Lowy, "The Group in Social Work with the Aged," *Social Work*, vol. 7, no. 10, pp. 43-50, October 1962.
27 Charles N. Lewis, "Reminiscing and Self-Concept in Old Age," *Journal of Gerontology*, vol. 26, no. 2, pp. 240-243, April 1971.
28 Robert J. Havighurst and Richard Glasser, "An Exploratory Study of Reminiscence," *Journal of Gerontology*, vol. 27, no. 2, pp. 245-253, April 1972.
29 Irvin D. Yalom and Florence Terrazas, "Group Therapy for Psychotic Elderly Patients," *American Journal of Nursing*, vol. 68, no. 8, pp. 1691-1694, August 1968.
30 Ibid., p. 1691.
31 Ibid., p. 1692.

32 Ibid.
33 Robert Frost, "The Road Not Taken," in *Complete Poems of Robert Frost*, Holt, Rinehart, and Winston, New York, 1949.
34 Butler, op. cit., p. 69.
35 Maurice E. Linden, "The Significance of Dual Leadership in Gerontologic Group Psychotherapy: Studies in Gerontologic Human Relations III," *International Journal of Group Psychotherapy*, vol. 4, no. 3, pp. 262–273, July 1954.
36 Ebersole, op. cit., p. 223.
37 Yalom and Terrazas, op. cit., p. 1692.
38 Ibid.
39 Irvin D. Yalom and Kenneth Rand, "Compatibility and Cohesiveness in Therapy Groups," *Archives of General Psychiatry*, vol. 15, no. 3, pp. 267–275, September 1966.
40 William C. Schutz, *The Interpersonal Underworld*, Science and Behavior Books, Palo Alto, Calif., 1966.
41 Dorothy Rinehart Blake, "Group Work with the Institutionalized Elderly," in Irene Mortenson Burnside (ed.), *Psychosocial Nursing Care of the Aged* (1st ed.). McGraw-Hill, New York, 1973, p. 158.
42 Yalom and Rand, op. cit., p. 267.
43 Ebersole, op. cit., p. 222.
44 Ibid., pp. 222–223.
45 Ibid., p. 222.
46 Janet Maney and Mark A. Edinberg, "Social Competency Groups: A Training and Treatment Modality for the Gerontological Nurse Practitioner," *Journal of Gerontological Nursing*, vol. 2, no. 6, pp. 31–33, November–December 1976.
47 Irene Mortenson Burnside, "Overview of Group Work with the Aged," *Journal of Gerontological Nursing,* vol. 2, no. 6, pp. 14–17, November–December 1976.

BIBLIOGRAPHY

Kubie, Susan H., and Gertrude Landau: *Group Work with the Aged*, International Universities Press, New York, 1953.
Linden, Maurice E.: "Group Psychotherapy with Institutionalized Senile Women: Study in Gerontologic Human Relations," *International Journal of Group Psychotherapy*, vol. 3, pp. 150–170, 1953.
Pincus, Allen: "Reminiscence in Aging and Its Implications for Social Work Practice," *Social Work*, vol. 15, pp. 42–51, October 1970.
Rechtschaffen, Allan: "Psychotherapy with Geriatric Patients: A Review of the Literature," *Journal of Gerontology*, vol. 14, pp. 73–84, 1959.
Yalom, Irvin D.: *The Theory and Practice of Group Psychotherapy*, Basic Books, New York, 1970.
Yalom, Irvin D., Peter S. Houts, Gary Newell, and Kenneth H. Rand: "Preparation of Patients for Group Therapy," *Archives of General Psychiatry*, vol. 17, pp. 416–427, October 1967.

Chapter 11

Day Care
for the Elderly

Marion B. Dolan

That which we are, we are,
and if we are to be any better,
now is the time to begin.

Alfred, Lord Tennyson

The newest and most rapidly growing minority in the United States is the aging—those 65 and over. Their number has grown from 4 million at the turn of the century to over 20 million today, representing 10 percent of the population. It is estimated that over a million, or 5 percent, live in institutions, with over 23,000 facilities providing long-term care. Many older persons are in need of institutional care because of special medical problems; however, several important studies have shown that, in many instances, patients in nursing care facilities or in mental hospitals do not require institutionalization—there is simply nowhere else for them to go.

Revision of a speech given at St. Anselms College, Manchester, N.H., April 1976.

One solution for older people who can no longer care for themselves completely is to live with their adult children and their families. This may well be a good arrangement for a minority; for most it is not because the older person loses independence, is often a financial burden, and may impede employment for the child (or child's spouse) with whom the aged person lives. The style of life for both the older person and the younger family is disrupted, and this may strain family relationships.

Despite the increase in home health services, meals-on-wheels, and homemaker services, an American family caring for an aged relative has few supports in either the community or the hospital system. In the United States, institutionalization, which is expensive in both human and financial terms, is forced upon the elderly because other alternatives do not exist. The individual loses independence and privacy; the family may feel guilty for putting an aged parent "away," and the financial cost to the older person, the family, and particularly the government is staggering. Unless America decides to seek solutions now, the situation in long-term care will continue to deteriorate as America's over-65 population grows to 30 million by the end of the twentieth century.

DAY CARE AS A SOLUTION

One possible solution is day care, which provides needed supervision and personal care services to older persons with physical, mental, or social impairments; day care solves some of the difficulties of daily living, and enables the elderly recipients to return home at night whether they live alone or with others. Thus, availability of day care affects a broad population: the aged themselves, adult children, their families, and possibly peers and neighbors.

Day care is neither a magic solution nor the answer to the multiple problems of the aging population; it is only one valuable component in the continuum of care. Day care centers are workable and less costly than other alternatives to those who must pay expenses for the chronically ill and disabled. Day care services are an alternative to long-term institutional care; they can also be used as a transitional phase for patients prior to their return to their community.

THE DAY CARE MOVEMENT

The day care movement began in Russia in 1942 for psychiatric patients as part of outpatient services. Day care has existed in the English-speaking world since 1946, when day care facilities for psychiatric patients opened in Montreal and London. The United States introduced day hospital service at the Menninger Clinic in 1947 and then at Yale Psychiatric Clinic in 1949 on an experimental basis; however, day care in the United States is still associated with psychiatric patients, as it was initially in the United Kingdom. The greatest thrust for the development of day hospital service came from Great Britain.

Day Care in the United Kingdom

In 1958–1959, when James Farndale conducted the first and only existing comprehensive survey of the day care system in the United Kingdom, there were only 10 geriatric day hospitals in Britain out of 65 day hospitals and day care centers of all types.[1] By 1969, there were over 90 geriatric day care centers, and 29 more had opened by 1970. These facilities are considered one of the fastest growing segments of the National Health Service. Because of the British experience, the British system of day care has served as a model for other developed countries. Cosin, the founder and planner of the first "purpose built" day hospital in a geriatric service in Oxford, England (1958),[2] is a member of the National Advisory Council of the National Council of Senior Citizens in this country and has given extensive testimony before the Senate Special Committee on Aging, advocating the use of day hospitals as part of the care continuum.

Day Care in the United States

Unfortunately, the United States has not kept pace with either Great Britain or the Scandinavian countries in providing services for the aged, and day care for the elderly is still not common in this country. In a bibliography from the U.S. Department of Health, Education and Welfare, Administration on Aging, "Words on Aging," published in 1972,[3] there is not a single mention of "day care" in over 500 titles! The earliest attempt at providing day care services in the United States seems to have been in Schenectady, New York, where in 1958 a 3-year project on a day hospital rehabilitation program was instituted. This service was an outgrowth of an extensive program of outpatient services at the Schenectady City Hospital.

A more recent program of day care services is that of the Levindale Hebrew Geriatric Center and Hospital in Baltimore. This facility is located in a home for the aged and attached to a hospital. In 1970, a day care program for disabled adults was established as part of the services of the facility and, in the beginning, an attempt was made to integrate the day care patients with similarly afflicted inpatients. Since this proved to be unsuccessful, the day care facility is now run separately; it is located in an area designated for that purpose, and has grown from 9 to about 30 patients daily. Levindale has received grants from the Social Rehabilitation Service of the Department of Health, Education and Welfare. Much of the knowledge about day care in the United States has come from the experience of this particular facility. Almost every article on day care in geriatrics and gerontology publications, as far back as 1970 (before that date there is almost nothing), was written by someone associated with Levindale. The remaining few published articles have dealt with psychogeriatric facilities. Most of the programs existing today are linked to a sponsoring institution whose facilities are easily available to the day care patient.

Funding and Legislation   The first state to enact day care legislation was Hawaii in April, 1972; this happened after two day care centers had already been operating successfully for a year. One of them, the Hale Ho'olai, was established by a group of concerned citizens; the other, the Kuakini, is under the Honolulu Model Cities Program.

Recently New York State initiated a program of day care services under Chapter V, Subchapter H, of the State Hospital Code, Nursing Home and Health Related Services for Non-Occupants.

Other forms of funding may be available through the following sources: Social Security Act, Titles I and XVI, under which funds are available on a 75 to 25 percent matching basis; Title XVIII, Medicare, and Title XIX, Medicaid.

Certainly the Department of Health, Education and Welfare, the Senate Administration on Aging, and the National Council on Aging should be helpful in locating sources of funding. Unfortunately, funding is the greatest problem facing day care today and, except for the many grants to the various institutions to determine the feasibility of the various components of day care, the financial arrangements are such that day care is still not economically possible for most individuals. Until the government makes it possible for Medicare and Medicaid and other third-party payees to pay for day care, private long-term care institutions will prevail, since the greatest profit is to be made in the private sector.

Range of Day Care Services

Day care services range from the very simple day center to the quite complex and complete day hospital. Day care may serve as a primarily social program for the frail, moderately handicapped, or slightly confused older person who lives alone and needs care for some part of the week, or to relieve a family and help keep the aged person living at home. Or a day hospital can be one that is usually filled with persons who require treatment following hospitalization, or who have impairments severe enough to require 8-hour supervision.

The day hospital is usually affiliated with a general hospital, mental hospital, nursing home, or health care facility, and provides in addition to the social and recreational programs at least some of the following services:

(1) group therapy, (2) occupational therapy, (3) physical therapy, (4) skilled nursing, (5) speech therapy, and, in some centers, even a sheltered workshop.

Both types of services—primarily social or primarily offering medical services—require that patients be transported, often in specially equipped vehicles and sometimes by their families, to the center, and both have a social component and a health component. The type of services available determine the degree of incapacity in individuals that makes them eligible. Day care centers will not usually accept either an incontinent or a severely disoriented person.

PURPOSES OF DAY CARE

Apart from the obvious objectives of providing convenience to the family concerned and of offering safety and socialization for the individual, what is the purpose of day care for the elderly? Each of the following reasons is of vital importance; however, there is no order of priority, since each individual and each community will establish their own. Usual reasons for day care include:

1 Provision of care for lonely, isolated, mildly confused, depressed, elderly persons utilizing a supervised program.

2 Prevention or retardation of physical deterioration.

3 Prevention or retardation of mental deterioration.

4 Prevention of institutionalization. Shanas and Townsend point out that 14 percent of the aged living at home in the United States are bedfast, homebound, or limited in mobility.[4] Many homebound elderly people do not bother or are not able to take care of themselves properly, which may lead to malnutrition and depression. Deterioration in functional ability occurs because incentives are often absent in the home environment. Necessary incentives for physical and mental activity can be provided by day care services. On the other hand, prevention of institutionalization among the elderly is a primary goal, since institutionalization can engender negative changes and reduce functional capacities. A comparison of the appearance and behavior of day patients with inpatients suffering from similar clinical conditions, shows that day patients tend to be happier, more active, better dressed, more interested in what is happening, and more communicative. These are reasons for the importance of working for social and political change; they are based on my observations made after many years of nursing experience and exposure to the plight of the elderly.

5 To give respite to relatives by relieving them of the care of the elderly during the day. Responsibility becomes onerous, indeed, when it appears that the caring tasks will be continuous without hope of relief. According to Townsend, the availability of the day hospital to care for burdensome cases

sometimes prevents the break-up of families by providing relief to exhausted families.[5] It is important to note that the supportive function is not recognized by most who adhere to the myth that most of the elderly are abandoned by their families.

6 To save hospital beds. In these days of increasing hospital costs and a desperate shortage of trained personnel, more effective use of hospital beds becomes an absolute necessity. It has been found that those institutions where the option of day care was available were able to discharge aging patients earlier and thus reduce the length of hospital stay; for aging patients who were awaiting admission to an institution, it was possible to begin treatment prior to admission and, for some individuals, the need for hospitalization was reduced.

7 To assist the institutionalized patient who could return home if day care were available. The management of geriatric patients is complicated because of the compound nature of their problems. Therefore, the setting up and management of a geriatric day care center has certain problems which do not exist in other day care centers for other age groups.

STARTING A DAY CARE PROGRAM

I would now like to discuss the logistics of beginning a day care center and the many practical considerations in such an undertaking, including (1) location, (2) size, (3) transportation, (4) publicity and outreach, (5) physical facilities and standards, (6) staff, and (7) programs and activities.

The facilities available in the community have to be considered. Since local needs require local solutions, there are bound to be differences in the planning and working of the various day hospitals; it is vital to obtain the support of the local general hospital and the welfare authorities.

The ideal number of patients for a day care center seems to be from 15 to 20. Fewer than this is too costly, and a greater number is unmanageable. It is important to remember that, because of "absenteeism," some centers enroll a few more patients than they are equipped to handle. Most centers operate on a 5-day week; the hours are usually 9 a.m. to 5 p.m. on weekdays. Participants do not usually come 5 days a week, although a few centers prefer or require it. It is generally agreed by health planners and service providers that 1 day a week is of little benefit. Also, there should be some way of knowing how many persons will attend each day so that staffing and supplies will be adequate.

Transportation

The greatest problem for day centers is transportation, and because of this a day care center cannot serve too large an area; sometimes they seem to be impractical in rural areas. Ideally, families should bring the patient on their way to work, and pick the patient up on their way home; unfortunately, this is not often the case. The majority of patients have to be transported, even in programs which do not furnish transportation, but rely on public transportation or arrangements with taxis. A 10 to 12 seat minibus is generally used as it is easier to maneuver and park than a large bus. One important consideration is the time spent coming and going; no one should travel more than a half-hour each way. The distance is not so much the problem as the time consumed in pickups. If wheelchair patients are accepted, the bus will have to have a specially built automatic lift; an assistant should accompany the driver to help the persons in and out of their homes.

One would think that with all the benefits, economy, and service day care centers provide a newly opened center would be overfilled. Such is not the case. People, especially old people, are resistant to new ideas, and in this country, day care is still a new idea. In order to publicize a day care program, the assistance of public health nurses, clergymen, senior citizens' groups, and social workers should be used. Frequently it is the family who, seeking some welcome relief, respond and convince the older person to use the service. The social worker often has to convince the individual, and the family, too, to give the program a trial period.

The admission process should be as short as possible. Once the older person attends, the level of satisfaction with day care centers is very high, both in the older person and in the family. *Since referral is usually through the family, day care centers must not forget to reach out to the lone older person who may be forgotten all too easily.*

Equipment and Services Needed

In planning to set up a day care center or day hospital, the following considerations, which relate to both safety and comfort, should be taken into account:

1 Telephone service must be provided.
2 Emergency first aid kit must be available.
3 There should be a proportionately greater number of exits (a minimum of two additional ones) than those required by safety regulations and space needs.
4 Toilets should be conveniently accessible to those older people whose movements are slow and unsteady and who have need of them more frequently than younger people.
5 Restrooms should be equipped with grab bars and call lights, and should be spacious enough to accommodate wheelchairs.
6 A first-floor, one-level location is essential. Non-skid carpet or floor covering of one color should be used, since designs tend to distract or confuse those with impaired vision. Rails along the walls are suggested, as are outside ramps in addition to stairs. The outside entrance needs a canopy for protection against inclement weather.

7   More than adequate lighting and heat should be provided.

8   Clocks, calendars, and notices should have extra-large numbers and letters, and visual aids should be employed to minimize confusion, i.e., restroom doors painted a different color than the other doors, and with explanatory pictures on them.

9   Suitable furniture is important, and furniture designed for the infirm is preferable; in any event, all chairs should be steady and have arms for leverage. Chairs should not tip or move easily when used for support while walking or sitting. Lounge chairs or couches should be provided for naps, and are preferable to beds.

10   The general atmosphere should be attractive and inviting. An outdoor garden, porch, or patio is desirable.

11   Meals should be served attractively in a pleasant setting, and each meal should contain one-third of the daily nutritional needs. Facilities should be available for therapeutic diets.

12   Setting up a number of smaller rooms as well as a room large enough for everyone to gather for movies, parties, etc. is preferable to having one large space. This provides space for different types of activity, and a quiet place where people can rest. If small rooms cannot be managed, a large room can be partitioned off with planters, bookcases, or other dividers at small cost without cutting off light.

13   Arrangements must be made with a local physician and/or hospital to deal with emergency illnesses or accidents.

Office Space

If the day center is autonomous, that is, not attached to a host institution, other items to be given consideration are: (1) office space for interviewing and files; (2) secretarial space if a secretary is employed; (3) storage space for supplies (the amount of which will vary depending on whether meals are prepared on the site); (4) space for occupational therapy, if given; and (5) an examining room, also depending on the emphasis to be given to health care.

Liaison with Family

An important ingredient of all day care is liaison with the family of the participant to learn what problems are being faced between visits to the day care program, and to assist the family in supporting the patient's progress. A social worker should interview the family and gather adequate information about the physical, social, and mental status of the patient, and then share this information with other professionals who provide care to the patient. Prior to admission, a thorough evaluation of the patient's physical, mental, and social status is essential.

Staffing the Center

The size of the staff will depend on the number of patients and the type of activities. An absolute essential is a paid director who, in a day hospital, should be a registered nurse; in a day care center, someone with professional training in social work, nursing, occupational therapy, or recreation is desirable, though not essential. Administrative skill and experience, however, are mandatory if the program as a whole is to function smoothly. Even in a small program, at least one other person should be employed full-time, and if 10 or more patients attend daily, there should be at least two staff members in addition to the director.

A team concept is important, and every day care program will probably want to have one nurse (RN), one recreation therapist, and a social worker, all of whom, either by training or experience, are familiar with the aged and understand their particular needs and problems. Nurses' aides are helpful if more basic staff is needed, and volunteers can be effectively used. Volunteers serve particularly well as a resource for special skills such as ceramics, art, and bridge, and to give more individual attention in groups led by staff members. In addition to the above, there may be specialized personnel such as speech therapists, physical therapists, and occupational therapists.

Required Skills and Knowledge   Staff should have the following skills and knowledge: (1) skill in group interaction, (2) knowledge about specific activities, e.g., crafts, exercises, (3) specialized knowledge of physical and emotional limitations of the impaired aged, (4) experience in family counseling, (5) some knowledge of community resources, and (6) skill in community organization.

In selecting staff, knowledge about the aged and experience in caring for them are essential, but the natural talents of humor and common sense, and the ability to talk easily to people and to work effectively and harmoniously with them are also important, and can make all the difference to a successful day care operation. A 2-year background in gerontology should be mandatory.

Although a physician should be available for emergencies, and participants' medical records should be kept on file with a record of medications to be administered, day care programs usually require participants to have their own private physician. Even in a day hospital, patients are required to have their own doctor, who may prescribe certain treatments to be administered by the day care staff. In my own investigations, I never found a full-time physician as part of a day center staff.

Activities for Participants

Activities can be as varied as the interests and capabilities of the patients, and the availability of staff or volunteers with special talents.

Most centers have a program of simple physical exercises to benefit those who sit so much of the day. Usually there is an arts and crafts program, both to encourage creativity and to increase or maintain dexterity. In arts and crafts and exercise programs, physical and occupational therapists are important, if only as consultants.

Educational programs on subjects such as current events, health education and Social Security benefits, safety in the home, lipreading, and sometimes even language instruction could be considered. Group activities such as games, cards, music, and movies are usually popular; old songs and movies of the 1930s are particularly enjoyed. In one center, it was learned that one patient had been an editor on a newspaper, and another a writer. The social worker initiated a small newsletter with their help, and eventually many people contributed—a life story, a poem, a drawing.

Health and Grooming Needs

Time should be set aside for taking care of certain health and grooming needs, including nail-cutting, and instruction or assistance in self-care tasks. Beauty school or barber students could come in regularly to cut and set hair. Group mending or sewing sessions can be set up. Some centers even have laundry facilities.

Older people may become very self-centered, and the opportunity to serve others can be provided in a day center. Participants can repair or paint toys, roll bandages, or knit or write letters for others whose vision or other incapacities make it impossible. Those well enough may even visit patients in a nursing home. An occasional trip away from the center for those who are able is worthwhile.

If the center is affiliated with a larger host institution some of the activities described above may be ongoing, in which case day patients can participate with inpatients. Most of the activities described create an opportunity for communication and for sharing. In addition, some time should be set aside for problem-centered discussion groups, sometimes with families attending.

The majority of the above programs are maintenance-oriented but, in a rehabilitative day hospital program, there are more comprehensive diagnostic and treatment services and all types of therapy are provided.

CASE EXAMPLE   My experience in the Manchester, New Hampshire, pilot day care center enhanced the research I had previously done.

The program was opened in 1976. As had been anticipated, interest and need ran high. It was my belief at that time that Title XVIII and Title XIX would begin to pay third-party reimbursement for eligible clients. Meetings were held with various people involved in both the public and private sector; however, after a year, the Medicare and Medicaid programs still did not recognize day care for the elderly as an important component of health care.

We had an average client census of 7 to 10 people who were in need of the service. One exception to the private pay patient was a man who was partially disabled because of multiple sclerosis. The Veterans' Administration paid for his daily day care because it was less expensive than our intermediate per diem rate. Noteworthy and sad is the fact that this patient became a resident at the Veterans' Hospital when the program folded due to lack of funding.

To keep financially solvent, the experiment needed 15 patients on a daily basis. The Medicaid district offices continually referred their patients to us, and we had over 80 applicants during the year. When the district social worker called with a new referral, we would take that opportunity to go over back cases from the previous quarter. Many times, when questioned on a particular patient, the same answer would be heard: "No, please delete that name, the patient has been placed in a county home."

We ran into a myriad of nursing challenges, among them bowel and bladder training, activities of daily living (ADL), maintenance care of stumps, ambulation, and active and passive range of motion. Anecdotal data was gathered from our best sources—the people using the services of the day care center. We applied all the techniques used in long-term care settings. Some of the services we provided were:

1   A one-to-one program, an innovative program which links all patients directly to the staff on a one-to-one basis. The volunteer staff act as advocate, surrogate family, or just friend to the patient. The whole staff are included, thus combining ancillary services, management, and administration with nursing to provide comprehensive care.
2   Reality orientation.
3   Art therapy.
4   Music therapy.
5   Reminiscing therapy.
6   Poetry groups.

Programs were well received and interest ran high as the groups were formed. In the poetry sector, all members participated and brought in favorite sayings from their past. There was great excitement when some of the members had increased self-esteem to a point where they started dabbling in new poems which dealt with the here and now.

It was an ominous day when we had to tell the patients and families we could no longer offer the service. The elderly, in their wisdom, took the closing of the day care center stoically; perhaps, to them, it was just one more of many losses. One very significant point to be noted is that *all of the day care residents were institutionalized within 6 months of the closing of the center.*

The role of the professional nurse was explored fully on a day-to-day basis. It became apparent in the first week we were established, that our most important impact would be as primary *preventative health providers.* Once the patients became familiar with the staff, they would begin to speak of symptoms they felt "no one else had time to listen to before." As a group, they overwhelmingly hated to be any more of a burden than they already felt themselves to be to their families and physicians. During the year's experience, we referred several patients to the physician for abnormal blood pressure, cardiac arrhythmias, weight loss, bowel and bladder changes, and mouth lesions, to name a few.

We also made the families more aware of the changes in vision and hearing of their aged relatives. In some cases these patients had not been to ophthalmologists or eye, ear, nose, and throat specialists even once during their lifetime. Seventy percent of the patient population in the center were helped after seeing a vision or hearing specialist.

Dental referrals were another area where we made an impact. For the residents who did not have a dentist of their own, we provided dental services on a monthly basis. In my experience, the elderly choose not to buy new dentures due to the cost involved. We did a great deal of patient teaching in this area to enable them to understand the importance of proper dentition to their overall health. A colleague wrote the following:

> Most older people I have come into contact with place so little value on themselves that it is not so much the expense of new dentures, or even the prospect of having the older ones adjusted to fit better (because of the natural atrophy of the gums, mouth tissues underlying such, and bone re-absorption, and the ill-fitting dentures themselves) than it is one of not being around long enough to justify the *bother.* Medicaid and other funds more than compensate for the expense, it's just that these old people have so little to look forward to, mushy tasting meals (because they won't wear their teeth) strangely flavored food (other than what they themselves have been accustomed to when they were able to cook) bibs to keep them clean, and other humiliating instances imposed upon them by the institution or family, that most of them are just hoping they will die soon, so they won't have to deal with the conflict of really wanting new teeth, but unable to assert their wishes against so bleak a future. They *are* worth the effort, but when they are a minority of one, why struggle? Staff reflect this: "Didn't eat, needs new teeth, won't be around long enough to bother. Won't wear old dentures, so why bother with new ones? Don't need to put in dentures today, not going anywhere," etc. Sad.[6]

We incorporated family conferences with patient teaching. All families agreed that their weekends went more smoothly after the first few weeks of day care. The main reason was the new interest the elderly persons had in living. Since there was somewhere for them to go on

Monday, their Saturdays and Sundays were caught up in a reminiscing over the events of last week or in a flurry of planning for the week ahead. Another factor was also brought up time and again. The families were no longer on "guilt trips." Actuarial data gathered from these families proved the cohesiveness that day care brought the family situation.

SUMMARY

Day care is so new in the United States that there have been few evaluations of either its effectiveness or its cost. Several research and demonstration projects have been funded by the various government agencies, but either they have not yet been completed, or the results have not yet been published. However, both the Canadian and the British experiences have indicated that day care in urban areas is economically viable, since there is a reduction of demand on hospital beds, and the per diem cost of maintaining patients in a day center is substantially less than that of maintaining them in a long-term care hospital. The cost is, however, comparable with present nursing home rates.

There are many reasons why alternatives to institutionalization should be more fully developed in this country, and I have tried to outline the most important ones: (1) safety, (2) socialization, (3) a means of continual assessment of the older person, thereby preventing or retarding his or her physical or mental deterioration, (4) convenience to the family, and (5) lower cost than institutionalization to all concerned.

With the aged population increasing so rapidly, day care as a component of the health care continuum will become an economic necessity. Unfortunately, Medicare has not yet recognized day care as a valid recipient of payments, day care guidelines have not been adequately defined, and payment mechanisms have favored nursing homes, and other institutional care. This seems to be the twentieth century version of the eighteenth century rejection of the deviant individual by the family and community. Until these legislative hurdles have been overcome, the outlook for day care as a reality in the United States is not promising.

Currently I am working as a consultant to the United Health Systems Agency in the state of New Hampshire. We are using the data I compiled in 1976 as the basis for planning in the future. The need for day care as an alternative to an institution is seen as paramount by our state health planners.

Momentum is picking up and research delegations have been set up to have meetings at the grass-roots level. Consumers' opinions about what they see as adequate health care are finally being sought. Old age is an unavoidable and irreversible phenomenon. Therefore, providing a more humane, dignified, and satisfying life for our handicapped aged citizens, who, as overwhelming evidence shows, prefer to remain at home, is our best insurance and ought to have our highest priority. Not taking immediate steps toward a concentrated, orchestrated effort to establish day care may be a form of cost containment, but it is surely not cost-effective. In the overall plan, cost containment takes its toll in the most vital area of health care—quality assurance.

REFERENCES

1 James Farndale, "Geriatric Day Hospitals," part 2, *Nursing Mirror and Midwives Journal*, vol. 113, no. 4, March 16, 1962.
2 Lionel Z. Cosin, Margaret Mort, F. Post, Celia Westropp, and Moyra Williams, "Experimental Treatment of Persistent Senile Confusion," *The International Journal of Social Psychiatry*, vol. 4, no. 2, pp. 24–42, April 1958.
3 United States Department of Health, Education and Welfare Administration on Aging, "Words on Aging," 1972.
4 Ethel Shanas and Peter Townsend, *Old People in Three Industrial Societies*, Atherton, Routledge and Kegan Paul, New York and London, 1968.
5 Peter Townsend, *The Family Life of Old People*, Routledge and Kegan Paul, London, 1957.
6 Rosemary McGhee Sylvester, personal letter, 1978.

BIBLIOGRAPHY

Butler, Robert N.: *Why Survive? Being Old in America*, Harper and Row, New York, 1975.
Clements, G.: "A Geriatric Day Hospital Serving a Rural Community," *Nursing Times*, London, vol. 64, no. 27, pp. 908–909, 1968.
Dolan, Marion B.: "1:2:1," *Nursing '78*, vol. 3, March 1978.
Hall, J., and B. Weaver: *Nursing of Families in Crisis*, Lippincott, Philadelphia, 1974.
Morris, Robert: "Alternatives to Nursing Home Care: A Proposal," U.S. Government Printing Office, Washington, D.C., 1971.
Mullen, Elaine: "Relocation of the Elderly; Implications for Nursing," *Journal of Gerontological Nursing*, vol. 3, no. 4, July–August 1977.
Pastorello, T.: "Relocation Stress: A Causal Model of Effect and Mitigation," Paper presented at 28th Scientific Meeting of the Gerontological Society, Louisville, Ky., October 1975.
Patrick, Maxine: "Little Things Mean a Lot in Geriatric Rehabilitation," *Nursing '73*, August 1973.

Preston, Caroline E., M. A. Helgerson and Steven Helgerson: "An Analysis of Survey Data Obtained by a Service Agency for Older People," *The Gerontologist*, vol. 12, no. 4, Winter 1972.

Rossman, Isadore: "Alternatives to Institutional Care," *Bulletin of the New York Academy of Medicine*, vol. 49, no. 12, pp. 1084–1092, 1973.

Shanas, Ethel: "Making Services for the Elderly Work: Some Lessons from the British Experience," U.S. Government Printing Office, Washington, D.C., 1971.

Turlow, Sandra: "Geriatric Group Day Care and Its Effect on Independent Living: A Thirty-Six Month Assessment," *The Gerontologist,* vol. 15, no. 6, pp. 508–510, December 1975.

Chapter 12

Utilization of Health Care Services by the Elderly

Barbara A. Moehrlin

Let us not be remembered as the generation that saved the whales and saved the trees but ignored our own kind.[1]

The above words appeared in an advertisement in a popular national magazine. The words were displayed with the picture of an old woman in an alley going through the garbage and are a sad commentary on a country as rich in resources as the United States. The role of the community health nurse can be directed toward "saving our own kind." One way of doing so is to influence positive use of the health care services by the aged.

This chapter is about a study done to determine whether persons over age 60 who receive public health nursing services utilize other health care services more or less than persons over age 60 who do not receive public health nursing services. The literature points to the multiple losses that the aging person faces; loss of health and the onset of chronic disease are major concerns for every elderly person. Most elderly persons have a real fear of being incapacitated, dependent on others, or institutionalized. Considering these factors, this study was designed to determine if public health nurses can positively influence older persons to use health care services.

HERMAN

"I'm well aware you're only 28 years old. That's why I'm telling you to take better care of yourself."

Copyright 1978, Universal Press Syndicate.

In analyzing the population used in this study, the theory of *symbolic interactionism* was used. This theory consists of three premises:

1 "Human beings act towards things on the basis of the meanings that the things have for them."[2] An older person may perceive the doctor as an all-knowing authority or as a "young upstart."

2 "The meaning of such things is derived from or arises out of the social interaction that one has with one's fellows."[3] An older person's respect for a doctor can come from what one's neighbors or friends have said about that doctor.

3 "These meanings are handled in, and modified through, an interpretive process used by the person in dealing with the things he encounters."[4] Thus, the older person may view the doctor differently if treatment for an illness or disease is required.

Social interaction involves more than one person. Blumer says:

> "Human beings interacting with one another have to take account of what each other is doing or is about to do; they are forced to direct their own conduct or handle situations in terms of what they take into account.[5]

Thus, what an older person's friends think about doctors and other health care providers influences what that person thinks about doctors and other health care providers. The theory of symbolic interactionism is supported by Shanas and Maddox, who said:

> There is reason to believe that the correlation among disability and illness and impairment is high and in any case, as far as social consequences are concerned, an individual is ill if he says he is ill and behaves as though he is ill."[6]

A public health nurse can then become part of the interaction between older persons and health care services. This interaction can produce change in the older person's behavior and positively influence the use of health care services.

THEORETICAL FRAMEWORK

Symbolic interactionism will be used to analyze the premise that public health nurses have an influence on the kind and amount of health care services that older people use. Using this framework, definitions of what health care services are and why they should be used must be determined in the context of their meaning to the older adult. Meanings may differ based on the older person's own experience or the experiences of their friends. Knowledge of the older individual's evaluation of the problem is also necessary. Kasl and Cobb distinguish between health behavior, activity undertaken for the purpose of preventing disease by persons who believe themselves well; illness behavior, activity undertaken by persons who feel ill for the purpose of diagnosis; and sick role behavior, activity undertaken for the purpose of cure by persons who consider themselves ill.[7] Archer and Fleshman point out that the main advantage of using symbolic interactionism "is that it provides the nurse with a clear, defendable, documented analysis of the client."[8]

POPULATION

Historical and Developmental Factors

History has shown that the United States has a youth-oriented culture in which age is not valued. The media promotes this youth-oriented culture through the images it portrays of the elderly as unattractive, senile, and uneducated. In 1900 only 4 out of every 100 persons in the United States were over age 65; in 1978 10 out of every 100 persons were over 65. This figure will increase by 40 percent by 1990 according to the U.S. Bureau of the Census.[9]

The National Institute on Aging divides the older population into two groups:

> the "young old"—persons in their sixties and early seventies who are relatively healthy and vigorous and active—and the "old-old"—persons in their mid-seventies, eighties, and nineties, an increasing minority of whom remain vigorous and active, but a majority of whom need a wide range of supportive and restorative health services.[10]

Many of the "old-old" persons today are people who grew up in the Victorian age, immigrated to the United States from Europe, frequently have less than 8 years of formal education, lived through two world wars and the Great Depression, and experienced an unprecedented advance in technology and science.

By the year 2000, increasing numbers of older people will have been born in the United States, will have higher education levels, and will experience and use daily advances in technology and science. They may also have available to them more government programs, such as an improved Social Security program and some form of national health insurance.[11]

Structure, Function, and Decision-Making Relationships

Due to the rising life expectancy in the United States, the aging population is dramatically increasing and older persons' voices are becoming louder and being heard more often. Many older persons are joining political and advocacy groups, and their attitudes and wishes are becoming known by legislators and other government officials. National, state, and local organizations to promote the well-being of the aging and distribute resources have been formed. As a result of increased numbers, the "vote" of the over-60 person has become an important one in today's society.

Older persons are also learning to take part in the decision-making process that influences their lives. They are becoming better informed consumers, particularly about their own health, about health care services, and health care providers; and they are learning to take responsibility for their own health care. They are learning that health, according to the National Institute on Aging,

> also depends on the willingness *and* the ability of the individual to care for themselves, and to apply the principles of preventive medicine by emphasizing in their lives those elements that foster health and the prevention of dependency and disability.[12]

Thus, the aged of today and of the future will have a definite effect not only on health care and its providers but on the formation of health care policies as well.

DESCRIPTION OF THE STUDY

Population Description

The population used for this study was persons over age 60 who reside in census tract 10 in the downtown area of a city on the West coast. This census tract lies within a larger area in which the over-60 population is 18 percent of the total population. This figure rises to 26 percent when census tract 10 (one of 27 census tracts) is considered alone. Of these persons over 60, 63 percent are female and 37 percent male, a ratio of 1.7 females for every male. Twenty percent of these persons have incomes below the poverty level—that is, single persons whose annual net income was $2590 or less, or four-person households with an income below $5050.[13] The specific population was taken from the residents of two large high-rise retirement residences located in the metropolitan area within census tract 10.

Residence A has 216 units including studio, one-bedroom, and two-bedroom apartments. The rents are federally subsidized. Meals are served in a central dining room. There are more women (176) than either single men (25) or couples (15). The average age in this residence is 75 years. The majority of the residents have at least one chronic health problem.

Residence B has 99 units housing 115 persons. Of these, 90 are single women, 5 are single men, and 10 are couples. This residence is not federally subsidized, but it is low-rent housing (owned by a nonprofit corporation and previously sponsored by the Episcopal Church). The average age of the residents is in the late seventies.

Purpose of the Study

The purpose of the study was to answer the question: Do persons over age 60 who live in census tract 10 and receive public health nursing services utilize other health care services more or less than persons over age 60 who do not receive public health nursing services? Health care, as defined by Lambersten, is

> the sum total of care provided by all health disciplines and comprises more than diagnosis, prescription and treatment of illness and disability; health care also includes health education, health maintenance, preventive measures, and restorative services in addition to therapeutic intervention.[14]

Public health nursing services are the services provided by a public health nurse during a home visit for the purpose of health education, health assessment, or screening. Preventive health, health maintenance and rehabilitative services, and health counseling, information, and referral are services provided to the older person on a regular basis of at least one time a month. Utilization of health care services refers specifically to the kind of health care service that is used and how often it is used. Blum states that "use of health care may be related to means, social class, knowledge, access, or acceptability of care," and that "medical care will be utilized according to other considerations, such as insurance, cultural beliefs, and availability of transportation."[15]

Selection of the Sample

The sample was selected on the basis of convenience. Residence A was selected because it was located in census tract 10; it received public health nursing services on a regular basis (in addition to home visits, the public health nurse held office hours and health education programs in the residence's conference room one time a week); and the district public health nurse was known to this author. This nurse provided the author with the names and apartment numbers of 22 persons open in her caseload, and gave the author permission to use the nurse's name as an introduction. Of the 22 persons, only 15 were interviewed; 5 were not home, 1 had moved, and 1 had gone to a nursing home.

Residence B was selected because of its proximity to residence A and because of the similar characteristics of the building and the residents. The author approached the manager of residence B, explained the purpose of the study, and received permission to use residence B as part of the study. The manager made a list of 40 residents who, in the manager's estimation, would respond positively to an outsider (a list of all the residents would have been ideal, but the manager was unwilling to provide this). The manager also gave permission for the author to use the manager's name as an entree. The 15 residents eventually used for the study were chosen simply because they were home on the day the study was conducted. A total of 30 residents were used for the study, 15 from each residence. All were Caucasian.

Assessment Tool

The assessment tool for this study was a form designed and implemented by the division of nursing of a county health department.* The form was used in combination with interviewing and observation. Two purposes described in the appendix to the form which are applicable to this study are: "(1) to establish a profile of families' and individuals' health status and identify the families' ability to deal with its health needs; (2) to establish a socioeconomic profile of families receiving

---

*B Form, Santa Clara County Public Health Nursing Department, San Jose, Calif. .

Public Health Nursing services (using measures comparable to those available from the U.S. Census) and to identify the families' ability to manage its situation.''

The form was completed by means of interviews. The interviews were unstandardized and unstructured.[16] Information requested from each respondent included number and kind of health conditions; educational level; amount and source of income; employment; place the person lived 1 year ago; source of payment for medical care; ownership of house; and transportation use. Five special questions were added for the purpose of this study:

1 What is your age and sex?
2 Do you use health care services?
3 If yes, what kind are they and how often do you use them?
4 If no, why not?
5 If it has been over one year since use, why?

These questions were open-end questions which gave the interviewer considerable discretion in determining how to ask the questions and in evaluating the answers. The interviews also used open-end items, specifically, to establish a frame of reference for the person's answers, but there were no restrictions on the answers.[17]

For instance, for the question, "Do you use health care services?" the following examples were supplied for each respondent: medical doctors (including GPs, surgeons, internists, and most other kinds), eye doctors, foot doctors, psychiatrists and/or other mental health professionals, chiropractors, acupuncturists, faith healers, Health Department services (includes multiphasic and immunization clinics), Public Health Nursing services (home visits and/or services in senior centers), home health agencies, dentists, and pharmacists.

This type of personal interview actualizes the theory of symbolic interactionism. In describing types of surveys, Kerlinger states:

A respondent's desires, values, and needs may influence his attitudes and actions . . . if the individual under study has accurately sounded his own desires, values, and needs—and can express them verbally—the personal interview can be very valuable.[18]

RESULTS OF THE STUDY

Number and Age of Participants

Thirty persons participated in this study: 15 (50 percent) were single females; 2 (7 percent) were single males; there were 6 couples (40 percent);

and 1 person (3 percent) was a separated woman whose husband lived in the same building.

The average age of the respondents was 78.4 years for both residences, 79.4 years for residence A, and 77.4 for residence B. This places the population of both residences in the "old-old" category discussed earlier, i.e., persons who need a wide range of supportive and restorative services. In addition, research by the National Health Survey in 1976 has shown that persons over the age of 65 years visit the physician much more frequently than other age groups.[19]

There were 23 females and 7 males who took part in the study—11 females and 4 males from residence A and 12 females and 3 males from residence B. This is a much higher percentage (77 percent) of females than either the national average or the statistics from census tract 10. The National Ambulatory Medical Care Survey indicates that visits by females accounted for 60 percent of all visits to physicians.[20]

Income Levels

The income levels of the respondents were as follows: 19 persons, or 63 percent, had incomes under $6000 a year; 8 persons, or 27 percent, had incomes between $6-8000 a year; 1 person's income was unknown; and 2 persons refused to answer the question. The two residences had similar income distributions. No one reported an income of over $8000.

The source of income of almost half the respondents was Social Security alone. Another 30 percent received full or supplemental welfare in addition to Social Security. Only 23 percent of the respondents had sources of income other than Social Security or welfare. It can be speculated that all of the single respondents on welfare and/or Social Security lived under the poverty level and that even those persons with incomes in the $6-8000 range had little left over for "luxuries," such as health services not covered by insurance. Residence A had two persons on Social Security only, six with Social Security and full or supplemental welfare, and six who had Social Security plus sources of income other than welfare. Residence B was less diversified; 80 percent were on Social Security alone and the other 20 percent had Social Security plus a welfare supplement. From these figures it appears that the respondents from residence B had lower incomes, which may have affected their utilization of health care services (see Table 12-1).

The source of payment for health care services was also predictable. Twelve persons had Medicare only; seven had Medicare plus a prepaid health insurance (includes Kaiser and VA); eight had Medicare and Medical; one paid for health care with personal funds; and one gave no information. Fewer persons in residence B had Medi-cal (3) than in residence A (6) which can be directly related to the sources of income listed previously.

Table 12-1 Comparison of Sex, Age, Income, and Education Characteristics by Residence

Characteristics	Residence A		Residence B		Total	
	Number	Percent	Number	Percent	Number	Percent
Average age	79.4	NA	77.4	NA	78.4	NA
Sex:						
Female	11	73	12	80	23	77
Male	4	27	3	20	7	23
Income:						
$6000	10	66	9	60	19	63
$6-8000	4	27	4	27	8	27
Refused	0	0	2	13	1	3
Unknown	1	7	0	0	2	7
Income source: *						
SS	2	13	12	80	14	47
SS/O	6	40	0	0	6	20
SS/WS	4	27	3	20	7	23
WF	2	13	0	0	2	7
Unknown	1	7	0	0	1	3
Education (years)						
Less than 8	5	33	4	27	9	30
8 to 11	5	33	5	33	10	33
12	1	7	4	27	5	17
12 +	3	20	2	13	5	17
Unknown	1	7	0	0	1	3

* SS   = Social Security
  SS/O   = Social Security/other
  SS/WS = Social Security/welfare supplement
  WF   = full welfare

Education Level

The education level of the respondents of both residences was similar. Overall, 30 percent had less than 12 years of education, while 17 percent had high school diplomas. Only 17 percent had education beyond high school. National statistics show that 28 percent of persons over 65 are high school graduates and 50 percent have completed less than 9 years of school. It has been predicted that by 1990 over 50 percent of the population of over 65 years will be high school graduates.[21] Blum had said that knowledge can be related to utilization of services[22] and Kalish states that "poorly educated elderly lack skills needed to manipulate the system to their advantage."[23]

All Respondents Retired

All respondents in this study indicated that they were no longer employed. All paid rent for their apartments and none owned any property. Over 80 percent of the respondents had lived in these two residences for over 1 year (a range of 1+ to 10 years); only 17 percent had recently moved to the residences (in the last 2–5 months); and all of these had lived in the same county before the move.

Transportation

Transportation was accessible to all the residents. Both residences are in the center of a city of 500,000 and have available frequent and regular bus service, taxis, and senior escort services. The bus was used by 50 percent of the people, and taxis and other cars by another 40 percent. Only 17 percent owned their own cars. People indicated that the problem of transportation was not inaccessibility, but rather their inability to use it. One man who regularly took the bus to a veterans hospital 35 miles from his home was physically unable to use it when he became acutely ill with the flu. Unaware that he had any other choices for transportation, he "doctored" himself for the 4-week duration of his illness. Other respondents expressed their frustration about dependence on others for transportation. One 92-year-old woman who used the bus and friends' cars for transportation stated that her greatest wish was that her osteopath, masseuse, and hairdresser should all have offices in the same building. If they did she would see them each once a week.

Specific Health Problems Identified

Each respondent was asked to identify the specific health problems or conditions that they had. Overall, 94 conditions were named. The conditions were categorized by the interviewer according to the instructions for preparation and use of the B Form. There was an average of 3.13 conditions per person. The 5 conditions cited most were: (1) heart disease, (2) arthritis, (3) musculoskeletal conditions, (4) hypertension, and (5) eye problems. This is similar to statistics reported by the National Ambulatory Medical Care Survey, which lists the principal conditions diagnosed during office visits in persons over 65 as: (1) chronic ischemic heart disease, (2) diabetes mellitus, (3) essential benign hypertension, (4) arthritis and rheumatism, and (5) diseases and conditions of the eye.[24]

Respondents in residence A identified almost twice as many conditions as those in residence B. Residence A had 3.9 conditions per person compared to 2.14 conditions in residence B. Residence B had three persons who

stated they had no identifiable conditions. No persons in residence B identified conditions related to depression, drugs, cancer, ear, psychosis, or
other neurology.

The sources of health care for all of the respondents were quite traditional. Twenty-three persons stated they had and used a medical doctor (includes surgeons and one psychiatrist). Fourteen persons said they had and
used an eye doctor and nine persons used a podiatrist. The only other frequent source utilized was the service of the public health nurse. Most of the
nurses' services (during home visits) were utilized by residence A. However,
four persons from residence B went to a neighborhood senior center to have
a nurse check their blood pressure. Three respondents had seen a dentist in
the last year. All were from residence B. Most other persons felt that since
they had dentures dental care was not necessary. Only three persons (two
from residence A and one from residence B) had used the services of a home
health agency (nurse and/or home health aide/homemaker). Surprisingly
only one person felt that a pharmacist was a source of health care. All
others felt that a pharmacist's only role was to fill prescriptions. Except for
one woman who saw a psychiatrist weekly, no one from either residence indicated use of any mental health service. No nontraditional health care providers such as acupuncturists and faith healers were used. See Table 12-2.

All 15 respondents in residence A stated that they had used health care
sources (mostly doctors) in the last year (many used them regularly on a 1–3
month basis). However, only eight persons in residence B had used a health
care source in the last year. In addition, one person had not used a source in
1–2 years; four had not used one in 2–5 years; and two had not used any
source in over 5 years.

The two persons who had not used a source in over 5 years were a married couple, one aged 70, the other 66. They stated that they didn't think
much of doctors or other health care providers. Since they felt they were

**Table 12-2 Summary of Most Frequently Used Sources
of Health Care by Residence**

Source of health care	Residence A	Residence B	Total
Physician	16	7	23
Eye doctor	7	7	14
Podiatrist	5	4	9
Public health nurse	12	4	16
Health department	0	3	3
Dentist	0	3	3
Home health agency	2	1	3

Table 12-3   Last Time Health Services Were Used in Each Residence

Number of years	Residence A		Residence B		Total	
	Number	Percent	Number	Percent	Number	Percent
Less than 1	8	53	15	100	23	77
1 to 2	1	7	0	–	1	3
2 to 5	4	27	0	–	4	13
5+	2	13	0	–	2	7

quite healthy, they saw no need to utilize any health care services. Of the four persons who had not utilized health care services for 2–5 years, one 73-year-old widow stated that she had lost all faith in doctors. This occurred because her husband's last illness was "misdiagnosed," and as a result he died. She had not been back to any health resource since, and said that she would do so in the future only in an emergency. A third woman, 86 years old, felt she was healthy and had no health conditions or problems, so "why go?" The fourth person, a 92-year-old woman, stated that she used to go to an osteopath but that now it was too difficult to get there on her own, and she did not like to bother friends. She stayed away from medical doctors as much as possible because she believed in "natural healing." She felt that she was quite healthy for her age and identified her only health problems as a prolapsed rectum (which she reinserted herself) and arthritic pains (which she felt were normal for her age and "you can't do anything about them anyway"). Table 12-3 shows the use of health services in the two residences.

Risk Factors

In interviewing the group, it became evident that the population was exposed to several risk factors. They include:

1   An overall increase in the morbidity and mortality rates for ages 65 and over.
2   A higher incidence of chronic disease and acute illness.
3   An increase in the rate of accidents (one woman had fallen in her apartment three times in one recent week).
4   A high neighborhood crime rate.
5   Inadequate incomes to pay for uninsured health care services.
6   An inability to use transportation services to get to health care services.
7   A lack of the education necessary to cope with the present health care system.
8   A lack of understanding and education by health care professionals to deal with the problems of the aged.

Health Care Needs

Several health care needs were identified as a result of this study:

    1   Lack of care and financial resources for eye, ear, and dental problems
    2   Need for transportation when ill and physically unable to use the usual sources of transportation
    3   Better knowledge of health care resources, especially those that are preventative, free or low-cost
    4   Acceptable mental health services in the home
    5   Health education about the aging process, chronic disease, and available resources
    6   Adequate income and insurance to finance needed services.

Persons who have these and other health care needs and cannot satisfy them are in danger of becoming disabled and eventually institutionalized. Some may become depressed and suicidal, others more isolated and lonely.

SUMMARY

Studies of the utilization of medical care among the elderly "show that the heavy users of such care, compared to other old people, are more likely to be over 75; they are more likely to be widowed; and they are more likely to be women."[25] Analysis of the data from this study supports this statement. Shanas states,

> The reasons many old people in the U.S. do not use medical care are primarily psychological, not financial. Many older people, despite their health complaints, believe that a doctor cannot heal them, or that they are not really sick enough to require medical attention.

Residence A in this study had the services of a public health nurse both for home visits and for the weekly counseling and health education session in the residence's conference room. During the interviews, it became apparent that participants from residence A were more knowledgeable about both their health and health care resources. This awareness may have led these people to seek out health care services in the first place, or they may have become more knowledgeable because they had more identified conditions. Though they were at approximately the same age, sex, and education level and had similar incomes as persons from residence B, the persons from residence A identified more health conditions or problems per person and all of them utilized health care sources at least once a year.

One reason why those from residence A utilized more health care services might be that the public health nurse specifically educated them about the services or identified new problems or problems needing additional care and services. Respondents from residence A related to the interviewer that the public health nurse was very respected, someone they could call on anytime they had a problem, were in a difficult situation, or had an emergency. In fact, most respondents from residence A considered the nurse as a friend. This was evident when the interviewer used the nurse's name as an introduction. The result was complete acceptance of both the interviewer and the study. All the respondents were friendly and gave open, uninhibited answers. Many asked the interviewer if she could return to visit, leading one to believe that loneliness and isolation factors are present whenever one deals with the elderly. From the results of the interviews in residence A, it can be concluded that the public health nurse had positively influenced the utilization of health care services.

The people from residence B were more wary of the interviewer and questioned the reason for the study even when the manager's name was used for an introduction. They did not give as many complete answers or supply as much unsolicited information about themselves. They seemed to have less knowledge about their health and utilized health care services much less frequently. More respondents from residence B did not see the need for health care services and some did not trust the providers. Some persons felt that they were totally healthy and had no identifiable health conditions or problems requiring utilization of services. Kalish says the reason for this may be that, while older people are "not as healthy as the young, most are for all practical purposes, quite healthy and are likely to maintain this state of health until very near the end."[27] However, Kalish further states that it can also mean that "some aged people believe that the symptoms of illness are normal and inevitable results of aging and therefore do not seek help. Others are aware of their need for help, but lack the knowledge or energy required to reach available services."[28]

The respondents from residence B, like those from residence A, exhibited signs of loneliness, asking the interviewer to come again. Indeed they seemed ready for health education and counseling as was evidenced by the questions asked and the referral sources requested. (In fact, this interviewer made three formal referrals to the health department to obtain services for two respondents from residence A and one from residence B.) The interviewer also spoke to the public health nurse whose district residence B was in. Though a former manager of the residence had previously refused the services of the health department, the interviewer informed the nurse that both the people and the present manager now seemed ready to accept public health nursing services. The nurse agreed to try again.

In both residences, other psychosocial factors may have influenced the respondents' use of health care services. Persons who had friends and relatives to call on for counseling and transportation seemed to have a slightly higher utilization rate than those who did not. This information was incidental to the study and was volunteered by several of the respondents. It can be speculated that utilization of services may be related to whether the elderly believe that anyone cares about what happens to them—i.e., "If someone cares about me, then I should care about and take care of myself."

Shanas and Maddox feel that the "elderly in the future will make more demands on the health establishment than they do now. They will require more physicians' care, more places in hospitals and nursing homes and more home health services."[29]

Since the elderly do use and need more health care services than any other age group, and therefore spend more money on them, public health nurses could educate the elderly about how and when to utilize services. This study has shown that a public health nurse did positively influence the utilization of health care services for persons over 60 in one retirement residence (residence A). The results also show that similar public health nursing services would probably influence residence B as well. A study reported by the National Center for Health Services Research and Development found that

> where people report they usually go when they are sick or for advice about their health influences whether or not they will seek care on a preventive basis. More importantly, once the decision to seek care is made, the regular source largely determines the type, amount, and continuity of care this patient receives.[30]

The role of the "regular source" could be assumed by the public health nurse as was done in the case of residence A.

REFERENCES

1 *Newsweek*, November 13, 1978.
2 H. Blumer, *Symbolic Interactionism Perspective and Method*, Prentice-Hall, Englewood Cliffs, N.J., 1969.
3 Ibid, p. 2.
4 Ibid, p. 2.
5 Ibid, p. 8.
6 E. Shanas and G. Maddox, "Aging, Health, and the Organizations of Health Resources," in R. H. Binstock and E. Shanas (eds.), *Handbook of Aging and the Social Sciences*, Van Nostrand Reinhold, New York, 1976, p. 604.
7 S. V. Kasl and S. J. Cobb, "Health Behaviors and Sick Role Behaviors," *Archives of Environmental Health,* vol. 12, no. 2, pp. 246–266, 1966.

8   S. E. Archer and R. Fleshman, *Community Health Nursing*, Wadsworth, Belmont, Calif., 1975, p. 69.

9   U.S. Bureau of the Census, *Current Population Reports*, Series P-23, No. 43, U.S. Government Printing Office, Washington, D.C., 1973.

10   National Institute on Aging, *Our Future Selves: A Research Plan Toward Understanding Aging*, Department of Health, Education and Welfare Publication No. 77-1096, Washington, D.C., 1977, p. 7.

11   Ibid, p. 7.

12   Ibid, p. 13.

13   Santa Clara County Planning Department, *1975 Santa Clara County Special Census*, San Jose, Calif., 1975.

14   E. C. Lambersten, "The Changing Role of Nursing and Its Regulation," in H. Creighton (ed.), *The Nursing Clinics of North America*, vol. 9, Saunders, Philadelphia, 1974, p. 396.

15   H. Blum, *Planning for Health, Developmental and Application of Social Change Theory*, Human Sciences Press, New York, 1974, p. 179.

16   F. N. Kerlinger, *Foundations of Behavioral Research*, Holt, Rinehart and Winston, New York, 1964, p. 469.

17   Ibid, p. 471.

18   Ibid, p. 396.

19   National Health Survey, *Home Interview Study*, Washington, D.C., 1976, p. 20.

20   National Center for Health Statistics, *The National Ambulatory Medical Care Survey: 1973 Summary*, Department of Health, Education and Welfare Publication No. (HRA) 76-1772, Md., 1975, p. 3.

21   U.S. Bureau of the Census, 1973, p. 25.

22   Blum, op. cit., p. 173.

23   R. Kalish, *The Later Years: Social Applications of Gerontology*, Brooks/Cole, Monterey, Calif., 1977, p. 299.

24   National Center for Health Statistics, op. cit., Table 17.

25   Shanas and Maddox, op. cit., p. 598.

26   Shanas and Maddox, op. cit., p. 599.

27   Kalish, op. cit., p. 292.

28   Kalish, op. cit., p. 299.

29   Shanas and Maddox, op. cit., p. 598.

30   National Center for Health Services Research and Development, *Health Services Use National Trends and Variations 1973-1974*, Department of Health, Education and Welfare Publication No. (HSM) 73-3004, U.S. Government Printing Office, Washington, D.C., 1972.

BIBLIOGRAPHY

Aday, L. A., and R. Eicharm: *The Utilization of Health Services: Indices and Correlates, a Research Bibliography*, National Center for Health Services, Research and Development, Washington, D.C., 1972.

Anderson, R.: *A Behavioral Model of Families' Use of Health Services*, University of Chicago Press, Chicago, 1968.

Babbie, E. R.: *Survey Research Methods*, Wadsworth, Belmont, Calif., 1973.

Birren, J. E., and K. W. Schaie: *The Handbook of the Psychology of Aging*, Van Nostrand Reinhold, New York, 1977.

Dresen, S. E.: "Autonomy: A Continuing Developmental Task," *American Journal of Nursing*, vol. 78, no. 8, pp. 1344–1346, 1978.

Freeman, H. E., S. Levine, and L. G. Rieder (eds.): *Handbook of Medical Sociology,* Prentice-Hall, Englewood Cliffs, N.J., 1972.

Igou, Jessie: "Health Education Curriculum with the Ambulatory Aged," paper presented at Spring Research Program, Pennsylvania State University, April 14, 1978.

National Center for Health Statistics: *Current Listing and Topical Index to the Vital and Health Statistics Series 1962–1976*, Department of Health, Education and Welfare Publication No. (HRA) 77-1301, Md., 1977.

Scitovsky, A., and N. Snyder: *Medical Care Use by a Group of Fully Insured Aged: A Case Study*, Department of Health, Education and Welfare Publication No. (HRA) 75-3129, Washington, D.C., 1975.

Shanas, E.: "Health Status of Older Persons—Cross-National Implications," *American Journal of Public Health*, vol. 64, no. 3, pp. 261–264, 1974.

Wadsworth, M. E., and R. B. Butterfield: *Health and Sickness The Choice of Treatment: Perception of Illness and Use of Services in an Urban Community*, Tavistock, London, 1971.

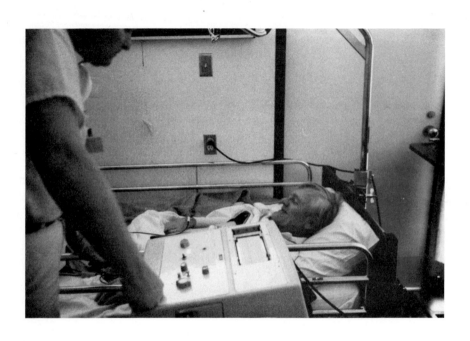

Part Three

The Aged Person in the Acute Care Setting

The Heart asks Pleasure—first—
And then—Excuse from Pain—
And then—those little Anodynes
That deaden suffering—

And then—to go to sleep—
And then—if it should be
The will of its Inquisitor
The privilege to die—

Emily Dickinson

INTRODUCTION

Part 3 deals with nursing problems in the acute facility, and current issues in acute care. Chapter 13 was first presented as a speech at the International Congress of Gerontology in Tokyo. Territoriality, an important aspect that is often forgotten in nursing the aged person, is described by Roberts in Chapter 14; the setting is the critical care unit. In Chapter 15, Roberts discusses death and dying of aged patients in the critical care unit.

Relocation Confusion: Intervention for Prevention

Mary Opal Wolanin
Janet Holloway

Procedure is swift; there follows a series of events which are routine for caring personnel but strange and frightening for the patient, for whom such an experience may be the first.

Mary Opal Wolanin and Janet Holloway

The unity of the physical structure of the human body and a person's emotional and behavioral functioning and cognition is not often considered in the theory and practice of medicine today.[1] The elderly person who is admitted to the acute care setting enters a health care belief system that continues to diagnose physical disorders with minute certainty yet continues to believe, as Palmore puts it, that "mental illness in old age is inevitable, untreatable, disabling, and irreversible." This becomes a self-fulfilling prophecy; it leads to lack of prevention and treatment which in turn tends to confirm the original belief.[2]

This chapter is a revision of the original paper, "Acute Confusional States Following Relocation of the Elderly: Nursing Intervention for Prevention" given at the International Congress of Gerontology, Tokyo, August 24, 1978.

The tendency to treat the pathological lesion only and overlook the whole person has resulted in the incorrect labeling of a large number of elderly persons as "senile." The real problems of such persons remain untreated. According to a recent report by Dr. Richard Besdine of Harvard University, the number of such persons who end up in institutions may range from 300,000 to 600,000. Many are persons who became confused during an illness or injury which required hospitalization, but were not diagnosed or treated because of a lack of recognition of their confusional state or, worse, because of the negative attitudes of health care personnel in acute settings.[3] *Treatment of confusion is within the scope of general hospital medical and nursing staff.*

A STUDY OF TRAUMATIC RELOCATION

In this chapter, the term *traumatic relocation* is used to describe an admission to a hospital under emergency conditions. Generally, an ambulance picks up the older patient, who is whisked to an emergency room with sirens blaring and paramedics attending. The patient may be suffering from a sudden illness or injury, or the illness may have been of long duration, but the decision to move the patient is sudden and dramatic. Procedure is swift; there follows a series of events which are routine for caring personnel but strange and frightening for the patient, for whom such an experience may be the first. The study reported in this chapter dealt with elderly persons with a hip fracture who underwent traumatic relocation. The rate of occurrence of confusion in such patients is based on data about 91 hip-fractured elderly persons between the ages of 60 and 94.* These persons were studied on the first, third, and fifth postoperative days.

Data Collection

Data were collected by means of: (1) record review; (2) openended questionnaires to explore patients' perception of their own mental status and find out what could have helped their confused state; (3) a structured test of patients' orientation, and recent, immediate, and past memory; and (4) their ability to follow two- and three-step directions. Care givers were questioned regarding patients' mental status as well as data for comparison between patients.[3] These four methods provided a multidimensional view of the patients' mental status as well as data for a comparison between patients' and

* The research study referred to is the "Relationship of Nursing Activities to Acute Confusional States in Elderly Hospitalized Patients," conducted by Margaret A. Williams, Janet Holloway, Mary C. Winn, Mary Opal Wolanin, Mariea Lawler, Carmen Westwick, and Marguerite Hsu under funding by a grant from the Division of Nursing, Department of Health, Education and Welfare to the Regional Program for Nursing Research Development, Western Interstate Commission for Higher Education, Boulder, Colo. It is reported in *Nursing Research*, January–February, 1979.

Table 13-1 Change in Mental Status of 91 Hip-fractured Elderly between Admission and Time of Surgery as Documented by the Nurses' Record

Mental Status of patient	On admission, percent	At time of surgery, percent
Alert and oriented	84	76
Some signs of confusion	12	14
Substantial signs of confusion	3	10
Unknown	1	0

care givers' perceptions of the same event. The patients were from five general hospitals located in the Rocky Mountain West.

Results of the Study

Table 13-1 compares the mental status of patients on admission and at the time of surgery (which is the same day as admission in many instances). The number of patients who were substantially confused increased in a very short time. Table 13-1 demonstrates that only 15 percent of patients who were admitted showed any evidence of confusion, but that this percentage had increased to 24 percent by the time of surgery. Care givers and patients reported that 36 percent were confused on the first postoperative day (POD) (Table 13-2). After the first POD, views of care givers and patients about the rate of confusion diverged, but there still remained a number of confused elderly by the fifth POD.

The results of the structured tests given to the patients show a steady increase in correct responses from the first to the fifth POD (Table 13-3). For 13 percent of those who were alert and oriented on admission (84 percent of the total) the confusional state persisted into the fifth POD. The 15 percent who had shown some to substantial confusion on admission (Table 13-1) increased to 36 percent on the first POD, but went down to 26 percent by the

Table 13-2 Comparison of Care Givers' and Patients' Perception of Confusional States as Measured by an Open-ended Questionnaire

Source of information	Percentage of patients who were confused		
	1st POD	3rd POD	5th POD
Care giver report	36	33	26
Patient report	36	25	19

Table 13-3   Results of Structured Tests of Patient Mental Status and Observed Orientation Expressed as Group Mean for 91 Hip-fractured Elderly

Results of structured tests of patients' mental status and nurses' recorded observations	Group mean		
	1st POD	3rd POD	5th POD
Structured tests			
Orientation (possible score—10)	7.6	8.1	8.4
Ability to follow directions (possible score—10)	5.9	6.45	6.7
Recent memory (possible score—10)	3.8	4.0	4.16
Immediate memory (possible score—4)	2.3	2.6	2.8
Observed incidents of confusional states as recorded on patient record	1.37	1.22	.934

fifth POD. Data analysis suggests that the critical period is from admission to surgery and following surgery through the fifth POD for the elderly patient who is suddenly relocated. This information alerts the nurse to recognize high-risk patients and to plan for prevention.

Attitudes of Patients and Staff

Patients were very open about their mental status, but when asked about what would have helped they were vague. Few had suggestions for nursing intervention; most felt that confusion was inevitable. When care givers were asked what interventions they had planned for their confused patients, many responded that they had no planned activities but reacted to each event as it occurred. No preventive measures were planned and most nurses and physicians felt that confusion was inevitable. Nevertheless, a few nurses gave examples of sensitivity and deliberative care. One example was suctioning the confused patient, who cleared mentally when airway patency was restored. Another nurse checked the electrolytes, and still another removed a catheter. A few called members of the family to stay with the patient, and in a few instances the patient was wheeled to a lighted area, e.g., the sun room during the day or the nurses' station at night.

NURSING THE ACUTE CARE PATIENT

We are concerned in this chapter with the nursing care that is given to the elderly patient with some pathology that requires instant relocation. Within the first 24 hours after admission the patient may be taken to an emergency ward, x-ray department, ward bed, operating suite, recovery room or critical care unit, and then back to the ward bed. During this period the patient may be seen as a diagnostic problem, a surgical wound, an unconscious patient, and finally a postoperative orthopedic case. But the elderly person's identity, unique life history, and highly specific needs are often lost in the acute care setting where the primary focus is on the lesion.

The patient will have pain and receive analgesics; there may be elevation of temperature, problems with urination and bowel elimination, immobility and position limitations, intubation in vein, wound, and often bladder, sensory deprivation or overload, and separation from significant others and from life history. And there will be a constant parade of intruding strangers through a life and space which is narrowed down to a tiny capsule. These are all threats to the elderly person with reduced reserves, and conditions which in themselves can cause confusion.

Maintain Mental Status

For the high-risk elderly person, maintenance of mental status should receive the same attention as the primary lesion. Care that heals the fracture, but leaves the patient with a confused mind which does not recognize reality, has missed the point. The crucial time from the moment of admission through the fifth POD should be planned to prevent confusion. Planning should start with the attitude that the elderly person will recover and that confusion is not inevitable. Care should continue with especial attention to the physiologic state: good hydration; prevention of iatrogenic nutritional deficiencies, which occur when food is restricted, by replacement of essential nutrients; control of pain; and attention to activity to restore the vertical position as soon as possible. It demands an assessment of the older person's ability to sense the environment, which may be impaired by visual or hearing deficits. It recognizes the loss of continuity with life history in the strange and foreign environment. The care plan senses the altered body image when the body feedback mechanism gives back pain and numbness instead of the usual proprioceptive cues. The nurse who sees that his or her patient's only view is of barren walls and bed curtains should plan to relocate the patient near windows, people, and light.

CRITICAL PROBLEMS

Critical patient problems that determine high risk are listed in Table 13-4, together with assessment and planning for prevention in three major categories: (1) physiologic function, (2) perceptual difficulties, and (3) loss of continuity with life history.

**Table 13-4   Assessment and Planned Interventions for Prevention
of Confusional States in the Elderly**

Patient problem	Areas for assessment	Planning for prevention
	Physiologic problems	
Hypoxia	Restlessness, cardiac function, respiratory function	Symptomatic relief should include reducing physical and emotional demands to level within patient's reserves. Provide supportive measures.
	Establishment of base line data vital signs	Recheck for minimal changes in the sensitive indicators of respiration rate, pulse, and blood pressure. Hypoxia should be suspected in the elderly, and intervention begun before overt signs.[4]
Hypothermia	Core temperature with a high degree of suspicion if temperature does not reach 97°F rectally. Cold extremities. Abdominal skin coldness. People who have fallen and remained in same position in cool room should be suspect. Check for long-term use of tranquilizers.[5]	Check core temperature for 10 minutes for base line value. Maintain warmth with close-fitting garments—socks, undergarments, pantyhose, sweaters, etc. Do not use heated appliances if temperature is below 97°F but raise ambient temperature to 80°F. Protect patients undergoing diagnostic tests or surgery which require moving from one place to another, from cold x-ray-table surfaces, cool operating and recovery rooms, swabbing with cold antiseptic solutions, and prolonged body inactivity during which body heat may be lost by evaporation, radiation, and convection. Frequent checks on body temperature should be made when patient is NPO, or given room temperature solutions intravenously.[6]
Hyperthermia	Flushed appearance. Core temperature 38.5°C or 101°F. Dry skin—no perspiration. Warm—hot ambient temperature. Excessive body covering. Increased pulse.	Reduce ambient temperature. Give cool fluids by mouth. Gradually reduce heat-retaining objects around body. Sponge face with tepid water. Sweat glands are reduced in number in the elderly and may not reduce body temperature through evaporation.

Table 13-4   Assessment and Planned Interventions for Prevention of Confusional States in the Elderly *(Continued)*

Patient problem	Areas for assessment	Planning for prevention
	Physiologic problems	
Hyperthermia		Aspirin, which acts through increased sweating, may not be effective.
Dehydration	History of living alone. Depression. Excessive use of tranquilizers. Use of diuretics. Observe saliva pool under the tongue, thickness of speech in dry mouth and, if available, BUN and hematocrit for signs of hemoconcentration. Specific gravity and amount of urine. Restraints which may prevent independent access to fluids. Every patient admitted with a poor history or no history should have a high degree of suspicion.	Hydrate patient while monitoring circulatory response and renal function. Ensure patient of independent access to fluids.
Hypotension	Establish base line blood pressure readings through serial readings at different times in the sleep-wake cycle, in both arms, and in lying, sitting, and upright positions. (Admission BP is rarely accurate.) Note signs of circulatory function, use of antihypertensive drugs or phenothiazines, and check for hypokalemia. Check for postural hypotension.	Establish monitoring base line with frequent checking until stable pattern emerges. For patient on drugs, a high level of suspicion is imperative. Prophylactic measures for confusional states in the elderly require guarding against hypotension.[7] Teach patients how to change from lying to upright positions.
Nutritional deficit	Appearance of recent weight loss. Edema. Lack of strength and/or alertness. Cheliosis. Periodontal disease (red, swollen, or spongy gums, retracted from teeth).	Iatrogenic nutritional deficits occur during institutionalization. Daily source of protein, glucose, essential vitamins, and minerals must be provided orally or parenterally. Replacement must be instituted by some route. The body has no

Table 13-4 Assessment and Planned Interventions for Prevention of Confusional States in the Elderly *(Continued)*

Patient problem	Areas for assessment	Planning for prevention
	Physiologic problems	
Nutritional deficit	Dental caries; edentulous. History of living alone. Depression, grief, loneliness. Low income. Drug history (especially tranquilizers, alcohol, and anticholinergic drugs). Special dietary restrictions—especially during surgery or diagnostic tests. Inability to feed self due to restraints, motor or sensory deficits.	reservoir for storing ascorbic acid, or K^+. Glycogen stores are limited; protein deficiencies must be made up from lean body mass (muscle).
Drug intoxication	Age: age-related changes pertaining to ingestion, absorption, assimilation, and excretion of drugs. Drug history including over-the-counter drugs and pattern of taking drugs: how many and when? Alcohol ingestion.	All drugs should be monitored to ensure that: 1 Action expected is taking place. 2 Action not expected is not taking place. 3 When a drug is not effective, it is discontinued before a second drug for the same problem is administered. 4 Minimal doses are given. 5 PRN medications are monitored for need and effectiveness. 6 Total number of drugs reviewed for interactions. All older persons taking drugs of any type are candidates for brain failure (lack of cerebral support).
Pain	Assess for occurrence of pain and for its lack. Look for numbness or lack of pain. All complaints of discomfort should be investigated by all means possible. If cause cannot be relieved by position, change, elimination, pressure reduction, or	Reduction of pressure, immobility, and other pain-causing stimuli. Small doses of pain-relieving medication should be given often enough to prevent pain cycle from beginning after 1 Relieving pressure 2 Ensuring that physiologic needs are met 3 Giving human care

Table 13-4   Assessment and Planned Interventions for Prevention of Confusional States in the Elderly *(Continued)*

Patient problem	Areas for assessment	Planning for prevention
	Physiologic problems	
Pain	movement, intensive investigation must be made.	4 Providing diversional activities[8] Pain is primary. It is distracting. It prevents meaningful interaction with human and material environment. Old age is not painful nor is it a disease. *Pain has a cause.*
Immobility	Determine activity level of of patient at ambulatory, wheelchair, or bed-bound level. Assess effects of immobility on: 1 Musculoskeletal system. 2 Circulatory system (hypotension, cardiac rate). 3 Respiratory system— shallow breathing—free airway. 4 Elimination—bowel and bladder (estimate renal function). 5 Feedback from proprioceptors. 6 Independence—ability to see and know environment. 7 Contraction of personal space. 8 Sensory deprivation.	Maintain highest level of physical and mental function. Provide meaningful sensory stimuli. All body needs remain the same but patient is dependent upon care to supplement restricted abilities. Care should be a deliberate effort to restore a normal environment and normal physiologic function, and to maintain normal body function in a limited and limiting situation.[9-11]
	Perceptual Difficulties	
Sensory deficits	Can the patient see the environment and the care givers? Functional vision is required at various levels—what level is required by patient's situation? Description of visual potential should include: 1 Best vision for print and color.	Care plan should state visual and hearing limitations and should be accessible to all care givers. Plan to potentiate limited senses should be known and used by all care givers. Wheelchairs of those with limited vision should have a symbol denoting the limitation to prevent surprising patient. A symbol of low vision worn on clothing will enable staff to adapt to the situation.

Table 13-4 Assessment and Planned Interventions for Prevention of Confusional States in the Elderly *(Continued)*

Patient problem	Areas for assessment	Planning for prevention
	Perceptual difficulties	
Sensory deficits	2 Black and white vision (or vision in shadow and darkness). 3 Peripheral vision. 4 Far and near vision. 5 Best vision with correction.	
	Description of hearing should include: 1 Ability to answer a question, asked in a normal speaking voice, which *cannot* be answered by "yes" or "no." 2 Ability to repeat an 11-word test after tester: smart, off, with, that, thin, well, cat, room, all, jaw, does. 3 Is hearing potential adequate to receive oral communication? If not, what other means of communication should be used?	The hearing handicapped should wear a special marking on the shoulder of the better hearing side. Staff should touch patient on hand when speaking, in order to ensure front view and good distance. Paper and pencil should be carried to communicate with those with adequate vision but poor hearing. More touch should be used in care giving with patients with sensory deficits. Prosthetic devices should be in good repair and accessible.
	Neurologic examination to determine taste and smell—as needed in patient's situation.	When taste is limited, attention must be given to color, texture, and temperature of food.
	Is patient overwhelmed by too much too fast?	Reduce quantity and intensity of input.
	How much has been presented and in what time space? Is orientation overwhelming?	Give primary nursing care (one care giver responsible for care).
	Is patient restless, distractable, fatigued or agitated? Is ratio of information to sensory deficits balanced?	Information should be given one item at a time with rest between items.

Table 13-4   Assessment and Planned Interventions for Prevention of Confusional States in the Elderly (Continued)

Patient problem	Areas for assessment	Planning for prevention
Perceptual difficulties		
Sensory overload	Physical environment may be overstimulating: lights, glare, noise (without pattern), activity, symbols, and signs.	Information should be offered after hearing and visual screening.
	How many staff persons has the patient had to react to within a 6-hour span? Are any physiologic problems competing for attention—i.e., pain, thirst, full bladder, rectal distention, or hunger?	Ensure that physiologic needs are cared for before increasing information. Tangible help is reassuring.[12] Increase meaning and pattern of input. Slow input to a point where patient can handle it. The greater the sensory deficit, the more difficult to handle information overload.
Sensory deprivation	To what extent does environment offer stimulation to the patient: human environment (staff and visitors), material environment (building furnishings, windows, food, sound, light, color contrasts and color)? What sensory-perceptual deficits require additional planning to enable the patient to have a rich environment? Help patient cope with "unreal" experiences.[13-15]	If deprivation or restriction is due to deficit, plan of care must include facilitation for other senses such as touch and taste, or accentuation of remaining senses. Environment must be planned with special needs of elderly in mind: plenty of light without glare, avoidance of distracting background noise. Environment should have pattern and meaning—familiar music, colors, pictures, contrasts, and day-night demarcation. Walking should be facilitated with aids; the floor finishes should assist in providing contrast. Calendars, clocks, television, or radios under the patient's control should be accessible.
	Spending time in a bland and ambiguous environment alone causes hallucinations.	
Interference with usual body feedback systems	Is there a change in body activity which interferes with body feedback (stroke, immobilization,	Assist with position change. Assist with feedback process by calling attention to body parts. Use touch extensively and intensively. Keep

Table 13-4   Assessment and Planned Interventions for Prevention of Confusional States in the Elderly *(Continued)*

Patient problem	Areas for assessment	Planning for prevention
Perceptual difficulties		
Interference with usual body feedback systems	fracture, pain, restraint)? Is body exposed to monotony of texture and shapes?	drugs which interfere with body sensing to minimal dose—ensure comfort but see that there is no interference with ability to sense body. Encourage use and exercise of all unaffected body parts and call attention to each as moved.
Lack of information	Does patient have access to information on which he or she will be expected to act? What usual information sources are present, and which need to be supplemented? (e.g., watches, radio, calendar, newspaper, window, temperature, time of day, meal schedule, location, weather, seasons)	Place next to window. Keep personal objects at hand. Do not curtain or screen except for privacy. Ensure good light without glare. Use large print on signs and reading material. Give information slowly, one item at a time. Use primary nursing system with one person preserving continuity and taking responsibility for maintaining patient's contact with reality.
Too rapid change	Is patient withdrawing? Overreacting?	"Must you always rush? We older people need time. A little patience is an investment in helping us keep in contact with our reality and yours." [16]
Loss of continuity with life history		
	Is there a family member or friend who can remind the person of present and past personal history? Does the patient have an article which links back to the past—a photograph, jewelry, clothing, furniture? Does the patient attempt to draw you into a reminiscence? Is the patient withdrawn from *today*?	Determine what persons can effect continuity with past either in person or by telephone. Help patients with telephone. Write down names, addresses, and phone numbers of any person the patient can mention. Be a listener with patient about the past. Call patients by their name and touch them as you talk—shake hands on greeting. Ask about their favorite music and arrange for them to hear it if possible. Introduce the patient to another patient of about the same age, bringing out some commonality in their pasts.

Table 13-4   Assessment and Planned Interventions for Prevention of Confusional States in the Elderly *(Continued)*

Patient problem	Areas for assessment	Planning for prevention
Loss of continuity with life history		
		Suggestions: old music; old, old catalogues; World War I books; reviewing the Depression; the first President voted for. It is necessary for care giver to be convinced that a person is continuous in time, space and becoming. A life history cannot be left behind, but it can be ignored, and then a part of the person dies as surely as if it were amputated.

REFERENCES

1   Phillip Ernst et al, "Isolation and Symptoms of Chronic Brain Syndome," *The Gerontologist*, vol. 18, no. 5, pp. 468–474, October 1978.

2   E. B. Palmore, in E. W. Busse (ed.), *Mental Illness in Later Life*, American Psychiatric Association, Washington, D.C., 1973.

3   Richard Besdine, report to the Department of Health, Education and Welfare, 1978 (draft form prior to publication).

4   Paola S. Timiras, "Biological Perspectives on Aging," *American Scientist*, vol. 66, no. 5, September–October 1978.

5   Isadore Rossman, *Clinical Geriatrics*, Lippincott, New York, 1971, pp. 374–375.

6   E. T. Allen, "Prolonged Immersion in Cold Water," *Nursing Times*, vol. 70, p. 1928, December 12, 1974.

7   Alvin Goldfarb, "Memory and Aging," in R. Goldman and M. Rockstein (eds.), *The Physiology and Pathology of Aging*, Academic Press, New York, 1975.

8   Margo McCaffery, *Nursing Management of the Patient with Pain*, Lippincott, New York, 1972.

9   John Deitrick et al, "Effects of Immobilization upon Various Metabolic and Physiologic Functions of Normal Men," *American Journal of Medicine*, vol. 4, no. 3, p. 36, 1948.

10 Ralph Ryback et al, "Psychobiologic Effects of Prolonged Bed-rest (Weightlessness) on Young Healthy Volunteers," *Aerospace Medicine*, vol. 42, no. 5, pp. 529–535, May 1971.

11 Pamela Holsclaw Mitchell, *Concepts Basic to Nursing*, 2d ed., McGraw-Hill, New York, 1977, Chaps. 11 and 12.

12   Judith Chodril and Barbara Williams, "The Concept of Sensory Deprivation," *Nursing Clinics of North America*, vol. 5, no. 3, pp. 453–465, September 1970.
13   Mitchell, op. cit., p. 287.
14   Lorraine Hiatt Snyder, "Environmental Changes for Socialization," *Journal of Nursing Administration*, vol. 1, no. 8, pp. 44–50, January 1978.
15   Florence Downs, "Bed-rest and Sensory Disturbances," *American Journal of Nursing*, vol. 74, no. 3, pp. 434–438, March 1974.
16   M. O. Wolanin and J. Holloway, "Acute Confusional States Following Traumatic Relocation of the Elderly: Nursing Intervention for Prevention," paper given at the International Congress on Gerontology, Tokyo, August 24, 1978.

BIBLIOGRAPHY

Eisdorfer, Carl, and Robert O. Friedel: *Cognitive and Emotional Disturbance in the Elderly*, Yearbook Medical Publishers, Chicago, 1978.
Prien, R. F.: *Organic Brain Syndrome*, A Review of the Therapeutic Literature with Special Emphasis on Chemotherapy, Washington, D.C., Veterans Administration, Department of Medicine and Surgery, 1972.

Chapter 14

Territoriality: Space and the Aged Patient in the Critical Care Unit

Sharon L. Roberts

Sometimes you get fighting over 'squatter's rights,' which makes staff members very uncomfortable. However, territorial behavior may be a response to resource scarceness, memory loss, unpredictable bladder control, etc.

Ruth Bennett and Carl Eisdorfer

Historically, in hospitals, interest and concern with space was limited to determining whether patients had enough closet or drawer space for their belongings, or if there was enough storage space for linen, equipment, and sterile supplies. There has been little attention given to feelings patients might have about the use or misuse of space. Now with the rapid development of critical care units, for example, intensive care, coronary care, respiratory care, trauma, and hemodialysis, there is more interest in the use of space in such areas. Space does not pertain only to physical use of space, such as arrangements of beds, chairs, cardioscopes, oxygen outlets, suction bottles, and respirators, but also to psychological use of space.

In our Western culture a "relationship between physical and social territory is frequently evident, the amount of space a person has is often related to his personal importance or economic status. For example, a large home on a double lot is generally symbolic of high income and status."[1] Therefore, if a patient has a private room in a hospital, this has some financial significance. On the other hand, if an aged patient has a private room the assumption may be made that the patient creates nursing care problems, for example, causing confusion or noise, bothering other patients, smelling bad, etc. If the aged patient has a private nurse, it is often true that this does represent a nursing care problem and the need for increased nursing care. In other words, what I have described indicates that what may imply status and dignity for patients as a whole may not do so for the aged patient.

Technological sophistication through man-made critical care environments tends to lessen the focus on the human aspect of care. The various routines in these units may be monotonous to the aged patient, but the environment may be both noisy and overstimulating. Current designs of critical care units have taken meaningful stimuli into consideration. This is especially significant to the aged patient with visual or auditory deprivation. For such patients colorful rooms with large windows, carpets, and clocks provide pleasant visual stimuli.

TERRITORIALITY, SPACE, AND PRIVACY

Those individuals who have studied the concept seem to categorize territoriality in two ways, first as a geographic or spatial phenomenon and second as a behavioral phenomenon. When applying territorial and spatial concepts to aged patients, it is best to view territoriality as a behavioral system.

Territoriality

Territorial behavior, according to Stea, "reflects the desire to possess and occupy portions of space and, when necessary, to defend it against intrusion by others."[2] Pastalan believes that "a territory is a delimited space which an individual or group uses and defends as an exclusive preserve. It involves psychological identification with the place, symbolized by attitudes of possessiveness and arrangements of objects in the area."[3] Hall believes that territoriality is "behavior by which an organism characteristically lays claim to an area and defends it against members of its own species."[4] He also maintains that territoriality is a basic behavioral system characteristic of living organisms, including man, which evolves in the same way anatomic structures evolved. He further believes that every living thing has a boundary which separates it from its external environment. A nonphysical boundary exists outside the physical one. This new boundary is harder to delineate than the first but it is just as real; it is called the organism's boundary.[5] Lorenz states that in all individuals the readiness to fight is greatest in the middle of their own territory, for it is there that they have the greatest chance of winning. The individual's readiness to fight decreases with the distance from the center of this familiar territory, and the increased proximity to strange territory.[6]

Space

There are people who view the individual's territory and personal space as being the same. Nevertheless, the two concepts have their own idiosyncrasies. Personal space is carried around by the aged individual. For some, the amount of personal space is greater due to excess body weight, canes, crutches, walkers, or wheelchairs. Individual territory is basically stationary and may be much larger in area. Pastalan points out that the aged patient in critical care will

> delineate the boundaries of his territory with a variety of environmental props, both fixed and mobile, so that they are visible to others, while the boundaries of personal space are invisible, though they may sometimes be inferred from self-markers such as facial expressions, body movements, gestures, olfaction, visual contact and voice intonation.[7]

Space has been defined as "room to move about in" and "room to put our bodies in." In and of itself space is a non-entity, but in relationships space has the power to convey meaning. Space is essentially that nothingness which exists between "self" as the point of departure and some object or person perceived in the world "out there."[8] Furthermore, spacing is also a function of dominance or high status; the more powerful the animal, the larger and more choice is his territory. According to Beck,

> Imminent space is inner, subjective space, the space of unconsciousness, of dreams, of fantasy; it includes the spatial styles and orientation of the individual, and the ingrained spatial notation systems of whole cultures. This is the basic space imposed upon us by the anatomy of our bodies. Consequently, it is also the space involved in the image of our body.[9]

Privacy

According to Pastalan, privacy may constitute a basic form of human territoriality because of its unique human behavioral state. Privacy may be defined as the right of the individuals to decide what information about themselves should be communicated to others and under what conditions.[10] Privacy serves the function of personal autonomy, emotional release or safety-valve effect, self-evaluation, and protected communication. There are four degrees of privacy: solitude, intimacy, anonymity, and reserve.

As the definitions of territoriality, space, and privacy indicate, each living thing has a physical boundary that separates it from its external environment. There is also a nonphysical boundary which exists outside the physical one. This new boundary is harder to delineate than the first, but is just as real. No matter how crowded the area in which the aged patient temporarily lives, he or she tries to maintain a zone or territory around self. The amount of personal space needed by each aged patient varies. Spatial needs are dependent upon emotional and physical status, cultural background, and position in the nonhospital environment.

AGED PATIENT IN CRITICAL CARE

Davis believes that the effects of unfamiliar territory are more rapidly induced in the elderly and more profound, leading to temporary states of confusion, anxiety, and disorientation.[11] Lorenz discovered in his studies that innate behavior mechanisms can be thrown completely out of balance by small, apparently insignificant changes in environmental conditions.[12] One should remember that for the aged client any change may be significant, since adaptability to change is greatly reduced in later years.

ENVIRONMENTAL FACTORS

Since the critical care unit is designed for the care of patients who are critically or seriously ill and who require continuous intensive nursing, assessment, and interventions, the space and territory of these units need to be large enough to accommodate various pieces of equipment. However, this is not always the case in practice. Critical care units are man-made, designed environments. "Designed environments are systems of energy and matter interposed between humans and ambivalent forces in the impinging macro environment."[13] Critical care units are environments designed in one of two ways: (1) with openness of space, where each patient unit is separated by an imaginary territorial boundary or curtain, and with about 4 to 5 feet between units; or (2) with closed-in space, with each patient in a private room. Closed units were originally constructed to offer the critically ill patient more privacy. Open units are less costly (saving wall space) and the nurse is able to see the patients visually at all times. The majority of units are now organized as open units. Patients have expressed feelings of security if they can look up and see their nurse, because they feel someone is watching them 24 hours a day. Furthermore, the critical care nurse also feels more secure because from any location in the unit he or she can see the critically ill patient and the equipment. For example, if an aged patient becomes confused and attempts to get out of bed, the nurse can notice this behavior before the cardioscope alarm fires, or before a fall or an injury occurs.

At present there seems to be little concern on the part of staff or architects who design these critical care units about the effects that space and territory have on one important segment of our patient population, the aged. Use of space and territory as it pertains to the aged patient is significant because a human being's sense of space is closely related to sense of self. It is important to realize the kind of space one is living in—not objective space, but lived, experienced space—"here." There is another important point to consider about aged patients in critical care units. They have had more years of experience in determining their own space than younger persons, and have learned through the years the kinds of territory and space that make them feel comfortable and secure, and the kinds which make them insecure.

For the aged patient, to be taken suddenly from the familiar, secure, and safe environment of home, or from a convalescent home or a community made up entirely of aged citizens, and placed in the tense and unfamiliar territory of critical care can be overwhelming. It has been my experience that aged patients find it difficult to adapt quickly; yet after admission to a critical care unit, they soon learn both nonverbally and verbally from staff that a quick adaptation is expected.

THE AGED PATIENT IN A CRITICAL CARE UNIT

Aged patients who arrive in a critical care unit enter an unknown environment that is tense, busy, and continually changing. They are taken by stretcher to a newly acquired territory which is either a bed in a private room or a bed in an open 8- to 10-bed unit. If the aged patient is placed in a private room, the nurse quite frequently hears, "My own room, how nice." I have noted that other patients in critical care units rarely comment on the openness or otherwise of their territory.

The aged frequently limit their comments to immediately liking or disliking the bed. DeLong conducted research on spatial-behavioral relationships among the elderly. In his research he discovered that private rooms decrease aggression and increase cooperation. He believes that the need for a space of one's own is bio-basic, rooted in man's phylogenetic past. "To deprive a person of a space of his own is, in a very real way, to deprive him of part of his identity."[14] When patients arrive in critical care, they are lying flat on their backs; therefore, the only spatial orientation is the ceiling, or possibly the faces of those pushing them. The unit is spatially confining, especially if various pieces of equipment are used. The equipment is usually located at the head of the patient's bed. If a respirator is needed, or ordered for "stand-by," or a nasal-gastric tube for intermittent suction, these items are usually kept at the head of the patient's bed. If the aged patient develops arrhythmias, the defibrillator may also be placed near the patient as an anticipatory nursing intervention. Often the aged patient may be receiving antiarrhythmic drugs, so an intravenous bottle is threaded through a machine which supplies a constant and small amount of fluid. The machine assures the nurse that only a preset number of drops will be given the patient. Further, if the aged patient's blood pressure drops, an arterial line may be inserted and connected to a machine which continuously monitors arterial pressure. If needed, blood gases can be drawn from the arterial line, which will eliminate repeated femoral artery punctures. All this equipment has strange noises, alarms, lights, and unfamiliar functions which only frighten, and certainly do not reassure, the elderly patient.

Since there are no walls or lines to separate each person's territory in the open ward, we, as nurses, create them by using artificial lines, for example, movable curtains or screens.

The stretcher is placed by the bed, and the aged patient is lifted into bed. An independent aged patient may feel humiliated when lifted like an infant. Other patients state their pleasure at being lifted into bed by saying, "Boy, what great service; I am going to love being spoiled." After the patient is in bed, the side rails are raised immediately to ensure safety. Again, the independent aged patient may feel like an infant just placed in a protective crib.

Depending on the nature and severity of the illness, and mental status, usually the next step is to apply cardioscope leads to the patient's chest so that cardiac rhythm can be continuously monitored. Most monitors are sensitive to external or environmental interferences which alter the patient's cardiac pattern, and they set off an alarm; therefore the patient is instructed not to touch the bed rails or leads, because such contact creates interferences which may trigger off the alarm mechanism. It is therefore impossible to assess the height of the bed rails, which further increases the patient's lack of territorial orientation and feelings of insecurity. The patient may, in fact, be afraid to reach out to touch anything at all after such instruction.

ANTECEDENT FACTORS

Antecedent factors of territoriality and space refer specifically to intrusion by others and by diagnostic or treatment procedures into the aged patient's personal territory and space. Intrusion by members of the critical care health team or by means of environmental props diminish the patient's sense of privacy. Privacy is important to most individuals, no matter where they are, and the critical care nurse should assess its meaning to the patient. Barton points out that "every patient, no matter how sick he is, needs some privacy and a place he can call his own where he may store his personal possessions. After all, man, like other animals, has territorial instincts.''[15]

Besides being connected to the cardioscope, the aged patient may be placed on intravenous feedings, oxygen therapy, and possibly nasal-gastric suction. The female patient will frequently need the bedpan if a diuretic has been administered, and the energy utilized getting on and off a bedpan increases metabolism and oxygen uptake. The male patient may be unsteady with his urinal and accidently spill it in bed. The aged patient may forget to call the nurse to help place the urinal or bedpan, or may forget to remain in bed. Younger patients manipulate the urinal better, or remember to call their nurse to place the bedpan. In order to protect the aged patient from physiological harm or prevent overactivity, a Foley catheter may be inserted. The Foley then becomes another intrusive tube which serves to further reduce the patient's mobility in bed. Moving an arm to touch the side rail may accidentally pull the patient's intravenous tube. When trying to turn, the patient must remember to move various tubes—nasal-gastric tube, oxygen tubing, or Foley catheter. Otherwise the tube may become disconnected, or cause pain from pulling. More frequently the aged patient will remain in one spot, on his or her back, so as not to disturb anything. The wires from the cardioscope and the tubes from intravenous feeding, oxygen, nasal-gastric, or Foley may limit the patient's mobility in bed and further decrease his or her territorial claim.

Because of the reduced agility that the normal aging process brings, and the possibility of a history of hip fracture, the nurse needs to make a concerted effort to assist and encourage mobility in the aged patient's limited territory—the bed. Younger patients are better able to protect all their wires and tubes while repositioning themselves in bed.

All the procedures discussed represent a direct intrusion into the personal territory of the patient. When personal territory is intruded upon, the aged person may react behaviorally by becoming angry, and refuse the procedures. On the other hand, the patient's defenses may become weakened by such intrusion, for ''when a man's territorial defenses are weakened or intruded upon, his self-assurance tends to grow weaker.''[16] The aged patient, who lives in a somewhat constricted world, may have only minimal day-to-day physical encounter with other people, and feel territorially intruded upon when *two* nurses enter the room to simultaneously apply cardioscope leads, intravenous therapy, and oxygen mask. Younger patients, who normally encounter the pushing, shoving, and touching activity of daily life, may not react to such intrusion; they almost expect it. Shortly after a young person's arrival in critical care, I have heard the patient ask, ''Well, when does all the action start?'' But the nurse often hears the aged patient say, "Please let me rest for a while." If there does not exist a life-threatening problem to the aged patient, this wish to be left alone for a while should be respected.

The elderly patient who is acutely ill may not be allowed to reach the night stand, which is territorially the patient's, because this motion (1) places an increased workload on the myocardium if there has been an infarction, (2) increases the possiblity of bleeding if the patient is a gastrointestinal bleeder, (3) displaces pacemaker wires, and (4) increases the workload of the pulmonary system if the problem is pulmonary embarrassment. The aged patient is again limited in ability to adapt territorially to the environment.

AGED PATIENTS' NEEDS IN CRITICAL CARE UNITS

The aged patient's needs in all critical care units are psychosocial and physiological in nature. The needs for protection, dominance, status, affection, and touch are all associated with the use of space and with territorial phenomena. The boundaries of the territories remain reasonably constant, as do the locations for specific activities within the territory, such as sleeping, eating, and resting.

Because of the severity of his or her illness, the aged patient is not able to hang up clothes in the closet, put belongings in a drawer, or even get in and out of bed alone. Hanging up clothes and putting belongings in their proper place are ways in which the aged patient lays a territorial claim. However, in critical care, someone else, usually the nurse, has claimed territorial rights for the patient. Therefore, the night stand will only symbolically be the patient's. Many patients have a wife or husband to tell them repeatedly where their belongings are and to help them obtain them. Elderly patients, on the other hand, often do not have a family member to tell them where their belongings are located; therefore, the nurses assume this responsibility. If they do not, the aged patients may feel disoriented in the new territory, because nothing seems to belong to *them*. The confusion may also serve to create anxiety within the older patient. "Man's sense of space is closely related to his sense of self, which is in intimate transaction with his environment."[17]

The nurse in critical care often finds environmental props in the aged patient's bed: glasses, purse, pictures, favorite pillow, sweater, tissues, address book, and even a piece of toast wrapped up from breakfast. Each prop has a certain space within the total territory of the bed. We who are determined to be professionally neat nurses have a tendency to remove these props in order to straighten the bed or simply to get them out of our way. If we do this, then the older patient may become bounded by a spatial mold that works against the establishment of a personal and social identity.

Another territorial characteristic of the aged patient is the tendency to collect many small objects. The nurse may find the night stand, like the bed, cluttered with various objects or props.

> The pattern of cluttering is very important in the organization of space for the elderly, and at the risk of sounding ludicrous must be one of the critical elements for achieving an *ordered space*. A cluttered spatial environment satisfies, not too surprisingly, most of the structure-points so far uncovered that the elderly use in environmental transactions, providing for: heightened peripheral visual stimulation, increased tactile involvement, greater kinesthetic awareness, and a sense of closeness so important in interpersonal transactions—by reducing the distance between objects to little more than an arm's length.[18]

Therefore, instead of straightening out the night stand and putting objects away, the nurse could be much more helpful to the elderly patient by simply leaving the stand cluttered.

As stated earlier, our sense of space is closely related to our sense of self; it is an intimate transaction with the environment. Human beings can be viewed as having visual, kinesthetic, tactile, and thermal aspects of self, which may be either inhibited or encouraged by the environment. Because of the aging process itself, the visual, kinesthetic, tactile, and thermal aspects of the aged patient are already limited. According to DeLong, underlying all perceptions of space are the senses, and an individual's perception and use of space is a function not only of the information available via sensory modalities, but also of the perceptual screen provided by the culture. In addition to the perceptual screen of culture, the elderly are forced to cope with a physiological screen. If there is a decreased sensitivity in the sensory apparatus, one might say that the sensory channels are affected by a greater degree of interference, or that the noise level relative to the information level is increased. "Either way, the sensory contact of the elderly with their social and spatial environment is diminished and they must negotiate with that environment with reduced information."[19] The aged patient's sensory apparatus is more limited than that of most other patients, and thus it affects what Hall describes as: "(1) distance receptors—those concerned with examination of distant objects—the eyes, ears, and nose; and (2) immediate receptors—those used to examine the world close up—the world of touch, the sensations we receive from the skin, membranes, and muscles."[20]

To cope with the environment of a critical care unit, the aged patient appears to depend upon quite different sensory information than do other patients. For example, the aged appear to pay more attention to information channeled through the peripheral receptors of the eye, which magnify movement. Therefore, since many aged have impaired vision, they have difficulty visually assessing the span of their territory. A common example is the older patient who uses peripheral vision and sees a "box" sitting above his or her head and thinks this is a television set. The patient doesn't realize it is a cardioscope. It is not unusual to find the aged patient standing at this "television set" turning the dial to another station saying, "The reception is poor; I only get a funny line." Even when patients are wearing glasses, they find it difficult to understand that this is not a television set, but rather a cardioscope. One reason may be because the machine has no meaning to the patient. Gelwicks states:

> People, regardless of age, relate to their environment only to the degree that it contains information relevant to them. The elderly individual whose sense receptors no longer function at full capacity may be receiving only partial messages and, therefore, faces a difficult task in relating appropriately to both his physical and social environment.[21]

If an explanation of the cardioscope is given, the aged patient may not hear the explanation, or even the noise made by the object of the explanation, the monitor. It is important to remember also that critical care environment equipment, such as cardioscopes, respirators, and aspirators, is highly complex apparatus and has highly patterned visual and auditory stimuli. Exposure to such complex apparatus may cause technological overload in the elderly person.

Frequently, older people who are anxious and hurrying to get to the hospital forget to bring their hearing aids. Those who do bring them discover the aids may not work because of functional failure. The nurse who does not call the family and tell them to bring the hearing aid and batteries may be forced to either yell in the patient's ear or to avoid verbal communication. If the nurse does not want to yell an explanation about the cardioscope to the patient, the latter may receive no explanation at all. The interpretation of the "machine" as a television set cannot always be blamed on the older patient.

Speaking loudly to patients in critical care may also disturb other patients who are in close proximity. Once again the nurse may avoid talking and the aged patient becomes alienated. In the case of the average patient who enters a critical care unit, if an explanation of the cardioscope is not offered immediately when the leads are applied, it is soon demanded!

As previously mentioned, the boundaries of territory remain reasonably constant. The territory is in every sense of the word an extension of the organism, which is marked by visual and invisible territorial markers.

Examples of extensions of territoriality in critical care are television sets and telephones, both of which are taboo in these units. The rationale may be that extensions of territory would serve to overexcite the acutely ill patient. However, the acuteness of the patient's illness needs to be continuously assessed, and I believe, if possible, a television set should be added to the patient's bedside. Many aged people I have known spend their mornings talking to friends on the telephone, and their afternoons watching television. A nurse in critical care interested in television may be able to keep the aged patients informed about what has been happening to their favorite characters on television. Telephone calls can be quickly made for the patient; such action demonstrates caring and helps the patient to keep contact with friends. Many aged have lost many friends so the few remaining ones may be very close to them.

The aged patient is immobilized because of complete bed rest and the various wires and tubes, and may have no idea about the spatial dimension surrounding the bed or encompassing the closet and night stand. Normally, as we move through space, we depend on messages received from our bodies to stabilize our visual world. Without such body feedback, a great many people lose contact with reality and hallucinate; the aged patient is certainly no exception.

Space perception is not only a matter of what can be perceived but also what can be screened out. Some older clients screen out one type of information while paying close attention to another. Aged patients should be allowed to have commode or bathroom privileges as soon as possible; this will serve to increase territorial orientation, and also provide a different perception of the environment—sitting instead of lying. As patients increase territorial claims and adaptations through exploration, they become very possessive about *their territory*. If the patient shares a bathroom with another patient, he or she wants the nurse to keep the other door locked. Most aged patients do not like sharing a bathroom with another patient, he or she wants the nurse to keep the other door locked. Most aged patients do not like sharing a bathroom or commode with any other patient. I've noticed that most other patients usually do not react this way; instead, they usually keep the bathroom door open and unlocked. The more space and territory is gained, the more significant and independent the patient feels.

BEHAVIOR

The last aspect of territoriality involves behavioral responses. Aged patients may use environmental props—objects and arrangements of objects in space. We have earlier referred to environmental props as various pieces of equipment around the patient's bed that give the impression of acute illness.

The aged patient may bring environmental props in order to mark territory. Patients may exhibit a broad range of responses to territorial intrusion, but usually they seem to emphasize verbal, communicative, and reactive mechanisms: argument, discussion, pleas, anger, and other forms of verbal behavior.

Aged patients in critical care units may also use gestures, facial expressions, and other forms of nonverbal behavior. When their personal territory is intruded upon, patients also use weapon props for reactive purposes. Occasionally patients have thrown their flowers against the wall or on the floor out of anger.

USE OF PROXEMICS IN NURSING INTERVENTIONS

The relationship between space and a feeling of freedom has potential therapeutic significance. "Spatial changes give a tone to communication, accent it, and at times even override the spoken word. The flow and shift of distance between people as they interact with each other is part and parcel of the communicative process."[22]

A willingness to be somewhat close in space conveys the message of a desire to be close in other human-to-human transactions. Such a message may serve to quiet the restless and agitated older patient as well as to support one who seems to be withdrawn.

I think the nurse has a primary responsibility for early detection of territorial deprivation and territorial disorientation, so as to either prevent its occurrence by manipulating environmental stimuli, or to help the aged patient to adapt better to the new environment. There is a reduction in meaningful and familiar stimuli for the aged patient. The need for self-esteem may be lowered; meaning and purpose have gone out of the patient's world. The older person in critical care is no longer registering the familiar world known through reception and perception of familiar sounds, sights, smells, tastes, and touch, and the patient who is severely ill may be territorially immobilized. Until contact with the critical care unit is increased through activity and exploration, enabling the patient to manipulate and experience the novelty of the nearby stimuli, the patient cannot meet higher needs. The nurse is a supportive figure who needs to constantly interpret the unfamiliar environment of strange sounds and equipment for the elderly patient.

Our sense of space has a bearing on our ability to relate to other people, to observe them as being close or far away. Hall has coined the term *proxemics* and identified four distance zones commonly used by people.[23] Two of these distances, *intimate distance far phase* and *personal distance close phase*, I believe apply to the aged patient in critical care.

Intimate Distance

At intimate distance, the presence of the other person is unmistakable and may at times be overwhelming because of the greatly stepped-up sensory inputs. Sight, olfaction, heat from the other person's body, sounds, and feel of breath all combine to signal unmistakable involvement with another body. According to DeLong:

> Intimate-personal transactions among the elderly are characterized by very high levels of sensory involvement. The inner boundary is at a point inside the skin, and the outer boundary falls at the distance of an extended forearm. Body orientation is generally at right angles or greater, with a side-to-side orientation not at all uncommon.[24]

There is a close phase and far phase of intimate distance, and the nurse working in critical care moves between them. Because nurses do technical procedures to the aged patient, they enter the close-phase intimate distance. When a nurse starts intravenous feeding, takes blood pressures, or inserts a Foley catheter, he or she has entered into an intimate distance close phase. The close phase involves touch and manipulation of the aged patient's skin, but too frequent intrusions upon intimate territory (for example, taking frequent vital signs) may cause anger. I have previously pointed out that the readiness to fight is greatest in the middle of a person's own territory. The patient must be verbally prepared before the nurse enters into his or her intimate-close phase territory. The nurse must also assess the appropriateness of frequent intrusions upon that territory. Rather than intruding into the patient's territory uninvited, it is wise for the nurse to ask permission to enter.

I have observed that the aged patient, more than other patients, relies heavily on tactile involvement; the nurse should use touch, and then the two territories, the nurse's and the patient's, overlap. Because touch has significance to both people involved, it may not be seen as intrusive. Important ways of using touch are: (1) ambulating the patient with arms around him or her, (2) combing the hair, (3) shaving him, (4) putting lotion on the feet, or (5) simply holding hands.

I myself have found the intimate-far phase extremely useful when working with aged patients in critical care. Hall defines intimate distance far phase as being a distance of 6 to 16 inches. At this distance the aged patient is able to see, touch, and hear the nurse. This is imperative for the aged patient who has loss of hearing or loss of vision. The patient is able to touch the nurse and know the voice is connected to a body. Also the close phase offers the aged patient a feeling of security and protection against harmful stimuli. This may well serve to meet needs for belonging, for closeness to a human being who has become significant. At the close phase, the nurse is able to touch the patient in an effort to convey warmth, caring, and understanding.

Personal Distance

As the severity of the illness subsides, and as the older client is able to increase activity and territorial exploration, the nurse may use personal distance close phase, a distance of $1\frac{1}{2}$ to $2\frac{1}{2}$ feet, which Hall describes as personal-close on his chart of informal distance classification.[25] The nurse uses personal-close phase to help the aged patient ambulate around the bed or to the bathroom.

It is at the personal close distance that the patient can reach the environment props located on the night stand. But the patient may not be allowed to reach the night stand if, for example, this activity would increase the need for oxygen, which in turn causes an increase in the workload of an already injured myocardium. The aged patient who no longer needs the bedpan, can be assisted to the bathroom and is able to lay territorial claim to it. This is also a good time for the nurse to increase the perception of territory by showing where the patient's clothes are hung and by allowing the patient to check out the night stand. As the older person increases immediate territorial adaptation—the area around bed and room—the chances of territorial disorientation are decreased. When the immediate territory is assimilated, the nurse may further increase the patient's awareness by ambulation around the critical care unit. If the critical care unit is a closed unit, or closed-in space, the patient can still be shown where the nurse's center of territory, the nurse's station, is located.

SUMMARY

The territorial and spatial adaptations of aged patients in critical care have been compared with those of younger patients. As pointed out earlier, one major difference the nurse finds between the average patient and the aged patient is the aged person's decreased sensory apparatus. All persons use their senses to lay territorial claim and maintain spatial orientation. I discussed ways the aged patient uses space uniquely; for example, clutter, environmental props, and possessiveness. I purposely used the word "uniquely" because *the aged patient does use territory and space differently than other patients.*

I believe that the nurse must intervene to decrease or control technological overstimulation and territorial deprivation, and to promote territorial adaptation as soon as possible. A skilled nurse brings together

Dr. Smock/George Lemont

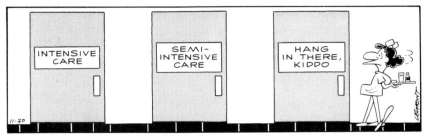

two territorial boundaries—the nurses's and the aged patient's. The nurse symbolically lays territorial claim for the aged patients until they are able to do so for themselves; this is especially important because, while younger patients usually have a significant other to help them with their territorial adaptation, older ones may not. Finally, the nurse uses the aged patient's sense of intimate and personal space to increase feelings of security, protection, and closeness, all of which are vitally important in broadening territorial orientation.

REFERENCES

1 Margaret L. Pluckhan, "Space: The Silent Language," *Nursing Forum*, vol. 7, no. 4, p. 393, 1969.
2 Irwin Altman, "Territorial Behavior in Humans: An Analysis of the Concept," in Leon Pastalan and Daniel H. Carson (eds.), *Spatial Behavior of Older People*, University of Michigan, Ann Arbor, 1970, p. 3.
3 Ibid., p. 4.
4 Edward T. Hall, *The Hidden Dimension*, Doubleday, Garden City, N.Y., 1966, p. 7.
5 Barbara Mickley, "Space and Place in Patient Care," *American Journal of Nursing*, vol. 68, no. 3, p. 511, March 1968.
6 Konrad Lorenz, *On Aggression*, Harcourt Brace and World, New York, 1966, p. 32.
7 Leon Pastalan, "Spatial Behavior: An Overview," *Spatial Behavior of Older People*, University of Michigan, Ann Arbor, 1970, p. 212.
8 Pluckhan, op. cit., pp. 386–387.
9 Robert Beck, "Spatial Meaning and the Properties of the Environment," in H. M. Proshansky, W. H. Ittleson, and L. G. Rivlin (eds), *Environmental Psychology: Man and His Physical Setting*, Holt, Rinehart and Winston, New York, 1970, p. 136.
10 Pastalan, op. cit., p. 89.
11 Robert W. Davis, "Psychologic Aspects of Geriatric Nursing," *American Journal of Nursing*, vol. 68, no. 4, p. 802, April 1968.

12 Lorenz, op. cit., p. 46.
13 Raymond Struder, "The Organizational Spatial Stimuli," *Spatial Behavior of Older People*, University of Michigan, Ann Arbor, 1970, p. 102.
14 Alton J. DeLong, "The Micro-Spatial Structure of the Older Person: Some Implications of Planning the Social and Spatial Environment," *Spatial Behavior of Older People*, University of Michigan, Ann Arbor, 1970, p. 83.
15 R. Barton, "The Patient's Personal Territory," *Hospital and Community Psychiatry*, vol. 17, p. 336, 1966.
16 Julius Fast, *Body Language*, M. Evans, New York, 1971, p. 43.
17 Hall, op. cit., p. 40.
18 DeLong, op. cit., p. 86.
19 Ibid., pp. 69-70.
20 Hall, op. cit., p. 40.
21 Louis Gelwicks, "Home Range and Use of Space by an Aging Population," *Spatial Behavior of Older People*, University of Michigan, Ann Arbor, 1970, p. 152.
22 Edward Hall, *The Silent Language*, Doubleday, New York, 1959, p. 160.
23 Ibid., pp. 110-120.
24 DeLong, op. cit., p. 72.
25 Hall, *The Silent Language,* op. cit., p. 118.

BIBLIOGRAPHY

Ardrey, Robert: *The Territorial Imperative*, Dell, New York, 1966, pp. 15-26.
Chodil, Judith: "The Concept of Sensory Deprivation," *Nursing Clinics of North America*, pp. 453-465, September 1970.
DeMeyer, JoAnna: "The Environment of the Intensive Care Unit," *Nursing Forum*, vol. 6, no. 3, pp. 262-272, 1967.
Engebretson, Darold: "Human Territorial Behavior: The Role of Interaction Distance in Therapeutic Interventions," *American Journal of Orthopsychiatry*, vol. 43, pp. 108-116, January 1973.
Felipe, N. J.: "Invasion of Personal Space," *Social Problems*, vol. 14, pp. 206-214, 1966.
Leigh, Hoyle: "A Psychological Comparison of Patients in Open and Closed Coronary Care Units," *Journal of Psychosomatic Research*, vol. 16, pp. 449-457, 1972.
Levine, Myra: "The Pursuit of Wholeness," *American Journal of Nursing,* vol. 69, no. 1, pp. 93-98, January 1969.
Roberts, Sharon L.: "The Patient's Adaptation to the Coronary Care Unit," *Nursing Forum*, vol. 9, no. 1, pp. 56-63, 1970.
_____: *Behavioral Concepts and the Critically Ill Patient*, Prentice-Hall, Englewood Cliffs, N.J., 1976.
_____: *Behavioral Concepts and Nursing Throughout the Life Span*, Prentice-Hall, Englewood Cliffs, N.J., 1978.
Roe, Anne: *Behavior and Evolution,* Yale University Press, New Haven, 1958.
Sommer, Robert: *Personal Space*, Prentice-Hall, Englewood Cliffs, N.J., 1969.

Chapter 15

To Die or Not to Die: Plight of the Aged Patient in the Critical Care Unit

Sharon L. Roberts

Anatomy of a Death

Tonight
a man was dying
I felt his life
as it slid away
I watched
the fear
in your faces,
coupled
with the drama.
You were very
well versed
in pathology
you taught me
very well,
but I couldn't
take away my eyes
from his door.
. . . .

I do not understand
these tears,

I hardly knew
this man
except inside
a part has changed—
to watch a man
die alone,
his family grieve
alone,
to run away
because I feared
I'd never fill
the space.
My life goes on
as it always has
except there'll
be one change
I'll never run away again.
You see—
he squeezed
my hand.

Carole Estabrooks

Reprinted with permission from *The Canadian Nurse*, vol. 73, no. 10, October 1977.

Traditionally, the attitude of a society toward death has been a function of its religious beliefs. To the extent that theological or sacred doctrines prevail within the society, death generally does not constitute an important challenge to human beings' self-concept. The individual regards death as natural and preordained. Within such a theoretical structure, we could stand relatively secure in the knowledge that death was a personal matter between God and ourselves. According to Fulton, "The very purposefulness of his death placed him at the center of existence and elevated him above all other creatures as the principal subject of creation."[1] Death could be confronted openly, spoken of freely, and treated as a natural phenomenon. The context within which death is experienced in the United States, and the general reaction to death, have changed dramatically within the last few decades. For example, in this country death is no longer exclusively a matter of religious concern, but increasingly a subject of scientific investigation.

Philosophers have assumed that death pertains to the essence of human life, to its existential fulfillment.

> Moreover, the comprehended acceptance of death was considered as the prerogative of man, the very token of his freedom. Death, and only death, brought existence into its own. Its final negation was considered as the affirmation of man's faculties and ends.[2]

> Death assumes the force of an institution which, because of its vital utility, should not be changed, even if it could perhaps be changed. The species perpetuates itself through the death of individuals; this is fact. Society perpetuates itself through the death of individuals; this is no longer a natural but an historical fact. The two facts are not equivalent. In the first proposition, death is a biological event: disintegration of organic into inorganic matter. In the second proposition, death is an institution and a value: the cohesion of the social order depends to a considerable extent on the effectiveness with which individuals comply with death as more than a natural necessity; on their willingness, even urge, to die many deaths which are not natural; on their agreement to sacrifice themselves and not to fight death "too much."[3]

Death remains a reality which relatively few people accept or face. We try to live as if it could not happen to us or to those whom we love. At the same time we live under a primitive shadow of fear. When the death of a parent, child, or loved one occurs, we suffer not only grief but also a sense of guilt for not having done more, or for past feelings and thoughts. During the present decade a new medical specialty has begun to emerge, known as *thanatology*, or the psychosociology of death. Nurses, physicians, psychologists, and social workers are studying and attending to the psychosocial problems faced by patients who are threatened with death,

"I noticed that shot was to sedate you. Are they getting you ready for an operation or checkout?"

Figure 15-1 Decisions in medicine and nursing must be made in light of the alternatives. There must be scrupulous attention to details, and knowledge and appreciation of the economic, social, moral, pathological, and psychological implications. The above cartoon speaks to the economic aspects of acute hospital care. *(Reprinted courtesy of the Chicago Tribune.)*

problems which also must be faced by their families, friends, and associates.

The individual realizes that death is inevitable. It is a phenomenon associated with life itself. What one doesn't know is when or how one's own death will occur. Many individuals intellectualize death as if it pertains to another death, and not to themselves. This is because we are basically future-oriented, planning the future as if we will live forever. While one is free of illness and the threat of a limited future, such behavior is normal. It does not imply denial. However, as losses of functions or parts of the body occur, death and denial sometimes become fused together. Denial for many individuals is a coping mechanism, one that enables them to guard against the threat of death or dying.

Few decisions in medicine can be made without thoughtful consideration of alternatives (see Fig. 15-1). The physician's role implies scrupulous attention to minute detail, as well as intimate knowledge of, and appreciation for, the economic, social, moral, pathological, and physiologic aspects of humanity. When medical science cannot make us well, it can often keep the catastrophic diseases from killing us, in the traditional sense. The machines await. When your lungs give out, a shiny new volume respirator will be wheeled in to pump air into your lungs and suck it back out again. If you cannot eat or even digest food, an ingenious process known as "total parenteral nutrition will catheterize your veins and inject nutrients directly into your bloodstream, drop by drop around the clock. If your heart refuses to beat, electric pacemakers will circulate your blood."[4]

The personal threat that death presents for the physician can best be illustrated by the enormous activity which is directed in hospitals toward the prolongation of life, and which acts as a mechanical barrier to the patient himself. One particular category of patient is almost inevitably confronted with the issue of prolongation of life. This is the aged patient who enters the highly technical, life-saving environment of the critical care unit. It should be emphasized that many aged patients enter critical care with the desire, will, and motivation to live as long as possible. They are usually people who have been relatively healthy all their lives and for whom illness is simply a nuisance or a waste of valuable time. Such patients are eager to return to their homes, families, social activities, dogs and cats, etc., no doubt motivated by several positive peripheral factors in their lives. One factor may be that they have been free from repeated, debilitating illness. Another may be that a spouse is home waiting for the aged patient to return. Because this portion of the aged population in critical care has a strong motivation to live, their wishes should be acknowledged and respected. On the other hand, I have seen and cared for aged patients who, because of chronic debilitating illnesses, enter critical care without the desire, will, or motivation to live. The nurse may hear these patients say, "Please let me alone," or "Let me die in peace." Often nurses will attempt to instill the desire to live, even though the patient has already chosen to die. Positive peripheral factors such as a spouse, or a family to give the desire to live, or social activities may not be operating in this group.

Death usually represents finality, the end of one's biological being, but for some it can represent a spiritual beginning. At some point in time the patient's fear of dying evolves into a fear of death. "Fear of death is not an immediate event, but rather a reflection about man's helplessness. . . . As a rule, fears about death are much stronger than the evidence produced by actual disease and invalidism."[5] Those who remain after the patient has died, usually the members of the family and the health team, go through the process of mourning.

The material presented and the stance I take apply only to those aged patients who desire to die. There are times when we, as professionals, go against the aged patients' wishes and prolong their death, thinking we are in fact prolonging their life. Death can be a beautiful, positive experience for elderly patients and their families. A crucial factor in helping the aged patient and family (if there is a family) prepare for death is the way in which the nurse accepts death.

PROLONGING LIFE OR DEATH
OF THE AGED PATIENT IN CRITICAL CARE

Many people think that the dying process only pertains to the aged and terminally ill. But terminal illness also applies to patients whose biological system progressively deteriorates toward total failure. The dying process is longer for some patients than for others.

> Dying becomes an important, noticeable process insofar as it serves to provide others, as well as the patient, with a way to orient to the future, to organize activities around the expectability of death, to prepare for it. The notion of dying appears to be a distinctly social one, for its central relevance is provided for by the fact that it establishes a way of attending a person.[6]

The American public in general has certain notions about what constitutes courageous behavior in the patient, as the possibility of death approaches. Such notions require that the patient maintain relative composure and cheerfulness or, at the very least, face death with dignity. The patient should not break contact with the world, nor turn away from the living; if there is a family, the patient should continue to be a good family member. The patient should be "nice" to other patients also, cooperate with the staff members who provide care, and avoid distressing either group. In critical care, nurses frequently hear family members say to the aged patient, "Now, Papa, be nice to the little nurse. Do what she says and don't complain." It may be, however, that complaining or arguing with the nurse is the only control "Papa" feels he has over the situation; he may be physically too weak to fight, so his control takes the form of verbal abuse. The nurse may be controlling him through pacemaker, dialysis, or intravenous feedings; in return, he is controlling his nurse through yelling, or pushing his light frequently.

Loss or the threat of loss can be a new experience for the aged patient. The loss can be the result of acute illness, chronic disability, or terminal process. Regardless of the cause, the patient may be unable to fulfill psychological or physiological needs. Illness is an inconvenience for the aged patient who must temporarily submit ownership of the body to others. The patient depends upon the nurse to be fed, bathed, turned, or assisted to the bathroom. As the illness or disease process increases in severity or chronicity, the patient may be totally dependent upon others. "For most people, sickness is uncomfortable, inconvenient, temporary, but rarely a menace. But, if sickness persists, enduring beyond the healing effects of treatment and time, the personal dimensions of being sick gradually become more conspicuous."[7]

Older patients do not always interpret the nurse's interventions as helping ones, especially if all they want to do is die. By treating them with the use of various pieces of equipment, exposing and manipulating their bodies, we destroy dignity in the aged. As Smith states, the elderly patient must relinquish

> ownership of his body and passively permit it to be handled and manipulated by those who purpose to nurse him back to health. He is dressed and undressed . . . he is washed like an infant; while his bed is made he is pulled and pushed from one side to the other; the process of urination and defecation are suddenly no longer private affairs; and he is subjected to the final indignity of having his nakedness exposed to the hospital personnel regardless of their sex.[8]

In critical care units, nurses further isolate this age group by limiting not only the number of visitors, but also who can visit. Only the immediate family is permitted; this is hospital policy. The family member rarely has time within the allotted 5 to 10 minutes to get comfortable with the environment. A visitor to a critical care unit may be appalled; typewriters tap away, bells ring, lights flash, and the whole milieu appears to be one of crisis, with very little human contact. At the time when patients are most critically ill, the support and visits of family, friends, and relatives are severely curtailed, and the closest thing to them is a monitoring machine. If family members do manage to adjust to stepping around pieces of cumbersome equipment, the aged patient may make them feel even more uncomfortable than before by statements like, "I wish they would let me die of old age."

Instead of orienting the patient to the new environment and thus encouraging cooperation, we may create confusion through overstimulation by strange sounds, lights, and equipment, or by giving tranquilizers which promote further isolation. In the world of sleep or withdrawal, the patient is not given the opportunity to talk about death with the family, or express love for them or satisfaction with their devotion, before a potential crisis occurs. As a result, those unsaid words may haunt the children during and after the crisis. The patient's inability to speak about death may motivate the family to seek heroics at any cost.

Critical care units in any hospital, with their atmosphere of heroic recovery, are geared towards prolonging life at almost any cost. Equipment is clustered near every bed, so that prolonging may be just a matter of leaning over and "hooking the patient up." The atmosphere in such units counters staff attempts to make the patients comfortable and let them die. As Fletcher has beautifully said, "It is the living that fear death, not the dying."[9]

Some doctors feel that a patient's death puts their professional competence, rather than the state of medical knowledge generally, in question, and as a consequence they will not relinquish the recovery goal until they feel assured that their own skills . . . are not at issue. A favorite rationale of the doctor who persists in the ideal of indefinite prolonging is the assertion that he is simply an instrument of society. He feels that society has vested in him the duty of sustaining life, and that he is therefore obligated to abdicate personal responsibility for judging the advisability of whether a particular life should or should not be prolonged.[10]

The aged, those most prone to die, are moving in increasing numbers toward segregated retirement communities to await their fate—almost in the same manner as lepers once did. However, many aged people become ill, sometimes critically ill, and so find themselves in critical care units. Prior to entering the critical care unit, aged persons had control over their destinies. If an elderly person had a heart condition and chose not to follow the doctor's orders, the consequences were known; the choice was voluntary. However, in critical care the choice, it seems, is no longer the patient's.

Although the medical ideal of prolonging life at any cost conflicts with the awareness that prolonging life may be both useless and unduly expensive, the ideal often wins out. According to Glaser and Strauss, one physician stated: "There are too many instances . . . in which patients in such a situation are kept alive indefinitely by means of tubes inserted into their stomachs, or into their veins, or into their bladder, or into their rectums—and the whole sad scene thus created is encompassed with a cocoon of oxygen which is the next thing to a shroud . . ."[11]

The patient whose loss results in denying and death becomes aware of a limited future sooner than the family or sometimes the health team. After all, the aged patient is living within the body that is experiencing a biological loss. Elmore points out: "To the extent that the individual perceives and interprets the nature of the internal messages and is consequently able to plot the rate of decline, and to extend this declining curve from the present into the future to a terminal point—to this extent we can speak of a premonition of death . . ."[12] The internal messages received by the patient are constant. They keep the aged patient continuously informed about biological stability or decline. No matter how hard a patient may try to deny it, he or she cannot avoid the close monitoring of biological events with the body. Therefore, the internal messages contribute to awareness. As the messages become more intense, the patient begins to accept the reality of death.

There follow three case studies of aged patients, all of whom had lost both their sense of dignity and their will to live. In each example, the aged patient specifically expressed the desire to die. This was manifested both verbally by such statements as, "Let me die; I have lived long enough," and nonverbally by attempting to pull out their pacemaker wires or tracheostomy tubes. All three had lost control over their own destiny and dignity. Nevertheless, the medical staff and family assumed the responsibility, delegated or not, to plan the aged patient's destiny. The original goal, of course, was to prolong life; however, after various crises developed, the goal was still not changed. But the medical staff and family, while thinking they were prolonging life, were actually prolonging death.

CASE EXAMPLE 1   Mrs. Z was an elderly woman in her seventies who had lived alone for 8 years after her husband died. She had two devoted married daughters. They checked on her at her home daily. Mrs. Z had a heart condition and had been forced to limit her activity. Since Mrs. Z seemed to function adequately within her limitations, the daughters decided their mother could continue to live alone. One day, after a morning's shopping, the daughters made their usual daily check to see if their mother needed anything from the grocery store. When they entered her home, they were horrified to find her lying on the living room floor. Mrs. Z's pulse was weak and thready, her color dusky, her skin cool and moist, and she was unconscious. Their impression was that she had fallen and hit her head. The daughters immediately called an ambulance and the mother was admitted to the critical care unit of a local hospital.

An electrocardiogram performed shortly after admission revealed that Mrs. Z had suffered an acute myocardial infarction. A skull series taken later revealed no cerebral damage. Shortly after Mrs. Z was admitted to critical care, she regained consciousness. During the next 24 hours her condition was critical. She experienced bradycardia with frequent premature ventricular contraction; her chest pain was unrelieved by a hypodermic of morphine sulfate $\frac{1}{6}$ g given intravenously. She finally experienced first degree heart block.

Mrs. Z's daughters remained at the hospital continuously. Visiting rules in critical care allowed them to see their mother for 5 minutes hourly. No other visitors were allowed to see her. Mrs. Z remained semiconscious, even though she was heavily sedated because of her continuous chest pain. During the daughters' allotted visits, she said repeatedly, "Tell them to let me die; I have lived long enough." At other times she would say both to her daughters, and to the staff as well, "I have been so lonely since George died." The daughters would try to lighten the situation, and perhaps their guilt feelings, by saying, "You are doing better, Mother; now don't talk; just rest."

In the subsequent hours Mrs. Z, still not free of pain, developed atrial-ventricular disassociation. Because Mrs. Z was heavily sedated with morphine, the physicians communicated the urgent new problem to Mrs. Z's daughters; they were told it was imperative that their mother have a temporary pacemaker. There was, moreover, the possiblity the pacemaker would be permanent. The daughters, well aware that if their mother were alert she would have refused the procedure, went ahead and signed the consent. During the insertion of her temporary pacemaker, Mrs. Z developed ventricular fibrillation; she was defibrillated three times. After the resuscitation, Mrs. Z lapsed into unconsciousness and it became necessary to intubate her and assist her respirations with a volume respirator. Later it was determined that Mrs. Z had developed a cardiovascular accident post-resuscitation. She remained unresponsive and was being kept alive by various pieces of equipment, the pacemaker, and the volume respirator.

CASE EXAMPLE 2   Mr. B was an 80-year-old man with chronic emphysema. He had lived with his son and daughter-in-law for the past 3 years. During that time Mr. B's condition rapidly deteriorated. His activity was greatly limited; he spent most of his time in front of a television set. Mr. B developed an upper respiratory tract infection which necessitated his admission to the hospital. While he was on the general floor, his condition worsened. His color was cyanotic, his breathing was labored, with sternal stridor, and he became increasingly more lethargic; blood gases revealed an increasing pCO_2 and decreasing pO_2. Because his clinical picture was rapidly deteriorating, and because his physicians felt a tracheostomy might be necessary, Mr. B was transferred to the critical care unit.

Mr. B seemed to understand what was happening to him. His son told the staff that his father simply "wants to die," that he "feels his life is useless this way." Approximately 2 hours after Mr. B arrived in critical care, the doctors decided on a tracheostomy to facilitate his breathing. Thirty minutes later, Mr. B had a tracheostomy and was breathing with the assistance of a volume respirator.

The nursing staff realized that this procedure only served to prolong Mr. B's dying, not his life. After 4 days of continuous use of the respirator, Mr. B was still unable to breathe independently. When he was taken off the respirator for tracheostomy care or suction, he became extremely cyanotic. Mr. B became discouraged; by the nonverbal communication of his nurses, doctors, and son he could tell that the situation was hopeless. Mr. B, with a shaking hand, wrote this question to his son, "Why don't they let me die?" The nurses knew that the longer Mr. B was dependent on the respirator, the less likely were his chances of being weaned off the machine. On the night shift Mr. B made several attempts to pull off his respirator and remove his tracheostomy tube. Mr. B became increasingly lethargic, and eventually comatose. The staff felt Mr. B had willed himself to die. His cardioscope pattern changed to bradycardia and finally asystole. Mr. B had finally achieved his goal—death.

CASE EXAMPLE 3 Mrs. A, a 74-year-old widow, was admitted to a critical care unit with a diagnosis of heart failure, pulmonary edema, and arrhythmias. Mrs. A was alone and without family. She lived in a senior citizen community several miles away from the hospital; therefore, it was almost impossible for her friends to see her. She had had previous infarctions over the past 3 years, and each time it took progressively longer for her to recover. During the first 12 hours, Mrs. A's arrhythmias varied between first and second degree heart block. Finally Mrs. A developed a complete heart block. The decision was made to insert an emergency pacemaker. The pacemaker was inserted without complications. Physiologically Mrs. A's pacemaker worked; however, psychologically Mrs. A deteriorated. The staff were unable to get her to eat, talk, or ambulate in her room. The staff noted that Mrs. A kept saying that she was ready to die. She finally told a nurse that "to live with a pacemaker is not really living at all—I wish I had died in peace at home." Mrs. A created much commotion as she attempted to pull out her pacemaker wires. The nursing staff restrained her hands, but Mrs. A had much strength and determination, and she continued to try to free herself from the restraints. Mrs. A chose to die sooner, rather than later, if she herself could succeed in making the decision. As the days progressed, Mrs. A became weaker and weaker. The nursing staff believed that Mrs. A, like Mr. B, had willed herself to die.

One must keep in mind that there are also those aged persons who enter critical care units with both the desire and the will to live. As I previously mentioned, their wish is respected by both medical and nursing personnel, because it corresponds to the medical staff's philosophy about saving lives.

However, when an aged patient wants to die, problems arise for the intensive care staff. The wish of such patients does not correspond to the wishes of the doctors and nurses; yet the latter largely control the destiny of the patient. The aged patient wants to die, as described in each of the case examples. Mrs. Z, Mr. B, and Mrs. A were also examples of the common problem of loss of the right to die with dignity. Mrs. Z, who was unconscious and dependent upon a respirator and pacemaker, suffered from a loss of self-respect. She continued in a state of absolute dependence upon doctors, nurses, family, and special equipment, long after the meaning of life had been lost. Each of these patients at some point in time expressed the desire to terminate their life by pulling out the pacemaker wires or tracheostomy tube. The right to choose death, it seemed, was taken away from the aged patient in all cases. For example, Mrs. Z's devoted daughters wanted a pacemaker inserted, even though they knew their mother would have refused it had she had the opportunity. The staff discouraged Mrs. A from pulling her pacemaker wires by restraining her hands.

In critical care units nurses do meet families like Mrs. Z's. Such families beg for impossible, heroic measures. The nursing and medical staff may need to go along with the family until the family can understand that such measures may not be the wisest choice. If the aged patient is being kept alive by equipment, the doctors have greater control over his life than in the case of natural prolonging of life. The doctor also has more time to plan, to calculate risks, and to negotiate with the family and nurses. Although the medical ideal of prolonging life at all costs and with all possible facilities conflicts with the awareness that prolonging life may be useless, unduly painful, and unduly expensive, the ideal often wins out.

THE NURSE'S ROLE

The nurse needs to assist the patient in adapting to the loss. The nurse realizes that the loss can imply a threatening fatal disease and a diminishing self-worth. Weisman states that "the healing effect of treatment and time are not his. Therefore, as his illness progresses, he is forced to settle for less and less, to compromise his expectations, and to become less than what he had been or might be. Finally, survival becomes an end in itself."[13]

When everyone, especially the family, is aware that there is "nothing more to do" the goal of recovery has, in effect, been changed to a goal of comfort. This seems to me the ideal time for ceasing to prolong the dying aged patient's life. In the case of Mrs. Z and Mr. B, the treatments were geared towards prolonging death. Of course, in critical care units the means by which the aged patient is allowed to die depend on whether life is being prolonged naturally or by equipment. In the case of Mrs. Z, the daughters practically begged for heroic measures. In such a case, the critical care nurse has a tremendous responsibility to aid the family to understand the hopelessness of the situation. The nurse can convey to the family how the terminally ill aged person is progressing. By keeping family or significant others continually informed of the acuteness of the situation, the nurse also psychologically prepares the family for the eventual death of the aged person. It is at this time that the nurse can be an attentive listener to the child, or children. Many times a member of the family will want to share memories of a parent with the nurse. Allowing the family to discuss pleasant memories, to reminisce, will help the family accept termination with the dying aged patient. This is part of facilitating their awareness of the aged patient's potential death; it initiates some of the "grief work," and perhaps makes it easier when the time comes to turn off the equipment.

Many times the patient is aware of a potential problem prior to its confirmation by a professional. Likewise, the same individual remains aware of the body's altered state throughout the illness or disease process. It is because of the aged patient's body perceptors that the patient is able to assess the seriousness of the illness or disease. This is a significant variable for the nurse to utilize when intervening to assist the aged patient and family through a difficult time.

There are times when the family requests that the patient not be informed of the seriousness of an illness or disease. The patient may realize that the illness or disease is serious, but wants to protect the family from the pain of potential or eventual death. Therefore, the loss is avoided through jovial behavior. As previously pointed out, the patient wants to maintain a positive self-image. Likewise, the family, thinking it is protecting the patient, avoids discussion of loss or threat of further loss. Both are aware of loss, but each avoids open discussion. The nurse should assess the readiness of each to begin sharing support with each other, and encourage patient and family to openly acknowledge the loss and its implications. Together they can begin resolving it.

The family often seeks reassurance that everything that can be done is currently being done for the aged patient. The nurse can reinforce their feelings, that, yes, everything is or has been done. Such feedback assists the family not to request heroics based on their own guilt feelings. Families who react, instead of act, because of feelings of having not done more for their parent often drain their financial resources. Hospitalization in critical care is expensive enough; but the expense of various pieces of equipment used to prolong death can be astronomical. In some instances families may pay financially for years for having tried to assuage guilt by requesting heroic measures.

The family may put the critical care nurse on the defensive by asking if their aged parent is better, or will get better. Many times, if it is hard to respond honestly, the nurse will resort to clichés such as, "You never know about these things," or "Why don't you ask your doctor?" Unfortunately the family may rarely see their physician, who may also have given up on the aged patient, as in the case of Mrs. Z, realizing that the prognosis was terminal. If the family does manage to get hold of their doctor, they may not understand the professional jargon. Nurses often act as translators for medical jargon.

The family may be caught in a double bind of wanting to do what is best, but not realizing what *is* best for their aged parent. As the family begins to understand that their aged parent is being kept alive by equipment, they may ask the staff to stop treatments which result in the useless prolonging of life. When the family or doctors decide to turn off the pacemaker or respirators, the family should be present in either the waiting room or the patient's room. If the family is at home when the doctors make their decision to turn off life-prolonging equipment, the family may have guilt feelings about their aged parent dying alone surrounded by unyielding pieces of equipment.

The nurse is usually the single individual who mediates between family, significant others, patient, and physicians, and who may support the physician in making the decision to turn off death-prolonging equipment. At the same time the nurse may help the family to see that the doctor's decision is the most humane one they could possibly make. Many nurses are caught in a pull between the task of lifesaving at all costs and a desire to provide the patient with a dignified and human death. I believe that in the future nurses will face more, rather than fewer, problems in which the central issue is whether to prolong the aged patient's life. For this reason, we need to move towards interdependence of medical and nursing staff. The physician and nurse must no longer function independently; instead, the responsibility should lie with both in critical care units. Sitting down together to assess each aged patient's potential for living or dying based upon the patient's prognosis and personal wishes and the family's feelings seems a good way to begin such a shared responsibility.

A patient's family can be a supportive asset throughout the illness or disease process. The patient can draw upon the family's strength. In this respect, they can help the patient cope with a difficult situation. The nurse realizes that "the response of the family and other meaningful people to the patient's illness or disability, to his communications of distress, and to his mobility to perform the usual social roles may spell the difference between optimal recovery or psychological invalidism."[14] However, the nurse should remember that the family can become emotionally depleted. Therefore, it becomes important to offer the family as much assistance as offered to the patient. The family needs to be continually apprised of the patient's biological status. If this is not done, the family may develop unrealistic expectations that the patient's loss is not serious but temporary. In the latter instance, the family may request heroic measures even when they will not alter the disease process.

There is a need for ministers, physicians, and nurses to discuss the concept of loss or humane death and the issue of prolonging life. As openness toward the once-taboo topic of death increases, nurses, physicians, and ministers may be able to decide under what conditions termination of life-prolonging techniques and procedures is appropriate for the aged patient, and they may also feel better about the decisions they shared in and carried out.

REFERENCES

1   Robert Fulton, "Death and the Self," *Journal of Religion and Health*, vol. 3, no. 4, p. 359, July 1964.
2   Herman Feifel, *The Meaning of Death*, McGraw-Hill, New York, 1959, p. 66.

3 Ibid., p. 74.
4 Wayne Sage, "Choosing the Good Death," in Harold Cox (ed.), *Focus: Aging,* Dushkin, Conn., 1978, p. 188.
5 Avery Weisman, *On Dying and Denying,* Behavioral Publications, New York, 1972, p. 14.
6 David Sudnow, *Passing On: The Social Organization of Dying,* Prentice-Hall, Englewood Cliffs, N.J., 1967, p. 68.
7 Weisman, op. cit., p. 52.
8 Sydney Smith, "The Psychology of Illness," *Nursing Forum,* vol. 3, no. 2, p. 39, 1964.
9 Joseph Fletcher, "The Patient's Right to Die," *Harper's Magazine,* October 1960, p. 139.
10 Barney Glaser and Anselm Strauss, *Awareness of Dying,* Aldine, Chicago, 1965, p. 202.
11 Ibid., p. 201.
12 James Elmore, "Psychological Reactions to Impending Death," *Hospital Topics,* November 1967, p. 36.
13 Weisman, op. cit., p. 57.
14 Z. J. Lipowski, "Psychosocial Aspects of Disease," *Annals of Internal Medicine,* vol. 71, p. 1200, December 1969.

BIBLIOGRAPHY

Agate, John: "Ethical Questions in Geriatric Care," *Nursing Mirror,* vol. 19, pp. 40–41, November 1971.

Aldrich, Knight: "The Dying Patient's Grief," *Journal of the American Medical Association,* pp. 329–331, May 4, 1963.

Baker, Joan: "A Patient's Concern with Death," *American Journal of Nursing,* vol. 63, no. 7, pp. 90–92, July 1963.

Burnside, Irene: "Multiple Losses in the Aged: Implications for Nursing Care," *The Gerontologist,* vol. 13, no. 2, pp. 157–162, Summer 1973.

Engel, George: "Is Grief a Disease?" *Psychosomatic Medicine,* pp. 18–22, 1961.

————: "Grief and Grieving," *American Journal of Nursing,* vol. 64, no. 9, pp. 93–98, September 1964.

Glaser, Barney: "The Social Loss of Dying Patients," *American Journal of Nursing,* vol. 64, no. 6, pp. 119–121, June 1964.

Gramlich, Edwin: "Recognition and Management of Grief in Elderly Patients," *Geriatrics,* pp. 87–92, July 1968.

Kneisl, Ren Carol: "Thoughtful Care for the Dying," *American Journal of Nursing,* vol. 68, no. 2, pp. 550–553, March 1968.

Popoff, David: "What Are Your Feelings about Death and Dying," *Nursing '75,* August 1975.

Roberts, Sharon L.: *Behavioral Concepts and Nursing Throughout the Life Span,* Prentice-Hall, Englewood Cliffs, N.J., 1968.

Schultz, Richard: "Clinical Research and the Stages of Dying," *Omega,* vol. 5, pp. 137–143, 1974.

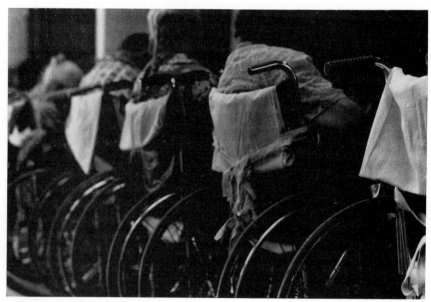

Courtesy of Harvey Finkle.

Part Four

The Aged Person in a Long-Term Care Facility

Being ill in a nursing home became my next task, a sombre dance in which I knew some of the steps. I must conform. I must be correct. I must be meek, obedient and grateful, on no account must I be surprising. If I deviated by the breadth of a toothbrush I would be in the wrong.

Florida Scott-Maxwell

Measure of My Days

This section of the book is about the patient who is in an extended care or intermediate care facility. While this often is meant to be only a temporary placement, it may become the final dying place for the aged person, especially the aged individual without an advocate. The sick role of the elderly is explored in Chapter 16 by Ness, who describes an elderly woman's adjustment to an extended care facility.

Group work by a social worker and a nurse to improve the lot of the aged stroke patient in a large metropolitan rehabilitation hospital is discussed in Chapter 17. Schwab, a pioneer in long-term care of the elderly, has written about the implementation of the Standards of Gerontological Nursing Practice. The standards can be found at the end of Chapter 18.

Courtesy of Harvey Finkle.

Chapter 16

The Sick Role
of the Elderly

Katherine M. Ness

What do you see, Nurse, what do you see?
Are you thinking when you look at me—
A crabbit old woman, not very wise

So open your eyes, nurses, open and see
Not a crabbit old woman. Look closer—SEE ME!!

Phyllis M. McCormack

Mrs. Allen, a widowed, retired nurse in her late seventies, was a patient in a nursing home at the time of her death. After years of independence and of "doing for others," she had become increasingly less able to care for herself. The aging process, advanced Parkinson's disease, and arthritis had diminished her capacity to meet even her most ordinary needs. For several months she had resisted the move to the nursing home, but eventually the necessity for the change became too obvious for her children to ignore any longer. "Mother never could accept the fact of her illness and dependency. She literally starved herself to death," reported her son.

A similar story is often told to the nurse or others who care for the elderly in the hospital, the nursing home, or the home. Although it is important to remember that chronic illness and disability are not synonymous with growing old, the fact remains that chronic disease is not distributed randomly in the population, but is associated with older age groups more commonly than with younger ones.[1] In later years, there may be a change in the way of life which is imposed by illness or disability; dependence, either full or partial, may occur.[2] As Ball has stated, "Nursing home residents are very old. Seventy-five percent are 75 or older, and 38% are 85 and older. Women outnumber men in nursing homes 7 to 3, and 64% are widows; for the group over 85, 80% are widows."*

For those of us who are concerned with the care of elderly patients, Mrs. Allen's story raises some crucial questions about the sick role and the adaptive process in long-term illness within the aging population. This chapter is directed to the exploration of these questions. What is the sick role? How does it differ from the role established by society for the acutely ill person? What are some of the adaptations the elderly person must make to the sick role? In order to understand the problems facing the elderly patient, it will be helpful to review the role expectations for the acutely ill patient and for the chronically ill patient.

THE ACUTELY SICK ROLE

The concept of the "social role of the sick person," reports Mechanic, was developed by Sigerist and elaborated by Parsons,[3] and can be defined as "the activity undertaken by those who consider themselves ill for the purpose of getting well. It includes receiving treatment from appropriate therapists, generally involves a whole range of dependent behaviors, and leads to some degree of neglect of one's usual duties."[4] This activity Mechanic has called "illness behavior."[5-7] One of the main criteria of illness, say Parsons and Fox, is that the sick individual is incapacitated, is not able, in some degree, to carry on normal functioning. The person becomes dependent, needing and expecting to be taken care of by stronger, more "adequate" persons. They compare the sick one's state to that of the child in our society. Both are dependent and incapable of meeting their needs through their own resources; both are states that are "legitimized" by society, but there are conditions attached. Thus, sick persons are not considered to be at fault if they fail to perform their normal functions; they are considered to have the "right" to exemption from duties and the "right" to care. However, the sick patient is also expected to "accept the definition of

*Robert M. Ball, "United States Policy toward the Elderly," in A. N. Exton-Smith and J. Grimley Evans (eds.), *Care of the Elderly*, Grune and Stratton, New York, 1977, p. 29.

his state as undesirable and the obligation to get well as expeditiously as possible."[8] Illness is deviant behavior, they say, because it entails passive withdrawal from normal activities and responsibilities, and too frequent resort to the sick role could present a serious danger to our social system.[9] The child, likewise, "is permitted to be childish only temporarily. He accepts the obligation to grow up, even though at times it is very painful, and to cooperate with his parents in helping him to achieve maturity."[10] This analogy between illness and childhood can be pressed too hard, as Parsons and Fox point out.[11] To view the doctor as a "father-figure," and the nurse's role as that of "mother-surrogate," could conceivably contribute to prolonged dependent states in some ill patients, and to the tendency to "talk down" to patients, or otherwise treat them as though, in fact, they were children. This is a danger particularly with elderly patients whose physical, sensory, and mental capacities are diminished.

The sick individual does not simply drop the usual social roles (such as father, student, breadwinner), but adopts a new role that supersedes the others for the duration of the illness. The concept of "role" implies expectations—how the individual in a particular role should behave and how others should behave toward that individual. These expectations are the norms or rules that establish what behavior is allowed, or even obligatory, and what is prohibited; and they apply both to persons in the role and to those who deal with them because they are in the role.[12] Thus the person is not held responsible for incapacity, and is excused from normal obligations. However, because the sick role, though sanctioned by society, is seen as undesirable, the patient is obligated to do all that is possible to get well. In fact, this is so important in our society that we often resort to terms like "malingerer," and "old crock" (especially when describing the aged), putting pressure on individuals to "encourage" them to want to get well.[13] The obligation to do all that is possible to get well means that the patient must engage in illness behavior for the purpose of obtaining help from appropriate and technically competent sources available. In our society technically competent help usually means the doctor, with whom the sick person "negotiates a contract"—agrees to cooperate to get well. Before consulting the doctor, the sick person may not uncommonly use a chain of resources, referred to by Friedson as the "lay referral system." These resources may include family members, friends, the local pharmacist, or other such informal "consultants" in the community.[14]

A number of factors operate in the decision to adopt the sick role and as to whether or not medical aid will be sought. These may be medical or nonmedical in nature. Medical factors are related to the person's perception of the threat the disease holds; perception of susceptibility to the disease; the importance attached to health; the urgency of the symptoms; past experiences with illness; and the value attached to the perceived therapy.[15]

Nonmedical factors may be psychological, social, or cultural in origin. In an extensive review of the literature on sick-role behavior, Kasl and Cobb have identified a number of these nonmedical factors:[16]

Age, sex, race
Marital status
Religious and ethnic background
Self-acceptance
Ways of coping with anxiety
Threshold for pain
Tolerance to disability

The psychological factors of fear and anxiety—and how one has learned to cope with them—are of major significance. Some persons' responsibilities may be so overwhelming to them that their anxiety may exceed their ability to cope. For them, assuming the sick role may provide a socially acceptable release from their responsibilities. Other people may fear the dependence of the sick role, or may be suspicious of doctors, hospitals, nurses, and other medical personnel. Still others may fear the symptoms they are experiencing and therefore refuse the sick role as a form of denial that they are ill. This is particularly true of cancer, as Blackwell found in her review of numerous studies on the delay in seeking medical care.[17] Fear is a potent factor in the delay or refusal to accept the sick role.

Social factors include age, sex, and marital status. The father may ignore or postpone the sick role as long as possible if this would mean missing work and result in hardship for his family. The mother may refuse to go to bed or to seek medical aid if it means disruption of the household and inadequate care of the family. One's social role in the community may interfere. The teacher or minister, for example, may find the pressure of the role in the community too great to assume the sick role, and may try to avoid it as long as possible. The person for whom money is not too great a problem and who can afford the time is more likely to seek medical advice, go to bed, and temporarily give up usual role demands.[18]

The influential relationship between cultural differences and illness behavior has been demonstrated in a number of studies (Saunders,[19] Clark and Anderson,[20] Zborowski,[21] Stoeckle et al.,[22] Apple,[23] and Philips[24]). How one defines illness, the behaviors one learns relating to illness, one's beliefs and attitudes toward particular disorders and symptoms, and one's value of health and wholeness of the body are all cultural determinants of illness behavior and of whether or not one assumes the sick role. Stoeckle et al. reported that a high prevalence of symptoms of bodily disorders in so-called "healthy" populations was the rule rather than the exception, indicating that the lay definitions of health and illness differed from the usual clinical definitions.[25] A study by Apple suggested that to some middle-class Americans "to be ill means to have an ailment of recent origin which interfered with one's usual activities.''[26] There is a potential danger inherent in this concept of illness, since behavior is likely to be delayed, particularly in seeking care for chronic diseases in which the onset of symptoms tends to be insidious. Self-reliance, too, has cultural significance for illness behavior and the sick role. To be self-reliant is a cherished ideal in our value system, and seems to be especially important among older age groups as a determinant of sick-role behavior. Philips found that there is a statistically significant inverse relationship between the emphasis upon self-reliance and the inclination to adopt the sick role, and that older people were less willing than younger ones to adopt it.[27]

THE CHRONICALLY SICK ROLE

> What of the chronically ill individual? Where reality insists that former role resumption is impossible or inadvisable, where circumstances dictate that some degree of dependency will have to be accepted, will some modification of expected sick role performance be necessary?[28]

In the past the problems associated with chronic illness have been little understood. In most general hospitals diagnosis, care, and treatment have been disproportionately dedicated to acute illness and acute episodes of chronic disease, and the "institutionalized professional-patient roles" have centered around the care of acutely ill patients. Now medical personnel who work with chronically diseased patients are recognizing that these roles, although functional with acutely ill patients, are inadequate with chronically ill patients.[29] Today, the complexity of the problems of chronically ill patients, and the frequency of their occurrence, place these problems among the most challenging ones facing the medical profession.[30] It is therefore imperative that more attention be given to the characteristics that differentiate the chronically sick role from the acutely sick role, so that the special needs of these patients can be better understood and met.

Kassebaum and Baumann point to several dimensions of chronic illness which distinguish it from acute illness.

1 By definition chronic illness is not temporary.
2 The performance of other roles is more partial than total, though the sick role may not be the dominant one throughout the illness.
3 The degree of permissiveness in the treatment of the chronically ill person and of exemption from other role obligations, will be different from that of the acutely ill, since prolonged adherence to the usual sick role would pose a threat to the role performance of the patient's family members.
4 The degree of alienation and dependency associated with chronic illness may be different than in the case of the temporary role of acute illness.
5 Chronic illness is associated to a large degree with advancing age.

Moreover, there are similarities between the "typical" expectations of the "aged" role and the "typical" expectations of the sick role, making distinctions between the two very ambiguous.[31] Exploring these dimensions in greater detail may serve to clarify further the differences between the acutely and chronically sick roles.

Chronic disease is not temporary. The character of chronic illness is clearly defined by the National Commission of Chronic Illness in the United States:

> All impairments or deviations from normal which have one or more of the following characteristics: Are permanent; leave residual disability; are caused by nonreversible pathological alterations; require special training of the patient for rehabilitation; may be expected to require a long period of supervision, observation, or care.[32]

The nonreversibility of its pathology, the permanence of disability leading to change in body image, and the long period of supervision, observation, or care are major medical determinants of the chronically sick role. Added to these characteristics is the insidiousness of the onset of symptoms. Whereas acute illness may have greater threat to the life of the individual, and the symptoms may require more urgent attention than in chronic disease, the delay in engaging in illness behavior to obtain treatment in the case of chronic disease may be just as detrimental in the long run to the health of the patient. Prolonged delay may mean that therapy is too late to be effective, and the chances of disability may be increased as with arthritis, cancer, and heart disease.

Psychologically, the implications of the indeterminate nature of the sick role for the chronically ill patient may be more devastating than for the acutely ill patient, whose role is clear and prescribed. The ambiguity implied in partial performance of the sick role and partial performance of normal social roles could certainly increase the patient's anxiety. Confusion on the part of the patient and those close to him or her about how the patient should perform may lead to unrealistic expectations for role performance. When encountering increasing difficulty in meeting the responsibilities of social roles, the patient is likely to become frustrated, give up, and sink into depression and hopelessness. Self-concept may be shattered as the patient becomes more and more dependent. If the individual is passive, with strong dependency needs, there may be lack of motivation to engage in illness behavior and the individual may be content to make the sick role and total dependence on others a way of life.[33] All of these points have special significance for the aged patient and need to be considered when planning for particular needs.

As previously mentioned, fear is a potent determinant of illness behavior. Fear of being totally disabled and of long and expensive medical care has a serious psychological impact on the chronically ill patient. Fear of being a burden to the family is often of prime concern to the elderly patient. Fear of pain and the symptoms experienced will also influence how the patient reacts and what course to take—to seek help or to ignore the symptoms. With disability and change in body image, self-identity may be threatened; and identity changes may be lasting in prolonged enactment of the sick role.[34]

Sociologically, differences between acutely and chronically sick roles are related to the view society takes of the sick role, to the impact of the illness upon the family, to patient-family relationships, and to patient-practitioner relationships. The permanent enactment of the sick role is viewed with disfavor in our society. Disabled persons are encouraged to make the most of their capabilities within the limits of their impairments. Motivation is the key word. The expectation is that the disabled person will realize his or her potentialities and "must 'accept' his impairment, the acceptance being nearly a necessary condition . . . to the proper realization of his capabilities."[35] This concept is basic to the philosophy of rehabilitation in which the goal of therapy is *control* of the condition rather than *cure* as in acute illness.[36]

Patient-family relationships will be affected in any illness. In acute illness family resources will have to be mobilized, to be sure, and patient-family dislocation will occur; but the duration of the illness is short-term, so that the impact upon patient-family interactions will be felt only temporarily. Under the stress of long-term illness, however, family disruption and conflict may have serious consequences for patient-family relationships. Miller points out the importance that consideration of the family as a unit has in the comprehensive care of the chronically ill patient. He states that the dynamics of the patient-family interaction cannot be ignored in planning patient therapy, except by denial.[37]

One further variation between the acutely and chronically sick roles is in the professional-patient relationship, or what Cogswell and Weir refer to as the "professional-patient role,"[38] and Thomas and Wright refer to as the "disability comanager" role.[39, 40] Cogswell and Weir see the patient-professional relationship in acute illness as one in which the patient is a passive recipient of care and treatment. Something is done *to* the patient; the focus is on the disease rather than on the patient, with the possibility of the patient being treated as an object. In the acute-illness perspective, they say, it is the professional who is in a position of authority and power. In the chronic-illness perspective, on the other hand, there is *mutual participation* by the professional and the patient. Although the professional remains the expert in treatment, the patient assumes responsibility for a considerable portion of the care. In this kind of relationship the patient gains considerable power as opposed to the professional.[41] As Wright says, the patient has not only voting privileges, but also veto power: both the right and the prerogative to make decisions regarding care and its outcome. The patient actively participates with the professional in the plans for treatment and care.[42] This ideal planning is not, however, the modus operandi one sees in the care of many elderly patients.

Cultural factors influencing the adoption of the sick role, such as one's definition of illness and self-reliance, have been mentioned earlier in this chapter, and these will not be repeated. There is one factor, however, that has special significance for the chronically sick role. This is the high value placed upon good health and wholeness of body physique in our culture. The disability incurred with chronic illness does not hold true with acute illness. The overtness of the handicap creates a special role for the disabled person that the nondisabled does not have. Thomas calls this the "Public Relations Man role." The uniqueness of the condition places a special burden on the disabled person to explain and interpret this condition to others, a burden the person in the acutely sick role does not have.[43] Moreover, the disability, if severe, may lead to pity and revulsion on the part of others for the disabled person, feelings that may be difficult to conceal. This places the disabled person in the position of being less valued than the whole person, with possible loss of self-esteem. The aged in our society already have experienced loss of self-esteem because of the negative view our society has taken of aging.

The major differences between the acutely sick role and the chronically sick role may be summarized as follows:

1 In the acutely sick role, the person temporarily gives up normal roles and adopts a new role for the duration of the illness; in the chronically sick role, role change is more partial than complete, and the person generally must give up the pre-illness role, adopt a new, less demanding role, or adopt the sick role on a permanent basis.

2 In the acutely sick role, the person is permitted to be dependent and accept the help of stronger, more adequate persons because it is a temporary dependence; in the chronically sick role, the degree of permissiveness and dependence allowed is smaller, or in some way changed, to avoid threat to the role performance of family members.

3 In the acutely sick role, the medical determinants of performance are more urgent and more immediately threatening to the patient's life, and treatment is directed to life-saving measures and cure; in the chronically sick role, the medical determinants hold less threat for life, but may lead to delay of illness behavior and therapy, thereby having long-range implications for the patient's life and health; therapy is directed towards control and rehabilitation.

4 In the acutely sick role, society has established clear-cut norms for behavior; in the chronically sick role, there are no established norms, so that conflicts may arise between the demands of society and the patients' expectations of themselves and of the sick role and the inability to move out of the sick role.

5 The acutely sick role may be performed primarily by younger age groups; the chronically sick role is primarily associated with older age groups.

Since, as Kassebaum and Baumann report, the similarity between the "typical" expectations for the chronically sick role and the "typical" expectations for the "aged" role makes distinctions between the two roles ambiguous, and since chronic illness commonly affects elderly people, it seems reasonable to assume that the chronically sick role model, in most respects, can be viewed as the sick role of the elderly. Expectations of role performance for the elderly, as with role performance in chronic illness, "may also involve impairment of capacity for certain types of role performance, exemptions from obligations, and other forms of permissiveness. Like the sick person, the aging individual is not held responsible for incurring his condition, nor can he arrest it by any act of volition."[44]

Using the chronic sick role as a model, then, we can explore the sick role of elderly patients and the adaptive mechanisms they may use in adopting the sick role. Mrs. Allen, who was introduced in the beginning of this chapter, is representative of individuals with illnesses which commonly occur with advancing age. These illnesses are long-term and chronic; they usually leave some residual disability; they prolong the patient role and interfere with a return to previous life-styles and social roles. Mrs. Allen had a handicap for which some kind of adjustment had to be made. A discussion of certain aspects of her adjustment will help to illustrate some of the dimensions of the sick role of the elderly patient.

CASE EXAMPLE: THE SICK ROLE OF THE ELDERLY Mrs. Allen's medical problems of arthritis and Parkinson's disease met the criteria established for chronic illness. Her disability was progressive and permanent; the pathological progress was nonreversible. The nature of her disability and its progress were such that confusion with the process of aging might well have been a factor in her delaying of illness behavior leading to diagnosis and therapy, because stiffness, rigidity, and palsy may also be experienced by aging individuals who do not have Parkinson's disease. Confusion of symptoms of chronic illness with the aging process itself may lead elderly persons to tolerate impairment unnecessarily because they may not attach medical significance to the symptoms until their capacity to perform usual roles is severely impaired.

The second dimension, that of a change in one's social role, either partial or total, took the form of a gradual change for Mrs. Allen because of the nature of her illness. Change in social roles, however, is not always gradual for elderly people. The person with a sudden stroke may find the change in roles overwhelming, even frightening. Since Mrs. Allen's roles of wife, mother, and wage earner were already changed, as is usually the case with elderly people, these social roles were not affected by her illness. The roles left to her in retirement were curtailed as a result of her illness. She had enjoyed cooking, baking, and entertaining; she had enjoyed maintaining her own apartment; she loved to knit and sew for herself, her children, and grandchildren; she traveled each year to spend time with family and friends in various parts of the country. With increasing disablement, these roles were gradually lost to her. She had previously been self-reliant, with a strong desire for independence; now she was increasingly dependent and had to remain in the sick role as a disabled person. Role change, which was partial in the beginning, eventually became complete.

As long as Mrs. Allen's disability did not interfere markedly with her independence, she was able to maintain her pre-illness roles very well. The goal of care for Parkinson's disease is to keep the patient functionally useful and productive as long as possible. Such care involves a program of medication, physical therapy, rehabilitation techniques, and education about the nature of the disease.[46] Mrs. Allen's program of therapy included these elements. She was encouraged to engage in activities to keep her joints mobile, such as taking daily walks and performing tasks to exercise her hands, and to develop interests that would take her mind off her problems. Enrolling in a painting class fulfilled this need for her. This is in keeping with the philosophy of rehabilitation, which encourages patients to make the most of their capabilities within the limits of the impairment. "One of the most important objectives of the program," say Nichols and Bogdonoff, "is to give the patient a feeling of improved physical vigor. This, in turn, will influence his attitude toward himself and his own sense of well-being."[47] It is important that health personnel who are involved in implementing the patient's program of therapy understand these objectives in order to be of greater aid as the patient attempts to move out of the dependency of the sick role.[48]

The third dimension, which relates to the impact of chronic illness on family members, has some special implications for the elderly patient. It is true that "a sick person in the home affects all habitants, and often family life may revolve around the sick member."[49] It is certainly the case when elderly patients are cared for in the home, because constant care and surveillance are required to protect them from the injuries which may occur as a result of the impaired sensory and motor functioning of aging. There may be disruption of family life, curtailment of social and recreational activities, and increased expenditure of physical, emotional, and financial resources.[50] Mrs. Allen was not cared for in the homes of her children, but, nonetheless, her illness affected them. There was the increased worry for her well-being, her safety, and the adequacy of her care. There was the need to make decisions to provide for her care and safety, since she could no longer make these decisions herself. This required uprooting her from her home in a distant city and placing her in a retirement complex near her son's home, where he could provide intermittent supervision of her as she became more feeble and disabled. Eventually, there was the need to provide for constant supervision which meant moving her to a nursing home. For her son these changes led to a drain on financial resources and increased time spent away from his usual roles.

For both Mrs. Allen and her son the changes in her role led to increased expenditure of emotional energy. She was extremely opposed to going to the nursing home, and the necessity for this move led to mental anguish for both of them. Profound depression resulted for Mrs. Allen, and for her son as well. It was difficult for him to see his mother, whom he had always known to be strong-willed and self-sufficient, now incapable of managing her own life. He was unsure about the wisdom of the move to the nursing home: "Have I done the right thing for Mother?" "Will she feel she has lost her right to independence and to her status as a valued member of the family?" "Each person, sick or well, ultimately wants to be valued as an individual with adult rights and independence, to keep status as a member of his family, to retain some sort of status in society."[51]

This brings us to the fourth dimension of the sick role of the elderly—the dependency and alienation dimension. Mrs. Allen, because of the combined effects of illness and the aging process, and through no choice of her own, had been thrust into a role repugnant to her. She had been separated from her normal roles in society, and "every separation is a reminder of death."[52] Her dependency needs were total; she would never again be able to abandon the sick role. Logically, then, her initial reactions were those of frustration and anger toward a situation over which she had no control. Her anger was directed toward those who were most concerned with her care—her son, the nursing-home personnel, and the physician. Her emotions became overwhelming for her. She had been hostile; subsequently, she became extremely depressed and apathetic. Her behavior indicated self-pity; she lost all interest in her surroundings, in her care, and in herself. She "turned toward the wall," "gave up"; it was as though she had told herself, "I might as well be dead, so I will die." In a sense, her hostility took the form of punishment of those closest to her. Professional personnel must provide the opportunity for the patient to express his or her feelings. Unless these feelings can be expressed, they cannot be reduced to a point where the patient can manage them successfully. Moreover, without management of feelings, the patient is in no position to establish a new set of feelings, decrease anger and frustration, and gain in self-confidence.[53]

It is equally important to provide for free expression of feelings on the part of family and friends. They, too, are experiencing the frustrations of the patient's prolonged therapy, separation, and the hopelessness of the outcome. They, too, may feel anger and resentment toward medical personnel, and toward the patient as well. Providing an outlet for these feelings will help to lessen the chance that these feelings will spill over to the patient. Full expression of anger and hostility toward those responsible for the patient's care is, however, usually short-circuited, because the patient is still dependent upon these people.[54] Mrs. Allen was disabled and helpless; she was on the receiving end of helping acts. This placed her in a vulnerable position, for she was dependent upon others for every need. In order to obtain satisfaction of their needs, aged patients, especially, learn that they must be gracious in their requests, appreciative of help, and must avoid complaining and finding fault—in short, behave in such a manner so as not to alienate their source of care. Mrs. Allen responded very passively to her care. She tolerated comfort measures provided and expressed her appreciation in a monotonous tone of voice. She neither praised nor criticized, but, rather, her behavior expressed indifference to what was done to and for her. "Do what you have to do," was a typical response. Though this response did not alienate the nursing staff from her, neither did it decrease her aloneness, for it is difficult to give of yourself when the offer is rejected.

Previously she had enjoyed and needed the companionship of others, and responded with pleasure to the visits of her family and friends; now she turned away and became more and more unresponsive to those about her. Elderly people, whether they live alone, in the home of their children, or in a nursing home, generally welcome visits from others. Often they will cling to the visitor's hand as though to retain the company as long as possible. Elderly people need a sense of belonging, a sense that someone cares, that they are recognized for themselves, have worth as human beings, and are not "put away" to be less bothersome to society or to family. To the lonely aged person a trip to the clinic or to the doctor's office may become the highlight of the day, for it provides the contact with others that may be lacking. Schwartz et al. cite a poignant example of this in their study of the elderly ambulatory patient. Asked whether a visiting nurse could save her a long and difficult trip to the clinic, one patient replied: "No, coming in to the clinic is my only chance to be myself. . . . It is something to look forward to, to come. . . . A long trip—trains and bus. But please don't tell me not to come. That's the only pleasure I have."[55]

The fifth dimension, the association of chronic illness with advancing age, had special pertinence in the case of Mrs. Allen. She had been widowed early in her marriage; she had raised her family alone; she had been the breadwinner for many years, and had helped her children through college. She had been housekeeper for her son until his marriage. In addition to the social roles relating to motherhood and wage earner, she had functioned as a professional nurse on whom others had been dependent for service and care. It is not difficult to see how adjustment to retirement and a life of decreased usefulness would diminish her feelings of self-worth. In our society the emphasis is on youthfulness. The end of childbearing and child raising, and retirement, are thought of as the end of productivity and usefulness. There are few, if any, roles allowed the elderly person that provide a sense of still being a valued member of society. One role, however, that is open is the sick role. Thus, it is not strange that "the individual who enters his senescent years without the complications of already existing chronic disease may nevertheless gravitate to the sick role *because* our society offers to those in their postretirement years readier access to this role than to any other."[56] This is a strong factor in the tendency to equate aging with illness, and it can be a most damaging component in the message of personal uselessness and worthlessness that is often relayed to the elderly person.

Since elderly people have been exposed to the stresses and strains of life for a longer period of time, they are particularly vulnerable to the impairment of mind and body resulting from chronic disease. This fact provides further evidence for the confusion between the aging role and the chronically sick role. The signs of aging develop slowly and insidiously, as do the symptoms of chronic disease. Mrs. Allen's symptoms developed slowly and insidiously, as has already been related. Several years passed during which slower, more halting gait, slower mentation, increased shakiness, changes in facies, and weakness progressed, paralleling the changes of advancing age. Here one can see the difficulties that may be encountered in attempts at rehabilitation of the elderly as compared to the younger person who is not yet faced with aging *and* illness.

NURSING INTERVENTION AND
THE SICK ROLE OF THE ELDERLY

Before discussing nursing intervention as it relates to the sick elderly person, it is appropriate to say something about social attitudes that may affect nurses who are charged with the care of elderly patients.

Attitudes

The rules of conduct for the disabled elderly person are unclear. The inability to move out of the sick role completely, the need to revise or give up former roles, and the inner conflicts that result, to say nothing of the conflicts that arise out of the "aged" role, make the sick role of the elderly a complex one. The conflicting feelings we exhibit in our society toward aging no doubt have done much to create this problem. We say that we respect the elderly for their years of experience and the knowledge they have gained, yet they have no important role to perform after retirement; "we value youth and fear old age, which in our society confers no dignity but only losses";[57] we have negative feelings toward growing old, yet we are ashamed of these feelings and try to hide them from ourselves by assuming a respect and interest in the elderly that we do not feel.[58] Sometimes, even a show of respect may be lacking in our approach to the sick elderly patient. Who has not heard the patient referred to as "cute," as though the patient were a child, or by the familiar titles of "grandma" or "grandpa," or first name, without the sanction of the patient.

Epstein expresses concern about the ambivalence our society exhibits toward aging and the elderly, especially as this ambivalence may be displayed by nurses who work with elderly people. She feels that it may lead to inappropriate behavior if the nurse is not sure how to relate to the patients. Confusion regarding expectations about the patients may result if the nurse "is not sure whether old people are all experienced, wise and capable of controlling their own lives, or childish, incompetent, and dependent."[59] The nurse may find him- or herself "seesawing between helping the patient maintain his independence and forcing him to submit completely to her will."[60]

Examining personal attitudes and feelings toward aging and the elderly is important if the nurse is to provide holistic care for older patients. In the words of Hirschfeld, "Genuine respect and non-possessive warmth are the basis for a relationship of trust and security, a *sine qua non* for helping a person rebuild his integrity."[61]

Interventions

How does one motivate elderly persons to persevere in treatment and rehabilitation when each week and month brings increasing loss of strength and increasing effort just to maintain the status quo? Great patience, tolerance, and empathy are required to stimulate elderly patients to try "just one more time." Elderly patients each day move closer to death, and ultimately, if they decide that death is more desirable than life without a purposeful role, is it not the patients' right to abandon that life? Sometimes an overwhelming sense of helplessness and hopelessness can bring on sudden, unexplained death. This has been demonstrated in studies of both humans and animals.[62] Seligman's studies point out the lethal consequences of helplessness and the importance of being able to have control of our lives.[63] Perhaps this was the case with Mrs. Allen. Loss of useful roles, loss of control of her life, and complete dependency upon others led to her wish to die. She exercised her right of veto power, refusing all life-sustaining measures. In this respect she did have control of her life. Paul Hunt, himself a victim of extensive disability, states that "even the most severely disabled people retain an ineradicable conviction that they are still fully human in all that is ultimately necessary. Yet even when he is most depressed, even when he says he would be better off dead, the underlying sense of his own worth remains."[64] One would like to think that this was true for Mrs. Allen.

Three major psychosocial problems are related to the sick role of the elderly for which nursing interventions could be brought to bear. They are feelings of *rolelessness*, *helplessness*, and *hopelessness*. All three problems have been referred to repeatedly throughout this chapter in relation to Mrs. Allen's situation. My intent here is to stress ways in which nurses and other helping persons may recognize these feelings and resultant behaviors in elderly patients and to enumerate ways in which they might be inhibited or decreased.

Rolelessness

Rolelessness implies that the elderly person has no useful role to perform in society upon reaching a certain age.[65] Yet there are many roles that can be performed despite age and disability, although they may of necessity be somewhat modified. The roles of parent and grandparent still existed for Mrs. Allen, although in a changed form from earlier years. Until her disease had progressed to the stage where she no longer was able to make decisions for herself, she did function in the roles of "disability co-manager" and decision maker. Together she and her doctor discussed ways in which she could help herself to maintain strength and function. He respected her knowledge of her disease; he answered her questions with honesty and with respect for her as a former nurse and individual. She respected his counsel and tried faithfully to follow the regimen planned for her. Perhaps the fact that she had been able to function as a co-manager in her therapy made it all the more difficult towards the end when she could no longer function in this role and her son had to make decisions for her. Because of the effects of illness and aging on her central nervous system, she failed to recognize this fact. This may have contributed to her feelings of worthlessness and self-denial, as evidenced through her attempts to hide her shaking hands and insistence on remaining in her own apartment.

During her stay in the nursing home, Mrs. Allen in effect became roleless, though meaningful roles were available to her. Among the roles she could have assumed with appropriate help and motivation were those of friend, group member, helper, decision maker, and hostess. These roles may be possible even for the severely impaired older person to maintain.[66] Helping elderly people to maintain such roles in the nursing home setting may stimulate them and keep their minds occupied, thus preventing boredom. People who are bored usually are not very happy, and unhappiness may lead to loneliness and self-denial.

To provide meaningful roles for the elderly in a nursing home, it is essential that a careful history of each person's special abilities and needs is taken. "Planning care and shaping the patient's environment, especially in an institution, is an important function of the nurse."[67] Skill in assessing the responses of elderly persons because of the multiple physiologic changes that occur with aging and the accompanying mental and emotional changes, becomes an especially important nursing function in working with the elderly. Care must be taken not to base assessments on half truths and stereotypes about aging. Each person's special abilities, disabilities, and psychosocial needs must be the basis of each care plan developed.

Elderly persons can be given the opportunity and encouraged to talk with lonely residents, to read to those whose vision is diminished, or to offer companionship to others. Such actions may foster a sense of usefulness, of being needed. Planning social activities, acting as host or hostess for various events, or in other ways making use of talents, skills, and interests of elderly residents should be encouraged. One nursing home has a council made up of residents and staff members which actively involves residents in decisions which affect them. Another nursing home provided residents with garden plots. Those who chose to be gardeners raised fresh flowers and vegetables for the enjoyment of all. Even more important, they enhanced their sense of worth and competence. Elderly residents can fill the role of helper by keeping their rooms tidy, making their own beds, and maintaining their own records, under supervision, of such things as intake and output, medication regimens, and food diaries. Such activities would help them feel useful and would also give them a sense that they are co-managers in their care, able to make some decisions about their own bodies and needs. The role of helper may have been possible for Mrs. Allen to perform in some measure. A nursing history would have been a valuable means of identifying activities that fell within the scope of her physical and mental limitations.

Obtaining a nursing history of the elderly person and diagnosing specific needs is not enough. The information must be used to improve patient care. One study has shown that the psychological and social information nurses had available about patients gathered through nursing histories was not used to improve care.[68] Nursing home personnel need to be helped to see that the psychosocial needs as well as the physical ones must be met if holistic care is to be given to patients. This can be done through example and through in-service programs. For example, one nursing home has developed a series of guides concerning all aspects of caring for elderly persons, including psychosocial aspects. These guides are used in staff development programs for all personnel who have contact with patients.[69]

Helplessness

Sensory loss, slower reaction time, and impaired mobility may contribute to a sense of helplessness and loss of control in the elderly. Loss of productive roles, of significant others, of self-esteem, and eventually of home and possessions surely increase this sense of helplessness. Relocation to a nursing home, often nonvoluntary (as was true for Mrs. Allen), may lead to a feeling of rejection and total loss of control of life.

"If one believes that the consequences of such events in aging are inevitable and nonreversible, then one need not wonder at the withdrawn, unmotivated, dependent, and depressed behavior often manifested in old age."[70] These behaviors were certainly evident in Mrs. Allen. Increasing dependency due to the progressive physical changes of Parkinson's disease and arthritis led her to a state of helplessness and depression. One can hypothesize that loss of control over what was happening to her caused her to withdraw and lose motivation to accept her place in the nursing home. She had opposed this move and had had no voice in the final decision. She probably never developed a sense of belonging, even though she had her personal possessions with her. Time to adjust to the idea of moving to a nursing home and some choice in the decision are important to one's self-image as a capable adult. This also holds true for moves within the institution, moves from one room to another or one unit to another. Often, however, the convenience of the staff takes priority in such moves. The patient is not consulted or given a choice, and the elderly person's possessions are not given proper regard.[71]

Helplessness is manifested by loss of motivation, withdrawal, anxiety, fear, and depression. Most of these behaviors were observed in Mrs. Allen. Helplessness diminishes the person's self-respect. One sees oneself as incapable and unworthy of the respect of others. It is not surprising that the elderly person finds it easier to take on the sick role, especially when helplessness is a factor, since it is often the only role available.

What can be done to minimize or inhibit this sense of helplessness in the elderly? It is most important to provide some means by which the elderly person has freedom to control the meaningful aspects of life. There are many ways in which this can be accomplished in the nursing home setting. Patients should be allowed to participate in care planning as much as possible. They should be consulted concerning likes and dislikes and made to feel that they have some power to make changes in some of the day-to-day activities. They should be allowed some decision making regarding their bodily needs. Independence should be fostered within the limitations of the patients' capabilities. Complete takeover of the patients' management when they are able to maintain at least a part of it makes them feel helpless and unworthy.[72] People of all ages need to feel that they make some difference in their environment, that they can choose the things they will do and the kind of environment they want to be in. Nursing home living tends to limit the choices available. Residents should be offered as many choices as possible, even though they may seem trivial. Allowing residents to personalize their rooms, to decide how they want their coffee and when they want their baths gives some sense of control. Providing choice in menus, as is done in most hospitals, could be initiated in nursing homes without too much difficulty. Recognizing when individuals need to be dependent and allowing that dependence also gives a sense of control. Fuller's review of the research on the relationship between the elderly nursing home residents' ability to control events and their level of happiness, activity, and improved physical condition demonstrated a significant increase in all three areas in the experimental group as compared to the comparison group. She cautions, however, that once elderly people have been afforded the opportunity to control their own lives to some degree, the options must be continued. Options cannot be available on one occasion and withdrawn on another.[73]

Hopelessness

If helplessness is allowed to continue, hopelessness and despair result, and eventually, to use Seligman's term, "submissive death." "Hope is generated in an atmosphere where there is freedom of choice, honesty, realistic goal setting, and a sense of control over oneself and one's environment."[74] Understanding and interest conveyed to patients by staff members can help patients to move from despair and hopelessness to hope. When a despairing, depressed patient, as Mrs. Allen became, shuts off communication with others by "turning to the wall," means other than verbal communication sometimes must be used to get through to the patient. Ruesch states: "Verbal and nonverbal language do not appeal to the same sensory modalities. Nonverbal language takes on prime importance in situations where words fail completely."[75] Burnside used the term "touch hunger,"[76] which expresses well the need for human touch so often demonstrated by elderly patients. A friend once asked me if I taught my students to use "the laying on of hands" in care of patients, or to give "tender loving care from the doorway." Both phrases say much. A caring attitude and a warm touch can make a difference to the lonely, depressed elderly person who is isolated from life and others.

Hopelessness can be initiated by prolonged illness with its invasion of privacy, loss of control, and helplessness; by loss of personal resources; by insult to independence; and by prolonged pain and weakness.[77] Mrs. Allen was affected by all of these factors. Nurses can recognize signs of hopelessness in patients if they are careful to observe for them, although the signs may frequently be vague. The patient may appear depressed or apathetic, volunteer little in the way of conversation. He or she may make no demands upon the nursing staff, and may be very passive. The patient may be cooperative when cared for but do little in the way of self-help.[78] Again, Mrs. Allen exhibited all of these signs.

Interventions to counteract hopelessness may include the following:

1 Validate with the patient that the assessment of hopelessness is correct. The nurse might say, "You seem depressed. Am I right? Is there something I can do?"

2 When one's assessment has been validated, plan an approach to care. An approach that will encourage the patient to "hang in there and fight" should be employed. Becoming involved in the care of such patients conveys the message to them "we care too much about you to let you give up."[79] Family members as well as the whole health team should participate in this planning. (It is emotionally draining to work with patients who have lost hope, and peer support is very necessary. Feelings of staff members should be discussed in conferences.)

3 Encourage visitors, both family members and others. This may provide a source of outside stimulation that may turn the hopelessness around.

4 Provide stimulation by external stimuli in the room. Music, pictures, clocks, and calendars are kinds of stimuli that could help to get the patient's interest aroused in other things. Opening windows to let the sunlight and outside sounds enter the room may be helpful as well.[80]

I do not know if this approach was used with Mrs. Allen. I suggest, however, that it was not. Such an approach might have been effective in alleviating her despair, making her situation more acceptable to her, or it might have made little difference. I do know that nursing care with a positive approach to the problem of hopelessness, one that emphasizes the patient's assets and starts with attainable goals, has a better chance of alleviating the distress experienced by Mrs. Allen than one that fails to deal with it. A realistic goal for her care might have been to help her to die with dignity.

In our care of elderly patients we have the responsibility to take our cues from the individual; what the patient's needs and expectations are; how the patient wants and expects to be addressed. Though senescence may be accompanied by senile changes, and the patient's behavior may present childlike qualities, we can provide the protective and supportive care needed and still accord the respect and dignified approach that the patient's status as an adult demands. Providing care based upon individual differences, with respect for the person and preservation of dignity will, I believe, do much to make the sick role of the elderly less confusing and easier for the elderly person to bear.

SUMMARY

In this chapter the dimensions of the sick role of the elderly patient have been described. The acutely sick role as established by society was reviewed, and variations between the acutely and chronically sick roles were delineated. An example of an elderly woman with chronic illness was used to illustrate the special problems of the aged person in the sick role and the problems of patient-family and patient-professional relationships that arise when the elderly individual must assume the sick role. Nursing interventions relating to rolelessness, helplessness, and hopelessness were emphasized. The patient and family are dependent on health team members for help and guidance in any illness situation. In order to provide the assistance they should be able to expect, it is important that we examine honestly our feelings toward the aged patient and toward the aging process. "Only through an understanding of the psychological factors which underlie our own needs and attitudes, and the patient's needs and attitudes, and those of society"[81] can we fulfill our responsibility to those we serve.

REFERENCES

1 Gene G. Kassebaum and Barbara O. Baumann, "Dimensions of the Sick Role in Chronic Illness," *Journal of Health and Human Behavior*, vol. 6, no. 1, pp. 16-27, Spring 1965.
2 Matilda Riley, John W. Riley, and Marilyn E. Johnson, *Aging and Society*, vol. 2, *Aging and the Professions*, Russell Sage Foundation, New York, 1969.
3 David Mechanic, "The Concept of Illness Behavior," *Journal of Chronic Diseases*, vol. 15, no. 2, pp. 189-194, February 1962.
4 Stanislav Kasl and Sidney Cobb, "Health Behavior, Illness Behavior, and Sick Role Behavior," *Archives of Environmental Health*, vol. 12, no. 2, pp. 246-266, February 1966.
5 Mechanic, op. cit., p. 192.
6 David Mechanic and Edmund H. Volkart, "Illness Behavior and Medical Diagnosis," *Journal of Health and Human Behavior*, vol. 1, no. 2, pp. 86-94, Summer 1960.
7 David Mechanic and Edmund H. Volkart, "Stress, Illness Behavior, and Sick Role," *American Sociological Review*, vol. 26, pp. 51-58, February 1961.
8 Eliot Friedson, "Client Control and Medical Practice," in Scott and Volkart (eds.), *Medical Care*, John Wiley, New York, 1966.
9 Talcott Parsons and Renee Fox, "Illness, Therapy and the Modern Urban American Family," *Journal of Social Issues*, vol. 8, no. 4, pp. 31-44, 1952.
10 Ibid., p. 33.
11 Ibid., p. 32.
12 Kasl and Cobb, op. cit.
13 Emily Mumford and J. K. Skipper, Jr., *Sociology in Hospital Care*, Harper and Row, New York, 1969.
14 Friedson, op. cit.
15 Kasl and Cobb, op. cit.
16 Ibid.
17 Barbara Blackwell, "The Literature of Delay in Seeking Medical Care for Chronic Illness," Health Education Monographs, 16, 1963.

18   Mechanic and Volkart, "Stress, Illness Behavior, and Sick Role," op. cit.

19   Lyle Saunders, *Cultural Differences and Medical Care*, Russell Sage Foundation, New York, 1954.

20   Margaret Clark and Barbara Gallatin Anderson, *Culture and Aging*, Charles C Thomas, Springfield, Ill., 1967.

21   Mark Zborowski, "Cultural Components in Responses to Pain," in E. G. Jaco (ed.), *Patients, Physicians and Illness*, Free Press, New York, 1958.

22   J. D. Stoeckle, I. K. Zola, and G. E. Davidson, "On Going to See the Doctor, Contributions of the Patient to the Decision to Seek Medical Aid: A Selective Review," *Journal of Chronic Diseases*, vol. 16, no. 9, pp. 975–989, September 1963.

23   Dorrian Apple, "How Laymen Define Illness," *Journal of Health and Human Behavior*, vol. 1, no. 3, pp. 219–225, Fall 1960.

24   Derek Phillips, "Self-Reliance and the Inclination to Adopt the Sick Role," *Social Forces*, vol. 43, no. 4, pp. 555–563, May 1965.

25   Stoeckle et al., op. cit., p. 976.

26   Apple, op. cit.

27   Phillips, op. cit.

28   Eileen Callahan et al., "The 'Sick Role' in Chronic Illness: Some Reactions," *Journal of Chronic Diseases*, vol. 19, p. 884, August 1966.

29   Betty E. Cogswell and Donald D. Weir, "A Role in Process: The Development of Medical Professionals' Role in Long-Term Care of Chronically Diseased Patients," *Journal of Health and Human Behavior*, vol. 5, pp. 95–103, Summer and Fall 1964.

30   Claude R. Nichols and Morton D. Bogdonoff, "Programming the Care of the Chronically Ill," *The New England Journal of Medicine*, vol. 266, no. 17, pp. 867–870, April 26, l962.

31   Kassebaum and Baumann, op. cit., p. 18.

32   Commission on Chronic Illness, *Chronic Illness in the United States: Care of the Long-Term Patient*, vol. 2, Harvard University Press, Cambridge, Mass., 1956.

33   Callahan, op. cit., p. 888.

34   Kasl and Cobb, op. cit.

35   Edwin J. Thomas, "Problems of Disability from the Perspective of Role Theory," *Journal of Health and Human Behavior*, vol. 7, no. 1, p. 5, Spring 1966.

36   Ibid.

37   Michael B. Miller, "The Chronically Ill Aged, Family Conflict, and Family Medicine," *Journal of the American Geriatrics Society*, vol. 17, no. 10, pp. 950–961, October 1969.

38   Cogswell and Weir, op. cit.

39   Thomas, op. cit., p. 3.

40   Beatrice A. Wright, *Physical Disability—A Psychological Approach*, Harper and Row, New York, 1960.

41   Cogswell and Weir, op. cit., pp. 97 and 102.

42   Wright, op. cit.

43   Thomas, op. cit., p. 6.

44 Kassebaum and Baumann, op. cit., p. 18.

45 Ibid., p. 19.

46 Lillian Sholtis Brunner et al., *Textbook of Medical-Surgical Nursing*, 2d ed, Lippincott, Philadelphia, 1970.

47 Nichols and Bogdonoff, op. cit., p. 868.

48 Ibid., p. 868.

49 Callahan, op. cit., p. 890.

50 Thomas, op. cit., p. 5.

51 Callahan, op. cit., p. 890.

52 Ibid., p. 888.

53 Nichols and Bogdonoff, op. cit., 868–869.

54 Ibid., p. 868.

55 Doris Schwartz, Barbara Henley, and Leonard Zeitz, *The Elderly Ambulatory Patient: Nursing and Psychosocial Needs*, Macmillan, New York, 1964.

56 J. Sanbourne Bockoven, "Aspects of Geriatric Care and Treatment: Moral, Amoral, and Immoral," in Robert Kastenbaum (ed.), *New Thoughts on Old Age*, Springer, New York, 1964, pp. 214–225.

57 Philip E. Slater, "Cross-Cultural Views of the Aged," in Robert Kastenbaum (ed.), *New Thoughts on Old Age*, Springer, New York, 1964, pp. 229–235.

58 Ibid.

59 Charlotte Epstein, *Learning to Care for the Aged*, Reston Publishing, Reston, Va., 1977, p. 19.

60 Ibid.

61 M. J. Hirschfeld, "The Cognitively Impaired Older Adult," *American Journal of Nursing*, vol. 77, no. 7, pp. 1187–1189, July 1977.

62 Martin E. D. Seligman, "Submissive Death: Giving Up on Life," *Psychology Today*, vol. 7, no. 2, pp. 80–85, May 1974.

63 Ibid., p. 85

64 Paul Hunt, *Stigma: The Experience of Disability*, Chapman, London, 1966.

65 Epstein, op. cit., p. 149.

66 Kathy Carroll (ed.), *Human Development in Aging: Understanding Psychosocial Needs of the Elderly*, Ebenezer Center for Aging and Human Development, Minneapolis, 1978, p. 29.

67 Sr. Marilyn Schwab, "Caring for the Aged," *American Journal of Nursing*, vol. 73, no. 12, pp. 2049–2053, December 1973.

68 Elizabeth A. Hefferin and Ruth E. Hunter, "Nursing Observation and Care Planning for the Hospitalized Aged," *The Gerontologist*, vol. 15, no. 1, part 1, pp. 57–60, February 1975.

69 Kathy Carroll (ed.), *Human Development in Aging: Psychosocial Aspects of Nursing Home Care*, Ebenezer Center for Aging and Human Development, Minneapolis, 1978.

70 Sarah S. Fuller, "Inhibiting Helplessness in Elderly People," *Journal of Gerontological Nursing*, vol. 4, no. 4, pp. 18–21, July/August 1978.

71 Schwab, op. cit., p. 2053.

72 Epstein, op. cit., p. 37.

73 Fuller, op. cit.

74 Brenda D. Brown, "An Innovative Approach to Health Care for the Elderly: An Approach of Hope," *Journal of Psychiatric Nursing and Mental Health Services*, vol. 15, no. 10, pp. 22–29 and 34–35, October 1977.

75 Jurgen Ruesch and Weldon Kees, *Nonverbal Communication*, University of California Press, Berkeley, 1956, p. 178.

76 Irene Mortenson Burnside, "Touching Is Talking," in M. H. Browning (comp.), *Contemporary Nursing Series: Nursing and the Aging Patient*, The American Journal of Nursing Company, New York, 1974, pp. 206–211.

77 Barbara J. Limandri and Diana W. Boyle, "Instilling Hope," *American Journal of Nursing*, vol. 78, no. 1, pp. 79–80, January 1978.

78 Ibid.

79 Ibid.

80 Ibid.

81 Callahan, op. cit., p. 895.

BIBLIOGRAPHY

Barker, R. G. and B. A. Wright: "The Social Psychology of Adjustment to Physical Disability," in J. F. Garrett (ed.), *Psychological Aspects of Physical Disability*, Department of Health, Education and Welfare, Rehabilitation Service Series, No. 210, Washington, D.C.

Cohn, Lucile: "Barriers and Values in the Nurse/Client Relationship," *American Rehabilitation Nursing*, pp. 3–8, November–December 1978.

Crandell, DeWitt, and Bruce Dohrenwent: "Some Relations among Psychiatric Symptoms, Organic Illness and Social Class," *American Journal of Psychiatry*, vol. 123, no. 12, pp. 1527–1536, June 1967.

Crate, Marjorie A.: "Nursing Functions in Adaptation to Chronic Illness," *American Journal of Nursing*, vol. 65, no. 10, pp. 72–76, October 1965.

Francois, Sr. D. C.: "The Philosophy of Rehabilitation," *Physical Therapy*, vol. 47, pp. 1132–1133, December 1967.

Huether, Sue E., and Roberta A. Acquaviva: "The Physically Disabled Patient in the General Hospital," *Nursing Clinics of North America*, vol. 2, no. 4, pp. 785–796, December 1967.

Kern, Richard A.: "Emotional Problems in Relation to Aging and Old Age," *Geriatrics*, vol. 26, no. 6, pp. 83–93, June 1971.

Lederer, Henry D.: "How the Sick View Their World," in James K. Skipper and Robert C. Leonard (eds.), *Social Interaction and Patient Care*, Lippincott, Philadelphia, 1965, pp. 155–167.

McGinty, Patrick J., and Bernard A. Stotsky: "The Patient in the Nursing Home," *Nursing Forum*, vol. 6, no. 3, pp. 238–261, 1967.

Miller, Michael B.: "Challenges of the Chronic Ill Aged," *Geriatrics*, vol. 15, no. 8, pp. 102–110, August 1970.

Neugarten, Bernice L., and Associates: *Personality in Middle and Late Life*, Atherton Press, New York, 1964.

Newton, Kathleen, and Helen C. Anderson: *Geriatric Nursing*, 4th ed., Mosby, St. Louis, 1966.

Riley, Matilda White, and Anne Foner: *Aging and Society*: vol. I, *An Inventory of Research*, Russell Sage Foundation, New York, 1968.

Shaw, D. M., C. R. Nichols, and M. D. Bogdonoff: "Problems in Comprehensive Medicine: A Distinction in Approach," *Journal of Medical Education*, vol. 36, pp. 148–153, 1961.

Shontz, Franklin S.: "Severe Chronic Illness," in James F. Garrett and Edna S. Levine (eds.), *Psychological Practices with the Physically Disabled*, Columbia University Press, New York, 1967, pp. 410–443.

Shontz, Franklin C., Stephen L. Fink, and Charles E. Hallenbeck: "Chronic Physical Illness as Threat," *Archives of Physical Medicine and Rehabilitation*, vol. 41, no. 1, pp. 143–148, January 1960.

Sobel, Ramond, and Ardis Ingalls: "Resistance to Treatment: Explorations of the Patient's Sick Role," *American Journal of Psychotherapy*, vol. 18, pp. 562–573, October 1964.

Sorensen, Karen M., and Dorothy B. Ames: "Understanding the World of the Chronically Ill," *American Journal of Nursing*, vol. 67, no. 4, pp. 811–817, April 1967.

Stenback, A., M. Kumpulainen, and M. L. Vauhkonen: "Illness and Health Behavior in Septuagenarians," *Journal of Gerontology*, vol. 33, no. 1, pp. 57–61, January 1978.

Twaddle, A. C.: "Health Decisions and Sick Role Variations," *Journal of Health and Social Behavior*, vol. 10, no. 2, pp. 105–115, June 1969.

Watson, Wilbur H., and Robert J. Maxwell: *Human Aging and Dying: A Study in Sociocultural Gerontology*, St. Martin's Press, New York, 1977.

Wilson, Robert N.: "Patient-Practitioner Relationships," in Howard E. Freeman et al. (eds.), *Handbook of Medical Sociology*, Prentice-Hall, Englewood Cliffs, N.J., 1963.

Wright, Beatrice A.: "Spread in Adjustment to Disability," *Bulletin of the Menninger Clinic*, vol. 28, no. 4, pp. 198–207, July 1964.

OTHER RESOURCES

Film

Peege, 16 mm, color, 28 min., 1974.
Phoenix Films
470 Park Avenue South
New York, N.Y. 10016

Chapter 17

Co-leadership with a Group of Stroke Patients

Diane Holland Puppolo

Shared experience is the greatest of human goods.

John Dewey

During my graduate work at a chronic disease rehabilitation hospital, I became involved in co-leading a group of stroke patients with a young social worker, whom I shall call Miss O.

This chapter describes my experience as a co-leader of this group. A basic analysis of the group process is described in addition to a presentation of the unique problems of stroke patients in a group. It is hoped that some of my observations and comments and the results of my efforts as co-leader may help others involved in similar group endeavors. The material presented here is drawn from data which I recorded after each meeting for the 11-week period during which I co-led the group. Since the group continued after I left, this chapter deals only with the beginning or initial phase of the group. This phase of group process is characterized by orientation, getting acquainted, cautious politeness, and much testing, in addition to a search for similarities, advice seeking and giving, and conflict, with open expressions of hostility.[1]

GROUP FORMATION

We agreed to include in our group (1) patients who had cerebrovascular accidents or strokes, (2) some patients with speech difficulties, and (3) patients we hoped would benefit from a group experience. In addition, the group was to be comprised of 5 to 10 patients, with no definite age range, and to have an equal number of males and females.

We planned to hold weekly meetings at the same hour; the meeting place would be the conference room in the occupational therapy department. We were able to form a cozy circle there with both wheelchairs and straight chairs.

The group was open-ended, permitting new members to join, since we expected that some patients would voluntarily leave the group or be discharged from the hospital. Because we had learned from earlier group experience that someone usually is absent from every meeting, we wanted to have at least 10 patients in the group. Selecting a larger number than is actually wanted allows for attrition and still leaves an appropriate number at each meeting.[2]

We asked social workers in the hospital to suggest appropriate patients for our group. Since one particular ward housed many stroke patients, we also asked the head nurse for a list from that ward.

After studying the lists submitted, we realized that some patients were inappropriate for our group. The ability to speak was the criterion for determining who was eliminated from the list of potential group participants. We felt that group members with speech impairments could benefit from the mere practice of talking before an audience; however, we thought group development would be retarded if there were too many patients with complete aphasia. As Yalom and Terrazas state, "A verbal group cannot absorb too many nonverbal members, however, and still maintain active interaction."[3] Miss O and I also included some talkative patients in the group, so they might help to carry the conversation.

MAKING THE CONTRACT

Miss O and I thought it best to approach the selected patients together so that they would become acquainted with both co-leaders. A statement about group goals, time, and purposes, as well as the place, frequency, and length of meetings, plus attendance and confidentiality was included in the initial contact with each patient.

Group goals included the following:

1 Expressing common concerns
2 Sharing ways to cope with similar problems
3 Decreasing social isolation
4 Developing morale
5 Increasing adjustment to the stroke

Seven patients consented to attend the first group meeting. However, that session was disrupted by Mrs. V, an elderly lady who could not always comprehend the conversation and who frequently interrupted group members. She tired in 15 minutes and had to be returned to her ward. Because Mrs. V was ill, she missed the next two sessions. I consulted with Miss O about Mrs. V's behavior and we decided that she was inappropriate for the group, particularly since the group already included patients who had communication difficulties.

GROUP DESCRIPTION

In the first 2 weeks, four more people were recruited for the group. Ages of members ranged from 41 to 82 years; the mean age was 57 years. The group consisted of six women and four men; six members were Caucasian and four Negro.

Seven group members had had cerebrovascular accidents; two may have had strokes. One man, Mr. E, had fallen off a bicycle, an accident which had resulted in a fractured skull and a subdural hematoma which severely affected his speech and reading. Speech impairment was evident in five patients; one showed complete verbal aphasia (expressive). One woman was blind. Because of poor vascular circulation in her affected side, another, Mrs. C, had had a leg amputated. Six patients had hemiparesis or weakness of one side of the body. One patient, Mrs. A, was hemiplegic.

The average hospital stay was 4 to 5 years; however, Mrs. L had lived in the chronic disease hospital for 24 years. Five patients in the group had been admitted to the hospital less than a year ago.

Six patients came to group meetings in wheelchairs, while the other four were ambulatory. Since wheelchairs take up more space than straight chairs, the meeting place had to be large enough to accommodate them. We considered this requirement carefully when we chose the conference room as a meeting place. See the chart of patient data (Table 17-1).

Table 17-1 Chart of Patient Data

Name of patient	Age	Sex	Race	Medical diagnosis	Length of time since stroke or fall	Length of time in hospital	Major disabilities	Method of mobility	Attendance
Mrs. L	56	F	W	CVA, hemiparesis, complete verbal expressive aphasia	24 years	24 years	Aphasia	Wheelchair	Absent 3 times
Mrs. A	56	F	B	CVA, hemiplegia, blind in both eyes	6 years	6 years	Blindness	Wheelchair	Absent 3 times
Mrs. W	57	F	B	CVA (?), pneumonia, expressive aphasia	4 months	4 months	Speech impairment	Ambulatory	Absent 3 times
Mrs. C	62	F	W	CVA, hemiparesis, amputation of right leg	4 years	4 years	Amputation	Wheelchair	Absent 3 times
Mrs. LU	47	F	B	CVA, hemiparesis, expressive aphasia	3 years	3 years	Speech impairment	Wheelchair	Absent once
Mr. JI	55	M	W	CVA, hemiparesis, expressive aphasia	10 months	10 months	Speech impairment	Ambulatory	Absent twice
Mr. R	41	M	B	CVA, hemiparesis, expressive aphasia	3 months	3 months	Speech impairment	Wheelchair	Discharged after fifth session
Mrs. J	65	F	W	CVA (?), rheumatoid arthritis	3 years	3 years	Chronic pain	Wheelchair	Attended 1 meeting
Mr. EW	82	M	W	CVA, hemiparesis	3 years	2 months	Weakness	Cane	Absent twice
Mr. E	49	M	W	Fell off bicycle, fractured skull, aphasia (both types)	2 months	2 months	Speech impairment	Ambulatory	Absent 3 times

SEATING ARRANGEMENT

The group usually formed a circle at every meeting so that patients could face one another. Any given group meeting included approximately equal numbers of male and female patients; numbers of black and white group members were also roughly equal. This racial balance may have eliminated the feelings of loneliness which a minority member in a group can experience.

As the weeks passed, the patients sat closer together, thus making the circle seem more tightly knit. As trust developed between members, the group moved toward the working phase of group process.

As co-leaders, Miss O and I sat across from each other in the circle, except during one group meeting in which a patient sat between us. I felt the focus of authority would be more dispersed if we sat apart, since we represented two opposite authority sites in the group. As we viewed group members differently from our seats, Miss O and I often picked up different cues and messages which were transmitted during the group process. Miss O often dealt with patients who were sitting near her, while I frequently focused on patients close to me. Through clinical observations, Yalom et al. found that "with physical separation of the therapists, the focal points of the communication pattern are dispersed, thus increasing the probability of including more of the patients in the network."[4]

The first four meetings were characterized by an interesting feature: certain people sat beside one another each time. This phenomenon is called *pairing*, or *subgrouping*[5]—a common feature of the initial phase of groups. The male group members often sat near one another, while the women also sat together. Black patients frequently sat next to one another. Three patients who were close friends, and also from the same unit, sat close to one another in those first group meetings. One reason for this phenomenon may have been the anxiety which occurs when strangers meet. Because group members were not too familiar with each other, they probably felt more comfortable sitting near someone with whom they could identify. An example of subgrouping is illustrated in Figure 17-1a, which represents the second group meeting.

In the fifth session, these identity groups were beginning to break up. As trust developed, patients felt comfortable enough to move away from their secure positions. Figure 17-1b illustrates the fifth group meeting.

The seventh group session is shown in Figure 17-1c. Mr. E was standing, since his hip made sitting too uncomfortable for him. A strange atmosphere was created by having one group member standing in that meeting; I had the feeling that the group was incomplete and not ready to

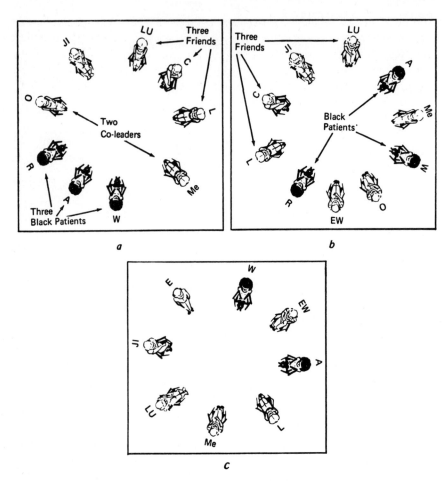

Figure 17-1 Seating arrangements in the (a) second, (b) fifth, and (c) seventh group meetings.

begin. It appeared to me that Mr. E was unwilling to be a part of the group, since he did not sit down with us. At a subsequent session, Mr. JI, who seemed concerned about Mr. E standing, told him to have a seat. Perhaps the patients also felt uncomfortable when one member did not join the group. (The co-leaders can, at this point, ask the group what it feels like to have one member standing during the session.)

ATTENDANCE

The size of the group varied, with four to nine patients attending each meeting. When Miss O went on vacation for a month, I led the group for four meetings. During this period, an exercise program on a female ward of the hospital was resumed, which led to a conflict of time. Several female group members chose to attend the exercise program instead of the group meeting. Patients tend to choose a familiar activity (such as the exercises) rather than a new and strange one (the group meetings). When the exercise program was discontinued after 3 weeks, there was no excuse for these women to stay away from the meetings. As a result, they soon returned to our group.

Attendance at a number of successive meetings was inconsistent as a result of various interferences that prevented the patients from coming to the group sessions. Two regular group members missed one meeting because of a picnic. One patient apparently "forgot" the group for 2 weeks; Mrs. A failed to come once because no one brought her to the meeting.

Another factor causing inconsistency of attendance throughout the group's history was a low level of motivation to attend the meetings. The patients had been asked initially by the co-leaders to join the group; their motivation would have been greater if they themselves had asked to join because they thought the group could meet some need.

STRENGTHS OF THE GROUP

One strength of this group was the prior familiarity of the six women who came from the same ward; this fact seemed to lessen the anxiety which is to be expected in a group of strangers. I also observed that more people spoke in this group compared to other groups with which I have worked where group members were strangers. Even so, it seemed to me that during the first five meetings this familiarity did not contribute to group cohesiveness. Cartwright and Zander define group cohesiveness as "the degree to which the members of a group desire to remain in the group."[6] The patients were not yet functioning as members of a group at that time, but more like separate people who knew each other slightly. However, group development was facilitated because the period of formalities was shortened.

The adaptability of the group members was also a strength. In time aphasic patients can learn unique ways of adapting to their situation. Mr. JI, for example, often left the hospital grounds during the day and rode the bus through the city. He managed to arrive back at the hospital in time for meals. To avoid talking to people he met on his adventures, he usually said, "Sorry, me no speak English." This tactic helped him to avoid the frustration and anxiety which an aphasic person often experiences in communicating with people. Thus, Mr. JI's ingenuity seemed to be a strength in helping him to adjust to his disabled role and in helping other group members with similar difficulties.

A particular strength was observed in one group member, Mr. EW. This man became interested in teaching speech therapy to patients who could use his assistance. He had been an art teacher for many years, and the task appealed to him. It also served two purposes: (1) to help other patients, and (2) to occupy Mr. EW's time. The idea was really encouraged by the group. In subsequent weeks, Mr. EW taught speech to three group members: Mr. E, Mrs. LU, and Mr. JI. As Mr. EW became involved in the rehabilitation of other group members, the unique situation brought those patients closer together. Mr. EW's behavior in this instance was a positive force in developing group cohesiveness.

INTERVENTIONS IN THE GROUP

We tried several techniques and interventions during the group work. When group meetings began, I mentioned who was missing and why. At the fifth session, I asked the group to name the absent members. Thus, instead of performing that task myself, I gave the responsibility to the patients; I think it helped them become more concerned about other group members. Also I hoped that the attention directed toward absent group members stressed the importance of everyone attending. This technique was successful because group members took on one of the functions of the co-leader.

In the second meeting, Miss O utilized an effective intervention which stimulated discussion in the initial phase of group development. Because Mrs. C had made good progress during the last 4 years in recovering from her stroke, Miss O asked her to give some hints to the group on coping with the usual problems and concerns of stroke patients. Since Mrs. C was talkative, she gladly volunteered that frequent exercises and determination were the keys to rehabilitation.

In the third meeting, Mrs. A, the blind woman, was verbally attacked by another patient. Mrs. C accused Mrs. A of being too lazy to exercise her paralyzed arm, and of having narrow interests. Since Mrs. C's hostility affected Mrs. A, I intervened by supporting the latter, saying, "I think it could be easy to lose your interests when your world is limited by being in a wheelchair and also by being blind." Mrs. A promptly agreed that her blindness certainly had a lot to do with it. This intervention demonstrated support for a group member who was attacked from within the group. It also seemed to reduce the anxiety of that member and to encourage her to express herself. Although persons who are verbally attacked may need protection, the co-leaders must not suppress direct expressions of feelings.

When several new patients came to the third meeting, I brought up the subject of group goals. Since the new people had "no idea" of the goals of the group, I asked if anyone in the group had an answer. The entire group seemed dumbfounded, even though Miss O and I had told them what the goals were when making the group contract with each of them. One useful intervention was made by Miss O.

Miss O: Mrs. C, why do you keep coming back if you get nothing from the meetings?

Mrs. C: Well, I do find it helpful to hear others talk about their problems.

(The group member can be asked how it has been helpful to him or her.)

Mr. EW, a new group member, expressed the thought that it was always valuable to learn just by listening to others speak. Group members were encouraged to think about the value of the group instead of waiting for the co-leaders to express the group goals. Either co-leaders or group members can restate the goals periodically throughout the group life. It is necessary for the group's goals to be clear to its members and shared by them in order for the group to work as a cohesive unit.[7]

Another effective technique was assigning a task to a group member which was to be completed by the next group session. Since Mr. EW's right hand was paralyzed, he wanted to learn to write with his left hand. He admitted to the group that he lacked the motivation to practice writing. When I suggested that he write a letter to his sister before the next session, he seemed amused and interested in accomplishing that task. At the following meeting, Mr. EW proudly announced that he had written a two-page letter. The technique of assigning tasks was successful with Mr. EW because it increased his motivation to write and also his interest in group attendance. I feel this technique can succeed in motivating some patients, and should be utilized whenever possible.

It is extremely important to provide positive reinforcement to patients who progress in their rehabilitation program. It is hoped that they will thus be encouraged to increase their efforts in rehabilitation. In the eighth meeting, I commented to Mrs. LU that her speech seemed more comprehensible and that she pronounced her words more clearly. Mrs. LU smiled with happiness; someone had noticed an improvement in her speech. Feedback helped to prevent Mrs. LU from getting discouraged; this was particularly important since she required many years of rehabilitation.

PROBLEMS IN GROUP WORK WITH STROKE PATIENTS

We encountered some problems which were unique to this group and some also which were unique to the individual patients; all of them affected the group process. *One concern of paralyzed persons is the help which is offered them by others, whether they want it or not.* In the second meeting it was mentioned that many people do too much for the disabled. I used myself as an example to demonstrate this point. When Mrs. L dropped her pad of paper on the floor, my first thought was to pick it up. I pointed out to the group that I realized Mrs. L might be capable of getting it for herself.

In spite of her hemiparesis, Mrs. L picked up her paper, although she had to expend more effort and time than I would have.

Since this particular group had major problems in communication, we concentrated more on the manifest, or spoken, meaning of verbal behavior than on the latent, or hidden, message.[8] The main task, we felt, was to comprehend the words being said. The most severe communication problems centered on (1) the blind woman, (2) the completely (verbal) aphasic patient, and (3) the five patients with speech impairments.

Mrs. A, the blind patient, had a problem in communicating with the group. She often appeared to fall asleep; her eyes were shut and her head hung low. This posture may have been because she could not see figures and objects to keep her alert and active. She had difficulty following the conversation, perhaps because she was unaware of who was speaking. Therefore, I occasionally told her who was talking, or who had walked in late to the group session. She was moderately deaf in her right ear, possibly from her stroke, and she could not always hear everything said, so I repeated to her certain phrases which she had misunderstood. I also placed her wheelchair further inside the circle than the others, with her right ear away from the center of the circle.

The completely (verbal) aphasic patient, Mrs. L, communicated by writing on a pad of paper which she carried to the group. She occasionally wrote a note which was read aloud by the person sitting beside her. I found it was easy to unintentionally ignore a silent member like Mrs. L. I felt it was important to give her attention at every meeting, so she would not feel left out. If she communicated nothing in the first part of the meeting, I often asked her a question. For example, I asked how her trip to the country had been. Another time I asked if she would care to bring up some topic for discussion in the group.

The third problem area in communication involved patients with speech impairments. *Feelings of frustration are common among patients with communication difficulties.*[9] Mrs. LU had expressive aphasia and often mispronounced her words. In session four, I sensed her frustration and anger at Mrs. C when she wrongly guessed the word Mrs. LU was trying to say. I commented: "It must be frustrating for you, LU, getting across what you are trying to say."

Mrs. LU: I don't care anymore, but used to.

Me: You once found it frustrating, but now you are used to it?

Mrs. LU: That's right.

Stokes indicates that it is a frequent mistake "to speak for the aphasic patient instead of waiting for him to speak."[10] Rather, aphasic patients need to receive patience, acceptance, and encouragement to speak at their own rate. I wanted to involve other patients in the discussion, so I asked the group, "Do others also feel frustrated at times trying to communicate?" Mr. R quickly responded, "Sure." (At this point, the co-leader can ask the group members to describe what it is like for them to be frustrated when trying to communicate.) I then focused on the aphasic group member by saying, "Mrs. L, do other people sometimes become impatient with you, since they have to wait while you write your words?" The up-and-down movement of her head indicated "yes."

Many stroke patients have defects in memory;[11] *this problem must be kept in mind.* One group member, Mrs. J, forgot one meeting until she saw me afterward. After that, I found her on the ward before each session to remind her. Another approach I used was to give Mr. E a note which specified the day and time of group meetings. Mrs. W showed some initiative in dealing with her memory difficulty. She asked Miss O three times before the first meeting to be sure she had the exact time and day.

Another common problem for the stroke patient is an uncontrollable emotional instability or lability.[12] Sudden crying spells or laughter may erupt for no apparent reason. For example, Mrs. L briefly cried in the seventh group session when the conversation was focused on Mrs. A. Mrs. L wrote me a note saying: "Mrs. A can hear, but doesn't think." Mrs. L was apparently saddened to think about Mrs. A, but overreacted emotionally by an outburst of crying. Since acceptance of this behavior is important, I would ask her, "What is wrong, Mrs. L?" or comment, "It is all right to cry, Mrs. L," An issue was not made about her sudden weeping; the stroke patient often does not know the reason for the emotional outburst.

Patients with recent strokes are apt to be very involved with themselves, since they are attempting to deal with a changed body image.[13] One goal which Miss O and I strived to achieve was to help the patients share ways of coping with common problems. However, in the first five group meetings, I felt that the group members did not care about anyone else's disability. Their behavior seemed to say: "It would not help me to know about anyone's stroke; besides, I am not interested." Perhaps this attitude reflected a protective mechanism on the part of group members against having to ask for help or having to share of themselves. However, as the group process developed over the weeks, patients began asking each other questions about their strokes. The co-leaders initiated the sharing of common concerns until group members felt enough trust to share their problems. In meeting five, Mr. EW was the first patient to show an interest in sharing information. He asked the group if anyone had eye trouble, since his stroke had left him with visual impairment. Their sharing, we hoped, would assist in adjustment to a new body image.

THEMES OF GROUP DISCUSSION

Several themes occurred frequently in the group discussions. The most common were the following:

1 Determination versus hopelessness
2 Progress versus status quo
3 Reality versus fantasy
4 Growth versus stagnation

The theme of determination versus hopelessness was one which was voiced in five meetings. For example, in the second meeting, Mrs. C said that determination was a key factor to successful rehabilitation. For the past few years, she and Mrs. LU had exercised together each day.

In the sixth meeting, Mr. EW admitted he should learn to write with his left hand, but said he lacked the motivation. Mrs. LU, who had practiced writing daily for the last two years, encouraged him to write a little each day. Her persistence in improving her writing skill provided an example for Mr. EW.

Mr. JI told the group his stroke had left him with a completely paralyzed right side. Even though the doctors gave him no hope of walking again, he did not accept that verdict. Through a positive attitude and much effort in rehabilitation, Mr. JI was ambulatory, with complete function in the affected side.

In the eighth meeting, Mr. E seemed depressed that his progress in speech therapy was slow. I mentioned that Mrs. LU had been practicing her speech for several years and had progressed a great deal. We conveyed to him that, even though the process was slow, the individual must continue practicing.

The second group theme—progress versus status quo—appeared frequently after the fourth group meeting. In the fifth session, Mr. R said he noticed improvement as a result of his walking and speech therapy. Perhaps this statement inspired other patients to discuss their own accomplishments and failures openly in the following meetings. Emphasis was placed upon progress in rehabilitation; we hoped to encourage the patients to try harder.

In session seven, Mr. JI complained about his slow progress in speech therapy. He was living in the hospital until his speech improved enough to get a job. He told the group that he realized a lot of time was necessary to relearn his speech.

The group frequently discussed progress in the following areas: (1) learning to write with the left hand, (2) learning to walk with crutches or a walker, (3) dressing oneself independently, and (4) relearning speech. The patients often gave support and encouragement to a group member who was progressing slowly in rehabilitation.

Another group theme—reality versus fantasy—appeared in four group meetings. In one session, Mrs. LU said her goal was to be completely well in five years, at which time she could, perhaps, return to barbering. Three weeks later, Mrs. LU decided it was too difficult to plan her future occupation since it was impossible to assess how much strength would return to her affected side.

A difference in Mr. R's behavior was noted in the fourth session. He had been fairly quiet, and rarely smiled. A denial of reality was evident in his behavior, as he said he had no fear of not walking again or of falling while learning to walk with crutches. Mr. R claimed that when he would be discharged from the hospital in the near future, he would find no problems he could not handle. His complete denial of problems and feelings broke down when he admitted frustration with his speech impairment.

In the seventh session, Mrs. W dealt with reality by discussing her future plans with the group. She wanted to live by herself in the city, and since her speech showed much improvement, she expected to be discharged from the hospital shortly. Her speech therapy would probably continue on an outpatient basis. When we asked her about returning to work, she said that she preferred to keep busy with a babysitting job.

The group members were encouraged to plan for the future when they seemed ready to look ahead, but first they had to be involved with rehabilitation and know some of their limitations, so that realistic goals could be set.

The last theme was growth versus stagnation. Patients frequently taught one another ways they could effect change in themselves. In some of the meetings, Mrs. LU and Mrs. C demonstrated their arm exercises. They stated they often exercised together while watching television. Other patients were encouraged to try those exercises and find some enjoyment in doing them. Perhaps Mr. EW, who claimed to be lazy, was motivated to exercise his affected arm.

In the fifth meeting, one patient asked how speech therapy was taught to patients at that hospital. Mrs. LU informed the group that sounds are first relearned, then syllables, and finally simple words. She imitated for the group how she practiced making sounds. As group members shared knowledge, they became more aware of one another's rehabilitation programs.

Some group members felt comfortable enough with their disability to discuss freely the devices they depended on for support. For example, one patient demonstrated removing and reapplying her leg brace, which had a shoe attached. Through a slow process, she applied the brace with one hand. Thus the group members became familiar with such a device, one which some of them might utilize in the future.

Other devices used by group members were commented on in subsequent meetings. For example, Mrs. LU wore a sling on her affected arm whenever she came to the group on crutches. Two patients commented on the use of the sling. Mrs. C, who had once used a sling, thought it was not difficult to apply by oneself, while Mr. EW felt it was too much effort for him to use a sling even if his shoulder did sag.

Mr. EW voluntarily told the group about his unique cane which had two additional legs to help maintain balance. He informed us that he received the cane two years ago when his stroke first occurred. He proudly admitted getting many comments about his cane.

We, as co-leaders, also functioned in an information-giving capacity when opportunities arose in the group. For example, when Mr. EW expressed concern about his defective vision, I used the opportunity to explain a visual problem called hemianopsia, or one-sided field blindness, which is common in stroke patients. Even though no group members had hemianopsia, they were better informed about that defect in other stroke patients, and thus were in a position to help explain hemianopsia to those afflicted with it. Another time, I asked a group member if his hearing was affected by his stroke. This question led to a discussion of how a hearing defect can result from a stroke. The patients then began to compare how their strokes had affected them. Learning more about their strokes helped the patients increase their awareness of what to expect from the disability.

MOODS IN THE GROUP

The mood or emotional climate in the group changed over the weeks. In the first two group meetings, anxiety was evident. Even though a little friendliness was shown, most patients remained withdrawn and unwilling to share.

Besides anxiety and nervous laughter, two new emotions appeared in the third meeting. Mrs. C, who valued self-motivation, showed hostility toward Mrs. A because of her lack of ambition by stating, "Mrs. A is lazy." On several other occasions, Mrs. C's hostility toward Mrs. A was expressed through sarcastic remarks.

The second new emotion expressed in the third session was frustration, which occurred when Mrs. LU attempted to communicate her thoughts. She became impatient and annoyed with group members who could not understand the words she said. When frustration about communication was evident at the next group session, the subject was openly discussed.

The atmosphere of the fifth meeting was somewhat anxious, yet the patients were more willing to learn about one another. For example, everyone mentioned the state where they were born. To know other group members better served a useful purpose because that knowledge helped to build new relationships and group cohesiveness.

A feeling of closeness was observed at this same session as more concern was shown by group members toward one another. For example, Mrs. LU suggested to Mr. EW that he use a sling, which would help to prevent a sagging shoulder on his affected side, thus showing a genuine concern for his appearance.

In the sixth group meeting, a happy atmosphere prevailed; joking and laughter were heard. The amount of anxiety had lessened as group members became better acquainted. More affection and concern were also shown, and patients began to direct the conversation toward other group members rather than toward the co-leaders. Moreover, the quieter patients were more willing to speak and share their thoughts.

After the sixth meeting, a more relaxed atmosphere was apparent, as group members began to share their feelings and thoughts. A feeling of comradeship or belonging began to develop among the group members as the weeks passed.

NONVERBAL COMMUNICATION IN THE GROUP

If there is a disturbance in verbal communication, nonverbal behavior becomes more important as a means of reaching others. For example, Mrs. L, the completely aphasic patient, utilized nonverbal modes of communication. In the group, she frequently shook her head to indicate "yes" and "no." She always carried paper and a pen so that she could write notes to be read to the group. Thus, writing and head motions were both effectively used by this patient in place of speech.

Because Mrs. L was fairly quiet throughout meetings, it was often difficult to detect her degree of involvement in the conversation. I did not realize what an astute observer she was until she wrote a note stating, "Mr. JI is getting fat." He *was* getting heavier, but I had not noticed. Other written comments by her revealed much nonverbal involvement which was concealed by her lack of speech. Mrs. L had deep empathy for group members. Facial expressions occasionally revealed feelings of joy, sorrow, or worry. Once she wrote a note to Miss O, which read, "Draw out Mr. E." As it was Mr. E's first group meeting, he appeared very tense and withdrawn. Mrs. L, who had had no previous contact with this man, showed a genuine concern for a distressed group member. Her empathy was evident without her speaking any words.

Another unique characteristic of Mrs. L was her nonverbal sense of humor. For example, when the group was talking about where everyone came from, she laughingly wrote, "I came from an egg." Once she jokingly stretched out her arms for my coat to pretend to steal it. I understood her joke without any verbal communication. We laughed together and I was intrigued by her sense of humor.

PROBLEMS OF SEPARATION ANXIETY

After five group meetings, Miss O went on vacation for a month. Her vacation was not announced to the group until the fifth session. It "slipped her mind" to tell them in earlier meetings. Perhaps her forgetfulness involved unconscious guilt feelings about leaving the group to go on a pleasure trip. When she told the group about her vacation, she said that she would return in four weeks. To prevent misunderstanding, I added clearly that the group would continue to meet.

It occurred to me that the group might be angry at Miss O for leaving. One way of expressing anger is not to attend group meetings. Some of the group members may have been unconsciously thinking: "The group can't be too important if a co-leader can leave us for a vacation. So why should I attend?" The next four group sessions without Miss O did, in fact, result in increased absenteeism. It is possible that the absentees were expressing their anger in this manner. A more constructive approach would be to prepare the group in advance for the co-leader's separation. The group should be told about the vacation at the first meeting or, at the least, several weeks in advance. This kind of preparation may help lessen the group's anger and acting-out behavior.

Because my clinical experience was to end after the eleventh group meeting, I discussed my termination with the group. In the ninth session, I reminded the group that Miss O would return from her vacation at the next group meeting, and also that I would be leaving the group in two weeks. I gave my reason for leaving, and told the group Miss O would continue to meet with them. The initial reaction was sadness about my departure, and at the following meeting, the group inquired about what I would be doing after I left.

CONCLUSION

The group took on a different character when Miss O was present, as compared to when she was away. Because of her background and group experience, Miss O influenced the patients to be verbal, but did not encourage physical activity. When Miss O was vacationing, I encouraged group members to become more activity-oriented. For example, at one meeting, from which Miss O was absent, Mrs. LU voluntarily demonstrated the application of her leg brace. Another time, the group asked several patients to write their names so the other members could determine their writing ability and encourage further practice.

In addition to its being more activity-oriented, a second difference was observed in the group during Miss O's absence: patients were more prone to request and utilize my nursing knowledge. For example, Mr. EW requested that I touch his cold hand to note the poor circulation in the affected side.

In another meeting, a patient who feared he had psoriasis asked me to look at the sores on his arm. It is my opinion that both approaches served a useful purpose for those patients. Pearlmutter says that co-leadership in a group actually benefits the patient by combining the insights and abilities of two trained leaders.[14]

Our group work with stroke patients proved to be effective as the group goals began to be realized. I felt the group experience demonstrated that there are tremendous rewards which patients can gain through support and encouragement from other stroke victims.

REFERENCES

1 Deanna Pearlmutter, "Conceiving and Nurturing the Group," in L. Joel and D. Collins (eds.), *Pyschiatric Nursing Theory and Application*, McGraw-Hill, New York, 1978, pp. 190–191.
2 Lisa Robinson, *Psychiatric Nursing as a Human Experience*, 2d ed., Saunders, Philadelphia, 1977, p. 278.
3 Irvin D. Yalom and Florence Terrazas, "Group Therapy for Psychotic Elderly Patients," *American Journal of Nursing*, vol. 68, no. 8, p. 1691, August 1968.
4 Ibid., p. 1693.
5 Suzanne Lego, "Group Dynamic Theory and Application," in J. Haber, A. Leach, S. Schudy, and B. Sideleau (eds.), *Comprehensive Psychiatric Nursing*, McGraw-Hill, New York, 1978, p. 149.
6 Dorwin Cartwright and Alvin Zander, *Group Dynamics*, Harper & Row, New York, 1968, p. 91.
7 Maxine E. Loomis and Judith T. Dodenhoff, "Working with Informal Patient Groups," *American Journal of Nursing*, vol. 70, no. 9, p. 1943, September 1970.
8 Dorothy Stock Whitaker and Morton S. Lieberman, *Psychotherapy Through the Group Process*, Atherton Press, New York, 1970, pp. 16–17.
9 Howard A. Grey, "The Aphasic Patient," *RN*, p. 48, July 1970.
10 Norma Stephenson Stokes, "Patients Recovering from Aphasia Seek Understanding," *Modern Nursing Home*, vol. 25, no. 3, p. 48, September 1970.
11 Ibid.
12 Lillian Sholtis Brunner and Doris Smith Suddarth, *Textbook of Medical-Surgical Nursing*, 3d ed., Lippincott, Philadelphia, 1975, p. 922.
13 Catherine M. Norris, "Body Image: Its Relevance to Professional Nursing," in C. Carlson and B. Blackwell (eds.), *Behavioral Concepts and Nursing Intervention*, Lippincott, Philadelphia, 1978, p. 32–33.
14 Pearlmutter, op. cit., p. 211.

BIBLIOGRAPHY

Corey, Marianne Schneider: "Groups for the Elderly," in Gerald Corey and Marianne Schneider (eds.), *Group Process and Practice*, Brooks/Cole, Monterey, Calif., 1977.

Fox, Madeline J.: "Talking with Patients Who Can't Answer," *American Journal of Nursing*, vol. 71, no. 6, pp. 1146–1149, June 1971.

Luft, Joseph: *Group Process: An Introduction to Group Dynamics*, National Press Books, Palo Alto, Calif., 1970.

Sampson, Edward E., and Marya Sampson Marthas: *Group Process for the Health Professions*, Wiley, New York, 1977.

Siev, Ellen, and Brenda Freishtat: *Perceptual Dysfunction in the Adult Stroke Patient*, Charles B. Slack, Thorofare, N.J., 1976.

Travis, Georgia: *Chronic Disease and Disability: A Basic Medical-Social Guide,* 2d ed., University of California Press, Berkeley, 1961.

Chapter 18

Implementation of Standards of Practice in Gerontological Nursing

Marilyn Schwab

I am less impressed by the nurse who can identify the patient who is throwing PVCs than with the nurse who can get a frightened, confused person to eat.

Sister Marilyn Schwab

I am well aware that there is great effort to move from the institutional model of care toward the care of people in their home settings, to health maintenance and health teaching, and to primary health services. I believe firmly in that approach. I believe that is the future of health care and the future of nursing, even though my practice has been exclusively in a nursing home.

However, I am equally convinced that nursing has not made sufficient impact on the small segment of our elderly population who suffer such overwhelming disability that inpatient care is necessary, either for a short

At the time this article was written, Sister Marilyn Schwab was administrator of Benedictine Nursing Center, Mount Angel, Oreg. Reprinted with permission from the *American Health Care Association Journal*, vol. 3, no. 5, 1977. Copyright © American Health Care Association, 1977. All rights reserved.

time or for the rest of their lives. Further, I am convinced that, given the patterns of health care delivery in our country, we must begin with the institution, or at least work at improving the quality of institutional care, at the same time that we are advocating and building an alternative network of services.

A major step toward improving the quality of nursing care in an institutional setting, specifically in a setting where the focus of care is on the elderly, is the implementation of the *Standards of Gerontological Nursing Practice* recently revised and published by the American Nurses' Association.[1] What happens to the severely disabled institutionalized patient has great impact on the health status of the entire cohort of the elderly chronically ill, wherever they may be.

I believe that this is true, not only because institutions serve as laboratories for testing treatment methods (e.g., reality-orientation and bladder-training methods), but also because what we do with the frailest and most vulnerable of our society betrays our deepest held values. What we do with the most confused, incontinent, immobile patient in our nursing homes in this country says a great deal about who and what we believe a human person really is.

We are all familiar with the statistic that only 4 to 5 percent of all people over 65 in the United States are in institutions. Recent studies have challenged the use of that figure. In 1973, Dr. Robert Kastenbaum wrote an article in *Aging and Human Development* on "The Four Percent Fallacy . . . ," in which he pointed out that 23 percent of all deaths of people over 65 occurred in institutions and 85 percent of those occurred in nursing homes.[2]

Certainly, many more than 4 percent of the elderly are affected by the quality of care in nursing homes. My strong belief is that until *nursing* is greatly improved in nursing homes, and until nursing as a profession takes its rightful leadership in delivering that care, elderly patients will continue to get into the dead-end street that the nursing home has become for them.

For all of those reasons, I have used the institutional setting as a framework for my discussion of the implementation of standards. I feel I also need to explain my concept of nursing prior to a discussion of the standards.

There are several legitimate conceptual models used by the profession to explain itself, and I suppose each of us chooses that which is most helpful to us in our practice. My concept is that nursing deals primarily with the *effect* of, or the *response* of an individual to an imbalance in the individual's health status, a disease process, or a disability or vulnerability. Thus, nursing is less focused on curing than on caring.

To be a nurse means to have the skills and science to care for people who cannot care for themselves; to assist people to cope with disability or the effects of pathological processes. Thus, I am less impressed with the nurse who can determine that a patient is "throwing PVCs" than I am with a nurse who can get a frightened confused patient to eat.

One of the reasons the general public and legislators seem to assume that nurse's aides *must* do most of the care in nursing homes is due to the fact that many in the nursing profession itself have lost sight of what nursing really is. We have undersold the degree of skill involved in "taking care of"—in *nursing*—people. I believe we need to refocus, and the long-term care situation in this country is one of the settings that might clarify our role for us, if we are willing to get involved.

The American Nurses' Association's *Standards of Gerontological Nursing Practice*, which have just been revised,[3] are a major way nurses can be involved in promoting better care of the frail, institutionalized elderly. The original set of standards, published in 1969, were beautifully articulated gerontological nursing principles. These standards represented the earliest official attempt by the profession to spell out the core content of the field.[4]

After the generic *Standards of Nursing Practice* were developed, however, the original *Standards of Geriatric Nursing Practice* were out of step, and efforts were begun to get them into the process model so that they would be consistent with the standards written by other ANA Divisions on Nursing Practice.

I do not think it was happenstance that the revisions took several years to accomplish. I believe that that time period is a reflection of the small number of practitioners prepared in both nursing theory and gerontological theory, who were actively translating content into their practice settings. Gerontological nursing is a very young specialty, and while many people are getting interested, gerontological nurses are still struggling to define their body of knowledge and their practice.

The phrase, "implementation of standards," can mean a variety of highly complex and theoretical activities. ANA has published several important reports about implementation.[5-7] I would like to use the term simply to mean "the use of" the standards. Therefore, I have chosen simply to review each standard and relate it to the practice situation in long term care. As we proceed, it may become obvious that, in fact, the use of the standards in this stage of the development of gerontological nursing may be to help nurses themselves clarify their function.

Standard I—Data are systematically and continuously collected about the health status of the older adult. The data are accessible, communicated, and recorded.

Rationale: In order to provide comprehensive nursing care for the older adult, the data are collected from a framework that includes the scientific findings and knowledge derived from the fields of gerontology and nursing.

Much work remains to be done about assessment and data gathering in the long term care setting. Nursing continues to be too concerned with medical care data and unsure of what constitutes nursing care data. Our skills in assessment of coping patterns, lifestyles, and life space needs, and even activities of daily living at functional levels are not very sophisticated and certainly not standardized.

We search for a medically diagnosed reason for bladder incontinence, for instance, instead of gathering our own data on fluid intake, distance to the bathroom, disorientation, or depression. Data collection by nursing must be truly autonomous.

The best example of what I mean by that is in the realm of mental functioning of the elderly patient. If the nurse builds her assessment around the assumption that the patient has an irreversible mental disorder because there is a diagnosis of chronic brain syndrome or cerebral arteriosclerosis, she will miss, or misinterpret, important patient data in her assessment.

There is evidence in our nursing literature and on our assessment forms that dietary habits, patterns of pain or sleep, and activity and elimination patterns are important areas of nursing assessment. But, too often, our assessment is heavily influenced by other data we already have from the medical diagnosis. With the elderly patient, medical diagnoses are often poorly made, and there are frequently a number of diagnoses. Thus, careful, autonomous nursing assessment is essential to good care.

Standard I reads, "The data are accessible, communicated, and recorded." Nurses have not yet mastered the skills of "naming the problem." The work of the group from St. Louis University on nursing diagnosis is extremely important for this reason. Nursing must develop its language. Just as the data gathering must be autonomous, so must the nomenclature be autonomous.

The word "autonomous" does not mean that nursing nomenclature would be in conflict with other data or diagnosis, nor would nursing nomenclature say the same thing in another way. The language of nursing would stand on its own merit. It means something by itself. And it would mean even more in relation to other data, because it would add something to other data. We cannot be colleagues or collaborators with other disciplines unless we know who we are, what our data and our diagnoses are, and what they mean.

The St. Louis University group cannot decide on nomenclature for the profession by itself, and that is why they have involved nurses from all over the country. Nurses in every setting must be thinking through the logic of the nomenclature, attempting to standardize it for their own setting, and contributing to the literature on the subject. It is a long range project for nursing, and it is more than an academic exercise for a few.

Again, the long term care setting provides all sorts of opportunities for nurses to develop this skill because of the nature of patient needs. Thus, the first standard points us in a direction, and gives us some general statement to guide our thinking. It must be implemented by nurses.

Standard II—Nursing diagnoses are derived from the identified normal responses of the individual to aging and the data collected about the health status of the older adult.

Rationale: Each person ages in an individual way. The individual's normal response to aging must be identified before deviations in response requiring nursing action can be identified.

The key elements in this standard are the ones having to do with normal aging and the normal responses of the individual. This standard speaks to one of the main reasons why I find gerontological nursing exciting.

Gerontology and the study of normal biological aging is only about 25 years old. We know very little about what normal aging really is. One of the very essential characteristics of gerontological nursing is the need to distinguish the normal aging process from pathology, so that one can intervene in potentially reversible pathology and assist the person to accept the irreversible changes of the normal aging process.

To deal with other reversible pathology, and ignore irreversible changes due to old age, is to fail the elderly person. To tell him that all his problems are due to old age, and that he should just accept it, results in frustration and custodialism.

Our past mistakes in the care of the aged have taken essentially one of two routes. We either treat the patient's broken hip and send him home, ignoring all else, because "Medicare doesn't pay for it"; or we turn over his care to a motherly nurse's aide who will keep him comfortable without needing to know what his potential function is. We err either in an extreme professionalism or in an ignorant but well-meaning protectiveness. We must learn to combine scientifically sound, quality health care intervention in reversing pathology with the caring warmth and empathy needed to help people accept irreversible deterioration when it occurs. We can only do that well when we know the difference, and strive always to distinguish it in individual older people with great care.

Nursing has the challenge, along with other health care professions, of adding to the existing body of knowledge about the aging process. An example of the developing nature of gerontological research is the relationship between physical fitness and neuromuscular decline. Numerous studies have been done over the years regarding muscular atrophy and infiltration of muscle with fat, resulting in a decrease in hand grip strength, work rate, speed, and endurance. Because this occurred so universally in tested subjects, tentative statements were made concerning the normal aging process and muscular activity. Recently, more gerontologists have suggested that reduction in exercise and fitness is culturally induced. We are culturally programmed to play tennis less, or ride bicycles less frequently as we get older. We say things like "I'm too old for this kind of thing." Perhaps the increase of fatty tissue in muscle and the muscle atrophy seen is not normal aging at all, but due to decreased activity. Nursing needs to be asking "cause and effect" questions such as that.

One of the statements in the introduction to the standards states this very well.

> In the practice of gerontological nursing, the nurse must continually question the assumptions upon which gerontological nursing practice is based, retaining those which are valid and searching for and utilizing new knowledge.

Gerontological nursing is characterized by a dynamic—almost tentative—base of knowledge. Nursing is an ideal discipline to test findings of basic research, not only in biology, but also in psychology and the sociology of aging.

Standard III—A plan of nursing care is developed in conjunction with the older adult and/or significant others that includes goals derived from the nursing diagnosis.

Rationale: Goals are a determination of the results to be achieved and are an essential part of planning care. All goals ultimately are directed toward maximizing achievable independence in everyday living.

Goal-setting in gerontological nursing has some special challenges. Few people want to give the elderly person the benefit of the ability to make his own decisions and set his own goals. Family goals are sometimes in direct conflict with the patient's goals for himself, which places the nurse in an advocacy/teaching/counseling role.

Probably the most difficult situation is that in which the patient's goals for himself are, in truth, unrealistic or impossible, and he cannot accept that this is so. Certainly there must be exquisite skill and empathy involved in coming to the conclusion that he is in fact unrealistic. The fine line between protecting the patient and interfering with his human rights is a very difficult one to discern.

When cure, and total return of function, is impossible, or when any return of function on any level is doubtful, then the skill of the nurse is truly tested in goal-setting. Gerontological nursing requires an ability on the part of the nurse to be willing to work with small goals and goals of preventing secondary or iatrogenic complications. The nurse must be committed to goal-directed nursing at all costs, because frequently other health disciplines (e.g., medicine, physical therapy) reach the point of having no goals left, and the nurse stands alone in defining and operationalizing goals. Without goals, care becomes custodial, which is never appropriate for a human person. Gerontological nurses must be comfortable with goals that state things like the achievement of a comfortable and dignified death.

One of the factors under this standard mentions congruency with other planned therapies. An interdisciplinary approach to patient care is essential because of the nature of the needs of the aged, chronically ill patient—needs which are multiple, collective, and interrelated. Participation of the frail elderly person in his own care-planning is frequently limited. That participation is so important that there is no real way to make up for it, but any attempt to come close to understanding his needs and intervening appropriately requires much more data, obtained by more than one person.

Standard IV—The plan of nursing care includes priorities and prescribed nursing approaches and measures to achieve the goals derived from the nursing diagnosis.

Rationale: Priorities and approaches are an integral part of the planning process and are necessary to the successful achievement of the goals.

Priority setting assumes some special problems in long term care of the frail elderly. First, we have some serious conflicts in our society about what desired outcomes and goals we really hold for these people, and that interferes with our priority setting. Secondly, the institutionalized elderly are characterized by a multiplicity of problems so that deciding *which* need or problem has priority is complicated.

By conflicts in society, I mean such things as our apparent goals to keep patients in nursing homes sanitary and safe from fire and at the same time be concerned for their individuality and autonomy. Does the priority of safety override the elderly man's individuality and life-style which includes smoking his pipe? Or the individuality involved in keeping a slightly soiled, favorite chair?

I believe that nurses should become the advocates for what I call the holistic or whole person approach to long term care of the elderly. If nurses gathered data about significant others, coping patterns, and favorite foods, as scientifically as they gather data about blood pressure and temperature, we would make great progress toward that goal. If nurses documented the effects of the visit of a significant other, or a cup of warm milk, as conscientiously as they chart medications and treatments, we would make even greater progress.

We must be convinced that these things are not somewhere down the scale of value from medicine—not just "frosting on the cake"—but an integral part of therapy. We make remarks about a new hairdo being better than medicine, but we never give it the same dignity in our documentation. Perhaps if we began to do that, the evidence would convince the world.

One of the greatest challenges of gerontological nursing is that of balancing the various needs, some of which are in conflict with each other. When the need for social interaction outweighs the need for absolute bedrest for the failing heart, we often recognize it, but feel like we are somehow being sympathetic, and not really scientific or professional by meeting that need.

We say things like, "Oh well, I let her cheat. At her age, what difference does it make?" That betrays a "medical" rather than holistic approach. I submit that those decisions, which involve placing some priority *other* than a medical one first, must be made with all of the knowledge and understanding and science and skill of gerontological nursing. We are *not* less than professional when we see other-than-medical needs as priorities.

Needless to say, such judgments must be based on thorough assessment, accurate diagnosis, and a constant and sensitive communication with the patient. Anything less than that is negligence. Our priorities can then be defended on the basis of good data and sound rationale.

Standard V—The plan of care is implemented, using appropriate nursing actions.

Rationale: Appropriate nursing actions are purposefully directed toward the stated goals.

The nursing process and the standards will remain an exercise in documentation and theorizing unless the nurse is truly involved in implementation. That means that the nurse does patient care. One of the most alarming signs of misunderstanding about nursing, both within and without the profession, is the assumption that it is all right that nurses' aides do most of the nursing in the nursing homes, and that one cannot expect the RN to know anything specific about the patient.

It is true that the multiplicity of nursing tasks and their frequency and repetition make the use of nursing assistants desirable in nursing homes. However, for nurses to delegate away patient care almost in its entirety has been disastrous for the patient. Professional nurses cannot do all the dressing, bathing, feeding, and toileting of patients in long-term care facilities. However, if the nurse refuses ever to be involved in these tasks, the nurse is unable to assess, diagnose, intervene, rehabilitate, or comfort. We must work vigorously for changes in licensing standards so that the ratio of professional to unprepared personnel is improved.

Standard VI—The older adult and/or significant other(s) participate in determining the progress attained in the achievement of established goals.

Rationale: The older adult and/or significant other(s) are essential components in the determination of nursing's impact upon the individual's health status.

Evaluation seems to be here to stay. Nursing must prove its ability to evaluate its own interventions, which, of course, presupposes measurable goals based on sound data and reliable diagnosis. Here the entire process is tested. In the evaluation, and in the measurements chosen to apply to data for the purpose of evaluation, nursing has an opportunity again to demonstrate the holistic nature of long term care.

Professional Standards Review Organizations (PSRO) are struggling with the differences between long term care and acute medical care. One of the glaring differences, of course, is that medical diagnosis by itself cannot be used as a justification for services rendered or as a basis for expected outcomes. Criteria such as discharge rates and length of stay are meaningless in long term care of the elderly.

Nursing, in developing standardized nursing data, nomenclature, and documented interventions which reach goals other than cure and discharge, could contribute in a unique and critical way to this developing science of evaluation of services in health care.

Institutional care of the frail elderly provides an ideal setting in which to demonstrate the effects of an holistic approach as opposed to a medical approach. Nursing must take a much more active role in developing this aspect of PSRO.

Standard VII—The older adult and/or significant other(s) participate in the ongoing process of assessment, the setting of new goals, the reordering of priorities, the revision of plans for nursing care, and the initiation of new nursing actions.

Standard VII, as well as Standard VI, emphasizes the importance of the ongoing involvement of the older adult and/or his significant others throughout all phases of the nursing process. In an institutional setting, the involvement of the elderly patient in evaluation of programs, resetting of priorities, and reviewing of goals and plans is often overlooked, because professionals assume that he is incapable of understanding or participating. Concurrently, relatives are too often only tolerated by the professional staff, usually just so that they do not create "too much disturbance."

In our program planning we rarely give the patient and/or his significant others his full place in our planning and evaluating processes. Nurses as well as other health professionals have some deeply ingrained attitudes about the superiority of their professional judgments, and they usually do not find involvement of the patient and his family in the caring process an easy thing to accomplish.

If the concept of an holistic versus a medical approach to care of the elderly is valuable, then the patient and his significant others must be involved in the whole process, and their involvement must be taken seriously. Again, the long-term setting could prove a good demonstration site for modeling the kind of involvement that should occur in all health care.

I have attempted to review the *Standards of Gerontological Nursing Practice* with a view toward some of their practical implications and implementation. Implementation of the practice standards at this point in the history of nursing care in institutions serving the frail elderly is still primarily one of clarifying the nursing role and the nursing process, and of teaching the practitioner some principles and care concepts of the specialty of gerontological nursing.

The standards hopefully will be used as a basis for institutional and agency standards, for development of peer review for nursing care audit, and for evaluations and improvement in patient care. But this will only be possible when *nurses* understand what the standards really demand in the way of knowledge and skill in nursing process *and* how to use the content of gerontology.

REFERENCES

1   Executive Committee of Division on Gerontological Nursing Practice, *Standards of Gerontological Nursing Practice*, American Nurses' Association, Kansas City, Mo., 1976.
2   R. S. Kastenbaum and S. Candy, "The Four Percent Fallacy: A Methodological and Empirical Critique of Extended Care Facility Program Statistics," *Aging and Human Development*, vol. 4, pp. 15–21, 1973.
3   *Standards of Gerontological Nursing Practice*, op. cit.
4   Executive Committee of Division on Geriatric Nursing Practice, *Standards of Geriatric Nursing Practice*, American Nurses' Association, Kansas City, Mo., 1973.
5   Congress on Nursing Practice, *A Plan for Implementation of the Standards of Nursing Practice*, American Nurses' Association, Kansas City, Mo., 1975.
6   *Recommendations for Involvement of Nurses in the PSRO Review Process*, submitted by American Nurses' Association to the Office of the Professional Standards Review and Bureau of Quality Assurance, Health Services Administration, Department of Health, Education and Welfare, under the provisions of contract #HSA 105-74-207, 1975.
7   *Guidelines for Review of Nursing Care at the Local Level*, submitted by American Nurses' Association to the Office of the Professional Standards Review and Bureau of Quality Assurance; Health Services Administration, Department of Health, Education and Welfare, under the provisions of contract #HSA 105-74-207, 1976.

Courtesy of Harvey Finkle

Part Five

Psychosocial Nursing: Special Concerns

Care permeates everything a nurse does.

Ruth Wu

INTRODUCTION

Part 5 includes problems nurses often must contend with in their nursing care of the older person. Harris, in Chapter 19, describes community health nursing and chronic disease, especially strokes and osteoarthritis. Chapter 20 focuses on the common problem of wandering. The psychosocial aspects of incontinence are discussed by Bartol in Chapter 21. Chapter 22 is written by Robinson, an Australian nurse, who describes the role she carved out for herself as a coordinator in a day care center and in a geriatric complex.

Chapter 19

Coping with Chronic Disease

Beverly Harris

Wish not so much to live long as to live well.

Benjamin Franklin

Living with a chronic disease is a fact of life for many older Americans. According to data reported by Weg, older people have more frequent and longer hospital stays, visit the physician more often, and spend more money on drugs (which are usually for a chronic disease). Over 75 percent of people over 65 years of age suffer from chronic conditions.[1] Data from noninstitutionalized elderly people reported that 43 percent had some limitation in activity, and 38 percent had limitation in a major activity as a result of a chronic condition.[2]

This chapter describes the coping behaviors of elderly persons who live in the community. Psychosocial adjustment to stroke and osteoarthritis will serve as primary examples because these two diseases are major disabling conditions in the older population. The onset of stroke is an acute crisis, offering a dramatic contrast to the more gradual onset of osteoarthritis. The community health nurse's role in working with older clients who are coping with chronicity will also be dealt with. See Table 19-1 for a list of common geriatric problems.

COPING WITH STROKE

The residual following a stroke can be minimal, devastating, or somewhere between these two extremes. Poststroke disabilities occur in the (1) physical, (2) cognitive, (3) emotional, and (4) social spheres. The spouse and the relatives of stroke patients are also affected by the stroke.

Review of the Literature

In 1962, Ullman published the results of an early study on the psychological consequences of stroke, which covered a wide range of behavioral manifestations. In this study, Ullman identified three major factors that influence the patient's reaction to a stroke: the extent of brain damage, the strengths and weaknesses of the prestroke personality, and the possibilities and limitations of the patient's current life situation.[3]

An article by Borden published the same year considered the psychological significance of stroke from the perspectives of the patient, the family, and the health professional. Borden states that depression and regression in mild to moderate forms are common, normal reactions to a stroke. Any situation that causes a loss of self-esteem may precipitate a depression, and illness can be a direct cause of loss of self-esteem.[4]

Borden emphasized the importance of the role of the family and community in the adjustment of the stroke patient, and maintained that the dangers of isolation are as great as those of paralysis.[5]

Tikofsky identified the patient's prestroke emotional, intellectual, educational, occupational, and social status as being among the variables that will influence the patient's adjustment and rehabilitation. Tikofsky included the family's reactions and attitudes as factors that significantly influence the patient's response to treatment.[6] He recommended a focus on the stroke patient's abilities, rather than on disabilities.

Leonard used cerebrovascular accident as an example of the causes of a disturbed body image. Family reactions to the chronic disability, ranging from panic to guilt because of ambivalent feelings toward the patient, were noted by Leonard,[7] who also raised the possibility that the family may use the altered status of the patient as an excuse for keeping the patient dependent.[8] Involving the family in the patient's care throughout the hospital period is one of the recommendations for successful rehabilitation that Leonard makes.

Schultz identified the patient's emotional reactions to stroke as fear, depression, anxiety, anger, and frustration. Schultz stated that "family members have similar reactions and, in addition, they may have strong feelings of guilt."[9] The importance of follow-up care to assist patients and

Table 19-1 Common Geriatric Problems

Most common reasons for office contact with patients 65 years of age or older in Wisconsin study

Reason	Patients No.	Patients %	Cumulative %
1 Essential benign hypertension	271	8.8	8.8
2 Chronic ischemic heart disease	213	6.9	15.7
3 Diabetes mellitus	168	5.5	21.2
4 Symptomatic heart disease	110	3.6	24.8
5 Osteoarthritis, allied conditions	88	2.9	27.7
6 Surgical aftercare	85	2.8	30.5
7 Arteriosclerosis	76	2.5	33.0
8 General medical examination	61	2.0	35.0
9 Neuroses	60	2.0	37.0
10 Arthritis, unspecified	58	1.9	38.9
11 Obesity not specified as of endocrine origin	56	1.8	40.7
12 Acute myocardial infarction	44	1.4	42.1
13 Emphysema	39	I.3	43.4
14 Generalized ischemic cerebrovascular disease	39	1.3	44.7
15 Prophylactic inoculation, vaccination	34	1.1	45.8
16 Hypertensive heart disease	32	1.0	46.8
17 Synovitis, bursitis, tenosynovitis	29	0.9	47.7
18 Acute upper respiratory infection of multiple or unspecified sites	29	0.9	48.6
19 Angina pectoris	28	0.9	49.5
20 Other general symptoms	28	0.9	50.4
21 Other deficiency anemias	26	0.8	51.2
22 Symptoms referable to cardiovascular, lymphatic system	25	0.8	52.0
23 Symptoms referable to limbs, joints	24	0.8	52.8
24 Asthma	23	0.7	53.5
25 Rheumatoid arthritis, allied conditions	23	0.7	54.2
26 Varicose veins of lower extremities	22	0.7	54.9

Source: Postgraduate Medicine, vol. 64, no. 1, p. 86, July 1978.

families with the problems that occur after discharge from the institution was emphasized by Schultz.

Steger, in discussing the psychological factors of rehabilitation, noted that the elderly are in a period of life in which they suffer many losses. Steger said "the life cycle issues confronting the elderly patient affect adjustment to disability."[10] He goes on to discuss the possibility that the older client may find the sick role more rewarding than the alternatives of loneliness, anxiety, and isolation.

The Onset of Stroke

The onset of a stroke is a crisis for most stroke victims. Although there may have been prior warning signs, the occurrence of a major stroke is usually rapid and frightening. Whether the stroke happens while the individual is awake or during sleep, the patient learns in a short time that something drastic has taken place.

Abilities that were intact just a few hours earlier begin to fail. This situation is met with extreme anxiety by most older patients. Borden describes this reaction of diffuse, disorganizing anxiety as an initial reaction to any illness which is experienced as a threat to life.[11] Patients will frequently talk of the fear, panic, and confusion that they felt at the onset of a stroke.

Coping with the onset of a stroke has been compared to coping with impending death or with the death of a loved one.[12] The patient must go through the stages of grieving in order to accept and adjust to an altered health status.

Family members and spouses of stroke patients also may experience the patient's stroke as a crisis, demonstrating the same feelings of panic, anxiety, and uncertainty. The significance of the onset of a stroke to the spouse is reflected in the comment made by many spouses, "Why has this happened to me?"

For the stroke patient who returns home, what started as a crisis becomes a chronic disease. The long-term adjustment process for both family members and patient may require permanent role changes.

Patterns of Coping with Stroke

Upon returning to the community the stroke patient is faced with adjusting to both a new self-image and the losses caused by the stroke. Spouses or other family members have to adjust to a person who may be very different from the prestroke individual. Often the family must take on new roles and responsibilities. Underlying the difficult adjustments for both patient and family is the anxiety caused by uncertainty. The extent of the patient's functional recovery is unknown; the occurrence of another stroke is unpredictable.

Different patterns of coping are found in stroke victims. Denial, withdrawal, dependency, or identification with a group of people in similar circumstances are some of the more common coping mechanisms. The same ways of coping are used by spouses of stroke victims. All of these coping mechanisms have potential for supporting either positive or negative adjustment patterns.

Living with Stroke

Positive Adjustments For a great many stroke patients, both those who live alone and those who live with spouses, returning to the community is followed by a positive adjustment to the crisis in their lives. There seem to be as many ways of making an adjustment to chronic changes as there are people who have strokes. A variety of the coping patterns come into use to support this adjustment.

Denial of the residual of stroke has allowed many a stroke victim to make a recovery far beyond that predicted by the medical profession. A stubborn refusal to admit that one's condition is permanent can lead to hard work aimed at regaining lost functions. The spouse's denial of the patient's disabilities may allow the patient to use remaining capabilities to the fullest.

Withdrawal from activities that are too stressful or too exhausting can be an important protective action. It is not uncommon to hear a stroke patient say that he or she never really enjoyed this or that activity (or those people) anyway, and that the stroke provides a good excuse to stop participating! After the stroke, patient and spouse may realize the limits of their time and energy and plan to spend both in the most enjoyable ways possible.

Dependency to the degree of being able to accept needed help from others can be a positive adjustment for both patient and spouse. For example, the patient who accepts the reality that driving is no longer within his or her capabilities may be more able to consent to using other forms of transportation. The spouse who realizes that total responsibility for housework and yard maintenance is too much may be more willing to accept help from a homemaker service.

Identifying with an individual or group with similar problems can be a positive adaptation. Association with other stroke families offers a supportive environment and an opportunity to see role models. Moreover, the practical information that is shared among stroke victims and spouses is seldom available from professionals.[13]

Religion plays a major role in coping with the losses suffered following a stroke. The patient may feel that "the Good Lord will give me the strength to do what is necessary."

Negative Adjustments   The same coping mechanisms that produce positive results for many stroke patients and families can lead to maladjustment for others. Denial is sometimes demonstrated by the patient to the extent that it interferes with the recovery process. The patient who refuses to admit that he or she has had a stroke often will not take the medication to control blood pressure.

Withdrawal may occur after a stroke to the exclusion of the majority of contacts between the patient and the outside world. The stroke victim may refuse to leave the house and discourage family members and friends from visiting. Often this extreme withdrawal is seen in stroke victims who are ashamed of their disability. An emotionally labile patient may cry inappropriately, then withdraw because of embarrassment. The spouse or patient who chooses to become isolated is often very depressed. Isolation from people and activity reinforces these feelings of depression. As the depression deepens, the withdrawal becomes more pronounced.

The stroke victim who becomes overly dependent after the stroke often assumes a position of control in the family setting. The patient who refuses to do anything alone ensures that someone will be available to help every minute. The spouse may encourage this dependency by refusing to allow the patient independence. Anger is common in families where dependency becomes a problem. The very dependent patient may be angry at a spouse who is still independent. One way to control that independence is to require the spouse's presence at all times. One spouse felt very angry toward the dependent patient because of the constant demands, but would not allow the patient to attempt any independent functioning. This anger is not always verbalized, but is frequently seen in the movements and facial expression of the spouse while he or she is tending to the demands of the patient.

Although the same coping techniques are used by patient and spouse, they seldom follow the same pattern at the same time. The coping behaviors work in the family system. It is as though a reciprocal arrangement has been established. A classic example of this is seen when a spouse who for years has made all decisions has a stroke. When the patient returns home, the previously dominated spouse assumes new roles and responsibilities, and may overreact to the altered relationship and begin to make all decisions for the patient. One wife assumed total control of her husband's life after his stroke, even choosing the shoes and socks he was to wear. This controlling behavior tends to increase the patient's dependent behavior, and both spouse and patient tend to feel strong anger and hostility toward each other.

> **CASE EXAMPLE 1** James G, a 70-year-old man, returned home after suffering a major stroke. His residual disabilities include right-sided hemiparesis and dysphasia. James had difficulty with walking and his speech was slow and halting. His wife, Mary, had actively participated in his care during his hospitalization.
>
> Upon arriving home James wanted very much to take a shower—his first full shower since the stroke. Mary got the shower prepared and helped James get into the shower. He had difficulty standing in the shower and began to feel faint. Mary had not been told about shower benches. With quick reactions, she got undressed and into the shower with James to assist him, whereupon he remarked with a twinkle in his eyes, "This stroke may not be so bad after all!" A supportive spouse and a sense of humor are great assets in coping with stroke.

NURSING INTERVENTION

The community health nurse works with the strengths and needs of the stroke patient. Patient capabilities, support of family and friends, and availability of community resources are part of the program for intervention.

Early involvement of the community health nurse (while the patient is in the hospital) is important because it allows time for a home and family assessment designed to identify the needs which will influence discharge planning. Information gathered about the prestroke coping mechanisms of the patient and family will yield insights into the ways both will cope with the crisis of stroke.

Facilitating Adjustment

A primary function of the community health nurse in facilitating the psychosocial adjustment of a stroke patient is to find out from the patient and family what their major problems and concerns are. Often these problems have not been discussed during the hospitalization period. The community health nurse provides the crucial link between the acute care period and the home, and can provide information and education in a setting where the stroke patient is more comfortable.

It is very reassuring for the patient and spouse to be able to anticipate problems and to have information on possible coping techniques. This educational process is long-term for many families. There is much to learn, and new problems have a way of developing just as old ones are resolved. It is important to reassure the patient and spouse that this is a part of the recovery process and that the nurse will be available to respond to the questions. A 75-year-old wife expressed her appreciation by saying, "I feel better just knowing you will come if we need you."

Encouragement and recognition of successes on the part of the nurse can be helpful to both spouse and patient. Encouragement about progress should, however, be realistic. "You are speaking more distinctly today," is recognition of the progress that the patient is making, while "Your speech will return to normal" may be incorrect and set up unrealistic expectations.

Working with Couples

The nurse can offer much encouragement to the spouse by recognizing the positive contributions made by the spouse to the patient's recovery. This is important, even if the spouse is not actively involved in rehabilitation. While teaching and demonstrating correct rehabilitation techniques to the spouse, praise those things which the spouse is doing properly.

Listening to the feelings of both the patient and spouse can be one of the most valuable activities of the community health nurse. The patient and spouse need to express the feelings of depression, frustration, anger, and discouragement that are part of the adjustment process. Knowing that these feelings are normal and acceptable is very reassuring. In order for these feelings to be discussed it is essential to plan to spend time with the patient and spouse separately. This creates an opportunity for each person to acknowledge feelings about their spouse which would otherwise not be mentioned. One husband of a stroke patient said to his nurse, "It helps just to be able to cry on your shoulder."

The Nurse as Link to the Community

The community health nurse is a link between the patient and the available community resources. The needs that occur in a home after a stroke patient returns from the hospital may be met through community service programs. Homemaking services, meals, transportation, and emotional support may be available, but unknown to the patient and spouse. The community health nurse can familiarize the patient and spouse with these resources. It may be necessary for the nurse to participate in the patient's first experience with a community resource. To be lifted up on a hydraulic lift, strapped into a van, and transported by a system identified for the physically handicapped is a devastating experience for a patient who has been accustomed to getting into a car and driving. The presence of the nurse can do a great deal to allay the patient's anxiety during this process.

Peer support and role models are additional mechanisms the community health nurse can use to help the patient's psychosocial adjustment. Visits from individuals who have had a stroke and have made a good adjustment can offer the patient encouragement. The visits should be planned with the patient's full cooperation. If a group, or stroke club, has been established in the community the patient can be invited to join the group. Like riding in a bus designed for the physically handicapped, going to a group meeting of a stroke club can be a frightening experience for a new stroke victim. It is important that a supportive person accompany the patient to at least the first meeting, whether it is the patient's spouse, an individual from the club who the patient knows, or the community health nurse.

COPING WITH OSTEOARTHRITIS

Osteoarthritis, also known as degenerative joint disease, is recognized by both the elderly and health professionals as a disease that is commonly seen with the aging process. It is estimated that 90 percent of the population will have some joint degeneration by the age of 40.[14] Pain is the most common symptom of osteoarthritis.

Review of the Literature

Vignos recognizes that the interrelationships between the physical and psychosocial aspects of chronic arthritis have received little attention.[15] Vignos considers the social adjustment of the patient and the patient's family to be as important as the medical management.

The choice between limiting movement or enduring pain is considered by Rodman.[16] How this conflict is resolved will influence the outcome of the medical program.

Clark mentions the importance of a psychological evaluation, including obtaining data on the reaction of the individual and family to chronic disease.[17] The relationship between the age of the individual and the adjustment to osteoarthritis is not covered in the material by Clark.

The Onset of Osteoarthritis

In sharp contrast to the dramatic onset of a stroke, the onset of osteoarthritis is gradual. Typically, the individual becomes aware of pain and stiffness on arising. These symptoms gradually clear as the joints are used. However, the pain may recur during the day if the involved joints are used extensively.

The longer interval between the onset of osteoarthritis and the resulting disability allows the individual more time to adapt to the losses involved. Although individuals may suffer significant functional loss as a result of osteoarthritis, they are able to alter habits and life-style to accommodate these losses. This gradual adjustment imposes less strain on the individual's coping skills than does a sudden disability.[18]

Patterns of Coping with Osteoarthritis

The patterns that older people use for coping with osteoarthritis involve some of the same mechanisms used for coping with stroke. They include reactions of anger, depression, denial, withdrawal, and dependency.

The adjustment that a person makes to living with pain and loss of function from arthritis will be similar to adjustments made to previous crises. Three coping patterns used by the majority of patients with osteoarthritis are (1) denial of the disease, (2) dependency as a result of the disease, and (3) compromise between the real loss of function and the need for independence. As with stroke, denial and dependency can result in either a positive or a negative adjustment. Denial of the pain and loss of function can be a mechanism for maintaining mobility, but, when carried to an extreme, denial can prevent an individual from following the therapeutic regime for joint protection. Dependency can result from the realistic recognition of the need for help, but it can also mean that the individual has given up roles and responsibilities still within his or her capabilities.

Living with Osteoarthritis

Older people living in the community use various techniques for adjusting to their osteoarthritis and continuing to live meaningfully. Often, the occurrence of osteoarthritis is thought to be an inevitable accompaniment to aging (sometimes to the frustration of the community health nurse who urges diagnosis and treatment!). Changes in habits and activities are made to accommodate the losses resulting from osteoarthritis.

These changes achieve two purposes: a simplification of the activities of daily living and a decrease in the number of activities. A 70-year-old woman spent time, energy, and money shopping for large earrings when she could no longer put on her small earrings. She also selected pullover blouses in order to free herself from the frustration caused by trying to button her clothing. She preferred that to using a button hook. A 73-year-old man decreased the length of his daily walks when the pain in his hips became troublesome. A 72-year-old typist limited the number of typing jobs she accepted in order to minimize the strain on her arthritic spine.

In each instance, the individual recognized loss of function by changing an important activity. Yet each person spoke with pleasure and pride about the activities which were still possible, indicating that a compromise had been accepted. Large earrings and slipover blouses replaced small earrings and buttoned blouses. Short walks provided a substitute for long walks. Fewer typing jobs were better than none. Such compromises allowed these individuals to continue involvement in meaningful activities. Each person mentioned the predictability of these changes; "You have to expect to slow down, to have some pain, when you get old." Each had achieved a balance between the physical pain of too much activity and the psychological pain of inactivity.

Often osteoarthritis leads to a selective withdrawal from activities that are unpleasant. A 79-year-old woman told her community health nurse that the onset of arthritis made it impossible to wash dishes any longer. She then went on to describe her busy schedule of card games and piano playing! This is a delightful example of an individual giving up activities that are not enjoyed, but retaining pleasurable hobbies. In this instance it was made possible by an elderly husband who assumed responsibility for washing dishes.

For some older people the onset of joint pain and stiffness from osteoarthritis may precipitate an extremely dependent status, one which is not required by the degree of joint pathology. A pronounced withdrawal from activities and socialization may take place. Such persons, like stroke patients who withdraw, are usually very depressed. One 73-year-old woman refused to walk from her mobile home to the clubhouse in her park, a distance of less than one block, stating that the pain from her arthritis made it impossible for her to walk that far. Her doctor diagnosed osteoarthritic joint changes in both hands! This woman was quite unhappy in the isolation of her mobile home, but adamantly refused to participate in neighborhood activities.

CASE EXAMPLE 2 John J exemplified the adjustments that an older individual makes in response to osteoarthritis. At 85, John had osteoarthritis of the weight-bearing joints, and was seldom without pain in his hips and knees. Yet he remained active, helped his wife with the housework, and in recent years, had taken on much of the responsibility for cooking. John had sought help for his arthritis from several physicians and numerous medications, but nothing had been successful in alleviating the pain he endured.

John got out of his home each day and, with his wife, was a regular member of a local senior group. When asked by the community health nurse how he managed to remain so active and to tolerate the discomfort, John replied, "I just don't let the pain get me down. I keep going 'cause if I give in and quit I might as well die. And, you know, I help some of these people that are worse off than I am. They need help. I've been lucky—I can still take care of myself." John smiled and cautiously attempted a waltz step to demonstrate that he could still "get around under his own steam."

NURSING INTERVENTION

In working with elderly clients in the community, the nurse will encounter some who, like John J, accept the limits of osteoarthritis and are thankful for what functions are intact, and others who focus on what has been lost and become withdrawn and depressed. In dealing with elderly clients suffering from osteoarthritis, the nurse should follow the same principle used with stroke clients: maximize the individual's capabilities.

In the case of a client who is coping well and making adjustments to accommodate to osteoarthritis, the community health nurse can aid the adjustment process in the following ways:

1   Listen to the client's fears and concern about losses resulting from osteoarthritis.

2   Discuss with the client ways in which these losses can be minimized, e.g., by replacing small earrings with large earrings that are easier to hold.

3   Provide the client with information that will help to make the medical regime more acceptable. For example, taking aspirin with food and taking long-acting aspirin at bedtime may increase the client's comfort.

4   Provide the client with information that will make activities of daily living easier, including education about adaptive equipment and community resources.

5   Emphasize the importance, both physical and psychosocial, of remaining mobile. Such things as teaching range of motion exercises to a group of clients in the same neighborhood may encourage both activity and socialization.

6   Make the client aware of the importance of those capabilities that remain. For a woman who had to give up crocheting, the ability to read to a blind neighbor was a source of satisfaction.

7   Demonstrate by role modeling that accepting can be as pleasant as giving. Often elderly clients will go to great lengths to prepare refreshments in anticipation of the nurse's arrival. It is important to accept this hospitality graciously and show pleasure.

For the client who is very depressed and withdrawn, nursing intervention must begin by focusing on the following issues. They are important for the client who is coping well, but essential for the client who is not, and in that case will have to precede the educational and adaptive processes.

1 Allow the client to express feelings of discouragement and depression.

2 Recognize and encourage the client's positive progress and statements. One depressed woman had made an effort to get dressed before the nurse's visit. When the nurse complimented her on her attractive appearance in brightly colored clothes, the client responded with a cheerful attitude and began to make plans for a shopping trip.

3 Make visits with clients contingent on a time schedule. Avoid making visits solely on the basis of the client's complaints of pain, since this will establish a reward of increased attention for the complaint. More attention and praise need to be given to what the client does well.

SUMMARY

In helping an elderly client to cope with stroke, osteoarthritis, or any other illness, the community health nurse will need to use a variety of supportive interventions. Listening, offering encouragement, teaching, and securing services for clients are equally important. The caring that is inherent in this process may be the most significant thing the nurse offers to an elderly client coping with chronic disease.

REFERENCES

1   Ruth B. Weg, "The Aged: Who, Where, How Well (Education, Health, Income, Marital Status)," unpublished paper, Leonard B. Davis School of Gerontology, Spring 1977, p. 5.

2   Ibid., p. 6.

3   Montague Ullman, *Behavioral Changes in Patients Following Strokes*, Charles C Thomas, Springfield, Ill., 1962, p. 29.

4   Walter A. Borden, "Psychological Aspects of Stroke: Patient and Family," *Annals of Internal Medicine*, vol. 57, no. 4, p. 689, October 1962.

5   Ibid., p. 692.

6   Ronald S. Tikofsky, "Emotional and Intellectual Considerations in the Rehabilitation of Stroke Patients," in William S. Fields and William A. Spencer (eds.), *Stroke Rehabilitation: Basic Concepts and Research Trends*, Warren H. Green, St. Louis, 1967, p, 107.

7   Beverly J. Leonard, "Body Image Changes in Chronic Illness," *Nursing Clinics of North America*, vol. 7, no. 4, p. 689, December 1972.

8   Ibid., p. 689.

9   Lucie C. M. Schultz, "Nursing Care of the Stroke Patient," *Nursing Clinics of North America*, vol. 8, no. 4, p. 640, December 1973.

10 Herbert G. Steger, "Understanding the Psychologic Factors in Rehabilitation," *Geriatrics*, vol. 31, no. 5, p. 68, May 1976.

11 Borden, op. cit., p. 689.

12 Steger, op. cit., p. 68.
13 George S. Tracy and Zachary Gussow, "Self-Help Health Groups: A Grass-Roots Response to a Need for Services," *Journal of Applied Behavioral Science*, vol. 12, no. 3, p. 388, July–September 1976.
14 Helen Clark, "Osteoarthritis: An Interesting Case," *Nursing Clinics of North America*, vol. 11, no. 1, p. 199, March 1976.
15 Paul J. Vignos, Jr., "Psychosocial Problems in Management of Chronic Arthritis," in George E. Ehrlich (ed.), *Total Management of the Arthritic Patient*, Lippincott, Philadelphia, 1973, p. 111.
16 Gerald P. Rodman, *Primer on the Rheumatic Diseases*, The Arthritis Foundation, New York, 1973, p. 128.
17 Clark, op. cit., p. 202.
18 Steger, op. cit., p. 69.

BIBLIOGRAPHY

Cobb, A. Beatrix: *Medical and Psychological Aspects of Disability,* Charles C Thomas, Springfield, Ill., 1973.

Colman, Hila: *Hanging On,* Atheneum, New York, 1977.

Ellor, James W., and Michele Rizzo: "Aging is Not a Disease: Caring for the Elderly Ostomate," *E. T. Journal*, vol. 5, no. 1, pp. 4–7, Winter 1978.

Fordyce, Wilber E.: "Evaluating and Managing Chronic Pain," *Geriatrics*, vol. 33, no. 1, pp. 59–62, January 1978.

Garret, James F., and Edna S. Levine: *Psychological Practices with the Physically Disabled*, Columbia University Press, New York, 1962.

Lehman, J. F., et al.: "Stroke: Does Rehabilitation Affect Outcome?" *Archives of Physical Medicine and Rehabilitation*, vol. 56, pp. 375–382, September 1975.

————: "Stroke Rehabilitation: Outcome and Prediction," *Archives of Physical Medicine and Rehabilitation*, vol. 56, pp. 383–389, September 1975.

McDaniel, James W.: *Physical Disability and Human Behavior*, Pergamon Press, New York, 1976.

OTHER RESOURCES

Films

Strokes, 16 mm, color, 7 min. Short graphic description of the physiology of strokes, with brief discussion of poststroke residuals. Produced by the American Heart Association. (Request from local chapter.)

Stroke-Counter Stroke, 16 mm, color, 28 min. Stars Patricia Neal and emphasizes the role of the family and community in the recovery process. Tells of the rehabilitation of a stroke victim in the community. Produced by Regional Medical Programs, California Area VIII, University of California, College of Medicine, Irvine, Calif. 92664.

Chapter 20

Wandering Behavior

Irene Mortenson Burnside

People are decidedly the hardest things we have to deal with.

Harry Stack Sullivan

Wandering is a common problem, and it can be a serious and even dangerous one for the elderly. In this chapter, I will try to explain various aspects and possible causes of wandering, incorporating into my discussion a review of the existing research. The end of the chapter will offer some guidelines for interventions extrapolated from the literature and from my own professional work as a nurse.

LACK OF RESEARCH ON WANDERING

Butler and Lewis have observed that "Much about old age is not known, but infinitely more is known than is applied."[1] To their observation it might

This chapter is a revised version of a speech presented at Rocky Mountain Gerontology Center, University of Utah, Salt Lake City, January 17, 1979.

be added that infinitely more is known about old age than is written. If our interest in any given subject concerning the elderly is reflected by the amount of material that is published on that subject, we must not be very interested in wandering behavior in the aged. My research has convinced me that this problem must be one of the least studied, least written-about problems. My Medlars computer search through the indexes of medicine and nursing texts for literature on wandering produced material on the following: (1) atrial pacemakers (especially in French hornists), (2) foreign bodies, (3) the oramylsalvoxyl-wanderer (used in post mastectomies), (4) the wandering fourth heart sound during atrioventricular dissociation, and (5) the wandering staghorn calculus in renal mass.

Articles on wandering, the kind done by people mainly with their feet, were almost impossible to find. There were only five articles on wandering people; one of them was published in 1941, three in the 1960s[2-5] (one of those was from Norway), and only one between 1970 and 1978.[6]

To date, there are no articles by nurses on the wandering behavior of aged people, nor are there any research studies. This is both surprising and discouraging. Wandering behavior occurs frequently among older people suffering from organic brain disturbance, and it occurs not only by day in the community, but also by night and in long-term care facilities. Nurses care for institutionalized patients around the clock, and are therefore in a particularly good position to observe and study wandering behavior.

There are as yet no studies of wandering behavior in the nursing home, even though such wandering can cause death or injury to aged patients and increase stress for staff members, relatives, roommates, and peers. Nursing home personnel can spend a great deal of time trying to locate a wanderer who leaves the facility, and the need to send people out to search the surrounding area can leave the facility short-handed.

One wonders why we, as nurses, have not given more attention to this pervasive problem. We can speculate that wandering might not be viewed as problematic because it is seen as simply capricious behavior and its seriousness is not understood. Perhaps also it is not a very interesting problem to nurses and care providers. Or care givers may believe that there isn't very much that can be done about wandering and so choose not to make a big issue out of it. Finally, it is also possible that the care givers who must handle the problem are not the ones who do the researching and writing.

Three books on dementia do not even mention wandering,[7-9] yet wandering is commonly seen in individuals suffering from organic brain syndrome. Moreover, wandering is often one of the first symptoms that gets an individual living in the community into trouble, or puts him or her in danger.

Authors allude to wandering in their writings, but never really go into the dynamics of wandering or spell out the details of possible interventions.[10-13]

No Precise Definition Exists

As yet, we do not even have a precise definition of wandering in the literature, although medical personnel continue to use the descriptive term frequently. The more common term, used of younger people, is "elopement," which is a euphemism for "escape." Webster's dictionary defines "wander" as "to move about without a fixed course, aim, or goal."[14] But even this definition does not precisely fit many aged wanderers, because they frequently have a definite goal. They may, for example, say they are "going home" and may be doing so in quite a determined manner, even though they don't know where they are or which direction to take to get home.

AN EARLY STUDY

One of the earliest studies on wandering was done in 1941 by Cameron, who studied the wandering confusion that some demented patients show at night.[15] He also discovered that the same disorganized behavior could be produced during daytime hours if patients were placed in a darkened room. He concluded that the confusion resulted because of the level of the background stimuli, that is, the demented patients he studied could not maintain a spatial image when they did not receive repeated stimulation. Cameron did not go further with this study, but his research is important because it shows the importance of the environment to the aged patient. I recall that I once put a group of regressed elderly in a darkened room one afternoon to show them slides of the group. One woman kept getting up and trying to walk through the lighted area where the screen was. She apparently thought that it was the doorway, and may have been unable to maintain spatial images. Her reaction seemed to parallel those described in Cameron's study.

CORNBLETH'S STUDY

Cornbleth studied wandering and nonwandering patients in a Veterans' Administration hospital,[16] evaluating subjects in terms of their physical, cognitive, and psychosocial functioning. He assessed 30 wanderers and 18 nonwanderers before they were transferred to the experimental and other wards. One wonders what impact the transfer itself had on the subsequent behavior of the subjects (see Chap. 13).

The sample consisted of 48 male patients in a geriatric division of a Veterans' Administration hospital. Almost all of them had a diagnosis of organic brain syndrome, and most of them had one or more physical disorders besides. Their ages ranged from 50 to 84 years. Nine patients fell into the age range of 80 to 84. The wanderers were identified by a consensus of nursing personnel, physicians, and corrective therapists.

The Findings

A major finding of the above study was the differential effect of the experimental ward on the physical functioning of wanderers and non-wanderers. The wanderers showed greater range of motion on the ward, while the nonwanderers showed greater range of motion off the ward. Cornbleth suggested that a protected ward area might be appropriate for wanderers, but that it might have a negative effect on nonwanderers; he also suggested that conditions which were beneficial to one group might be detrimental to the other.

Cornbleth concluded that special safeguards were necessary to provide activity for wanderers and to increase the wanderers' opportunity to move about without jeopardizing their safety.

He also noted that the wanderers showed less improvement than the nonwanderers in the psychosocial function, as assessed by the nurses. Wandering is a psychosocial indicator, and could be used as a prognostic signal that a wanderer should be placed in a treatment program geared to improve psychosocial functioning.

The criteria for wandering were not precisely defined in this study, nor were the words "wandering" and "nonwandering." Wandering behavior needs a more precise definition than we presently have. Nor did the study describe how wandering was treated and which personnel intervened. The time of day when the people wandered, or whether they wandered alone or with another person, were not discussed either. (I recall two confused old ladies in a back ward of a state hospital who were inseparable; they wandered arm-in-arm constantly through the halls and dayroom of the large ward.)

Because women are outliving men by 7 or 8 years, nurses will be dealing with increased numbers of elderly women, so a study is needed to describe the wanderings of elderly women. Subjects should also be studied in settings other than institutions.

OTHER REFERENCES TO WANDERING

In my search, I found other writers, mainly psychiatrists, who mention wandering briefly; as I noted earlier, nurses have not written about wandering.

Excessive Wandering

In *Clinical Geropsychiatry*, Verwoerdt mentions "excessive wandering" in connection with organic brain syndrome individuals.[17] He includes in his analysis regressive sexual behavior, combative behavior, loss of social graces, incontinence, the tendency to hoard, and deterioration in personal appearance and environment. Although Verwoerdt does not elaborate on excessive wandering, later in the same textbook he says, "An aged person becomes a source of social nuisance when he is mentally so impaired that he continuously wanders away, exposes himself, is incontinent, is very boisterous, hoards a multitude of senseless items, and so on."[18]

Nocturnal Wandering

Stotsky discusses the problems of nocturnal restlessness and wanderers, and reminds us that these persons create chronic problems in nursing homes.[19] Any nurse who has worked the night shift in a long-term care facility or a Veterans' hospital will welcome new research findings in this particular area. Stotsky says that residents walk aimlessly at night and that this aimless wandering, plus decreased vision, hearing, and mental ability contribute to confusion, agitation, and uncooperativeness. He suggests properly chosen nighttime activities for such patients. Overworked activity directors will hardly welcome that suggestion, and night staff will need in-service education about effective ways to handle uncooperative, difficult nighttime wanderers. It is easy to write such persons off as confused. But when one sees so many of them seek a warmer, or at least different, bed at night, one sometimes wonders whether they are truly confused or merely trying to satisfy real needs.

Stotsky suggests letting the wanderers and restless ones nap in comfortable chairs if they desire, or allowing them to stay up if they do not disturb other residents.

Stotsky also writes about individuals who walk aimlessly around the neighborhood in an apparent daze. He suggests that such persons may experience a desire to travel and are out searching for new experience, and that wandering could be one means of relieving tension. Boredom is discussed later in this chapter.

Nocturnal Wandering as a Sign of Cardiac Decompensation Anderson mentions that nocturnal wandering might be an indication of cardiac decompensation, and that it is important for normal sleep rhythms to be reestablished. Mental confusion nearly always precipitates a crisis in the family of the old person, writes Anderson. It is important to remember that medical advice is not always sought, and Anderson warns that if the confused state is of sudden onset, it should not be treated lightly.[20] The police department in a community may know more than the medical personnel about who the wanderers are, since policemen often bring wanderers home.

The following is an example of a man who was not actually a wanderer, but who knew how to use the behavior to his own advantage!

CASE EXAMPLE 1: EXPLOITING WANDERING BEHAVIOR Mr. G was an alert man in his eighties, at least 6 feet tall, and strongly built. He alternated living with his two daughters, moving from one part of California to another every few months.

Since he could be rather bad-tempered on occasion, it must have been a relief to one daughter when he left her home to find his own entertainment. However, the daughters were not especially pleased at his choice—a day at the horse races! Each time he went, he bet all the money he had, and never saved enough for bus fare home. He solved the problem quite easily. He put his hat on a bit crooked, pulled it down over both ears, then walked over to a nearby freeway, knowing quite well that pedestrians were not permitted on California freeways. He then began to shuffle down the side of the freeway until a police car came along. Invariably one stopped and the officers took him home, since he could always tell them where he lived.

It is true that Mr. G is the uncommon wanderer; many of those who are out in the community or on the roadways are lost. If they are wearing dark clothing in inclement weather or at night, they are in jeopardy. Local papers frequently describe people in California who have wandered off and perished in bad weather. Enlisting community support systems can turn the search into a costly venture, as once happened in southern California when a man wandered off from an outlying nursing home and went into the foothills. He was found by a helicopter because he was wearing a brightly colored poncho, and was thus easily spotted from the air. When picked up, he said he was going home to Mexico. He was headed in the right direction.

Wandering in a Car

Some old people who are in institutions think that they are going home and that they can find their way by themselves. Stotsky describes institutionalized elderly people who still have their driver's license who get lost in their cars and end up getting into accidents.[21]

The Jury brothers have described and photographed a poignant example of "Gramp" wandering in his car, aware that something was wrong, and quite afraid.[22] Since driving is so important to many elderly men and women, the loss of a driver's license can be a real blow. Yet, for those who begin to lose their directions and cannot maneuver well in a vehicle, the decision to stop driving may be unavoidable. Wandering behavior among elderly drivers is an area to consider carefully in making an assessment of psychosocial behavior in the elderly client.

A Dangerous Symptom

A psychiatric text by Whitehead covers wandering briefly in two paragraphs and calls it "a dangerous symptom." Whitehead uses the term wandering to

Figure 20-1 A wandering person can create havoc in both the acute care setting and the nursing home, especially when the facilities are located on busy streets. Much time is spent in locating the person and the police often have to be notified and asked to help. In inclement weather, some wandering persons perish. In the above photograph, it has taken two staff members to locate a missing resident. *(Courtesy of Anthony J. Skirlick, Jr.)*

describe restlessness, agitation, and a type of mental confusion in both acute and subacute toxic confusional states. He also uses it to mean walking away from home and having a proclivity for getting lost.[23] Night wandering in particular provokes anxiety in the family, neighbors, and peers. The following is an example of the beginning wandering of an 86-year-old man.

CASE EXAMPLE 2: A SUCCESSFUL WANDERER A widow in her sixties lived on a quiet street in a small town. Her next-door neighbor was a man of 94 who lived alone; with the support service of a local nutri-lon site and two devoted sons, he managed quite well. One night at about 10 p.m., he went for a walk on his quiet, one-block street. He fell and broke his glasses and was found by a teen-aged boy who was driving past. The boy brought the man to the widow's home, but refused to stay when she said she would call the man's son, afraid that "they" would think he had hit the old man while driving. The old man continued to be maintained at home.

About a year later, the same woman was outside working in her garden. The old man came through her house—she had left the front door open—sat down on a brick wall, and said, "Well, are you ready to go? I am." The neighbor explained that they were not going anywhere and that she had not discussed anything like that with him. He shook his head, slowly got up, and said matter-of-factly, "Well, I certainly am confused; I guess I had better go home."

The old man is still at home in spite of the above two wandering incidents. His sons check on him frequently on their way home from work, or on weekends. He is taken to a nutrition site for noon meals and social events by a volunteer. The neighbors on the street are alerted, and know that he lives alone and has wandered a couple of times. Yet, with the tremendous support system around him, he does well. Not all old people who experience wandering incidents are that lucky.

The wanderer can be helped by day center care, even when wandering from home occurs at night. Treatment is aimed at getting to both the symptom and the underlying pathology.[24]

The dangers of wandering can be seen in the following example, which describes the deaths of two confused wanderers, as reported in a local paper.[25]

CASE EXAMPLE 3: TWO DEATHS FROM WANDERING A 77-year-old woman left a nursing home on Thanksgiving day, without money or identification. The local paper said that she was lucid and conversant, but that she sometimes got confused, and had wandered away from the nursing home on several previous occasions, although she had always been found a short distance away. This time, on the day after Thanksgiving, her body was found lying partially submerged in a creek, in a clump of reeds about four blocks from the hospital. She died of exposure.

Another elderly woman from the same facility had died three months previously when she wandered into an unlocked utility room, turned on the hot water tap, slipped and fell, and was scalded to death.

While not all wandering results in such tragic endings, the wandering aged person, whether at home or in an institution, is in jeopardy.

FEAR AS A BASIS FOR WANDERING

My own professional background included student experience in a state hospital. At that time, a great deal of electric shock therapy was done, often on women suffering from melancholia, as it was called then. The patients disliked shock treatment intensely and many of them would saunter off across the field when we walked the group to the shock therapy room. It occurs to me that fear may be one of the reasons why an aged individual leaves a strange place, and special efforts must be made to provide a "settling-in" period for the person admitted to a long-term care facility or an acute hospital.

BOREDOM AS A REASON FOR WANDERING

Boredom and ennui are other aspects of wandering that should be considered more fully. In one case, a farmer was hospitalized at age 85 for the first time in his life. He had fallen from the top of a hayload and was brought to the hospital in an unconscious state. He was furious that he had been brought to the hospital; as he said, "I could have come to in the hayfield just as well as here." He was placed under observation and put on bedrest. One Sunday afternoon when the hospital was very quiet, he got up and dressed and went for a walk around the block. He would not have been found out if he had not climbed back into bed with all of his clothes on and kept them on until the nurse's aide appeared for the backrub routine. He had been active all of his life, and was not used to being a bed patient. He was also in a strange environment and found it quite boring. Many of the present generation of old people must feel the same way when they are hospitalized or institutionalized.

IMPLICATIONS FOR NURSES

Wandering behavior should be one of the areas that nurses check out carefully in the examination, both for the possible etiology and for ways to prevent the behavior or to ensure the safety of the wanderer. Nurses should also be aware of the strain wandering puts on the family members who have to cope with such behavior. And, difficult as it is in the daytime, wandering creates real havoc at night when it prevents other family members from getting adequate rest. Wandering behavior in persons with Alzheimer's disease can cause endless frustration and worry for families of the patients. Police are often involved in returning confused old people either to a nursing home or a police station; perhaps police files should be studied to understand who the problematic wanderers are in a community. I know of no health professionals who work closely with the police in this area.

WANDERING PERSONS AND RESTRAINTS

The use of restraints to quell the wandering aged is still a controversial issue. The geriatric wheelchair (usually called the Gerichair) can perpetuate unresolved service problems, states Lorraine Snyder, who was director of the Human Development Program at Ebenezer Society in Minneapolis. Such confinement to a chair can put off "working effectively with a person who wanders," she wrote.[26] Gerichairs are often used to restrain wanderers, and while this is preferable to tranquillizing them with drugs, it still is a poor solution to the problem of wandering.

Wells states:

> A lot of people have the concept of the chair in care of the elderly as a limited concept, like something you sit in . . . it is a therapeutic tool. It can easily facilitate their rehabilitation and their mobility and it can also facilitate modification of their behavior. For example, in wandering, disoriented, elderly people, there is a tendency to feel that one has to tie them into a chair with a Posey belt or put them into a chair that's got a cable in front and restrain them.
>
> I don't see this as very satisfactory for the elderly person or their families. Rather, you try to put them in a chair that is still a good chair, an acceptable chair, but it's the reverse of restraining them. It facilitates their mobility. It does slow them down, but they can still get out. They are their own free agent.[27]

The following list of possible interventions for wandering behavior is based on my review of the scant literature on the subject. Readers who have worked in long-term care may be able to add interventions that have worked for them.

GUIDELINES FOR INTERVENTION

1 A protected ward is appropriate for wanderers (Cornbleth, 1977).

2 The wanderer must have room to move about in but not have his or her safety jeopardized (Cornbleth, 1977).

3 Proper nighttime activities must be chosen for the nocturnal wanderer (Stotsky, 1968).

4 Wanderers and restless ones can be allowed to nap in comfortable chairs if they are nocturnal wanderers (Stotsky, 1969).

5 Do not let the nocturnal wanderer disturb other residents by staying up or wandering (Stotsky, 1968).

6 Help reduce boredom for the aged person. Boredom is one reason for wandering in a neighborhood, and those who do it may be expressing a wish to travel, or to search for new experiences (Stotsky, 1968).

7 Wandering could be a means of relieving tension (Stotsky, 1968). Spend time with the individual to ascertain if this is the case.

8   Nocturnal wandering may be an indication of cardiac decompensation (Anderson, 1971). A physical checkup may be indicated.

9   Wandering is a dangerous symptom and the wanderers can be helped by day care if they are still resident in the community. Day care will help even when the wandering from home occurs at night (Whitehead, 1974).

10   Treatment must be aimed at both the symptoms and the underlying pathology (Whitehead, 1974).

11   Be discreet about the use of restraints with the wandering aged. Is the Posey belt or tying to chair necessary? (Wells, 1975).

SUMMARY

This chapter surveyed what current literature there is on wandering behavior. To date, there is no writing by nurses on wandering behavior. Medical and psychosocial aspects of wandering were briefly discussed. Wandering behavior is a fertile area for research, and one that nurses can monitor while caring for aged clients.

REFERENCES

1   Robert N. Butler and Myrna I. Lewis, *Aging and Mental Health,* Mosby, St. Louis, 1977, p. 9.

2   D. E. Cameron, "Studies in Senile-Nocturnal Delirium," *Psychiatric Quarterly,* vol. 15, no. 1, pp. 47–53, 1941.

3   S. Soverni and E. Borghesi, "On a Strange Case of Wandering in an Arteriosclerotic Demented Patient," *Gerontology,* vol. 16, no. 8, pp. 846–851, August 1968.

4   Robert Cancro, "Elopements from the C. F. Menninger Memorial Hospital," *Bulletin Menninger Clinic,* vol. 32, no. 4, pp. 228–238, July 1968.

5   Kjell Noreik, "Hospitalized Psychoses among Wandering People in Norway," *ACTA Psychiatr. Scand.,* vol. 41, no. 2, pp. 157–176, 1965.

6   Terry Cornbleth, "Effect of a Protected Hospital Ward Area on Wandering and Non-Wandering Geriatric Patients," *Journal of Gerontology*, vol. 35, no. 5, pp. 573–577, September 1977.

7   Nandy Kalidas, *Senile Dementia: A Biomedical Approach*, Elsevier/North Holland Biomedical Press, New York, 1978.

8   Andrew E. Slaby and Richard J. Wyatt, *Dementia in the Presenium*, Charles C Thomas, Springfield, Ill., 1974.

9   Charles E. Wells, *Dementia*, 2d ed., Davis, Philadelphia, 1977.

10   Adrian Verwoerdt, *Clinical Geropsychiatry*, Williams and Wilkins, Baltimore, 1976.

11   Bernard A. Stotsky, *The Elderly Patient*, Grune and Stratton, New York, 1978.

12   W. Ferguson Anderson, *Practical Management of the Elderly*, 2nd ed., Blackwell Scientific Publications, Oxford and Edinburgh, 1971.

13 J. A. Whitehead, *Psychiatric Disorders in Old Age*, Springer, New York, 1974.
14 *Webster's New Collegiate Dictionary*, G. & C. Merriam Company, Springfield, Mass., 1973.
15 Cameron, op. cit., pp. 47–53.
16 Cornbleth, op. cit., p. 573.
17 Verwoerdt, op. cit., p. 90.
18 Ibid., p. 243.
19 Stotsky, op. cit., p. 106.
20 Anderson, op. cit., p. 71.
21 Stotsky, op. cit., p. 106.
22 Mark Jury and Dan Jury, *Gramp*, Grossman Publishers, New York, 1976.
23 Whitehead, op. cit., p. 17.
24 Ibid.
25 *Contra Costa Times*, Concord, Calif., December 1, 1978.
26 Lorraine Hiatt Snyder, "Living Environments: Geriatric Wheelchairs and Older Persons' Rehabilitation," *Human Ecology*, vol. 3, no. 2, Autumn 1972. Autumn 1972.
27 Thelma Wells, quoted by Loretta Ford in "Strategy of Clinical and Health Services," papers presented at the annual meeting of American Academy of Nurses, September 22–23, 1975, pp. 80–92.

BIBLIOGRAPHY

Carroll, Kathy: *Psychosocial Aspects of Nursing Home Care*, Ebenezer Center for Aging and Human Development, Minneapolis, 1978.
_____: *Understanding Psychosocial Needs of the Elderly*, Ebenezer Center for Aging and Human Development, Minneapolis, 1978.
Fish, Mayer, Alvin I. Goldfarb, Siroon S. Shahinian, and Helen Turner: "Chronic Brain Syndrome in the Community Aged," *Archives of General Psychiatry*, vol. 18, no. 6, pp. 739–745, June 1968.
Grubisich, Thomas: "Aged Wanderer Baffles State," *Washington Post*, September 15, 1976.
Miller, Edgar: *Abnormal Aging: The Psychology of Senile and Presenile Dementia*, Wiley, New York, 1977.
Sadowski, Adam, and Paul Weinsaft: "Behavioral Disorders in the Elderly," *Journal of the American Geriatrics Society*, vol. 23, no. 2, February 1975.
Snyder, Lorraine Hiatt, Peter Kupprecht, Janine Pyrek, Sandra Brekhus, and Tom Moss: "Wandering," *The Gerontologist*, vol. 18, no. 3, pp. 272–280, June 1978.
Storlie, Frances: "Unit 5: The Aged Poor," in *Nursing and the Social Conscience*, Appleton-Century-Crofts, New York, 1970, pp. 147–194.

Chapter 21

Psychosocial Aspects of Incontinence in the Aged Person

Mari Anne Bartol

The social implications of incontinence have received scant attention in writing, but produce profound changes in the life-style of the sufferer and of the relatives who may have to look after them.

F. L. Willington

Incontinence is a problem that has plagued both the elderly and nursing care givers for years. Effective means of treatment or care for incontinent elderly persons (both at home and in an institutional setting) have not been found. Significant strides have, however, been made in finding the causes of incontinence,[1-4] which range from constipation to severe neurological disorders. Because some causative factors have been identified, we are now in a position to treat effectively and eliminate successfully some states of incontinence. Nevertheless, the average practitioner will find that the number of persons treated successfully is not so great as the number still suffering from intractable incontinence.

What of these people and the nursing staff and family members who care for them? This chapter is about the psychosocial aspects of incontinence in the aged; its intent is to examine the psychosocial factors that are important in caring for the chronically incontinent older person. The first part of the chapter discusses current literature and the psychological mechanisms, while the latter part deals with interventions that might be helpful to nurses. We can care for, but not cure, incontinence, and the temptation is strong to say that somehow we have failed. There tends to be ignorance about the psychosocial impact which chronic incontinence has on the individual and all others involved, including family and care givers. Little has been written about the emotional impact and psychological dynamics of the chronic incontinent person. If we are to treat the whole person we have to remember that incontinence, like any other physiologic failure of the body, will have an impact on the emotional and social well-being of the individual,[5-7] regardless of age. Although the application of psychiatric principles has limitations, these principles must be considered if we are to treat the whole person and accord him or her dignity and respect.[8]

Pathologically-induced intractable incontinence is a sad, and to most people, unpleasant situation. Although it is not a normal physiologic occurrence that comes with age, many elderly individuals suffer its indignity. Sometimes the condition cannot be cured, since the devices and equipment available at this time are inadequate, not always effective, and at times even dangerous.

DEFINITION OF INCONTINENCE

Urinary incontinence is defined as "in practical terms . . . the voiding of urine at unsuitable times, and elsewhere than in a suitable receptacle."[9]

Psychiatric syndromes commonly found in the aged and aging population (particularly those in institutions) in conjunction with incontinence are: (1) hypomanic or agitated states, (2) senile and presenile dementias (neuronal loss dementias) such as Pick's disease and Alzheimer's disease, (3) arteriosclerotic dementia, (4) schizophrenia, (5) toxic confusional states, and (6) psychotic depression.[10] It is important to note that the dementias are in a grey area that may include some aspects of neurological impairment, as well as emotional factors, as precipitants to incontinence. Emotional distress associated with incontinence will tend to lessen as the disease progressively impairs insight, perception, and social consciousness. The symptoms of incontinence tend to accompany other signs of uninhibited behavior and reflexes.

PSYCHOLOGICAL MECHANISMS

Sutherland describes some of the psychological mechanisms which can result in incontinence or appear concomitantly with incontinence:[11]

• Regression: emotional lability, temper tantrums, irritability, are a logical accompaniment to incontinence. Regression becomes a coping mechanism for dealing with the stress of increasing infirmity.

• Dependency: a reversal of roles in which older adults perceive themselves in a dependent situation. This situation can be precipitated by "putting the individual to bed" unnecessarily. A bed-bound person by necessity becomes dependent on the care giver for every nuance of existence. The dependency role thus becomes circular and reinforcing.

• Rebellion: anger and resentment expressed in a very primitive manner. Rebellion is a nonverbal cue that care givers should attend to. The individual is not usually aware, on a conscious level, of the anger and resentment that are present. This situation may recall comments on the part of staff members that the patient is "just being stubborn."

• Insecurity: elderly persons usually find themselves in an insecure situation, at best, and expend much psychic energy to maintain equilibrium. A sudden change of environment or of state of health, or sudden excitement, can bring about incontinence, which, if not recognized as having its etiology in anxiety, could easily result in a chronic state.

• Attention seeking: this particular mechanism has a hysterical nature to it and is the individual's way of manipulating or controlling the environment. Staff may claim that the patient is "doing it on purpose." It is equally likely that this is an unconscious mechanism, but it will nevertheless engender staff hostility. In fact it is rare for persons to willfully soil themselves in the absence of structural brain damage. The situation is compounded by an environment perceived as uncaring.

• Disturbance of conditioned reflexes: a situation in which the usual cues for elimination are missing, e.g., privacy, lack of sufficient time, uncustomary positions, unusual stress, and strange bathrooms. Persons with dementia in particular are prone to exhibiting a symptom known as ultraparadoxical inhibition.[14] In this case, positive cues become reversed, and dry clothes or bed stimulate urination. The toilet or commode depresses the urge to void, a positively frustrating situation for care givers and one that the affected individual is unable to control.

• Sensory deprivation: this situation can exist most easily in the confused and disoriented individual. Without adequate and appropriate stimulation, the individual loses the sense of being in a social relationship with the environment.

CASE EXAMPLE A 58-year-old male, Mr. B, was admitted to the hospital with a diagnosis of Alzheimer's disease. He was ambulatory, and exhibited agitated pacing behavior, impulsiveness, disrupted nighttime sleeping patterns, partial global aphasia, and frequent incontinent episodes of which he was totally unaware. Initially the staff felt he had no understanding of verbal or nonverbal communication. The ongoing nursing assessment later revealed that he could in fact grasp the meaning of some situations, and renewed efforts were made to find a method of communicating with him. During this process the frequency of his incontinence decreased. The staff was bewildered until they discovered that Mr. B had found the staff bathroom, which "looked like" a bathroom. It was not a stall, but a room with a door that closed, roll toilet paper, and peace and quiet. The nursing staff was delighted, but the cleaning staff and "the powers that be" were not pleased and demanded that he use his "own" bathroom (which with his memory deficit, he could not recognize very well). The staff set about weaning Mr. B away from his chosen spot. Continuing efforts to communicate with Mr. B led to the discovery by nursing staff that, in spite of his very frequent laughter and generally "high" behavior, Mr. B was not happy, but actually very sad, and his agitated behavior represented a manic state. Collaboration with the physician resulted in an initial trial treatment of lithium carbonate, combined with renewed efforts to acquaint Mr. B with "his" bathroom. The results were successful and episodes of incontinence were reduced to occasional nighttime wetting and incontinence during ward activities that generated excitement. A year later Mr. B was sitting in a chair in the day room. He looked over to witness another resident next to him urinating while sitting in a chair, causing a large puddle to form under the chair. Mr. B looked away, and said to no one in particular, "I don't know if that's the best way to do it or not!"

This case example shows that several psychological mechanisms were operating to contribute to the symptom of incontinence: manic state, insecurity, and disturbance of conditioned reflexes. Understanding these psychological factors assisted the staff to intervene in the incontinence symptom and to understand better what they could not control.

INDIVIDUAL REACTIONS TO INCONTINENCE

Since individual reactions to incontinence are about as variable as reactions to aging or illness, it is important to know the meaning incontinence has for a particular individual. If the incontinence has begun insidiously in a person whose self-esteem and self-concept are already low, it may seem to the individual to be further evidence of worthlessness and loss of control. Much of an individual's psychological reaction to incontinence results from pre-existing attitudes toward self, aging, and the life situation; it will also depend on how much of the current situation he or she comprehends. The individual may or may not be motivated to maintain continence. The individual's attitude cannot be assumed, but must be solicited, directly when possible. As was mentioned before, few people soil themselves intentionally without a reason.

Reactions of Those Living at Home

It is easy to see how incontinence can affect body image, self-esteem, personal integrity, social image, and social functioning. Less obvious is its effect on emotional stability. The cognitively intact, community-based elderly person is likely to stay home rather than risk being in a social setting when incontinence occurs. The circular sequence of events includes embarrassment in discussing the problem with anyone, self-imposed isolation, depression, apathy, anger, a decline in personal care and nutritional status, and physical illness. These events sometimes result in institutionalization.

Reactions in an Institutional Setting

The individual who is already in an institutional setting presents a different problem. Sutherland states: "In the patient with advanced cerebral deterioration the response to the symptom of incontinence is minimal since awareness of the incontinence, let alone of its significance to interpersonal relationships, is negligible."[12] This is in part true for some individuals with dementia, but we must be very careful of the diagnosis of severe cerebral deterioration and not simply assume that lack of insight is secondary to cerebral deterioration. Many, if not most, cognitively impaired aged individuals have intact social skills and some insight. When I worked with a group of Alzheimer's patients it was painfully apparent that many of them were aware of incontinence and its significance. These patients were in a general state that could be described as severe cerebral deterioration. The majority of ill elderly persons living in institutions are insecure, and feel they are unable to depend on the support of relatives, friends, or care givers. This situational framework may contribute to an exaggerated response to incontinence, which may be difficult for nursing staff to understand. Three of the more common responses that are discussed in detail by Sutherland are depressive reaction, insecurity, and apathy.[13] These reactions do not occur in isolation; they are responses directly related to the individual's involvement with other people. Incontinence is a physiologic event which has profound social consequences. Because of incontinence and its attendant odor, people are excluded from group activities, become offensive to other people, and generally are not accepted by their peers. A further psychological consequence may be the assumption on the individual's part that not being able to control even body excretion is additional evidence of loss of control and powerlessness. A possible reaction from some individuals is aggression. It is not infrequent to hear statements such as "You clean it up, that's your job." Other reactions may include embarrassment, self-recrimination, shame, a sense of increasing dependency, inability to discuss the problem, and withdrawal.

REACTIONS OF CARE GIVERS TO INCONTINENCE

The individual who is incontinent will be involved primarily with three groups of people: family, friends, and the nursing profession. These people are considered here as care givers. The initial reaction to incontinence is a normal healthy disgust or revulsion. Even within the higher mammal group, hygienic measures with regard to excretion can be observed. It is a natural and normal feeling to be repulsed by the smell of feces and urine or by waste next to the skin. This is true for the care giver as well as for the incontinent individual. The following table indicates the gamut of reactions.

Nurses' Reactions

Nurses have been taught not to allow their feelings about a situation to interfere with the quality of nursing care delivered. This leads to a conflict in the care giver between a natural aversion to the symptom of incontinence and a conditioned response to avoid such feelings about the patient or the symptom.[14] The result is a sense of guilt, since all past training has taught nonaversion or uninvolved tolerance. Healthy disgust is not in and of itself destructive, but an individual's reactions to the feelings of guilt can be. Commonly, what happens is that negative feelings regarding the symptom become displaced onto the incontinent person. Another reaction is to push negative feelings into the unconscious level in an effort to lessen anxiety.

Table 21-1 Reactions of Nursing Staff and Family to Incontinence

Nursing staff reactions to incontinence	Staff's perceptions of patient's feelings	Family's reaction to incontinence
Anger	Ashamed	Denial
Frustration	Angry	Frustration
Disgust	Sad	Sadness
Irritation	Depressed	Resentment
Helplessness	Unaware	Acceptance and understanding
Sadness	Feeling "less of a person"	
Feelings of inadequacy		Anger at staff for being unable to control
Guilt	Anxious	
Depression	Disgusted	Ignoring
Nausea	Feeling a loss of control	Anger
Revulsion	Embarrassed	Anxiety
Understanding, empathy	Worried about being a burden	Despondency
Loss of control	Apologetic	
	Apathetic	

These two reactions are particularly common when there is no outlet for care givers to discuss their feelings about incontinence honestly and openly.

Other reactions include reaction formation whereby the care giver will try to compensate for negative feelings by overindulgence, ultra-permissiveness, and excessive "caring." A result of this pattern is seen when the older adult falls into the regressive-dependency behavior pattern.

Reactions of Other Care Givers

Care givers other than nurses are also prone to suffer pangs of frustration, anger, hostility, and helplessness, particularly when faced with intractable incontinence. Family members are faced with feelings of disgust, which are healthy and normal, followed by unhealthy guilt feelings based on their initial reaction. The conflict is even more intense for family members than for nurses, since they struggle to maintain their feelings of respect and love for the patient. If the individual is at home, and care for the older adult is provided by children, a dependency relationship reminiscent of a child-parent relationship develops.

Additional Consequences of Incontinence

Another aspect of intractable incontinence which engenders hostility and anger is the inordinate amount of time, energy, and resources necessary to maintain the incontinent patient in a stable state. Expenses are heavy, and include nursing staff time, housekeeping staff, laundry, quantities of personal clothes, and extra supplies, i.e., incontinence pads.

When conflict occurs, there is a general level of discomfort and anxiety until the conflict is resolved by the emergence of a successful defense mechanism. If the conflict is allowed to go on without change, depression will result.

Avoidance is a mechanism which is commonly seen initially. It is difficult, sometimes impossible, to acquire staff for wards where there is a high incidence of incontinence. Rationalization is used, and it is for the most part a benign mechanism.

There are consequences of other defense mechanisms. The care giver may accept incontinence as a symptom by denying the interpersonal aspects and taking an "ultraprofessional" stance. Sutherland describes this phenomenon: "The symptom comes to be treated as a technical exercise . . . efforts become diverted away from rehabilitation of the patient in an attempt to overcome the incontinence, and concentrate instead on reduction of unpleasant sequelae."[15] It is in this situation that the abuse of indwelling catheters is seen. Much time and effort is spent in identifying and classifying the types of incontinence. The end result is usually an inadequate solution to the incontinence problem and a thoroughly dissatisfied, demoralized staff and patient. The destruction of person-to-person communication and interpersonal relationships leads to a situation in which the patient feels isolated and the staff feels frustrated and helpless. Particularly dangerous aspects of denial in the staff may dehumanize the older adult. Very impersonal behavior on the part of the staff may lead to a loss of sensitivity for a patient's need for privacy, respect, and emotional support.

Projection and Displacement

Projection and displacement are two other potentially dangerous and destructive defense mechanisms. Unexpressed feelings of anger, hostility, and frustration may find their outlet within staff groups; or staff may turn against families, and families against staff. Families frequently feel a loss of control over care of their loved one. They may be displeased with the care the nursing staff is giving and somehow fantasize that if they were the ones giving care, the situation would not exist, or would not be as bad as they perceive it to be. Inevitably, these reactions lead to complaints from family about nursing care. The nursing staff feels harassed, defensive, and unable to verbalize their helplessness adequately to the family. The staff and family become estranged, making productive problem solving, mutual support, or therapeutic interaction difficult or impossible.

It must be stressed that the initial reactions to incontinence are reactions which are held in common by all three groups: affected individuals, nursing staff, and families. The psychodynamics of how each individual handles and responds to his reactions is the area in which potential destructive relationships may develop.

INTERVENTION IN THE PSYCHOLOGICAL ASPECTS OF INCONTINENCE

The initial recognition of the need for psychological intervention is of prime importance. Psychological etiology, psychological response to incontinence, and the psychodynamics of care givers' reactions are the initial issues to be raised through in-service education with staff and as part of general health education with family members. *The approach to education regarding incontinence is not accomplished in a single in-service session or class; it is an ongoing issue of care, especially on a ward or with a family in which incontinence is an ongoing event.* Through education it is possible to focus the attention of staff and family in a constructive manner on the multifaceted aspects of incontinence. The aim of in-service education is to stress that the problem of incontinence is a problem for *all* persons who are involved with the incontinent person, not just for the individual who is incontinent. It is important that both staff and family share information on incontinence from the standpoint of physiology, psychology, and normal aging processes.

The individual who is incontinent needs to be thoroughly assessed to ascertain the etiology of the incontinence, and a well-organized, well-executed treatment should follow the assessment. Without a well-organized specific approach, the outcome of intervention can be more disastrous than if the problem were treated only with supportive care. *It must be remembered that to intervene in an elderly person's care is to affect the total system and to apply stress.* Unless there is good reason to believe that the benefit to be gained is worth the risk one takes, it may be preferable not to intervene.

INCONTINENCE IS NOT ALWAYS REVERSIBLE

The fact that intractable incontinence is rarely discussed makes it seem that all incontinence is reversible. It has been my experience that there are forms and stages of an illness, particularly in the case of diffuse brain damage, in which incontinence as a symptom is intractable. The symptom may not be reversible, but it is treatable. It is this grey area of the treatable, but not curable, chronic problem which tends to cause the most ambivalence on the part of staff and families. Intervention in this situation must be discussed in terms of realistic goals for patient, staff, and families. When expectations are too high, reactions of frustration, anger, hostility, helplessness, and hopelessness are most likely to occur. When staff are dealing with incontinence that is not curable, or when it is occurring frequently with many patients, it is important to have discussions at regular intervals at which all staff can share their reactions and feelings honestly. Such discussions provide an acceptable outlet for the ventilation of conflicts and bring relief of tension. One adaptive tension release is humor. Staff members, family, and patients should be encouraged to maintain and utilize their sense of humor. When good taste is used and the setting is appropriate, humor can be very valuable.

BASIC INTERVENTIONS

There are a few basic interventions which can be used in the management of the incontinent patient. Incontinence is an abnormal state and as such will tend to foster neurotic needs.

1 Awareness of the individual's neurotic needs makes it easier for them to be met. The need for attention is normal, but in the ill elderly person it can become neurotic if the environment is perceived as neglectful and uncaring. By meeting the individual's need for attention, destructive behavior can be prevented and perception altered.

2 Care givers should be aware of the tendency of the incontinent to suffer sensory deprivation and social isolation. Promote a caring, stimulating environment through mobility, "people therapy," reality orientation, contact with reality, and sensory stimulation. Continue with these treatment modalities even if they provoke some physical discomfort. It is time that we recognize that it may be unrealistic to try to create a discomfort-free life-style for aged persons. Most of us, including the aged, have lived with both comfort and discomfort, and an environment where both ends of the pain/comfort continuum did not exist would be an artificial one.

3 Understanding the tendency on the part of the patient to return to earlier primitive behavior will lessen the immediacy of automatic reactions on the part of care givers.

4 Placing the incontinent individual in an appropriate environment will promote caring. Avoid the "grand shuffle" of patients at staff convenience, which leads to disorientation, low self-esteem, and feelings of being unwanted and uncared for on the part of the patients.

5 Modify the environment so that it is supportive of the individual with incontinence.

6 Work with family members to make sure that there are always enough clothes available for changes.

7 Use chlorophyll tablets to reduce odor.

8 Talk honestly, directly, and with empathy to incontinent individuals about their problem and how they feel about it.

9 Share with the incontinent individual how you would feel if you yourself had the problem.

10 Form an alliance with the incontinent person to work against incontinence; assist individuals to separate themselves from incontinence.

SUMMARY

Incontinence is a common problem among the institutionalized aged as well as for aging persons in the community. Episodes of incontinence, particularly if chronic and intractable, may have their etiologic basis in diffuse brain damage. Up to the present time, nursing research has not been directed toward the psychological impact of incontinence on both the affected individual and on care givers and families. It is hoped that this chapter will stimulate some awareness of the psychological significance of incontinence for patient, families, and care givers.

REFERENCES

1 B. Isaacs and F. A. Walkey, "A Survey of Incontinence in Elderly Hospital Patients," *Gerontologia Clinica*, vol. 6, no. 15, pp. 367–376, 1964.
2 S. M. Thompson, "Managing the Problems of Elimination," *Nursing Outlook*, vol. 14, no. 9, pp. 58–60, September 1963.
3 F. L. Willington, "Incontinence 5: Training and Retraining for Continence," *Nursing Times*, vol. 71, no. 13, pp. 500–503, March 27, 1975.
4 F. L. Willington, "The Prevention of Soiling," *Nursing Times*, vol. 17, no. 14, pp. 545–548, April 3, 1975.
5 J. Whyte and N. Thistle, "Male Incontinence: The Inside Story on External Collection," *Nursing 76*, vol. 4, no. 9, pp. 66–67, September 1976.
6 F. L. Willington, "Incontinence 3: Psychological and Psychogenic Aspects," *Nursing Times*, vol. 71, no. 11, pp. 422–423, March 13, 1975.
7 S. S. Sutherland, "The Psychology of Incontinence," in F. L. Willington (ed.), *Incontinence in the Elderly*, Academic Press, London, 1976.
8 Ibid., p. 52.
9 J. Agate, *The Practice of Geriatrics*, 2d ed., Heinemann, London, 1970, p. 54.
10 Sutherland, op. cit., pp. 54–56.
11 Ibid., pp. 56–61.
12 Ibid., p. 61.
13 Ibid., pp. 62–63.
14 Ibid., p. 64.
15 Ibid., p. 66.

BIBLIOGRAPHY

Brocklehurst, J. C.: "Causes of Urinary Incontinence in Old Age," in *Textbook of Geriatric Medicine and Gerontology*, Churchill Livingstone, Edinburgh and London, 1973.
DuFault, Sr. Karin: "Urinary Incontinence: United States and British Nursing Perspectives," *Journal of Gerontological Nursing*, vol. 4, no. 2, pp. 28–33, March-April 1978.
Field, Mildred A.: "Urinary Incontinence in the Elderly: An Overview," *Journal of Gerontological Nursing*, vol. 5, no. 1, pp. 12–19, January-February 1979.
Grosicki, J.: "Effect of Operant Conditioning on Modification of Incontinence in Neuropsychiatric Geriatric Patients," in *Nursing and the Aging Patient*, American Journal of Nursing Company, New York, 1974.
Habeeb, M., and M. Kallstrom: "Bowel Program for Institutionalized Adults," *American Journal of Nursing*, vol. 76, no. 4, pp. 606–608, April 1975.
Hartie, Anthony, and David Black: "A Dry Bed Is the Objective," *Nursing Times*, vol. 71, no. 47, pp. 1874–1876, November 20, 1975.
Hodkinson, H. M.: "Nursing Care," in *An Outline of Geriatrics*, Academic Press, London, 1975.
Maney, J.: "A Behavioral Therapy Approach to Bladder Retraining," *Nursing Clinics of North America*, vol. 2, no. 1, pp. 179–189, March 1976.

Norton, Doreen, Rhoda McLaren, and A. N. Exton-Smith: "The Problem of Incontinence," in *An Investigation of Geriatric Nursing Problems in Hospitals*, Churchill Livingstone, Edinburgh, 1975.

Pinel, C.: "Disorders of Micturition in the Elderly," *Nursing Times*, vol. 71, no. 51, pp. 2019–2021, December 18, 1975.

Rudd, T. N.: "Urinary Incontinence in Old Age," *Gerontologica Clinica*, vol. 10, no. 6, pp. 340–344, 1968.

Wells, Thelma: "Promoting Urinary Continence in the Elderly in Hospital," *Nursing Times*, vol. 71, no. 48, pp. 1908–1909, November 27, 1975.

Willington, F. L.: "Incontinence 1: Significance of Incompetence of Personal Sanitary Habits," *Nursing Times*, vol. 71, no. 9, pp. 340–341, February 27, 1975.

_____: "Incontinence 2: Problems in the Aetiology of Urinary Incontinence," *Nursing Times*, vol. 71, no. 10, pp. 378–381, March 6, 1975.

_____: "Incontinence 4: The Nursing Component Diagnosis and Treatment," *Nursing Times*, vol. 71, no. 12, pp. 464–467, March 1975.

_____ (ed.): *Incontinence in the Elderly*, Academic Press, San Francisco, 1976.

Chapter 22

The Role of a Nurse Coordinator in a Geriatric Setting

Noël Robinson

Without the willing support of the people being helped, treatment is unpleasant, inefficient, and sometimes ineffective.

Franklin C. Shontz

My role as a nurse coordinator in two geriatric programs in Australia has convinced me that coordination is vital to the continuing success of such programs. In this chapter I would like to use my experiences to describe the role and functions of a nurse coordinator. A coordinator is, according to the dictionary, "one who brings parts together."[1] This definition is certainly applicable to the role of a nurse coordinator of geriatric care; in this context the "parts" are, of course, the various long-term services and programs that are available to the elderly.

.n their book *Adult Day Care*, Weiler and Rathbone-McCuan describe two functions of health care in a geriatric day care setting: providing direct

This chapter is a revision of a speech presented at the Gerontology Association Annual Conference, Tasmania, Australia, October 1976.

nursing care and providing nursing coordination.[2] The authors point out that nurses fulfilling both of these functions must "have the ability to engage in inter-disciplinary communications, and a diverse array of inter-actions with participants, families, and other day care staff."[3] "The nurse coordinator," according to these writers, "must have the ability to par-ticipate in health care as a collaborative effort, and to assume ad-ministrative and leadership responsibilities."[4] The writers further note that guiding the planning process for geriatric care is an important function of the coordinator. A nurse who works in an adult day care setting is in a posi-tion to provide valuable assistance to clients who need additional communi-ty services; he or she should therefore be familiar with local community health and social resources.[5]

My own experiences as a nurse coordinator bear out the observations of Weiler and Rathbone-McCuan and enable me to add some observations of my own.

EXPERIENCE IN A DAY CARE CENTER

My first experience as a coordinator was in a day care center in Kew, Melbourne, Australia, which opened in 1966 with 25 clients, and was under the auspices of the Mental Health Authority of Australia. (See Chapter 11 for an account of day care centers in the United States.) After 5 years, there were approximately 200 clients and the average daily attendance was 60. The center was open 5 days a week from 9 a.m. to 3:30 p.m. We provided hot lunch, morning and afternoon tea, and transportation to and from the center. Those eligible for day care admission were:

1 Individuals with a functional disease for which partial recovery or remission had been achieved, but who needed constant reassessment.
2 Individuals suffering moderate dementia.
3 Clients who had recovered enough to be discharged from the hospital, but who had no family and faced a return to a solitary and un-supervised life.
4 Clients accepted on a trial period, after temporary discharge from the hospital, to assess the degree of recovery. Final discharge and perma-nent return to the community followed.

The therapeutic climate provided the patient with constant, measured, and absorbable stimulation of considerable variety. The stimulation was ac-tive, since it required patients to share with others an experience in a group situation. Whether they are at home or in an institution, the activity of the elderly is generally limited, and stimulation is qualitatively and quantitative-ly poor, passive (television, radio, reading), and unshared.

We saw the day care center as an indispensable therapeutic modality in geriatric psychiatry, forming one link in the chain of comprehensive care, which consisted of home, outpatient clinic, domiciliary visiting, special home unit for the aged, old people's home, and short- and long-term hospitalization.

The program consisted of counseling and individual psychotherapy, often dispensed by all staff members in an ambulatory fashion, over tea, on the grounds, during the occupational therapy sessions, or in a structured group environment. Clinical assessment and follow-up sessions were held weekly, as were staff and coordinator meetings. Every 3 months, the patients' continued involvement in the various programs was assessed by the heads of all areas except psychiatry.

The coordinator, the responsible person in the absence of the psychiatrist, acted as liaison between staff and programs, with the community, with relatives, and of course, with the all-important patient; sometimes the coordinator also was involved in follow-up after discharge. Documenting of all aspects of the center was the coordinator's responsibility.

Staff at this day center concluded that a therapeutic team can be welded into an extremely efficient group. Even unqualified individuals, when highly motivated and under experienced leadership, can give high-quality service in a complex area such as psychiatric nursing. The relaxed and happy atmosphere brought astonishing results for the patients. I reported these results in a paper at the International Conference of Gerontology in Kiev.[6]

The following case example will serve to illustrate how a coordinator can function to provide holistic care to the elderly patient.

CASE EXAMPLE FROM A PSYCHOGERIATRIC DAY CENTER   Mrs. H, age 67, a day care client, made a parasuicide attempt; it was a call for help, and was not the first. The attempt was made late in the evening after a family Christmas dinner gathering. Mrs. H took an overdose after the Christmas dinner and was admitted to a general hospital. She was later transferred to a psychogeriatric hospital, and while there continued to attend the day care center. When she returned home, she visited the day center three times a week as before.

In retrospect, Mrs. H had presented herself to staff and family members in a certain way during other parasuicide attempts. She appeared to be in full control of herself and to be reasoning well. Yet she repeatedly asked one person after another over a period of time, "Do you think it a good idea if I visit my sister?" or a similar question. She had a tendency toward overactivity, and stated, "I am fine, it is great. My children are all taking their young families away for school holidays after Christmas. I'll be lonely, but not for long."

The younger daughter contacted the coordinator immediately when the center reopened after Christmas and asked for support. We saw a very distressed family, whose holiday had been marred.

I had had a good relationship with all the family, so I "drew parts together." Mrs. H had been deserted many years before. She had been a fashion buyer for a large department store for some years, had retired about two years earlier and had then enrolled in the day care center. She was prone to periods of depression, had strong feelings of unworthiness, little insight, and was full of hopelessness. Until she commenced at the center these feelings were almost unrelieved. Mrs. H lived with her son (who had also been deserted) and had been housekeeper and "gran" to his two daughters, since his marriage broke up some years previously.

I checked out the treatment being given in each department as well as staff attitudes to patient and family, which varied greatly. I finally brought Mrs. H to a team clinic meeting which was headed by the day center psychiatrist. The staff saw Mrs. H as manipulative, selfish, generous, lonely, vindictive, lovable, and so on. A care plan was formulated, medication reassessed, and behavioral patterns discussed. The patient's cooperation was sought, as well as her family's. As a result of these actions, the patient stabilized, gained more insight, and accepted her situation with the help of the increased support.

I learned from this case that it is vital to be aware of *all aspects* and not to rely only on "the team." *Care givers do not always function as a cohesive group; attitudes vary, and misconceptions occur.* There was some truth in all the attitudes, but the staff needed coordination and discussion to place their feelings and help in perspective.

With the help of staff in crisis situations (real or otherwise), Mrs. H remained stabilized until she succumbed to an organic illness in her seventies.

EXPERIENCE IN A HOME FOR THE AGED

The Montefiore Home for the Jewish Aged in Melbourne, Australia, is a setting very different from the day care center described above. For several years I have been the coordinator there. It provides 363 beds, 150 in the nursing home unit and the rest in hostel/motel-style residential units. Montefiore is a pluralistic community, with 19 nationalities represented. Criteria for admission require that females be 60 years of age or older, males 65 or older, or that applicants be on an invalid pension. Costs vary with the ability to pay, and some government funding is available. The domestic staff is mainly of southern Mediterranean origin, with some from

Northern Europe. One can imagine the difficulties of communication between patients and personnel, and an important task for the coordinator was to reduce racism and improve communication among people of diverse national and regional backgrounds.

Accent for Residents

As in the day care center, the emphasis at Montefiore is on providing stimulation for residents, and avoiding the isolation of individuals. Extensive psychosocial programs are offered on varying levels, among them simple movement programs, music programs, and discussion groups on the arts, current affairs, and general subjects. Entertainment, varied occupational therapy programs, physiotherapy, and excellent nursing care are also available.

Volunteers are an important part of the programs. I work extensively with volunteers to help them become liaison personnel or leaders; they provide social entertainment outside the home, serve tea, act as escorts, and so on. The doctors at Montefiore continuously request the involvement of volunteers and reassess their performance. Since the coordinator is the person in charge of the volunteers, he or she can do much to ensure that their contributions are effective.

The case example that follows describes a problem which the coordinator worked to solve.

CASE EXAMPLE FROM JEWISH HOMES FOR THE AGED   Mr. T, age 73, was reported by his wife and daughter as "being wrongly treated at the Homes." The report was made to the medical superintendent of the Jewish Homes for the Aged, and presented to him by the daughter at his home.

It appeared that the patient had been placed on the ward for demented residents. He was reported to be aggressive, and since he was impossible for the staff to manage, he had been sedated and restricted. His wife appeared to be histrionic. She could not accept his placement on a ward for the demented. Throughout her life she had been unable to show consideration for her family (or for anyone else). The staff did not listen to her, and the patient was later returned to his home.

I had just begun work as coordinator, but my background in psychogeriatric nursing care and administration was most helpful. I made an individual assessment of the gentleman (and gentleman he was) and found him suffering a tremendous amount of frustration, which was presented as aggression, and which was largely due to his aphasia. The nursing home staff had had little or no experience of such a situation.

I discussed the situation as I saw it with the superintendent, and we devised a plan which provided more challenge for Mr. T. Mr. T was moved from the ward for demented residents and placed in a single room on another unit. His wife and daughter were encouraged to join the proposed activity program. The social worker began counseling both the mother and daughter, while I worked on regular contacts with Mr. T and had his medication regimen revised.

The program continued for many months, and Mr. T was progressively transferred to units with individuals who were functioning at higher levels. Finally, at the request of his wife, he was discharged to family care. He was returned for a short period to day care and physiotherapy, but now manages at home. He is still disoriented at times and also shows some confusion; however, his aphasia is not a deterrent to communication. His family gives him support and seems able to cope most of the time. If there had been no coordinator available to piece together all of the information, this man, like many others before him, would not have had a complete team assessment, and it is likely that his deterioration would have been rapid.

FUNCTIONS OF A NURSE COORDINATOR

As nurse coordinator, I discovered that the elderly people whose care I helped provide had had a wealth of life experiences. They had often lived 70 years or more, and had experienced two wars, a depression, inflation, and some good fortune as well as some tragedy and loss. Yet, in spite of their vast experience of life, elderly people in institutions are often treated as "pets" or as children, and surrounded by an atmosphere of cleanliness, solicitude, and enforced rest. Is it sufficient to meet only the physical needs of the elderly, without seeing them as complete individuals? I think not.

The coordinator must be particularly sensitive and responsive to the psychosocial needs of the elderly person. Coordinators are in a particularly good position to ensure that the needs of the whole person are attended to, because their primary responsibility is to the aged patient as an individual, and not to the performance of any specific health care function (e.g., physical therapy).

I view my role as coordinator as an opportunity to take a holistic approach to patient care. In my experience I have noted that the time of the staff of various departments is usually taken up by specific functions, and they generally do not communicate very much with the staff of other departments. Often, in giving instructions, and in clinics, team meetings, and administration meetings, staff are concerned with zealously protecting their own "turf." This attitude is encountered all the way from the medical staff to the maintenance crew. Departments often function well, but seem to work independently of one another, and often department staff members seem unaware of the roles of the other disciplines in the spectrum of treatment and care.

Required Characteristics

Several qualities are required of a coordinator, but the ability to build trust is the most essential. The coordinator must be seen as accessible to all and available where needed, within, of course, the constraints of time and schedules. An attitude of neutrality is also essential. Rapport must be established with individuals so that the initiator of the problem is not embarrassed about exposing attitudes or feelings, and will not fear reprisals. *Reprisals very often occur when residents complain, or voice a problem regarding institutional life.*

Flexibility is another important characteristic of a coordinator, and it goes without saying that the coordinator will need to be an attentive listener.

Ability to Function Well

What helps a coordinator to function well? First of all, a coordinator must have the full support and loyalty of those in authority. A coordinator should also have varied experiences at different levels in the health field, and should be willing, when necessary, to operate on a trial and error basis. It has been my experience that the coordinator must work to reduce prejudices and always endeavor to improve and increase communication. At times the coordinator will have to be forceful without being overly aggressive. The stress involved in this role will be reduced if the coordinator does not always expect to be liked.

I would recommend the following steps to a coordinator:

• Get to know colleagues, personnel at all levels, volunteers, relatives, residents, and other community workers.
• Ask continuously what constitutes the whole of the problem being presented.
• Accept some of the difficulties as inevitable—especially when they result from human frailties.
• Build a good public image of the facility, particularly in the eyes of outside agencies, so that as many persons as possible may share its advantages.

The Position in the Hierarchy

Where does the coordinator stand with regard to the hierarchy? What authority does the coordinator have within that framework? On the surface, very little. The coordinator is the "presenter" of the situation, offering one or more possible solutions, but he or she must be able to accept whatever decisions are ultimately made.

SUMMARY

This chapter described the characteristics and role of a nurse coordinator in a geriatric complex. Experience has shown the need for psychosocial nursing care and a holistic approach to the elderly client. I have briefly described my own experiences as a coordinator in Melbourne, Australia, first in a day care center and then in a long-term care facility.

REFERENCES

1 *Oxford Concise Dictionary*, Clarendon Press, Oxford, United Kingdom, 1958.
2 Philip G. Weiler and Eloise Rathbone-McCuan, *Adult Day Care: Community Work with the Elderly*, Springer, New York, 1978.
3 Ibid., p. 65.
4 Ibid.
5 Ibid., p. 72.
6 Noël Robinson and P. Ots, "First Psychogeriatric Day Center in Victoria," paper presented at International Congress of Gerontology, Kiev, U.S.S.R., June 1972.

BIBLIOGRAPHY

Bower, Herbert M.: "Sensory Stimulation and the Treatment of Senile Dementia," *The Medical Journal of Australia*, vol. 1, no. 22, pp. 1113–1117, 1967.

_____: "The First Psychogeriatric Day-Centre in Victoria," *The Medical Journal of Australia*, vol. 1, pp. 1047–1050, May 17, 1969.

Clements, G.: "A Geriatric Day Hospital Serving a Rural Community," *Nursing Times* (London), vol. 64, no. 27, pp. 908–909, 1968.

Hodges, Eileen L.: "A Chance to Start Again," *Nursing Mirror and Midwives Journal* (London), vol. 134, no. 22, pp. 37–44, 1973.

Preston, Caroline E., M. A. Helgerson, and Steven Helgerson: "An Analysis of Survey Data Obtained by a Service Agency for Older People," *The Gerontologist*, vol. 12, no. 4, Winter 1972.

Rathbone-McCuan, Eloise, and Julia Levenson: "Know Your Community Resources," *Journal of Gerontological Nursing*, vol. 3, no. 4, July–August 1977.

Rossman, Isadore: "Alternatives to Institutional Care," *Bulletin of the New York Academy of Medicine*, vol. 49, no. 12, pp. 1084–1092, December 1973.

State of Washington, Department of Social and Health Services, Office on Aging, *Handbook: Adult Day Health Program*, February 1978.

Name Index

Subject Index